Sexual Freedom
and
The Constitution

Sexual Freedom and The Constitution

An Inquiry into the Constitutionality
of Repressive Sex Laws

Walter Barnett

University of New Mexico Press
Albuquerque

Preface

This book is the outcome of an idea I conceived in the fall of 1969. It was intended to be only part of a larger study of legal and other factors in American society that discriminate on the basis of marital status and sexual orientation. The favoritism shown by our social arrangements to married persons and to heterosexuals generally, and the discouragement given to single persons and to homosexuals in particular, were to be explored, documented, and critically evaluated. The justification for such a study, in my own mind, was simply that people have a right to the pursuit of happiness, as our Declaration of Independence recognizes. Many people are not capable of finding happiness within the confines of marriage or even of heterosexuality. Why not free them from those confines? It had always seemed to me that the only defensible restriction society could place on a person's pursuit of his own happiness is the one outlined in John Stuart Mill's essay *On Liberty*—that his actions shall not hurt others. I could not see any way in which remaining single, or engaging in homosexual behavior with other consenting adults, harmed anybody or even society in general.

Unfortunately, such justifications in terms of expanding the frontiers of human liberty seem no longer fashionable. Only those studies can find subsidy which serve some particular *social* need. The needs of individuals are considered insignificant. The justification I therefore proposed for the study was the untoward effect such discrimination might be having on population growth. So justified, it succeeded in winning the Harlan Fiske Stone Fellowship of Columbia University School of Law, a half-year sabbatical grant from the University of New Mexico, and a supplementary stipend from the Ford Foundation. These funds enabled me to devote most of an entire academic year (1970–71) to the project. I wish to express my gratitude to these institutions for their support.

v

I undertook this part of the project first, largely because an appeal to the United States Supreme Court was then pending (that is, during the fall and winter of 1970–71) in a federal case which raised the very issue of constitutionality with which this book deals. (The case—*Buchanan v. Batchelor*—is discussed in Chapter 3.) Having been asked to represent the National Committee for Sexual Civil Liberties as amicus curiae in the matter, I wanted to get this part completed in time for the appeal. As events turned out, the substantive issues were never heard, because the Court vacated and remanded the lower decision for reconsideration on jurisdictional grounds. Meanwhile, it had become apparent that this subject was complex and difficult enough in itself to demand book-length treatment.

Work was interrupted in the summer of 1971 when I returned to the University of New Mexico School of Law to resume teaching. However, I was able to devote the entire spring and summer of 1972 to completing the book, thanks to a grant from the Playboy Foundation. I am most grateful for this additional support, without which the work would still be unfinished.

I want to express my appreciation to Columbia University School of Law, the University of New Mexico School of Law, and Hastings College of the Law of the University of California, each of which provided in turn their libraries, office facilities, and other administrative support. I also want to thank the following persons, who read and criticized all or part of the manuscript: Professor Harold Edgar of Columbia University Law School; Professors Henry Weihofen and Leo Kanowitz of the University of New Mexico Law School; Dr. Evelyn G. Hooker, formerly research psychologist of the University of California, Los Angeles; Professor Laud Humphreys of the Department of Sociology of Pitzer College, Claremont, California; Dr. Donald J. West of the Institute of Criminology of Cambridge University, England; Dr. Donald T. Lunde of the Department of Psychiatry of Stanford University Medical Center; Dr. Paul H. Gebhard, Director of the Institute for Sex Research, Indiana University; and Professor Louis Crompton of the Department of English of the University of Nebraska. Invaluable assistance was also obtained from William Parker, whose book *Homosexuality—A Selective Bibliography* (1971) proved to be an essential research tool in the field, and from the Information Service of the Institute for Sex Research, Indiana University. However, I take sole responsibility for the contents of this book. I also want to thank Scott Rosien, a law student at Hastings, for his research assistance during the final weeks of work and Marvin R. Montney for helping me with the proofreading.

Whether the viewpoints here urged ultimately win general concurrence or not, I hope the book will serve to promote wider understanding and acceptance of human beings whose emotional needs diverge from the majority pattern, thereby enabling more and more people to pursue their happiness free from fear and the threat of punishment.

Walter Barnett

Contents

Contents

1

The Scope of, and Reasons for, the Inquiry

Many people may be surprised by the title of this book. What possible relevance could the Constitution have to sexual behavior? Even to mention them in the same breath smacks of profanity. Admittedly, some word of explanation is in order.

It seems safe to say that the traditional attitudes of American culture make monogamous heterosexual marriage the moral norm, and all expression of sexuality outside that institution morally deviant.[1] The American states possess a battery of criminal statutes whose overall design, if not effect, appears to be to confine all interpersonal sexuality to marriage.[2] Although it is not considered immoral to remain unmarried, the unmarried person who has coitus with another single person is guilty of fornication under the statutes of a number of states. If he or she engages in intercourse with a married person, one or both of them may also have committed the crime of adultery. In either situation if the partners engage in any form of genital stimulation other than coitus, they may violate the various criminal statutes prohibiting "unnatural" sex acts. These same statutes are almost invariably violated by any form of homosexual activity. If either partner pays the other for his sexual favors, the crimes of prostitution and patronizing a prostitute may have been committed. And if the two individuals are within certain degrees of kinship to one another, they could be guilty of incest. In a number of states, unmarried people who desire contraceptives for the prevention of pregnancy may find themselves barred by law from obtaining them for such purposes.[3] Even

Even if no evidence of sexual connection is present, a male and a female who live together without the benefit of marriage can be prosecuted for illicit cohabitation.

That the behavior in all these instances occurs in private and involves only consenting adults is immaterial. The behavior is criminal notwithstanding the lack of any victim to make a complaint.[4] Sexual deviance, in its legal connotation, then, encompasses at least these instances of private consensual adult behavior that our society has labeled criminal. It could, of course, also cover sexual behavior that is criminal because of victimization, such as rape, but criminalizing these other categories does not in itself pose any constitutional issue. The victimless forms of deviance are those with which this book is concerned.

The point has been made over and over again by legal and other commentators that these criminal laws are unjustifiable in a society founded upon the principle of individual liberty.[5] Regardless of one's views on the morality of such behavior, there should be no crime where there is no victim. Efforts to enforce such laws use up police, prosecutorial, judicial, and correctional resources needed to combat crime for which a victim really exists. Yet these laws generally remain on the statute books for fear that their repeal would be taken to condone immorality.

My objective is to explore the possibilities of attacking such "morals" laws on constitutional grounds. Occasionally, suggestions have been made that constitutional limits do exist on the state's power to restrict the private sexual behavior of consenting adults, but the subject has not been explored in depth.[6] This effort is in the nature of an essay. It does not pretend to be a definitive statement on the matter, because, as will later become more apparent, the application of a number of constitutional doctrines to these laws is a rather novel approach, which must proceed by way of analogy from established positions in cases dealing with other areas of civil liberties.

Such an exploration is peculiarly timely. We are beginning to realize that effective population control in America may depend more upon encouraging people to remain single than upon efforts to disseminate birth control information and techniques more widely. According to demographer Judith Blake Davis, one of the two most influential and universal factors in producing an over-supply of babies is "the standardization of both the male and the female sexual roles in terms of reproductive functions, obligations, and activities."

> With regard to sex roles, it is generally recognized that potential human variability is greater than is normally permitted *within* each sex category. Existing societies have tended to suppress and extinguish such variability and to standardize sexual roles in ways that imply that all "normal" persons will attain the status of parents. This coercion takes many forms, including one-sided indoctrination in schools, legal barriers and penalties for deviation, and the threats of loneliness, ostracism, and ridicule that are implied in the unavailability of alternatives. Individuals who—by temperament, health, or constitution—do not fit the ideal sex-role pattern are nonetheless coerced into attempting to achieve it, at least to the extent of having demographic impact by becoming parents.

> Therefore, a policy that sought out the ways in which coercion regarding sex roles is at present manifesting itself could find numerous avenues for relieving the coercion and for allowing life styles different from marriage and parenthood to find free and legitimized expression. Such a policy would have an effect on the content of expectations regarding sex roles as presented and enforced in schools, on laws concerning sexual activity between consenting adults, on taxation with respect to marital status and number of children, on residential building policies, and on just about every facet of existence that is now organized so as exclusively to favor and reward a pattern of sex roles based on marriage and parenthood.[7]

In other words, the notion that everyone should marry and raise a family was important in an era when infant-mortality rates were high and life expectancy short, but it is detrimental in an already overcrowded world in which the reduction of infant mortality and the extension of life expectancy are doubling the population every thirty to forty years.[8] Yet if people are to be encouraged to remain single, the legal hindrances that society opposes to satisfaction of the sex drive outside marriage must be removed. None but a select few can be expected to remain single and continent as well; if a law of nature exists, this is it.

Admittedly, the birth rate in the United States has been declining recently, but Professor Davis believes this recent decline is due, in large part, to nonmarriage and to delayed marriage and childbearing, although there has also been a sharp drop in the average family size desired by Americans.[9]

It is impossible to do justice in a single book to all the criminal laws in question. For this reason, the discussion is focused on one type of law—that which prohibits "unnatural" sex acts—although some of the approaches here outlined may serve equally well to attack the others. Criminal laws that prohibit "unnatural" sex acts will be referred to hereafter as "sodomy" laws, for lack of a more inclusive term, even though the category "sodomy" does not in a number of states cover all such prohibited acts.[10]

There are good reasons for choosing the sodomy laws. It is true that the increasing availability of effective contraceptives and of abortion has diminished the importance for population control of allowing people sexual gratification in ways other than ordinary vaginal intercourse. The significance of sodomy law reform for confining the population explosion thus is not a major reason for the choice. The significance of reform even in this respect can be underestimated, however. As one, and perhaps the most crucial, manifestation of the social taboo on homosexuality, the existing sodomy laws aid in coercing a certain percentage of homosexuals to attempt marriage and parenthood.[11] If the taboo were absent or even less severe, these people might never add their quota of offspring to the population explosion. We have no means of estimating just how many may be in this category, but indications exist that the number is not negligible.

One good reason for picking the sodomy laws is that the variety of constitutional arguments capable of being marshalled against them is probably greater than for any of the other crimes. This choice thus may furnish a kaleidoscope of the range of arguments available against repressive sex laws generally.

A second reason is that the likelihood of genuine reform of these laws through the legislature is nil in many states. Reform in this sense—the decriminalization of private consensual adult be-havior—has so far been enacted in only seven of the fifty states, despite the recommendation of such reform by the American Law Institute since 1955.[12] Even in those seven states (with the possible exception of Delaware), reform was effected not by any lobby of interested citizens but as one facet of a complete revision of the criminal code. Its only proponents, if one could call them that, were the experts on the law revision commission itself or the legislators responsible for guiding the package through. The vehicle of a new criminal code may have facilitated legislative approval of the reform by deflecting public attention to larger and more controversial issues. In at least one state—California—where the proposed reform had to stand on its own merits in a separate bill, it was easily defeated.[13] In another state—Idaho—where the reform did slip through as part of a new code,[14] the focusing of public attention on it after passage appears to have been a major reason why the new code was then scuttled.[15] Of course, a new criminal code does not necessarily import liberalization. It can effect retrenchment just as easily.[16] Some legislators share the feelings of loathing and disgust experienced by many other people at the thought of the principal acts in question—anal-genital and oral-genital contacts. Moreover, in considering bills dealing with matters of sexual morality, most legislators seem prone to take an estimate of their constituents' attitudes that errs, if at all, on the side of greater strictness, or at least to give lip service to the more conventional viewpoints. Few legislators would relish the prospect of facing a political rally, accused of favoring immorality and having to justify themselves against that charge.[17] In states where the political balance of the two-party system is a close one, few office seekers dare earn the enmity of any sizable body of people whose membership cuts across party lines, such as those religious groups whose voices are most consistently heard on the side of strict morals legislation.[18]

A third reason is that removal of penal sanctions on consensual sodomy between adults in private, through constitutional invalidation, might well break the logjam for legislative repeal of the laws against fornication and illicit cohabitation.[19] These crimes are usually bracketed together as strictly "morals" legislation. If the one which is the most intractable to legislative reform is removed by whatever means, it would be anomalous for a legislature to retain the others on the books. The same chain reaction might sweep away the laws banning contraceptives for unmarried persons in those states that still have them.[20]

The fourth and final reason is the major one. Although our constitutional protections have emphasized the requirement of fairness largely in the context of procedural matters, substantive laws can just as easily be fundamentally unfair to human beings. A sense of moral outrage has undoubtedly been the driving force behind the constitutional attacks on abortion laws and on capital punishment, just as it provided the impetus for assaults on the segregation and miscegenation laws in our recent past. Someone who is convinced in his own conscience that reasonable people cannot differ on the question of whether such a law is an acceptable legislative judgment within our constitutional framework will scarcely sit by quietly and let the injustice be perpetuated. In such a situation, appeal to the courts may serve as the only safety valve preventing the outrage from building into open rebellion and defiance of the law.

It is, admittedly, a serious charge to bring against legislators that they have acted so unreasonably as to overstep the Constitution, not one to be made lightly. Now it seems clear that the extent to which population ought to be controlled, or *needs* controlling, is a matter for legislative judgment. One may have strong feelings on this issue, but how much is too much is a question of degree, which can be answered only by a legislature. To the extent, therefore, that someone's justification for a constitutional attack against any of these laws rests on that ground, he is wasting the courts' time. His arguments are being addressed to the wrong forum, though they may be garbed in the concepts and terminology of constitutional law. On the other hand, if the ground of his attack is an overwhelming conviction that the law in question violates fundamental human rights, that it perpetrates an intolerable injustice, his appeal is for protection of the individual against the tyranny of the majority—a function our judiciary has long exercised.

I am convinced that the sodomy laws are such laws. Of the other crimes mentioned, only the laws against fornication and those prohibiting the dissemination and use of contraceptives come close to meeting the same test. The reader is therefore entitled to know my stand from the outset. This book is not intended as a coldly dispassionate analysis of the subject. The viewpoint that such laws are constitutional has gone unquestioned for so long that there is no need to offer it further support. What is needed is a piece of serious advocacy challenging that viewpoint, and this book seeks to supply it. I believe, however, that the arguments and positions here presented are sound and reasonable, even granting allowance for my personal bias, if one wishes to call it that. The reader is invited to judge for himself. Although this effort is directed primarily to the legal profession—to judges and to other lawyers—I hope that laymen, and particularly legislators, will read it and think seriously about the issues it discusses. Ultimately, all Americans hold the responsibility for preserving and promoting human rights and civil liberties.

On what basis does my conviction rest? On the basis that these laws stigmatize as criminals, nay, as felons, a group of people who feel that their only real crime consists of being attracted exclusively to members of their own sex—the homosexuals. The reasons for regarding these laws as such a fundamental outrage to the human personality as to be ranked unconstitutional will become more apparent later in the book. At this point all that can be given is a hint of the dimensions of the outrage.

The sodomy laws do not, in so many words, make criminal the condition of being attracted only to the members of one's own sex. They make criminal certain acts, regardless of with whom those acts are performed. In most states the acts are a crime even when they occur in a heterosexual context, and even between husband and wife.[21] It happens, however, that these prohibited acts are almost the only means by which homosexuals can find sexual expression with each other. No convincing reason can be given why in a homosexual context the *acts* should be deemed more antisocial than the *condition* of which they are merely the manifestation; thus it is hard to deny that the sodomy laws serve as an indirect way of branding the condition itself criminal. Of course, prosecutions under these laws for acts not involving force, minors, or public places are almost as scarce as hens' teeth,[22] and no one suggests that acts involving such factors are outside the constitutional prerogatives of the state's police power. If, then, the law goes largely unenforced except in areas where it cannot be constitutionally questioned, why all the fuss?[23]

The laws have three consequences for the homosexual that are often overlooked.[24] One is that the *threat* of criminal prosecution hangs like a sword of Damocles over his head. Americans are only beginning to perceive what a destructive impact conviction of crime can have on a person's life, even a prosecution that results in acquittal, even a mere arrest never leading to prosecution.[25] An arrest record, especially on a "morals" charge, can form a permanent blot on a person's life, marking him as one of doubtful character.[26] It may bar him from government service, from the professions, and even from the lowliest of occupations for which a license must be obtained from some official board.

Besides such direct detriments flowing from this "record," the person never knows how awareness of its existence may affect other people's assessment of him, whether in applications for employment, for insurance, for bonding, for the extension of credit, or for a coveted membership in some organization. It is difficult to imagine any threat our society might make that could dry up the wellsprings of ambition and creative energy more effectively than this one of criminal prosecution. When that threat is tied directly to an urge that is an insistent, almost daily, part of life—the sex drive—the dimensions of the outrage begin to be revealed. If a similar threat hung over ordinary heterosexual intercourse, and people were convinced, as the homosexual is, that society would indeed catch and pillory them if it could, they would begin to realize the degree of cruelty inflicted. It becomes possible to enjoy one of the principal satisfactions of life only by building a thick wall of insensitivity around the tenderest of emotions. Love and fear do not mix.

A second consequence is that such laws serve to support a number of explicit legal disabilities of the homosexual: ineligibility to be employed by the federal government, whether in the foreign service or in the civil service, or by private businesses engaged in defense procurement contracts with the government;[27] ineligibility to serve in the armed forces;[28] ineligibility to immigrate to the United States.[29] As long as homosexuals bear the stigma of criminality, not much progress can be made toward removing these other disabilities. For example, the reason often given for the federal employment disability, especially in the foreign service, is that the homosexual's orientation make him peculiarly liable to blackmail, thus raising the possibility of betrayal of government secrets from fear of exposure. Yet the criminal law itself, together with the governmentally instigated ineligibility, creates the major stimulus to blackmail. Were the criminal law reformed, and the government to adopt a policy not just of eligibility but of affirmative job protection for homosexuals, the potential for blackmail would be drastically reduced, if not eliminated.[30] In other words, the justification for discriminating against these people builds on itself, and the criminal law forms its central pillar.

The third consequence is that the criminal law supplies the warrant for countless public and private discriminations, lacking any explicit permission from the law, of sorts that our consciences have long since stopped tolerating against other fellow citizens. For the sake of brevity, only three recent examples, taken from widely separated parts of the country, will be cited.

In early June 1970, a coalition of thirty-four homosexual and sexual freedom groups in Los Angeles County and the San Francisco Bay Area applied to the Police Commission of Los Angeles for a parade permit to conduct a procession with floats down Hollywood Boulevard the evening of June 28.[31] It was advertised as "a joyous affirmation of self-respect."[32] At the hearing Police Chief Edward M. Davis opposed the parade altogether. He told the commission that as long as felony laws against oral copulation and sodomy are on the books, "we would be ill-advised to discommode the people to have a burglars' or robbers' parade or homosexuals' parade from a legal standpoint."[33] After this equation of homosexuals with robbers and burglars, the commission voted to grant the permit only if the sponsors put up a $1 million liability insurance policy against damage anticipated from the reaction of Los Angeles's version of the hard hats, plus a $1,500 fee to pay for extra police services supposedly necessary to protect the paraders against them. These extravagant conditions on an exercise of the right of peaceful assembly were struck off by court order, and the parade took place without incident.[34]

The second example, almost contemporaneous, comes from Minneapolis. There, on May 18, 1970, two young men, one of whom had been offered a librarian's position at the University of Minnesota, applied for a license to marry each other, both freely admitting to the news media that they were homosexuals. The resultant publicity brought a meeting of a committee of the university's board of regents, whose recommendation was adopted that the man's appointment "not be approved on the ground that his personal conduct, as represented in the public and University news media, is not consistent with the best interest of the University." The regents' position, with no dissenting vote, was that, though the young man might be a very capable librarian, his professed homosexuality connoted to the public generally that he practiced acts of sodomy, a crime under Minnesota law; that the regents had a right to presume that by his applying for a license to marry another man he intended, were the license granted, to engage in such sodomous criminal activities; that the regents cannot condone the commission of criminal acts by university employees; and that consequently the young man had rendered himself unfit to be employed. Unemployment, perhaps the destruction of an entire career, thus befell an attempt not only to be open and aboveboard about one's sexual orientation but also to bring it within the ambit of society's requirement for sexual morality—monogamous marriage. The university's action was declared unconstitutional by a federal court, but the decision was subsequently reversed.[35]

The third example is from New York. The Gay Activists Alliance, a homosexual civil rights association whose objectives are to work for peaceful change of the antihomosexual laws and for protection of homosexuals against discrimination, applied for a certificate of incorporation from the state of New York. On November 5, 1970, the application was rejected by the secretary of state, who commented:

> The name of the corporation is not acceptable since it is not an appropriate name for a corporation when one considers the connotation in which the words are being used.
>
> The purposes of the corporation also raise a serious question whether a corporation may be formed to promote activities which are contrary to the avowed public policy of the State of New York and are in fact contrary to the penal laws of the State. . . .
>
> While individuals or groups have every right to seek changes in the laws and public policies of our state, the filing of the certificate which you submitted would be tantamount to a public sanction of the activities which are presently in violation of our public policy and penal statute.

On February 24, 1971, the association filed suit in New York supreme court to force the secretary of state to grant them the certificate of incorporation.[36] On May 21, the court denied their petition, saying,

> . . . . by identifying themselves as a "homosexual civil rights

organization," they are professing a present or future intent to disobey a penal statute of the State of New York. . . . [I]t would seem that in order to be a homosexual, the prohibited act must have at some time been committed or at least presently contemplated. It would therefore follow that the Secretary of State properly refused to provide the petitioners with "the imprimatur of incorporation" in the legitimate exercise of his discretion.[37]

This decision was later unanimously reversed by the Appellate Division of the New York Supreme Court.[38]

If such blatant discriminations are indulged by public agencies who must operate in full view of the news media and whose actions are easily subjected to further scrutiny by the courts,[39] one can imagine what is going on in the way of private discrimination. It has not yet become fashionable to champion the cause of this minority group. It is easy to stand up for the rights of a black as a human being, but hard to side with a "queer." No matter how closely the white civil rights enthusiast tries to identify with the plight of the Negro, blackness can never rub off on him. The aura of "immorality" can. Yet "queers" are human beings who suffer from their niggerdom as much as any black man ever did, even more so.[40] Discriminations based on one's race obviously do not reflect on one's real worth as an individual by any rational standard. They bespeak only the pettiness and bigotry of the actor. But to imply that someone is not "a real man" or "a real woman"[41] is, in our society at least, to inflict the deepest wounds of which words are capable. And when to words are added actions against which there is no redress, what grosser forms of persecution are possible, short of total outlawry? Is it not time to begin righting these wrongs?

NOTES

1. *See* Mead, *Cultural Determinants of Sexual Behavior*, in 2 SEX AND INTERNAL SECRETIONS 1474 (3d ed. W. C. Young 1961). I am using the words "deviance" and "deviation" throughout this book simply in the sociological sense of behavior that the majority in society has condemned. No pejorative connotation is implied.

2. This pattern is described in M. PLOSCOWE, SEX AND THE LAW (rev. ed.

1962); G. MUELLER, LEGAL REGULATION OF SEXUAL CONDUCT (1961); Slovenko, *A Panoramic View: Sexual Behavior and the Law*, in SEXUAL BEHAVIOR AND THE LAW 5 (R. Slovenko ed. 1965); and S. G. KLING, SEXUAL BEHAVIOR AND THE LAW (1965). An excellent, more recent, review of the statutory regulations on sexual behavior in the various states appears in Hefner, *The Legal Enforcement of Morality*, 40 U. COLO. L. REV. 199 (1968). A table summarizing the current laws in all fifty states appears in PLAYBOY, August 1972, at 188–89.

3. The constitutionality of these anticontraceptive laws has been brought into serious question by *Eisenstadt v. Baird*, 405 U.S. 438 (1972), which ruled unconstitutional the Massachusetts law of this type. *See* the discussion and notes at pp. 64–67, Chapter 3 *infra*. A *New York Times* article discussing this case noted that Massachusetts' attorney general claimed there were 25 other states with similar laws. N.Y. Times, March 2, 1971, at 22, col. 3. The lower federal decision, which also had ruled in favor of Baird's application for habeas corpus, and from which Massachusetts had appealed to the United States Supreme Court, is reported in 429 F.2d 1398 (1st Cir. 1970). Even in Massachusetts, though, condoms were legally available for the purpose of preventing the spread of venereal disease.

4. It is, of course, possible to argue that adultery has a victim, even though it may be consensual as between the participants, because it violates the specific marital vow of fidelity to one's spouse. Indeed, some states so treat it by providing that prosecution may be instigated only upon complaint of the "wronged" spouse. Our society does not, however, generally criminalize the violation of promises. Incest, on the other hand, has no victim at all if the conduct occurs between consenting adults neither of whom is married to another. However, both adultery and incest may demand special consideration for other reasons.

Formerly, the prohibition on incest between blood relatives was thought to be justifiable on the genetic theory that sexual unions between individuals who were closely related would be more likely to produce defective offspring—a theory now rendered more debatable by modern genetic science and in any event made largely irrelevant by the availability of effective contraception. *See* H. L. PACKER, THE LIMITS OF THE CRIMINAL SANCTION 315 (1968). It seems clear that the incest taboo is not instinctive but the product of cultural conditioning, because no aversion to sexual intercourse between relatives exists in animals other than man. The taboo is, however, almost universal in the human societies of which we have knowledge, though there is great variation in which relationships are tabooed beyond those of parent-child and brother-sister.

The suggestion has been made that the incest taboo is valuable to human societies because it encourages exogamous mating, thereby strengthening the ties *between* families. A more likely justification, however, is that it tends to hold intrafamilial sexual jealousies and conflicts to a minimum. This might explain why the taboo often extends to in-laws. Among all animals, human young undergo the longest period of helplessness and dependence. Without the nurture and protection of adults, they could not survive. In times past this nurture was likely to be provided only by parents or other relatives. The stability of family life was therefore essential to the propagation of the species. Disturbance of that stability by sexual conflicts within the family could not be tolerated. *See* C. S. FORD & F. A.

BEACH, PATTERNS OF SEXUAL BEHAVIOR 264–65 (1951); also Mead, *supra* note 1. If this hypothesis is correct, the worldwide variations in the range of incest taboos may be a function of the relative importance in the various societies of kinships beyond the nuclear family. Likewise, the taboo on adultery, by discouraging sexual jealousies that could split husband and wife, may serve the objective of family stability in much the same way. But to admit that taboos on adultery and incest can serve an important social need does not require one to admit that use of the criminal sanction is justifiable. In any event, both these restrictions on sexual behavior constitute rather insignificant limitations on human freedom. So it is not terribly important whether they be deemed constitutional or not. The person who cannot or will not confine his sexual activity to a single partner generally possesses the options of remaining single or getting a divorce. And one's relatives who stand within the prohibited degrees of kinship make up but an infinitesimal fraction of the potential sexual partners available in American society.

5. *See, e.g.,* J. S. MILL, ON LIBERTY (various editions); H. L. A. HART, LAW, LIBERTY AND MORALITY (1963); E. M. SCHUR, CRIMES WITHOUT VICTIMS (1965).

6. Throughout this book, the three concepts of "consent," "adult," and "private" are used to divide sexual conduct that the state should not have power to criminalize from that which it may. Nowhere have I attempted to define them. Yet no one of these concepts is free from difficulty.

When should a person be deemed an adult for the purpose of consenting to sexual acts? This is a question to which the various states have given different answers. Only if the age of consent for sexual acts is raised above that set by the state for all other purposes would the question seem to reach constitutional dimensions.

Is conduct private if the participants reasonably expect to be alone, even when it occurs in a "public" place? Is it public even though occurring in a "private" place, if a single nonparticipant can and does view it? And which places are "public," which "private"? Or should the test be whether the participants could reasonably foresee that others might view their conduct *who would likely be affronted or alarmed,* regardless of how one might characterize the place of its occurrence?

With regard even to the issue of consent, is conduct nonconsensual only if force was employed? Or is consent lacking if coerced by a threat likely to overcome the resistance of a normally resolute person? And if so, must the threat be express, or may it be implied? In prison, for example, homosexual relations often may appear to be consensual but are not in fact, because a long line of prior contacts between the partners has convinced one of them that he faces a risk of serious injury unless he consents. Imprisonment makes total escape from involvement with the aggressor impossible, thus diminishing one's will to resist. On the other hand, if someone has been offered some immense benefit to gain his consent, is the consent really voluntary? The consent to experimentation and other medical procedures obtained from prisoners is a nonsexual case in point. I have not attempted to resolve all these difficulties because I am convinced that despite them, the three concepts have a meaning definite enough for drawing lines in constitutional law.

7. Blake, *Population Policy for Americans: Is the Government Being Misled?*, 164 SCIENCE 528–29 (1969).

8. This state of affairs is gaining increasing recognition in government circles, as witness the following excerpt from *Time Magazine:*

> Population planners hope that, at least in the U.S., pills and other contraceptive devices will soon be available to every couple that wants them. Yet even then, the nation's population will keep growing at an alarming rate. The reason is simple but often overlooked, according to Dr. Roger O. Egeberg, HEW's Assistant Secretary for health and scientific affairs. "The typical American family," he told a Planned Parenthood conference last week, "will elect to have three children, not two."
>
> Egeberg proposed a radical solution, involving nothing less than a change in prevailing attitudes about marriage and children. The notion that everyone should marry and raise a family was important in an era when infant-mortality rates were high and life expectancy short. Now it is important, he warned, to remove the stigma that society attaches to remaining unmarried and to somehow change the feelings of comfort and security that many Americans derive from having large families. "This is going to shock a lot of people," he conceded, "but we have to get the discussion started."

TIME, Nov. 7, 1969, at 80.

9. Letter from Judith Blake Davis to the author, June 30, 1972.

10. The crime of "sodomy" in English jurisprudence, from which our American legal concepts sprang, covered only anal intercourse between humans (whether the partners were of the same sex or of opposite sexes), and any form of sexual gratification by a human being with a member of another species. Conduct of the latter sort was also often termed "bestiality." In England, "buggery" is a synonym for "sodomy" and is the official name for the crime, whereas in Scots law "sodomy" is the official term. In both England and Scotland, however, these terms do not cover acts between humans other than anal intercourse. Fellatio, cunnilingus, and all the additional sexual acts between humans that anyone might conceivably regard as "unnatural" were not criminal in Great Britain, regardless of the sex of the partners, until the Labouchère amendment of 1885. This amendment, offered to the Criminal Law Amendment Act of that date by one Henry Labouchère, and adopted by Parliament without any real consideration of its significance, made criminal any act of "gross indecency" between males. Thus, all sexual activities *between males* besides anal intercourse also became a crime, but the same or similar acts were perfectly lawful if performed between a man and a woman or between two women. The law remained so in Britain until the reform of 1967. *See* note 19, Chapter 2 *infra;* WOLFENDEN REPORT, REPORT OF THE COMMITTEE ON HOMOSEXUAL OFFENCES AND PROSTITUTION *passim,* but particularly para. 77 (authorized Amer. ed. 1963) [hereinafter cited as WOLFENDEN]; and H. M. HYDE, THE LOVE THAT DARED NOT SPEAK ITS NAME—A CANDID HISTORY OF HOMOSEXUALITY IN BRITAIN (1970).

In the United States, legislatures typically enacted statutes denouncing the crime without defining it. The statutory language simply prohibited "sodomy" or "buggery" or "the abominable and detestable crime against nature" and prescribed a penalty. Legislatures in some of the states were more explicit, but even their attempts at definition were hardly models of clarity and precision. In some states, the courts construed the statutes to include various acts in addition to anal intercourse. In other states, the statute was held restricted to that one act. Generally, in the latter states, the legislature either amended the statute to broaden its scope, or enacted a separate statute, to cover other types of sexual acts such as fellatio. In order to avoid boring the reader with a lengthy and detailed survey of the statutes in all American jurisdictions, I have collected examples of the various kinds of sodomy statutes in the appendix. References to the citations of all the American sodomy statutes can be found in the first seven notes to Chapter 10. Anyone interested in the law of a particular jurisdiction can find its statute by consulting these notes. Most of the reported appellate opinions that have decided which acts are and are not covered by these various provisions are cited and discussed in Chapter 2. The only form of sexual gratification clearly not prohibited by these laws in any state is coitus—the penis of a man in the vagina of a woman.

11. See text and notes at pp. 223–24 and note 105, Chapter 7 infra.

12. See Model Penal Code §207.5, Comment at 276-91 (Tent. Draft No. 4, 1955). The seven states having aligned their laws with the Model Penal Code in this respect are Illinois, Connecticut, Colorado, Oregon, Hawaii, Delaware and Ohio. The new laws in the latter three states are effective on January 1, 1973, April 1, 1973, and January 1, 1974, respectively. See ILL. ANN. STAT. 38 §§11-4 and 11-5 (1964); CONN. GEN. STAT. ANN. §§53a-65 (2), 53a-70, 53a-71, 53a-75, 53a-77 (1972); ORE. REV. STAT. §§ 163.305(1), 163.385, 163.395, and 163.405 (1971); COLO. SESS. LAWS 1971, ch. 121, §§ 40-3-403, 40-3-404, 40-3-405, 40-3-410, and 40-7-301; new HAWAII PENAL CODE §§ 700(8), 733, 734, and 735; new DELAWARE CRIMINAL CODE §§762, 763, 766, and 773(2) and (3); and new OHIO CRIMINAL CODE §§ 2907.01(A), 2907.02, 2907.03, 2907.04, and 2907.09.

In New York, Minnesota, Kansas, and Utah, the offense between consenting adults has been reduced to a misdemeanor—a step in the right direction. See N. Y. PENAL LAW § 130.38 (McKinney 1967); MINN. STAT. ANN. § 609.293, subd. 5 (Supp. 1971); KAN. STAT. ANN. §21-3505 (Supp. 1970); and UTAH CODE ANN. § 76-53-22 (Supp. 1969). Section 3124 of the new Pennsylvania Criminal Code adopted December 5, 1972, will also reduce the offense to a misdemeanor there. Although in New Jersey the offense is denominated a "high misdemeanor," this category of crime in that state carries a penalty of felony dimensions. N. J. STAT. 2A:143-1 (1969).

13. See note 48, Chapter 4 infra.

14. See IDAHO CODE 18-901(2), 18-903, 18-904 (1971 Supp.).

15. See The Advocate, May 10, 1972.

16. What happened in Georgia's recent penal code revision may furnish an omen of the future in many other states. In its section on sodomy, the new code ignored the recommendations of the Model Penal Code and retained consensual sodomy between adults as a felony carrying a maximum penalty of 20 years. The offense was redefined so as to make the language unambiguous and to cover lesbian conduct, which had been held outside the purview of the old statute. The

old law had allowed a maximum penalty of only 10 years for the first offense between consenting adults. Thus the new law, if anything, represents a regression to greater barbarity in its treatment of sexual deviation. *Compare* GA. CODE ANN. § 26-2002 (Crim. Code 1970 Revision) *with* Ga. Code Ann. § 26-5901 (1953).

17. The development of adult sexual consensus about acceptable overt behavior through the interaction of pairs of individuals [generally husbands and wives] rather than among larger social groups in the community has serious consequences for the nature of public discussion of sexuality, especially in times of controversy. The privatization of sexual consensus means that no one can be sure of the behavior of others, and this insecurity is accompanied by a belief that statements that differ from the conventional norms will be taken as evidence of sexual deviation. The only system of values that can be invoked in a time of sexual controversy is the most conservative. . . . This lack of consensus makes it very difficult for a body of disinterested opinion about sexuality to exist. Any statement by an individual about sexuality is commonly presumed to be related to the sexual preferences and desires of that individual.

Gagnon, *Sexuality and Sexual Learning in the Child,* in SEXUAL DEVIANCE 20–21 (J. H. Gagnon & W. Simon eds. 1967). *See also* T. SZASZ, LAW, LIBERTY AND PSYCHIATRY 249 (1963).

18. Homosexuality, too, cuts across party lines, and in some states, notably New York and California, homosexuals have begun to organize for political action and to force politicians to listen. So far, these efforts have not managed to produce reform in either state. But the situation in these states, which may hold some promise of success, is a far cry from that in, say, South Carolina or New Hampshire, where "gay liberation" seems confined to some student group here and there on a college campus. Effective political militancy seems light years away in states like those. *See* note 4, Chapter 11 *infra.*

19. The Model Penal Code was to have included a section on illicit cohabitation but none on adultery or fornication as such. In the final draft, however, even the section on illicit cohabitation was eliminated. R. M. PERKINS, CRIMINAL LAW 379 (2d ed. 1969).

20. As noted before, these laws may already have been effectively undermined. *See* note 3 *supra.*

21. At the time of this writing, the only legislatures which have expressly excluded sexual activities between husband and wife from the coverage of their sodomy statutes are those of Kansas, New York, and Pennsylvania. The Kansas law, but not those of New York or Pennsylvania, also excludes activities between unmarried consenting adults of opposite sexes. *See* KAN. STAT. ANN. 21-3505 (Supp. 1970); N.Y. PENAL LAW §§130.00(2), 130.38 (McKinney 1967); new PENNSYLVANIA CRIMINAL CODE §§3101, 3124. In Illinois, sodomy between consenting adults in private is not a crime. If one of the partners is underage but they are validly married, the conduct likewise must not be criminal because otherwise normal sexual intercourse between them would be equally a crime. *See* ILL. ANN. STAT. 38 §§11-4 and 11-5 (1964). The new criminal codes of Connecticut, Colorado, Oregon, Hawaii, Delaware, and Ohio likewise do not

make sodomy between consenting adults in private a crime. If one of the partners is underage but they are validly married to each other, the marriage precludes criminal responsibility because these codes' definition of the offense or of the term "deviate sexual intercourse" excludes conduct between husband and wife. *See* citations note 12 *supra*. Of course, wherever sodomy is legitimated by the existence of the marital relationship between the partners, as in New York, an invisible discrimination exists against homosexuals, because their liaisons have not qualified for such legitimation. *See* note 48, Chapter 5 *infra*.

22. The great bulk of appellate opinions in sodomy cases involves force, minors, or a place where the participants could be and were viewed by others. This pattern is partly due to the fact that the police rarely learn of private adult consensual behavior (whether homosexual *or* heterosexual). Neither participant is likely to report it. And if they try to discover such "crime" through direct observation of it, their testimony is usually inadmissible on constitutional grounds. The law is becoming established that obtaining evidence without a warrant by means of direct police surveillance of any place—even a public place—where the occupants reasonably expect privacy violates the fourth amendment's proscription of unreasonable searches and seizures. *See* Katz v. United States, 389 U.S. 347 (1967). In *Katz*, the Supreme Court rejected the old notion that there must be a physical trespass or intrusion into such a "private" place to constitute a violation of the fourth amendment. The case involved the bugging of a telephone booth from which the incriminating call was made. *Katz's* overruling of prior law was made to operate prospectively only, in Desist v. United States, 394 U.S. 244 (1969), but Mapp v. Ohio, 367 U.S. 643 (1961), indicates that the new *Katz* principle is applicable to the states as well as the federal government.

A number of cases have raised the question of whether visual surveillance by the police of enclosed toilet stalls in public restrooms violates the fourth amendment. It would seem that if auditory surveillance of a telephone booth without a warrant, as in *Katz*, violates the fourth amendment, then visual surveillance of a completely enclosed toilet stall (usually from some concealed position in the woodwork) is equally unconstitutional if conducted without a warrant. The leading case denying the unconstitutionality of such surveillance is Smayda v. United States, 352 F.2d 251 (9th Cir. 1965), *cert. denied*, 382 U.S. 981. But *Smayda* was decided before *Katz* and a reading of the opinion reveals that the decision was based on a view of the law which is inconsistent with *Katz* and therefore now erroneous. Several cases involving visual surveillance have been decided by state appellate courts in line with the *Katz* reasoning, thus preventing the police from impairing, by such means of crime detection, the public's general expectation of privacy in using enclosed toilet stalls. *See* Bielicki v. Superior Court, 57 Cal.2d 602, 371 P.2d 288, 21 Cal. Rptr. 552 (1962); Britt v. Superior Court, 58 Cal.2d 469, 374 P.2d 817, 24 Cal. Rptr. 849 (1962); Brown v. State, 3 Md. App. 90, 238 A.2d 147 (1968); State v. Bryant, 177 N.W.2d 800 (Minn. 1970); Buchanan v. State, 471 S.W.2d 401 (Tex. Crim. App. 1971); and State v. Kent, 20 Utah 2d 1, 432 P.2d 64 (1967). In a unanimous decision, the Supreme Court of California has extended this line of reasoning to include open toilet stalls. People

v. Triggs, Crim. No. 16486 (Cal. Sup. Ct., filed Feb. 22, 1973). For a recent case
that follows the *Smayda* result and rationale, *see* Mitchell v. State, 120 Ga. App.
447, 170 S.E.2d 765 (1969).

Almost the only means by which the police can thus obtain legally admissible
evidence of truly *private* activities between consenting adults are (1) the
voluntary confession of the defendant, and (2) the testimony of the other party to
the "crime." The first means requires corroboration in almost all states. *See* C. T.
McCormick, Handbook of the Law of Evidence § 110 (1954). The second
requires corroboration in most. *See* 7 J. H. Wigmore, Evidence § 2056 (3d ed.
1940). Even where the other party to the "crime" is a police officer, his
testimony may demand corroboration no less than that of any other accomplice.
See People v. Brocklehurst, 14 Cal. App.3d 473, 92 Cal. Rptr. 340 (1971). If the
other party is the spouse of the defendant, his or her testimony is excludable in a
number of states under the old principle that a wife cannot testify against her
husband in a criminal prosecution and vice-versa. *See* McCormick, *supra* § 66.
Consequently, even when such "crimes" come to the attention of the police, they
find it difficult to obtain proof sufficient to justify prosecution.

The difficulty inherent in enforcement of the law against consensual acts of
adults in private does not prevent occasional prosecutions, though. Two of the
most outrageous instances—one heterosexual, the other homosexual—are Cotner
v. Henry, 394 F.2d 873 (7th Cir. 1968), and State v. Edwards, 243 Ore. 440, 412
P.2d 526 (1966). In the *Cotner* case, the petitioner had been prosecuted at the
instigation of his wife for a consensual act of anal intercourse, and sentenced to
the statutory term of 2 to 14 years' imprisonment! In the *Edwards* case, the
defendant and the prosecuting witness met in a "gay" bar in Portland in February
1962, and soon thereafter began living together, first in Oregon, then in San
Francisco. In the latter part of December 1962, they went to Reno, Nevada, and
were ostensibly married there, the prosecuting witness using a feminine alias.
They returned to Medford, Oregon, and lived together as "husband" and "wife,"
the witness continuing to use a female alias and to dress in women's clothes. The
testimony of the "wife" in this homosexual marriage was the basis for convicting
the "husband" of sodomy (anal intercourse). Their representations to others that
they were husband and wife were deemed sufficient corroboration of "her"
testimony. One suspects that what happened in both cases was that the
prosecuting witness developed a grudge against the defendant, and then, by
offering to turn state's witness in return for immunity from prosecution, enlisted
the aid of the authorities in wreaking his or her private vengeance. Plainly, if any
"crime" was committed, the prosecuting witness was as guilty as the defendant.
Neither was any more a "victim" than the other. That such perversions of justice
are permitted to take place in this day and age is a far greater outrage than these
harmless "perversions" of sex.

23. Slovenko, *Sex Mores and the Enforcement of the Law on Sex Crimes: A
Study of the Status Quo*, 15 U. Kan. L. Rev. 265 (1967), seems to be asking this
question and finding no answer.

24. The most comprehensive yet concise summaries of the consequences for
homosexuals of the present state of American criminal law are Note, *Homosexuality and the Law—An Overview*, 17 N.Y. Law Forum 273 (1971), and The

Challenge and Progress of Homosexual Law Reform, 1968 (pamphlet published by the Council on Religion and the Homosexual, the Daughters of Bilitis, the Society for Individual Rights, and the Tavern Guild, San Francisco). Another good summary is found in Cantor, *Deviation and the Criminal Law*, 55 J. CRIM. L., C. & P. S. 441 (1964). One who wishes to get an accurate picture of how the criminal justice system impinges on homosexuals can do no better than to read the massive study by the UCLA Law Review staff in Note, *The Consenting Adult Homosexual and the Law: An Empirical Study of Enforcement and Administration in Los Angeles County*, 13 U.C.L.A. L. REV. 644 (1966).

25. For a first-hand account by a sociologist of his harrowing arrest by vice-squad officers, which is probably typical of such experiences, *see* L. HUMPHREYS, TEAROOM TRADE—IMPERSONAL SEX IN PUBLIC PLACES 93–96 (1970).

26. *See* Note, *Discrimination on the Basis of Arrest Records*, 56 CORNELL L. REV. 470 (1971).

27. *See* Note, *Government-Created Employment Disabilities of the Homosexual*, 82 HARV. L. REV. 1738 (1969); and W. Parker, Homosexuals and Employment, 1970 (pamphlet published by the Corinthian Foundation, San Francisco).

28. See Army Regulation 635-89, Air Force Regulation 35-66, Air Force Manual 39-12, and Secretary of the Navy Instruction 1900.9; Society for Individual Rights, The Armed Services and Homosexuality, no date (pamphlet published by the Society for Individual Rights, San Francisco); and C. J. WILLIAMS & M. S. WEINBERG, HOMOSEXUALS AND THE MILITARY: A STUDY OF LESS THAN HONORABLE DISCHARGE (1971). The Veterans Administration denies most veterans' benefits to any serviceman given an Undesirable Discharge for homosexuality. *See* Note, *Homosexuals in the Military*, 37 FORDHAM L. REV. 465, 473 (1969).

29. Immigration and Nationality Act of 1952, § 212(a) (4), 8 U.S.C. §1182(a) (4) (1970), as construed in Boutilier v. Immigration and Naturalization Service, 387 U.S. 118 (1967).

30. The extent to which the threat of blackmail is a product of the criminal sanctions against homosexual acts can be overstated. A lot of noncriminal behavior would be very embarrassing if publicly known, and may consequently supply the pretext for blackmail. For instance, Parker, *supra* note 27, at 17-19, shows that far more heterosexuals than homosexuals have been blackmailed into handing over secret information to an enemy nation. In all likelihood, few if any of these heterosexual cases involved criminal sexual behavior. Nonetheless, if a person is being blackmailed for criminal conduct, he will be far less likely to call the police. The risk of undergoing prosecution himself, with its much surer effect on his livelihood, is too frightening. He may resist the blackmailer, but he must do so on his own. He gets no help from society.

31. The incident is reported in L.A. Times, June 13, 1970, Part II, at 1, col. 1. The parade, which was arranged to be contemporaneous with a similar one in New York, was noted in TIME, July 13, 1970, at 1.

32. L.A. Times, June 13, 1970, Part II, at 1, col. 1.

33. *Ibid.*, and at 10, col. 1.

34. *See* L.A. Times, June 29, 1970, Part I, at 3, col. 3.

35. The case, in which the facts here set out are reported, is McConnell v. Anderson, 316 F.Supp. 809 (D. Minn. 1970), *rev'd* 451 F.2d 193 (8th Cir. 1971), *cert. denied,* 40 U.S.L.W. 3484 (1972). A story on the decision appears in N.Y. Times, Sept. 20, 1970, at 56, col. 1, and on the "marriage" of the two young men in question, in LOOK, Jan. 26, 1971, at 69. *See* note 48, Chapter 5 *infra.*

36. The facts here reported are taken from the N.Y. Times, Feb. 25, 1971, at 32, col. 2.

37. Gay Activists Alliance v. Lomenzo, 66 Misc.2d 456, 320 N.Y. Supp.2d 994 (1971).

38. Owles v. Lomenzo, 38 App. Div.2d 981, 329 N.Y. Supp.2d 181 (1972). Surprisingly, the secretary of state appealed this decision to New York's highest court—the Court of Appeals. That court unanimously affirmed the Appellate Division. The Advocate, Feb. 14, 1973, at 19.

39. Another example of official discrimination is the Miami, Florida, city ordinance which prohibits bars from knowingly employing homosexuals, serving them, or allowing them to congregate on their premises. This ordinance had been previously sustained against constitutional attack. *See* Inman v. City of Miami, 197 So.2d 50 (1967), *cert. denied,* 389 U.S. 1048 (1968). *But see* One Eleven Wines and Liquors, Inc. v. Division of Alcoholic Beverage Control, 50 N.J. 329, 235 A.2d 12 (1967), which reached an opposite conclusion on somewhat similar facts. In November 1971, the Miami police attempted to enforce the ordinance, but a municipal judge declared it unconstitutional and urged city officials to appeal his decision in order to test the conclusion reached in the *Inman* case. *See* The Advocate, Dec. 8, 1971, at 12, and Jan. 5, 1972, at 2.

40. Certainly, in terms of the objective, quantifiable effects of discrimination, blacks suffer more than homosexuals because the latter can and do, on the whole, pass for "straight." But for those homosexuals whose identity is publicly known, the effects may be greater because blacks are now, formally at least, protected by law from the more blatant kinds of economic discrimination. The only formal protection yet enacted for homosexuals consists of city ordinances banning discrimination against them in a tiny handful of locales, such as Ann Arbor and East Lansing, Michigan and San Francisco, California. In the latter city, the ordinance covers only employment by the municipal government and by private companies doing business with it. *See* The Advocate, August 16, 1972, at 1, 16; May 24, 1972, at 3, 17; May 10, 1972, at 1, 4. In terms of the psychic effects of discrimination, it is debatable whether one group suffers more than the other. Concealment, for instance, may exact a heavier psychic toll than outright confrontation of hatred or contempt.

41. *E.g.,* Wyden, *How to Raise Your Son to Be a Real Man,* FAMILY CIRCLE, July 1970, at 22.

2

The Void-for-Vagueness Doctrine

In 1931, in *McBoyle v. United States,*[1] one of the greatest of America's men of the coif said:

> Although it is not likely that a criminal will carefully consider the text of the law before he murders or steals, it is reasonable that a fair warning should be given to the world *in language that the common world will understand,* of what the law intends to do if a certain line is passed. To make the warning fair, so far as possible the line should be clear.[2]

Oliver Wendell Holmes, Jr., was not announcing a novel idea. The maxim *ubi jus incertum, ibi jus nullum* has come down to us from ancient times, and the cases are legion which hold that a criminal statute drawn so vaguely as to give no, or inadequate, notice of what is proscribed violates the due process clauses of the fifth and fourteenth amendments.[3] These cases have been analyzed, sifted, and resifted enough already.[4] What is needed for the purposes of this essay is to review briefly some of the reasons behind the doctrine, and to point out how plainly the typical sodomy statute violates them.

Despite the current fad for looking at law as a *process* of conflict resolution, it is still also a set of *rules* for the guidance of conduct. This is particularly true of the criminal law, and, as the quotation from Mr. Justice Holmes indicates, the rule's language must be directed at the common man, because it is *his* conduct that the lawgiver is seeking to guide. It is immaterial whether the common man is likely ever to consult that language and thus rely on it. The fact that the language may say something to those trained in the law—judges, prosecutors, and defense counsel—is not enough, especially when the rule regulates behavior that is part and parcel

21

of everyday life, as sexual behavior is. The corporate executive knows that his company's activities are subject to a mass of regulatory legislation. He can be expected to consult legal counsel about possible technical meanings of words and to explore all avenues for resolving ambiguities before acting upon any one interpretation. Not so the ordinary individual where the satisfaction of a powerful natural drive and the expression of his most intimate feelings are concerned.[5]

Professor Fuller in his book *The Morality of Law* identifies eight canons as essential to realizing the ideal of "the rule of law."[6] The fourth of these—that rules should be understandable—corresponds with the void-for-vagueness doctrine. It is worth noting, however, that a violation of this fourth canon may result in violations of the first three as well.

If a rule is not understandable, one result may be that no rule at all is achieved, the issues being decided on an ad hoc basis by the adjudicators (the first canon). Of course, to the extent that those affected by the rule are able to take such varying ad hoc applications up to the state's supreme court, the rule over a period of time acquires a measure of definition by the gradual process of inclusion and exclusion. In such a process, however, Fuller's third canon—the ban upon retroactive lawmaking—is commonly violated. If acts A, B, C, and D are as reasonably susceptible of being regarded outside the rule as within it, and the supreme court progressively includes them, the result is about the same as if the legislature had prohibited each of them specifically but made the prohibition retroactive. It cannot be discovered that, say, act B is within the prohibition until somebody has already committed it and been prosecuted and convicted and the conviction sustained by the supreme court. In other words, the rule offers no guide for future conduct. The hapless defendant finds out that his conduct was prohibited by it only *ex post facto*.

This process also violates the second canon—the requirement that the rules a person is expected to observe be publicized, or at least made available to him. However unlikely a layman may be to check through the statutory law, it is the limit of what he should be held to know, at least in an area regulating a universal facet of life. Only those trained in the law and legal research can be expected to ferret out the gloss that appellate courts have placed on statutory language. Logically, this analysis would also mean that the constitutional requirement of due process of law excludes the very notion of common-law crimes. This may go against traditional wisdom, but a group of ancient judicial precedents hardly gives laymen notice of a criminal rule adequate to satisfy the requirements of due process.[7] Significantly, a number of current penal code revisions assert that no conduct can be considered a crime unless defined as such by the code.[8]

The requirements formulated in Fuller's canons are, admittedly, general guidelines at best. They give us no hard and fast tests for determining when a rule is so vague as to be void. All language is to some extent plastic. Let us take a look at the sodomy statutes to see how they measure up to these guidelines.

The most typical sodomy statute reads like section 286 of the California Penal Code. It contains no definition of the crime:

> Every person who is guilty of the infamous crime against nature, committed with mankind or with any animal, is punishable by imprisonment in the state prison not less than one year.[9]

With differences in the penalty, and minor variations of language that should not affect the interpretation, this provision appears in the current statutes of Alabama, Arizona, Delaware, Florida, Idaho, Maine, Massachusetts, Michigan, Mississippi, Montana, Nevada, North Carolina, Oklahoma, Puerto Rico, Rhode Island, South Dakota, and Tennessee.[10] Some of these states use the term "sodomy" or "buggery" in the title of the section. One other—New Jersey—uses the same language in the body of its section but adds the word "sodomy" in such fashion as to indicate equivalence between that term and the phrase "crime against nature."[11] The statutes of Arkansas, Kentucky, Maryland, and South Carolina are the same, except that they omit the phrase "crime against nature," substituting for it the phrase "crime of sodomy," "crime of buggery," or "sodomy or buggery."[12]

The term "crime against nature" is meaningless to the average layman.[13] If the language quoted above from the California law did not appear among the sex offenses of the penal code and did not carry such a stiff penalty, one might think that its purpose is to keep people from walking horses on the grass, or that its enactment was prompted by the Sierra Club to prevent the spoliation of Nature.[14] On the other hand, the term "sodomy" may connote something to a layman, because of widespread acquaintance with the biblical tale of Sodom and Gomorrah[15] and its frequent interpretation that their fate involved the sin of homosexual acts. Even lacking such familiarity with the Bible, a layman could be expected to learn the core meaning of the word, since it is defined in lay dictionaries. But how can he be expected to know what is "the crime against nature"? This is a legal term of art. It has no currency in common parlance and is not found in lay dictionaries. Alabama's statute is even worse: By speaking of "*a* crime against nature," it does not even give warning that the phrase used may *be* a legal term of art.[16]

So much for what the statutory language may signify to a layman. Contrary to the suggestion offered above as to what due process ought to require, the United States Supreme Court has indicated more than once that a vague word or a legal term of art will pass muster if it is defined by the common law, that is, if it has a commonly accepted meaning derived from the common law. Under this test neither "crime against nature" nor "sodomy" will pass, except as regards their single agreed "core" meaning: anal intercourse between humans, and any type of sexual act between a human being and an animal.[17] Whether other forms of sexual conduct between humans are covered by the terms has been so much a subject of disagreement that the courts of the various states have not been able even to reach accord on whether oral stimulation of the penis—fellatio—is within their scope. In England, the controlling precedent of *Rex v. Jacobs*[18] held that it is not. Parliament later enacted another statute covering fellatio, mutual masturbation, and other practices between males, all of which are subsumed under the category of acts "of gross indecency."[19]

In America, the courts of the states of Arizona, California Colorado, Kentucky, Louisiana, Michigan, Nebraska, New Jersey, New Mexico, Texas, Utah, and Virginia have held that fellatio is not within the common-law meaning of "crime against nature," "sodomy," or "buggery," in construing statutory provisions giving no further definition of the offense.[20] The opposite conclusion has been reached in Alabama, Delaware, Florida, Hawaii, Idaho, Kansas, Maine, Mississippi, Montana, Nevada, North Carolina, Oklahoma, Oregon, Rhode Island, South Dakota, and Tennessee.[21] The Arkansas supreme court has sustained a conviction for sodomy, involving fellatio, under its statute, which likewise does not define the offense (beyond terming it "sodomy or buggery"). The court apparently assumed without discussion that fellatio falls within those terms.[22] In Georgia, Indiana, and Missouri, the courts reached the conclusion that fellatio was included in the offense, but relied on language peculiar to their statutes, which defined the offense further and thus furnished some ground for presuming the legislature intended to expand it beyond its common-law "core" meaning.[23] In two other jurisdictions—Puerto Rico and South Carolina—where one would expect to find some precedent one way or the other (because the only statute is of this general type that gives no definition of the offense), no precedent has been found. In Maryland and Massachusetts, sodomy apparently was thought not to cover fellatio since supplemental statutes were enacted in those states to cover it, leaving the sodomy statutes still lacking a statutory definition of the offense.[24] Vermont, lacking any sodomy statute at all, has held sodomy indictable as a common-law crime[25] and has enacted a statute specifically covering "Fellation."[26]

The approach taken in most cases that have extended sodomy to include fellatio is to look at the statute like any *civil* statute, that is, to construe it according to what the court thinks the legislature meant the ambiguous words to cover. Since these statutes were generally enacted at a time when records of a bill's legislative history were not kept, no evidence of the legislative intent exists beyond the statutory language itself. The courts have ignored what a layman might think the language means, or what it meant at English common law according to case authority. The courts also have disregarded whether the meaning they ascribe to the language is an accepted one under American common law. Their reasoning runs like this: When the legislature penalized the "crime against nature," it must have intended to make criminal all sexual behavior which is against the order of nature. Since penis-in-vagina is the only mode of sexual gratification that accords with the order of nature, the legislature must have intended to include fellatio within its proscription of sodomy, fellatio being just as unnatural as anal intercourse.[27] In some states, misgivings have been expressed in later cases about whether this approach was correct, but reluctance to overturn an established precedent prevented overruling of the earlier decision.[28]

The significant question is not which line of cases represents the majority view or the more correct approach to statutory interpretation. Rather, it is whether one can say that the terms "crime against nature," "sodomy," and "buggery" have an agreed definition at common law which includes fellatio. The evidence is incontrovertible that they do *not*. And if they do not, then to apply them so as to sustain the conviction of someone who has performed fellatio would seem to violate due process by convicting him for conduct which he could not have been expected to know was covered by the statutory language.

This particular variant of the challenge on void-for-vagueness grounds is not available in those states which narrowly construed their sodomy statutes. Their legislatures either amended the statute or added an additional one to cover oral-genital contacts.[29] How has the challenge fared in the other states? The response of Nevada is typical. In the 1968 case of *Hogan v. State*,[30] in which this challenge was made, the court's response was that, although the term "crime against nature" is not defined in the Nevada statute, the statute is not unconstitutionally vague because the term is defined by *Nevada* common law. In other words, since the Nevada supreme court had previously held, in the *Benites* case,[31] that fellatio was within the term "crime against nature," the term is now adequately defined so that anyone in Nevada should know that fellatio is proscribed.

The courts may succeed in such legerdemain,[32] but it is hardly justifiable. Unless statutory definitions of crime exist only for the instruction of prosecutors, defense counsel, and judges, variations from English common law created by appellate decisions should not be included within them. Only lawyers can be expected to know such decisions and how to interpret them. Even if Nevada laymen know the peculiar way in which their supreme court has interpreted "crime against nature," what about the multitude of people who visit Nevada annually from other states where that phrase has been held to its meaning at English common law? In view of the mobility of modern Americans, a judicial definition of vague statutory terms should salvage the law only when that definition is generally accepted across America; "common law" for this purpose ought to mean the common law of America, not the judge-made law of Nevada.

Although the United States Supreme Court has often held that, in testing the constitutionality of state statutes, the statute must be viewed in the light of its interpretation by the state's highest appellate court, the Supreme Court cannot have intended that a term in common use to refer to a common crime throughout the states can have as many different meanings as there are state supreme courts to define it. If so, all vagueness would become curable by judicial construction and a primary policy behind the void-for-vagueness doctrine would be totally frustrated.

Anthony Amsterdam, in his exhaustive review of the cases involving the void-for-vagueness doctrine in the United States Supreme Court,[33] argues that the objective behind the doctrine is not so much to give laymen clear guidelines for conduct as it is to ensure that a definite rule exists within the judicial system in question, whether federal or that of any particular state. Lower officials—prosecutors and judges—are thus prevented from holding the same conduct criminal in one time or place but not in another. A statute is not unconstitutionally vague if a definite meaning has been or can be conclusively affixed to it in one state, though that same meaning has been conclusively excluded from the identical ambiguous statute of another. In short, the doctrine exists primarily to limit discretion among lower judicial officials; it serves as a defense against arbitrary and capricious enforcement.

However sound this analysis may be as a general description of the results reached in void-for-vagueness cases, it may not be the proper analysis to apply to the sodomy laws.[34] The Supreme Court, as already noted, has often stated that the policy of the doctrine *is* to assure statutory language clear enough to guide laymen.[35] It may thus be safer to rely on what the Court says and thinks it is doing when it uses the doctrine than to rely exclusively on some pattern deducible from the overall results it has in fact accomplished. In one of the most crucial recent cases involving the doctrine—*United States v. Vuitch*[36] in which an abortion statute was claimed to be unconstitutionally vague—the justices seemed fully as concerned with what the statutory language would mean to laymen untutored in the law, *i.e.*, physicians deciding whether or not they could legally perform abortions, as with what it would mean to judges, prosecutors, and juries. This concern with "the lack of notice given a potential offender" is also evident in *Papachristou v. City of Jacksonville*,[37] in which the Supreme Court overturned a vagrancy ordinance as unconstitutionally vague.

The doctrine can serve different policy objectives in different contexts. Many of the void-for-vagueness cases in the United States

Supreme Court involved regulatory statutes over business conditions and practices in which the vagueness lay in language of degree. The same conduct could be criminal and noncriminal, depending on where it fell along a continuum of varying magnitudes. Defining in advance a precise point along that continuum dividing criminal from noncriminal conduct would be a difficult if not impossible legislative feat; that task is better left to the judiciary in the process of applying the law to concrete situations. In these cases, there is no social advantage in encouraging potential offenders to come as close to the line of criminality as possible. If, for example, a businessman suspects that his activities may effect an "unreasonable" restraint of trade in violation of the antitrust laws, he should cease and desist until he is assured his plan is legal, not proceed to take the risk and then plead ambiguity when he is prosecuted.

In the statutes concerning murder, manslaughter, and justifiable homicide, a considerable diversity can be tolerated among the states in their judicially reached distinctions between the various circumstances that cast the act of killing into one or the other of these pigeonholes. The act of killing another human being is known by all to be a crime unless special circumstances excuse or mitigate it. Therefore, laying down the precise distinctions in the statutory language itself is not required to protect any important social interest. No one who is contemplating taking another's life deserves to be scrupulously forewarned so that he can plan circumstances to make his action fall into one pigeonhole rather than another.

The sodomy statutes are a different matter. They involve questions neither of the degree to which an activity is indulged nor of which circumstances make the same act an offense of the first order or of some inferior order or even no crime at all. In the sodomy statutes the very issue is which sexual acts are criminal and which are not. Everyone is entitled to assume that some such acts are licit; and, because the sex drive is an appetite common to all humankind, we can safely predict that just about everybody, at least at some point in his life, will engage in some sexual acts. If a legislature is going to make certain of them illicit, we are entitled to a comprehensible description of them.

Do the words "crime against nature" describe anything? Do they permit one to kiss the lips, but not the penis? To tongue the inside of the mouth, but not the labia? To caress the breasts, but not the anus? To ejaculate in the vagina, but nowhere else? To lie with the male on top of the female, but not vice versa? To practice birth control by the rhythm method, but not by coitus interruptus or artificial contraceptive devices? The implication of the statutory terms that the criterion is "naturalness" does not help, because there is no consensus in our society on what is and what is not "natural."[38] Science cannot tell us, because every sex act that is anatomically feasible is "natural" in the sense that it occurs in nature. If we ask what it is that people consider "natural" for themselves, the answer is "everything"; for every person who finds a particular act "unnatural" there will be another who finds it "natural." As will be noted at more length later in this book, the only consensus that ever existed in Western culture on this issue (and one may doubt how widespread it was even in its heyday) was built on a Judeo-Christian theological construct that the sole "purpose" of human sexuality is procreation, and therefore any sexual act incapable of serving that purpose is "unnatural." In our modern, secular, and pluralistic society, that consensus (assuming it once existed in America), has long since disappeared. Although nobody has tested the assumption, it seems likely that a question-naire asking all Americans to identify natural and unnatural sex acts would elicit amazingly diverse answers. In the absence of such empirical evidence of common attitudes, how can anyone, includ-ing judges, be expected to know what is and what is not "against nature"?

In this area, there is an important social interest in precise definition of the line, one that does not hold in many other realms of life. In regulations involving speech, our constitutional jurispru-dence has abundantly recognized special cause for concern if vagueness is not strictly controlled. Vaguely drawn restrictions in that area can induce self-censorship and result in a poverty of communication, and communication is deemed so vital to human life that in our society it has a preferred rank even among fundamental freedoms. Sexual activity is not exactly speech, but it is a profound means of communication. It can express love and communion in a dimension of which words give only a faint echo. Since sexual acts can be a deeply significant nonverbal means of expression,[39] a substantial social interest exists in knowing precisely the boundaries of prohibited conduct, unless we are to subscribe to the limited view that inhibiting communication can impoverish life only in the political and intellectual spheres. This interest demands that no more vagueness be tolerated in statutes regulating sexual behavior than is absolutely necessary. Individuals should be encouraged, rather than discouraged, to venture as close to the line as they wish.

We should not assume that the state statutes which have been amended to include oral-genital contacts explicitly are immune to the void-for-vagueness challenge. New Mexico's is a good example. After *Bennett v. Abram*,[40] the New Mexico legislature enacted a new statute defining "sodomy" as "any person intentionally taking into his or her mouth or anus the sexual organ of any other person or animal or intentionally placing his or her sexual organ in the mouth or anus of any other person or animal, or coitus with an animal."[41] In *State v. Putman*,[42] the question was whether cunnilingus is within this statutory definition of the crime. Two judges held that it was, but the third judge dissented on the ground that he could not see how a man's placing his tongue in a woman's vagina could be deemed to constitute "taking into his or her mouth . . . the sexual organ of any other person." Oddly enough, the void-for-vagueness issue was not raised. But if three learned appellate judges could disagree so completely on whether the statutory language prohibited cunnilingus, it seems unfair to expect a layman like the defendant to realize that it did.[43]

How have such other "perversions" as cunnilingus fared in those states where there was no need to amend the statute to include fellatio because the courts had held it already within the crime? Presumably, extension of the offense by judicial interpolation would proceed to encompass *all* modes of sexual gratification other than penis-in-vagina, since inclusion of fellatio rested on the rationale that the legislative intent was plainly to prohibit all "unnatural" sex acts. A few examples will illustrate the crazy-quilt patterns that developed.

In Georgia, the statute until 1969 read, "Sodomy is the carnal knowledge and connection against the order of nature, by man with man, or in the same unnatural manner with woman."[44] *Thompson v. Aldredge*[45] held that cunnilingus performed between women was not within the statute. Warrant for such a holding did exist in the words of the statute, but it is curious to see this court paying such close heed to the language—a court that in the *Herring* case[46] dwelt largely on the presumed intent of the legislature to ban all sex which is "against the order of nature." Ten years after *Thompson*, a Georgia court, noting the inconsistency of approach between that case and *Herring*, admitted that the earlier case had created by judicial fiat a definition for sodomy in Georgia that went beyond the common law to include some, *but not all*, perversions.[47] Before *Thompson*, a Georgia decision had held cunnilingus *was* within the statute if performed by a man.[48] But this decision was overruled in 1963 on the reasoning that it was highly unlikely the legislature had intended to penalize between man and woman an act which would not be criminal if performed between two women.[49]

Interfemoral stimulation of the penis (*i.e.*, between the thighs) was held to be outside the Georgia statute,[50] though this particular form of "unnatural" sexual gratification can be performed by the combinations of partners contemplated by the statute's language. The reason given for the exclusion was that at common law the offense required penetration of some orifice of the body (which orifice, and by what, apparently being thought immaterial). Why this anomalous requirement should have been used in this case to defeat the "presumed" legislative intent, while an equally anomalous requirement—that the orifice be the anus—was ignored in the *Herring* case in order to effectuate that intent, is a puzzle.

Actually, there is good cause for disputing the view that the common law required penetration. The leading English case on buggery—which remained impeccable authority until well after the date of American independence—was decided in 1631. In that year Mervyn Touchet, twelfth Lord Audley in the English peerage and second Earl of Castlehaven in the Irish, was tried before the House of Lords, convicted, and executed for having emitted between the thighs of his manservant while the latter was engaged in intercourse with Castlehaven's wife.[51] Their lordships referred to the justices the question of whether buggery had been committed where there was proof not of penetration but only of emission, and received back an affirmative answer. The case appeared to establish that *either* penetration *or* emission sufficed to complete the offense. In the latter part of the eighteenth century, some confusion apparently existed in rape cases concerning what had to be proven in order to establish that offense. In *Hill's Case* in 1781, a majority of the justices finally gave their opinion that *both* penetration *and* emission were required for rape. Sir Edward Hyde East, in his treatise published in 1803, appears to have analogized

the requirements for proof of buggery to those for rape, and his
view seems to have been taken as authoritative because in 1828, at
the instance of Sir Robert Peel, Parliament enacted a statute
providing that penetration alone sufficed to complete either
crime.[52] It is interesting to note that the new Georgia statute,
which defines sodomy as "any sexual act involving the sex organs of
one person and the mouth or anus of another," has been construed
not to require penetration,[53] even though there seems to be little
warrant in the difference between the old and new definitions for
this change in the coverage of the offense.

In Maine, following the precedent of the *Cyr* case[54] that the
crime comprehended fellatio, cunnilingus was also held included.[55]
Then, when faced with the issue of whether masturbation of a male
by a female was within the crime, the Maine court reneged on its
approach and refused to extend the crime that far, again because of
the absence of "penetration."[56] The same development occurred in
Florida. Following the *Ephraim* case,[57] which had held fellatio
included, the Florida courts brought in cunnilingus as well.[58] Then
when urged to extend the "crime against nature" to include
contact between the mouth and the vulva where there was no
evidence of "penetration," a Florida court balked. It pointed out
that cunnilingus had not been included in the crime at common
law, and that now to sweep aside the requirement of "penetration"
as well would open the door to judicial legislation of crimes.[59] In
California, the sodomy statute having been held limited to anal
intercourse,[60] the legislature enacted another statute penalizing
"any person participating in an act of copulating the mouth of one
person with the sexual organ of another."[61] The courts at first held
that penetration was required under this latter statute.[62] Then they
backtracked and determined that any contact between the mouth
of one and the sexual organ of another was within the statutory
terms.[63] In Virginia, on the other hand, where the statute forbids
anyone to "carnally know any . . . person by the anus or by or
with the mouth," penetration is required.[64]

In Indiana, the statute since 1905 has read, "Whoever commits
the abominable and detestable crime against nature with mankind
or beast; or whoever entices, allures, instigates or aids any person
under the age of twenty-one (21) years to commit masturbation or
self-pollution, shall be deemed guilty of sodomy. . . . "[65] It has
already been noted that the Indiana courts construed the term

"crime against nature" to include fellatio, relying on the additional clause of the statute as supplying evidence of a legislative intent to include acts in addition to anal intercourse.[66] The reasoning was that the legislature surely could not have intended to punish anal intercourse *and* the enticing of minors to commit masturbation, yet leave unpunished the "vilest and, if possible, most unnatural" sex act.[67] Later, in two successive steps, the Indiana courts brought cunnilingus within the second clause of the statute ("self-pollution")[68] and then within the first clause ("crime against nature").[69] Anyone engaging in an act of cunnilingus thus is guilty of the crime, regardless of whether the partner is under *or over* 21. Unless the Indiana courts resurrect the common-law requirement of "penetration" for the first clause of the statute, it is difficult to see any obstacle to a similar development with respect to mutual masturbation and other forms of "unnatural" sexual gratification as well.

In Alabama, Missouri, and Oklahoma, where the statutes are of the undefined "crime against nature" type,[70] the courts have deemed cunnilingus included.[71] The same result has been reached in Pennsylvania,[72] where the statute defines sodomy as *carnal knowledge* of any person "by the anus or by or with the mouth,"[73] and in Colorado,[74] under the former statute that proscribed "any unnatural carnal copulation committed per anus [sic] or per os or in any other way whatsoever."[75] On the other hand, in Ohio, where the definition is in terms of "carnal copulation . . . in any opening of the body, except sexual parts, with another human being,"[76] a court has held cunnilingus excluded.[77] The differences in language between these statutes hardly seem to warrant the differences in the resulting treatment of cunnilingus.

As for mutual masturbation, apart from the Maine case already noted,[78] no decisions have been found posing the question of its inclusion under a statute of the undefined "crime against nature" variety. But cases under other vague formulations hold that it *is* included.[79] It is not unfair to say that the only obstacle to including solitary masturbation within the crime of sodomy, apart from any requirement of "penetration," is that the statutes of the great majority of states require the crime to be committed "with mankind or beast" or "with another," so that some partner to the act is essential. The former statute of Delaware[80] did not, however, expressly require either a partner or penetration. If the crime is indeed "against nature" rather than against a person, a conviction for solitary masturbation might have been a real possibility in that state. In Arkansas and Nevada, the statutes also contain no express requirement of a partner, but do contain an express requirement of penetration.[81] In those states, although a man could not be convicted for solitary masturbation, a woman presumably could be.

A recent case in Oregon has held that urinating on another person can constitute the crime of sodomy under the former Oregon statutory language, which included "any act of sexual perversity."[82] Other instances come to mind of harmless acts that, at the whim of some court, could be brought within the statutory term "crime against nature." Artificial insemination performed by a physician, using the semen of an undisclosed donor, is classifiable as a sex act, and one which is against the "order of nature" as that concept is used in the sodomy statutes. It certainly involves "penetration." An act of ordinary intercourse performed by or with a transsexual after a sex-change operation would presumably be a "crime against nature." These operations themselves—currently much in the public eye—might even be so viewed.

The ultimate nonsense in this area comes from New Hampshire. That state has two statutes, one a felony law simply proscribing the commission of "any unnatural and lascivious act with another person,"[83] the other a misdemeanor law simply proscribing "gross lewdness or lascivious behavior."[84] Since the latter statute, contrary to what one might expect, has been held to cover conduct in private as well as in public,[85] there is no apparent difference in coverage between the two laws except that the former requires a partner to the act and that the act be unnatural. In two cases, the Supreme Court of New Hampshire, faced with the problem of which acts the felony statute covered, held that it was more comprehensive than the common-law crime of sodomy.[86] In neither case, however, could the court bring itself to say *what* the additional acts were. Then, in the recent case of *State v. Wickey*,[87] the same court, faced with apparently still another type of "deviate" conduct, held that this conduct was not included within the felony statute but was within the misdemeanor statute. Again the court did not disclose in its opinion what the conduct was. It contented itself with referring the reader to the attorneys' briefs on file in these cases. History recounts that the mad emperor Caligula used to publish his laws by posting them so high up and in such fine print that nobody could read them.[88] The New Hampshire supreme court has gone Caligula one better.

Enough has been said to demonstrate how blind the courts have been to elementary requirements of fairness in dealing with these statutes. The question is: Why such total insensitivity to those requirements in this area? A quotation from one of America's most respected and illustrious courts—the Supreme Judicial Court of Massachusetts—tells the story:

> They[89] signify irregular indulgence in sexual behavior, illicit sexual relations, and infamous conduct which is lustful, obscene, and in deviation of accepted customs and manners. . . . Numerous decisions of the Supreme Court of the United States and of other jurisdictions have sustained statutes similar in form and phraseology to the one with which we are here concerned. . . . It is enough to say that it generally has been held that the common sense of the community, as well as the sense of decency, propriety, and morality which all respectable persons usually entertain, is sufficient to apply the statute to a situation and determine what particular kind of conduct offends. Further specifications in the indictments would be an offense against common decency.[90]

Later in this book, we will explore more fully the question of whether there are any accepted customs and manners, or any community sense of decency, propriety, and morality in this realm of behavior.[91] Without reiterating here what is said there, one can state that there is considerable evidence that no such consensus now exists. What has happened in the application of these vague statutes is judicial legislation of the worst kind. The legislatures have written a blank check, and the judges have filled in *their* notions of sexual propriety. If this accords with the American Constitution, then so does the Nazi law of 1935 which empowered judges to inflict punishment "in accordance with the sound instincts of the people."[92]

Since most language is subject to the charge of imprecision, the decisions of the United States Supreme Court in the void-for-vagueness area indicate that it is not enough to challenge a law on the basis of its imprecise words alone. Several tests have been gleaned from these cases to furnish guidance to when such attacks will be successful and when not.[93] One such test is whether every layman ought to know that the conduct in question is *so* wrong that it is likely to carry a criminal penalty. Where consensual acts between adults in private are concerned, this test is not met. Most people realize that obtaining sexual gratification by force, or by capitalizing on the immaturity of children, or in reckless disregard of the presence of others who might be alarmed or offended, may well be criminal.[94] It may be because many of the cases raising the void-for-vagueness challenge have involved these factors that the courts have often turned a deaf ear to it. But the ways in which two mature people seek mutually to fulfill their sexual desires in private are not regarded generally by laymen as inherently "criminal." Everyone knows that physical injury to another person is probably criminal, but it demands considerable sophistry to think that private consensual sex acts between adults harm anybody.[95] If this estimate of lay reaction to the likely criminality of deviate sex acts is in error, then a very great proportion of the population must be near-wilful "criminals."[96]

A second test is whether the conduct is capable of more precise definition. If greater specificity is impossible, the statute will pass muster. Legislatures cannot be asked to do the impossible—define the ineffable. Sodomy is not, however, in this category. New York's new penal law demonstrates how easy it is to define the offense in crystal-clear terms. In section 130.38, it proscribes engaging in "deviate sexual intercourse." In section 130.00(2), this is defined as "sexual conduct between persons not married to each other consisting of contact between the penis and the anus, the mouth and penis, or the mouth and the vulva." Though such a definition may not cover every form of sexual gratification other than penis-in-vagina, it certainly is not subject to the criticism that it leaves anything to conjecture.

A third test is whether the statute is more uncertain than the mine run of statutes. If not, a void-for-vagueness attack is unlikely to succeed; otherwise the great bulk of legislative law would be called into question. In this respect, one can only say that it would be hard to find any statute *more* uncertain than the typical sodomy statute.

Finally, can one whose case clearly comes within the statute claim that it is void for vagueness because another's case may or may not? Courts would be understandably reluctant to hold a sodomy statute void for vagueness at the instance of a defendant convicted of anal intercourse performed by force. This reluctance probably explains in large part the tendency of many of the cases to dismiss the void-for-vagueness argument lightly.

One case that treats this challenge seriously and fairly is *Harris v. State*,[97] decided in 1969 by the Supreme Court of Alaska. In that case, the defendant had been convicted of forcible sodomy *per anum* under the Alaska statute, which at that time read, "A person who commits sodomy, or the crime against nature, or has unnatural carnal copulation by means of the mouth, or otherwise, either with a beast or human being, upon conviction, is punishable by imprisonment in the penitentiary for not less than one year nor more than ten years."[98] The court agreed that the phrase "crime against nature" was void for vagueness, but refused to hold the term "sodomy" equally vague. It said that, at the very least, the latter term covered unconsented anal intercourse—the act for which the defendant had been convicted. The opinion did not say what else the term "sodomy" might cover, but implied that the court would be reluctant to extend its meaning beyond that. The decision obviously had minimal impact on the coverage of the Alaska statute, which contained other language reasonably capable of being construed to cover additional types of deviate sex acts. At least it served notice on the legislators that they had better clarify the statute. In other states, though, the decision can be cited as persuasive authority for voiding statutes of the typical undefined "crime against nature" variety.[99]

Other appellate judges are beginning to see the light. The 1971 reports of the Supreme Court of Indiana reflect a running battle between two judges who are convinced that the phrase "crime against nature" is unconstitutionally vague, and the rest of the members of that bench.[100] A federal district court in Tennessee has intimated that the state's sodomy law may be subject to the same constitutional infirmity. It has, however, abstained from deciding the question until the state courts have had an opportunity to pass on it.[101]

The void-for-vagueness attack can be described as a "diversionary tactic." The reason, of course, is that, if successful, its only effect is to force the legislature to rewrite the statute in clear terms, as in New York.[102] Why, then, belabor this issue? The answer is that, in today's climate of opinion, any tactic which compels a reconsideration of the sodomy laws holds a fair chance of bringing about substantive, as well as formal, revision. The opportunity it affords for bringing into existence a rational and sensible law (*i.e.*, one that covers only acts by force or other imposition, with minors, or in public) can hardly be ignored.

This potential of the void-for-vagueness attack is illustrated by developments in Florida. On December 17, 1971, the Supreme Court of Florida held the Florida sodomy statute unconstitutional for vagueness.[103] This statute was of the typical undefined "crime against nature" variety. The court overruled its own prior decisions, which had held the statute not unconstitutionally vague.[104] The test it applied was whether the statute informs the average person of common intelligence what is prohibited so that he need not speculate as to the meaning. The Florida statute did not, in the court's opinion, meet this test:

> One reason which makes this apparent is the transition of language over the span of the past 100 years of this law's existence. The change and upheaval of modern times are of drastic proportions. People's understanding of subjects, expressions and experiences are different than they were even a decade ago.[105]

In response to the argument that the meaning of the "crime against nature" had already been settled by prior judicial decisions in Florida, the court said,

> Those who are versed in the law may understand the statute's meaning because of their knowledge of legal interpretations in court opinions, but it seems to us that if today's world is to have brought home to it what it is that the statute prohibits, it must be set forth in language which is relevant to today's society and is understandable to the average citizen of common intelligence. . . .
>
> . . . .
>
> Common law definitions are of course resorted to when the forbidden conduct is not defined. This may supply the deficiency for a *legal* understanding of a vague statute, but it cannot meet the constitutional requirement that the language of the statute be understandable to the common man.[106]

Also influential in the court's mind was the constitutional right of privacy.[107]

A further reason dictating our reexamination here is the expansion of constitutional rulings on the invasion of private rights by state intrusion. . . . The language in this statute could entrap unsuspecting citizens and subject them to 20-year sentences. . . . Such a sentence is equal to that for manslaughter and would no doubt be a shocking revelation to persons who do not have an understanding of the meaning of the statute.[108]

In the wake of this decision, the Florida senate passed a bill redefining the crime of sodomy, with only misdemeanor penalties for acts between consenting adults. An amendment that would have reinstated felony penalties for such acts was defeated. But a number of legislators wanted all penalties removed for consensual acts between adults, and succeeded in passing such a measure in the house of representatives. When the senate then refused to accept the house version, the house stood firm and the legislature adjourned without enacting any replacement for the voided law.[109] It is surprising that such a legislative deadlock over no penalties versus misdemeanor penalties should come to pass in the state which only a few years ago produced the infamous Johns Committee Report.[110]

NOTES

1. 283 U.S. 25 (1931).
2. *Id.* at 27 (emphasis added).
3. Other frequently cited formulations of the doctrine, besides that quoted in the text, are:

> . . . . [A] statute which either forbids or requires the doing of an act in terms so vague that men of common intelligence must necessarily guess at its meaning and differ as to its application, violates the first essential of due process of law.

Connally v. General Construction Co., 269 U.S. 385, 391 (1926).

> If on its face the challenged provision is repugnant to the due process clause, specification of details of the offense intended to be charged would not serve to validate it. . . . It is the statute, not the accusation under it, that prescribes the rule to govern conduct and warns against transgression. . . . No one may be required at peril of life, liberty or property to speculate as to the meaning of penal statutes. All are entitled to be informed as to what the State commands or forbids.

Lanzetta v. New Jersey, 306 U.S. 444, 453 (1939).

> [A defendant has the right] to have available, through a sufficiently precise statute, information revealing the standard of criminality before the commission of the alleged offense.

Watkins v. United States, 354 U.S. 178, 208 (1957).

> A state may not issue commands to its citizens, under criminal sanctions, in language so vague and undefined as to afford no fair warning of what conduct might transgress them.

Raley v. Ohio, 360 U.S. 423, 438 (1959).

4. *See* Note, *The Void-for-Vagueness Doctrine in the Supreme Court,* 109 U. PA. L. REV. 67 (1960), which also cites a number of other similar studies.

5. This differential analysis has been applied by the Supreme Court to the closely analogous case of vagrancy laws. Such laws applicable to everybody, even people in the most humble walks of life, are subject to a stricter test of definiteness.

> This ordinance is void-for-vagueness, both in the sense that it fails to give a person of ordinary intelligence fair notice that his contemplated conduct is forbidden by the statute . . . and because it encourages arbitrary and erratic arrests and convictions. . . .

> Living under a rule of law entails various suppositions, one of which is that 'All [persons] are entitled to be informed as to what the State commands or forbids' [citing Lanzetta v. New Jersey, note 3 *supra*].

> *Lanzetta* is one of a well-recognized group of cases insisting that the law give fair notice of the offending conduct. . . . In the field of regulatory statutes governing business activities, where the acts limited are in a narrow category, greater leeway is allowed. . . .

> The poor among us, the minorities, the average householder are not in business and not alerted to the regulatory schemes of vagrancy laws; and we assume they would have no understanding of their meaning and impact if they read them. Nor are they protected from being caught in the vagrancy net by the necessity of having a specific intent to commit an unlawful act. . . .

Papachristou v. City of Jacksonville, 405 U.S. 157, 162–63 (1972). These quotations from Mr. Justice Douglas's opinion for the Court would be just as apropos if a reference to the sodomy laws were substituted for the reference to vagrancy laws.

6. L. FULLER, THE MORALITY OF LAW 33–94 and particularly 38–39 (rev. ed. 1969).

7. The notion that conduct could be a crime at common law, without any legislative definition, may have had some justification in a country like that from which ours sprang (England). There the legislature developed its lawmaking prerogatives and its competence over a long period of time, during which society could hardly wait for a full-blown legislative code before acting to protect itself from crime. There, too, the populace may have been sufficiently homogeneous in ethnic, religious, and cultural background to provide a "morality" common

enough to be taken as "common *law.*" It is also important to realize that in those times no clear distinction existed between "morality" and "law."

The notion was transplanted to America when America was almost equally homogeneous, and when legislatures, though possessing fully developed prerogatives, were still incapable of committing to writing the entire penal law. Nevertheless, the day has arrived when this anachronistic notion ought finally to be laid to rest, as contravening our "developing sense" of due process. The Supreme Court may unwittingly have already encouraged such a development. In Musser v. Utah, 333 U.S. 95 (1948), the Court indicated that a Utah statute proscribing conspiracy "to commit any act injurious . . . to public morals" appeared to be unconstitutionally vague. It vacated and remanded the case to the Supreme Court of Utah to permit that court to pass on this question. The Utah court held the statute unconstitutional. *See* State v. Musser, 118 Utah 537, 223 P.2d 193 (1950). Oddly enough, conspiracy to corrupt the public morals is a common-law crime, and prosecutions for it are still occurring in England. *See* Shaw v. Director of Public Prosecutions, [1962] A.C. 220 (1961); and Regina v. Knuller (Publishing, Printing and Promotions) Ltd., [1971] 3 All E.R. 314 (C.A.). We are thus treated to the spectacle of a statute being held unconstitutional even though it denounces a common-law crime and in terms no more vague than the common-law definition.

8. This statement is drawn from my own knowledge of these revisions, both enacted and proposed. The citations would be too voluminous to include here.

9. CAL. PENAL CODE §286 (West 1970). California is one of the states where such language has been held restricted in meaning to the English common-law definition of sodomy—anal intercourse, where humans are involved. See People v. Boyle, note 20 *infra.* An additional statute, §228a, was therefore added to cover oral-genital contacts.

10. *See* CODE ALA. tit. 14, § 106 (1959); ARIZ. REV. STAT. ANN. § 13-651 (1956); DEL. CODE ANN. 11 §831 (1953); FLA. STAT. ANN. §800.01 (1965); IDAHO CODE 18-6605 (1948); ME. REV. STAT. 17 §1001 (1965); ANN. LAWS MASS. c. 272 §34 (1968); MICH. COMP. LAWS ANN. §750.158 (1968); MISS. CODE tit. 11, c. 1, § 2413 (1957); REV. CODES MONT. 94-4118 (1969); NEV. REV. STAT. 201.190 (1967); GEN. STAT. N.C. §14-177 (1969); OKLA. STAT. tit. 21 §886 (1958); LAWS P.R. ANN. tit. 33 §1118 (1969); GEN. LAWS. R.I. §11-10-1 (1970); S.D. COMP. LAWS 1967 ANN. 22-22-21 (1969); TENN. CODE ANN. 39-707 (1955). The Delaware statute here cited is superseded by a new criminal code as of April 1, 1973. The Florida statute here cited has been declared unconstitutional, but no replacement for it has yet been enacted. *See* pp. 38–39 *supra.*

11. N.J. STAT. ANN. 2A:143-1 (1969).

12. ARK. STAT. 1947 ANN. 41-813 (1964); KY. REV. STAT. ANN. 436.050 (1969); ANN. CODE MD. art. 27, § 553 (1971); CODE LAWS S.C. §16-412 (1962).

13. Any lawyer who does not believe this is invited to test it on his lay acquaintances. Ask them simply and without further explanation, "What is the crime against nature?"

14. The Supreme Court of California once stated baldly, "Every person of ordinary intelligence understands what the crime against nature with a human being is." *See* People v. Williams, 59 Cal. 397, 398 (1881). Presumably, the court

was referring to anal intercourse, since that is what the term means *in California*. *See* People v. Boyle, *infra* note 20. Also presumably, judges in other states must lack ordinary intelligence, since they have not been able to agree on what the crime against nature is.

15. *Genesis* 18:16 to 19:29.

16. CODE ALA. tit. 14, §106 (1959) (emphasis added).

17. For authority that such is the "core" meaning of the terms, *see* R. M. PERKINS, CRIMINAL LAW 389, and especially n. 4 (2d ed. 1969).

18. 168 Eng. Rep. 830 (1817).

19. The Criminal Law Amendment Act of 1885, 48 & 49 Vict., c. 69, §11. The British Parliament recently removed from the purview of the criminal law in England and Wales deviate sex acts between partners at least 21 years old, regardless of their gender. *See* the Sexual Offences Act, 1967.

20. State v. Potts, 75 Ariz. 211, 254 P.2d 1023 (1953); People v. Boyle, 116 Cal. 658, 48 P. 800 (1897); Koontz v. People, 82 Colo. 589, 263 P. 19 (1927); Commonwealth v. Poindexter, 133 Ky. 720, 118 S.W. 943 (1909); State v. Murry, 136 La. 253, 66 So. 963 (1914); People v. Schmitt, 275 Mich. 575, 267 N.W. 741 (1936); Kinnan v. State, 86 Neb. 234, 125 N.W. 594 (1910); State v. Morrison, 25 N.J. Super. 534, 96 A.2d 723 (1953); Bennett v. Abram, 57 N.M. 28, 253 P.2d 316 (1953); Prindle v. State, 31 Tex. Crim. 551, 21 S.W. 360 (1893); Muñoz v. State, 103 Tex. Crim. 439, 281 S.W. 857 (1926); State v. Johnson, 44 Utah 18, 137 P. 632 (1913); and Wise v. Commonwealth, 135 Va. 757, 115 S.E. 508 (1923).

21. Woods v. State, 10 Ala. App. 96, 64 So. 508 (1914); State v. Maida, 6 Boyce 40, 29 Del.-40, 96 A. 207 (Ct. Gen. Sess. 1915); Ephraim v. State, 82 Fla. 93, 89 So. 344 (1921); Territory v. Wilson, 26 Hawaii 360 (1922); State v. Altwater, 29 Idaho 107, 157 P. 256 (1916); State v. Hurlbert, 118 Kan. 362, 234 P. 945 (1925); State v. Cyr, 139 Me. 513, 198 A. 743 (1938); State v. Davis, 223 Miss. 862, 79 So.2d 452 (1955); State v. Guerin, 51 Mont. 250, 152 P. 747 (1915); *In re* Benites, 37 Nev. 145, 140 P. 436 (1914); State v. Fenner, 166 N.C. 247, 80 S.E. 970 (1914); State v. Griffin, 175 N.C. 767, 94 S.E. 678 (1917); *Ex parte* De Ford, 14 Okla. Crim. 133, 168 P. 58 (1917); Berryman v. State, 283 P.2d 558 (Okla. Crim. App. 1955); State v. Start, 65 Ore. 178, 132 P. 512 (1913); State v. Milne, 95 R.I. 315, 187 A.2d 136 (1962); State v. Whitmarsh, 26 S.D. 426, 128 N.W. 580 (1910); and Fisher v. State, 197 Tenn. 594, 277 S.W.2d 340 (1955).

22. Mangrum v. State. 227 Ark. 381, 299 S.W.2d 80 (1957).

23. Herring v. State, 119 Ga. 709, 46 S.E. 876 (1904); Glover v. State, 179 Ind. 459, 101 N.E. 629 (1913); State v. Katz, 266 Mo. 493, 181 S.W. 425 (1916).

24. For Maryland, *compare* ANN. CODE MD. art. 27, §553 (1971) ("sodomy"), *construed in* Daniels v. State, 237 Md. 71, 205 A.2d 295 (1964), *with* ANN. CODE MD. art. 27, §554 (1971) ("unnatural or perverted sexual practices"), *construed in* Blake v. State, 210 Md. 459, 124 A.2d 273 (1956). For Massachusetts, *compare* ANN. LAWS·MASS. c. 272, §34 (1968) ("Sodomy and Buggery"), *with* ANN. LAWS MASS. c. 272, §35 (1968) ("Unnatural and Lascivious Acts").

25. State v. La Forrest, 71 Vt. 311, 45 A. 225 (1899).

26. VT. STAT. tit. 13, §2603 (1958).

27. This is a perfect example of a court's ascribing to the legislature a fairly complex intention in the face of a simple explanation for its choice of language.

The explanation is that *some* language was needed for this statutory denunciation of a common-law crime, so the scrivener lifted the language from Blackstone's *Commentaries*. Blackstone's only description of the crime is "the infamous *crime against nature*, committed either with man or beast." 4 W. BLACKSTONE, COMMENTARIES °215. He says the indictments in English law refer to it as "a crime not fit to be named." *Ibid*. American lawyers in the late eighteenth and early nineteenth centuries teethed on Blackstone, his book having been the only generally available authoritative work on the common law; so he is without doubt the source of this statutory euphemism. He should not be credited with too much originality in coining the phrase. The medieval church had customarily referred to these acts as *peccata contra naturam*—"sins against nature." In secular parlance, substitution of the word "crime" for "sin" was to be expected.

28. *See, e.g.,* Territory v. Bell, 43 Hawaii 23 (1958); and State v. Dietz, 135 Mont. 496, 343 P.2d 539 (1959), in which two of the judges joined in a long dissent criticizing the *Guerin* case, *supra* note 21, and urging that it be overruled despite the long period over which its precedent had remained unchallenged.

29. In Arizona, California, Kentucky, Michigan, and New Jersey, the original sodomy statute remains on the books and another one or more have been added. *See* ARIZ. REV. STAT. ANN. § 13-651 and 13-652 (1956); CAL. PENAL CODE §286 and 288a (West 1970); KY. REV. STAT. ANN. 436.050 and 435.105 (1969); MICH. COMP. LAWS ANN. §750.158 and 750.338, 750.338a and 750.338b (1968); and N.J. STAT. ANN. 2A:143-1 and 2A:115-1 (1969). In Colorado, Louisiana, Nebraska, New Mexico, Texas, Utah, and Virginia, the single statute was amended to cover both anal-genital and oral-genital contacts. *See* COLO. REV. STAT. 1963 ANN. 40-2-31 (1964); LA. REV. STAT. 14:89 (1951); REV. STAT. NEB. 1943, §28-919 (1965); N.M. STAT. 1953 ANN. §40A-9-6 (1964); TEX. PENAL CODE art. 524 (Vernon 1952); UTAH CODE ANN. §76-53-22 (Supp. 1969); and CODE VA. §18.1-212 (1960). The Colorado statute here cited was superseded on July 1, 1972, by a new criminal code that does not penalize private consensual adult behavior.

30. 84 Nev. 372, 441 P.2d 620 (1968).

31. *Supra* note 21.

32. In Perkins v. North Carolina, 234 F.Supp. 333 (W.D.N.C. 1964), the court said flatly that if the North Carolina statute, which contains no definition of the "crime against nature," were a new one, it would be obviously unconstitutional for vagueness. Since, however, it had previously been construed many times by the North Carolina supreme court, it must be read as though it incorporates those judicial interpretations, which make clear that it does not cover "walking on the grass." Another variant on this same theme is to say that the statute was intended to embrace all carnal copulations that are unnatural, the crime being too well known and too disgusting to require other definition or further description. *See* Boyington v. State, 45 Ala. App. 176, 227 So.2d 807 (1969).

In accord with the *Hogan* and *Perkins* cases are Delaney v. State, 190 So.2d 578 (Fla. 1966); Phillips v. State, 248 Ind. 150, 222 N.E.2d 821 (1967); State v. White, 217 A.2d 212 (Me. 1966); State v. Crawford, 478 S.W.2d 314 (Mo. 1972) (the Missouri statute, unlike the others, however, does say explicitly that the crime against nature can be committed "with the sexual organs or with the mouth"); State v. O'Keefe, 263 N.C. 53, 138 S.E.2d 767 (1964); Berryman v. State, 283 P.2d

558 (Okla. Crim. App. 1955); and Warner v. State, 489 P.2d 526 (Okla. Crim. App. 1971). The *Delaney* case has since been overruled. *See* note 103 *infra.*

In State v. Milne, 95 R.I. 315, 187 A.2d 136 (1962), the court did not explicitly decide whether the Rhode Island sodomy statute was unconstitutionally vague. The statute merely proscribes the "crime against nature" without defining it. However, the court did construe that statute to cover fellatio. It then proceeded to uphold against the void-for-vagueness challenge another statute making it an offense to receive anyone into a house or room for the purpose of committing an "indecent act." Thus it is difficult not to regard the case as authority for upholding the Rhode Island sodomy statute against the void-for-vagueness objection.

33. *See* his *Note* in the *University of Pennsylvania Law Review, supra* note 4.

34. Actually, the Michigan statutes which make criminal any "act of gross indecency" between males, between females, and between a male and a female are unconstitutionally vague even under Amsterdam's analysis. A Michigan court has held that the question of whether fellatio is a crime under these statutes is not one of law but one of fact. The jury in each case must determine whether it is "conduct which the common sense of society regards as indecent and improper." *See* People v. McCaleb, 37 Mich. App. 502, 195 N.W.2d 17 (1972).

35. *See* notes 1–3 *supra.*

36. 402 U.S. 62 (1971).

37. 405 U.S. 156, 168 (1972). *See* note 5 *supra.*

38. To take only one example of how attitudes can vary drastically, even within the same culture, about what is and what is not "natural," the Kinsey group revealed an interesting division of opinion about "deep kissing" at the same time of its survey of the sexual behavior of American males:

> Deep kissing is utilized as a prime source of erotic arousal by many persons in the better educated and top social levels. A deep kiss may involve considerable tongue contacts, deep lip contacts, and extended explorations of the interior of the partner's mouth. Such behavior is . . . a regular concomitant of coital activity among many of the vertebrates, and particularly among the mammals. . . . In the human mammal, at the upper level, oral eroticism may still be considered a bit sophisticated, but deep kissing is in the experience of 87 per cent of the group. . . . Its sanitary implications seem no obstacle to its acceptance. This group accepts mouth contacts in its erotic play, although it objects to the use of a common drinking glass.

> On the other hand, the lower level male considers such oral contacts to be dirty, filthy, and a source of disease, although he may drink from a common cup which hangs in the water pail, and he may utilize common utensils in eating and drinking. . . . Once again, it is the upper level which first reverted, through a considerable sophistication, to behavior which is biologically natural and basic.

A. C. KINSEY, W. B. POMEROY, & C. E. MARTIN, SEXUAL BEHAVIOR IN THE HUMAN MALE 369 (1948) [hereinafter cited as KINSEY, MALE].

When one compares differences between cultures, it becomes hopeless to arrive at a consensus on what is "natural" in human sexual behavior. Consider the Kinsey group's observations on coital position:

> Most persons will be surprised to learn that positions in intercourse are as much a product of human cultures as languages and clothing, and that the common English-American position is rare in some other cultures. Among the several thousand portrayals of human coitus in the art left by ancient civilizations, there is hardly a single portrayal of the English-American position. . . . Malinowski . . . records the nearly universal use of a totally different position among the Trobrianders in the Southwestern Pacific; and he notes that caricatures of the English-American position are performed around the communal campfires, to the great amusement of the natives who refer to the position as the "missionary position."

Id. at 373. The position almost universally shown by the ancient art of Greece, Rome, Peru, India, China, Japan, and Mesopotamia is with the female above the male. *Id.* at 374. *See also* A. C. KINSEY, W. B. POMEROY, C. E. MARTIN, & P. H. GEBHARD, SEXUAL BEHAVIOR IN THE HUMAN FEMALE 362–64 (1953) [hereinafter cited as KINSEY, FEMALE].

39. Sexual behavior contains a nonverbal language through which an individual expresses and conveys meanings; sensory exploration and gestures outweigh words as sign and symbol vehicles. Removal of clothing beyond the degree necessary for coitus itself exemplifies the significance of tactile communication. Any sexual act may carry several social and personal meanings.

Klausner, *Sexual Behavior: Social Aspects,* in 14 INT'L ENCY. SOCIAL SCIENCES 201 (1968).

40. *Supra* note 20.

41. N.M. STAT. 1953 ANN. § 40A-9-6 (1964).

42. 78 N.M. 552, 434 P.2d. 77 (Ct. App. 1968).

43. Since *Putman,* a New Mexico appellate judge has indeed taken the position that the New Mexico sodomy statute is void for vagueness. *See* State v. Trejo, 83 N.M. 511, 494 P.2d 173 (Ct. App. 1972) (dissenting opinion of Judge Sutin).

It is difficult to see how any judge could have come to a conclusion other than that of the dissenter in *Putman,* except by disregarding the express words of the statute in favor of some more general "supposed" intent of the legislature. One suspects that the other judges were sure the legislature meant to include cunnilingus, and were embarrassed to come up with another decision like the *Bennett* case, telling the legislature that the language it had used was inadequate. That very language had been suggested for the statute by their fellow appellate judges in the *Bennett* opinion. *See* 57 N.M. at 30, 253 P.2d at 317. *Bennett* indicates the suggested language was drawn from the definition of sodomy contained in the United States Army Manual for Courts Martial, a definition which for obvious reasons probably never had cunnilingus in mind.

44. GA. CODE ANN. §26-5901 (1953) (repealed effective July 1, 1969).

45. 187 Ga. 467, 200 S.E. 799 (1939).

46. *Supra* note 23.

47. *See* Barton v. State, 79 Ga. App. 380, 53 S.E.2d 707 (1949).

48. Comer v. State, 21 Ga. App. 306, 94 S.E. 314 (1917).

49. Riley v. Garrett, 219 Ga. 345, 133 S.E.2d 367 (1963).

50. Wharton v. State, 58 Ga. App. 439, 198 S.E. 823 (1938). *Accord,* Rozar v. State, 93 Ga. App. 207, 91 S.E.2d 131 (1956).

51. Castlehaven was apparently one of those who become sexually excited through watching the activities of others; in modern terms a "voyeur."

52. *See* H. M. HYDE, THE LOVE THAT DARED NOT SPEAK ITS NAME—A CANDID HISTORY OF HOMOSEXUALITY IN BRITAIN 44–57, 65, 68–69, and 90–92 (1970); 1 E. H. EAST, A TREATISE OF THE PLEAS OF THE CROWN 436–41, 480 (1803).

53. Carter v. State, 122 Ga. App. 21, 176 S.E.2d 238 (1970).

54. *Supra* note 21.

55. State v. Townsend, 145 Me. 384, 71 A.2d 517 (1950).

56. State v. Pratt, 151 Me. 236, 116 A.2d 924 (1955). Presumably, the conviction would have been sustained if the roles of the two participants had been reversed, because then "penetration" would have occurred.

57. *Supra* note 21.

58. Lason v. State, 152 Fla. 440, 12 So.2d 305 (1943); Fine v. State, 153 Fla. 297, 14 So.2d 408 (1943). The Florida statute has since been ruled unconstitutional. *See* note 103 *infra.*

59. Swain v. State, 172 So.2d 3 (Fla. Dist. Ct. App. 1965). For cases in other states that have taken precisely this same position, *see* State v. Hill, 179 Miss. 732, 176 So. 719 (1937); State v. Whittemore, 255 N.C. 583, 122 S.E. 2d 396 (1961); and State v. Withrow, 142 W. Va. 522, 96 S.E. 2d 913 (1957).

60. *See* People v. Boyle, *supra* note 20.

61. CAL. PENAL CODE § 288a (West 1970).

62. People v. Angier, 44 Cal. App.2d 417, 112 P.2d 659 (1941).

63. People v. Coleman, 53 Cal. App.2d 18, 127 P.2d 309 (1942); People v. Harris, 108 Cal. App.2d 84, 238 P.2d 158 (1952); People v. Hunter, 158 Cal. App.2d 500, 322 P.2d 942 (1958); and People v. Wilson, 20 Cal. App.3d 507, 97 Cal. Rptr. 774 (1971). *See also* People v. Triplett, 70 Cal. App.2d 534, 161 P.2d 397 (1945).

64. Ashby v. Commonwealth, 208 Va. 443, 158 S.E.2d 657 (1968).

65. IND. STAT. ANN. 10-4221 (1956).

66. *See* the *Glover* case, *supra* note 23.

67. 179 Ind. at 466, 101 N.E. at 632.

68. Young v. State, 194 Ind. 221, 141 N.E. 309 (1923).

69. Connell v. State, 215 Ind. 318, 19 N.E.2d 267 (1939).

70. CODE ALA. tit. 14, § 106 (1959); ANN. MO. STAT. § 563.230 (1953); OKLA. STAT. tit. 21, § 886 (1958).

71. *See* Brown v. State, 32 Ala. App. 131, 22 So.2d 445 (1945); Parris v. State, 43 Ala. App. 351, 190 So.2d 564 (1966); State v. Wellman, 253 Mo. 302, 161 S.W. 795 (1913); Roberts v. State, 57 Okla. Crim. 24, 47 P.2d 607 (1935); Warner v. State, 489 P.2d 526 (Okla. Crim. App. 1971).

72. Comm'r *ex rel.* McDonnell v. Rundle, 188 A.2d 843 (Pa. Super. Ct. 1963).

73. PA. STAT. ANN. 18, § 4501 (1963).

74. Gilmore v. People, 467 P.2d 828 (Colo. 1970).

75. COLO. REV. STAT. 1963 ANN. 40-2-31 (1964). This statute was superseded as of July 1, 1972, by the new Colorado criminal code, which does not criminalize private adult consensual behavior.

76. OHIO REV. CODE ANN. 2905.44 (1971). This statute is superseded as of Jan. 1, 1974, by the new Ohio criminal code, which does not criminalize private adult consensual behavior.

77. State v. Forquer, 74 Ohio App. 293, 58 N.E.2d 696 (1944). The Iowa and Nebraska statutes are virtually identical to Ohio's. See IOWA CODE ANN. § 705.1 (1950); REV. STAT. NEB. 1943, § 28-919 (1965). Presumably, the same interpretation would be placed on the statutes there. Fellatio, on the other hand, has been held included in this statutory language. See, e.g., State v. Simpson, 50 N.W.2d 601 (Iowa 1951).

78. State v. Pratt, supra note 56.

79. See State v. Mortimer, 105 Ariz. 472, 467 P.2d 60 (1970) [construing ARIZ. REV. STAT. ANN. § 13-652 (1956), which reads, "A person who wilfully commits, in any unnatural manner, any lewd or lascivious act upon or with the body or any part or member thereof of a male or female person, with the intent of arousing, appealing to or gratifying the lust, passion, or sexual desires of either of such persons, is guilty of a felony. . . ."]; State v. Brazell, 126 Ore. 579, 269 P. 884 (1928) [construing the former Oregon law—ORE. REV. STAT. § 167.040 (1969) —which read, "Any person who commits . . . any act or practice of sexual perversity . . . shall be punished . . . by imprisonment. . . ."]. Although the opinion does not tell us what acts were involved, the case of Blake v. State, 210 Md. 459, 124 A.2d 273 (1956), probably involved acts of masturbation. At any rate, the opinion indicates they were acts in addition to oral perversions and to sodomy in its restricted common-law sense. The statute in question was ANN. CODE MD. art. 27, § 554 (1971), which reads, "Every person . . . who shall be convicted of committing any other unnatural or perverted sexual practice with any other person or animal, shall be . . . imprisoned. . . ."

80. DEL. CODE ANN. 11 § 821 (1953). This statute is superseded on April 1, 1973, by the new Delaware criminal code, which does not criminalize private acts between consenting adults.

81. ARK. STAT. 1947 ANN. 41-813 and 814 (1964); NEV. REV. STAT. 201.190 (1967).

82. Jellum v. Cupp, 476 P.2d 205 (Ore. Ct. App. 1970), construing ORE. REV. STAT. § 167.040 (1969).

83. N.H. REV. STAT. ANN. 579:9 (1955).

84. N.H. REV. STAT. ANN. 579:3 (1955).

85. State v. Lizotte, 101 N.H. 494, 148 A.2d 91 (1959).

86. State. v. Vredenburg, 91 N.H. 372, 19 A.2d 414 (1941); State v. Desilets, 96 N.H. 245, 73 A.2d 800 (1950).

87. 108 N.H. 336, 235 A.2d 527 (1967).

88. SUETONIUS, LIVES OF THE TWELVE CAESARS 192 (J. Gavorse transl. 1931). See Fuller, supra note 6, at 93.

89. The court is referring to the words of ANN. LAWS MASS. c. 272, § 35 (1968), which proscribe the commission of "any unnatural and lascivious act with

another person. . . ." The Massachusetts statute on "sodomy and buggery" is ANN. LAWS MASS. c. 272, §34 (1968), which is of the typical undefined "crime against nature" variety.

90. Jaquith v. Commonwealth, 331 Mass. 439, at 442–43, 120 N.E.2d 189, at 192 (1954). *Cf.* People v. Hicks, 98 Mich. 86, 90, 56 N.W. 1102, 1104 (1893), which contains an almost identical justification of a statute prohibiting "indecent liberties" with a child but lacking any definition of the term "indecent liberties."

91. *See* note 46, Chapter 5 *infra*, and pp. 233–35, Chapter 7 *infra*.

92. *See* W. FRIEDMANN, LEGAL THEORY 40 (5th ed. 1967). *Cf.* Giaccio v. Pennsylvania, 382 U.S. 399, 403–4 (1966).

93. *See* Note, *The Void-for-Vagueness Doctrine in the Supreme Court*, 109 U. PA. L. REV. 67 (1960).

94. I do not believe that 'this statement is seriously debatable, and therefore deem it needless to cite either authority or evidence. This is not to deny that laymen may be uncertain where one draws the line between children and adults. Whether the age of consent for sexual activity should be the age of majority (formerly 21, but now 18 in many states), or should be 16, 14, or some other figure in the general range of adolescence is a rather arbitrary question, to which different states have given different answers. *See* Reiss, *Sex Offenses: The Marginal Status of the Adolescent*, 25 LAW & CONTEMP. PROB. 309 (1960). But surely no one in American society is unaware that there *is* a difference between children and adults with regard to one's freedom to take them on as sexual partners. Likewise, there may be a large measure of uncertainty about just what kind of public conduct is likely to be offensive and therefore criminal. Some people may think that wearing a bikini on the street is offensive enough to be criminal; others may not be offended by total nudity. The point is that it is not unreasonable to expect people to know that they are running some *risk* of criminality when they engage in *sexual behavior* in a place where it could be viewed by others or with a partner who is not yet clearly an adult, and that the use of force makes criminality virtually certain.

95. These last two statements in the text are put forth as general propositions, and then only tentatively. Applied to specific behavior, they may be more debatable. For instance, one could argue that most American laymen do regard *homosexual* activities as inherently criminal. I thought so too until I ran into a third-year law student who was totally unaware that there were any criminal laws against homosexual acts between two consenting adults. *He* had taken the law school's course in criminal law. The belief may also be general among laymen that the infliction of pain is likely to be criminal even though the recipient consents, as in the case of various sado-masochistic sexual practices such as whipping. Without large-scale empirical surveys, it is impossible to make confident generalizations about lay attitudes on this subject, and no such surveys exist. My contention is, however, that in the absence of hard empirical data, my estimate of lay attitudes is just as likely to be true as, for instance, the former estimate of some judges that "everybody can be expected to realize that sodomy is a crime." (I would even assert that in today's context, my estimate is *more* likely to be true than theirs). The Kinsey group, discussing instances in which the police accidentally stumble upon American young people in parked cars engaging in

genital manipulations, mouth-genital contacts and other forms of premarital petting, make the following statement: "Few American youth are aware that any legal question is involved; and if they were aware, most of them would deliberately ignore the law." KINSEY, FEMALE at 262–63.

96. *See* pp. 233–35, Chapter 7 *infra*. This is not to ignore the conclusion that some empirical studies have reached: *most* people at some point or another in their lives engage knowingly in prohibited conduct. Violations of the sex laws are often repetitive rather than one-time offenses, and may even be felonies, yet the violators generally remain law-abiding citizens in all other respects.

97. 457 P.2d 638 (Alaska 1969). For a case that held void for vagueness a statute making it a crime to solicit another for an "unnatural sex act," *see* State v. Sharpe, 1 Ohio App.2d 425, 205 N.E.2d 113 (1965).

98. ALASKA STAT. § 11.40.120 (1970). This statute has since been amended to delete all language of definition of the crime but the word "sodomy." *See* ALASKA STAT. § 11.40.120 (1971).

99. Several such statutes have faced the void-for-vagueness challenge in the courts of their states and been upheld. For the cases concerning statutes held to cover more than anal intercourse, *see* notes 30 and 32 *supra*. For those concerning statutes held restricted to anal intercourse, *see* People v. Gann, 259 Cal. App.2d 706, 66 Cal. Rptr. 508 (Dist. Ct. App. 1968); and People v. Green, 14 Mich. App. 250, 65 N.W.2d 270 (1968). For cases upholding against the void-for-vagueness challenge statutes worded in other ways than the typical undefined "crime against nature" variety, *see* Lovelace v. Clark, 83 Ariz. 27, 315 P.2d 876 (1957), and State v. Jones, 8 Ariz. App. 38, 446 P.2d 487 (1968) [ARIZ. REV. STAT. ANN. § 13-652 (1956), proscribing the commission of, "in any unnatural manner, any lewd or lascivious act"]; People v. Parsons, 82 Cal. App. 17, 255 P. 212 (Dist. Ct. App. 1927) [CAL. PENAL CODE § 288a (West 1970), proscribing participation in "an act of copulating the mouth of one person with the sexual organ of another"]; Gilmore v. People, 467 P.2d 828 (Colo. 1970) [former Colorado law, COLO. REV. STAT. 1963 ANN. 40-2-31 (1964), proscribing, in addition to the crime against nature, "any unnatural carnal copulation committed per anus [sic] or per os or in any other way whatsoever"]; State v. Bonanno, 245 La. 1117, 163 So.2d 72 (1964) [LA. REV. STAT. 14:89 (1951), defining the "crime against nature"]; Blake v. State, 210 Md. 459, 124 A.2d 273 (1956) [ANN. CODE MD. art. 27, § 553 (1971), proscribing "unnatural or perverted sexual practices"]; People v. Dexter, 6 Mich. App. 247, 148 N.W.2d 915 (1967) [MICH. COMP. LAWS ANN. § 750.338 (1968), proscribing "any act of gross indecency" between males]; People *ex rel*. Farr v. Mancusi, 335 N.Y. Supp.2d 161 (County Ct. 1972) [former New York statute, N.Y. PENAL LAW § 690 (1963), forbidding carnal knowledge of a minor "by the anus or by or with the mouth"]; State v. Anthony, 179 Ore. 282, 169 P.2d 587 (1946), and Jellum v. Cupp, 476 P.2d 205 (Ore. Ct. App. 1970) [former Oregon law, ORE. REV. STAT. § 167.040 (1969), proscribing, in addition to sodomy and "osculatory relations" with any person's private parts, "any act or practice of sexual perversity"]; Furstonburg v. State, 148 Tex. Crim. 638 190 S.W.2d 362 (1945) [TEX. PENAL CODE art. 524 (Vernon 1952), defining sodomy]; State v. Rhinehart, 70 Wash. 2d 649, 424 P.2d 906 (1967) [REV. CODE WASH. ANN. 9.79.100 (1961), defining sodomy]; and Jones v. State, 55 Wis.2d 742, 200 N.W.2d 587 (1972) [WIS.

STAT. 944.17 (1958), proscribing any "abnormal act of sexual gratification involving the sex organ of one person and the mouth or anus of another"]. The ruling in the *Dexter* case, *supra*, seems now no longer valid, in view of a later holding that sexual acts constitute "gross indecency" or not depending on the jury's view in each case. *See* note 34 *supra*. The early Texas case of Fennell v. State, 32 Tex. 378 (1869), refused to uphold any convictions under the Texas sodomy statute, not because of unconstitutional vagueness but because of the general provision of the early Texas penal code that no one could be convicted of a crime not defined by that code. The sodomy provision was held to conflict with this general principle, because it failed to define the offense. When the general provision was later amended to require only that the crime be denominated an offense by the code, the common law being permitted to supply the definition, the *Fennell* holding ceased to be applied. *See Ex parte* Bergen, 14 Tex. App. 52 (1883).

100. *See* Barnes v. State, 266 N.E.2d 617 (Ind. 1971); Dixon v. State, 268 N.E.2d 84 (Ind. 1971); and Miller v. State, 268 N.E.2d 299 (Ind. 1971).

101. Polk v. Ellington, 309 F.Supp. 1349, 1353 (W.D. Tenn. 1970). This case may prove to be a very important one on the void-for-vagueness challenge, because Tennessee's statute is one of the typical undefined "crime against nature" variety and there are no prior state cases giving it a limiting construction. The federal court's opinion indicates an awareness of the statute's vulnerability on this score. Indeed, the federal court appears to have retained jurisdiction of the case to pass on the question in the event the state courts fail to resolve it satisfactorily.

102. Among the statutes that cover private consensual adult behavior, those of two other states—Georgia and Wisconsin—now approach that of New York in clarity and comprehensiveness. *See* GA. CODE ANN. §26-2002 (Crim. Code 1970 Revision); WIS. STAT. ANN. 944.17 (1958). The statutes of the District of Columbia and New Mexico, which employ almost identical language in their definitions of the offense, are equally clear, but, as indicated in the text at note calls 40–43 *supra*, they can be construed as equally comprehensive only by stretching the language beyond recognition. *See* D.C. CODE ANN. §22-3502 (1967); N.M. STAT. 1953 ANN. §40A-9-6 (1964). (The D.C. law is apparently deemed inapplicable to private acts between consenting adults. *See* pp. 67–68, Chapter 3 *infra*.) The definitions of the Illinois law and of the new Connecticut, Colorado, Oregon, Hawaii, Delaware, and Ohio codes are clear, but these laws do not criminalize private conduct between consenting adults. *See* note 12, Chapter 1 *supra*. The statutes of the remaining states, apart from those simply proscribing sodomy or the crime against nature without any definition of it, vary considerably in clarity. In this latter group, two variations of language predominate. The statutes of Iowa, Nebraska, Ohio, and Texas speak of "carnal copulation in any opening of the body, except sexual parts, with another human being." *See* notes 76 and 77 *supra*, and TEX. PENAL CODE art. 524 (Vernon 1952). The statutes of Minnesota, North Dakota, Pennsylvania, Virginia, Washington, West Virginia, Wyoming, and the Virgin Islands speak of anyone who "carnally knows" another by the anus or by or with the mouth, or in any unnatural manner. *See* MINN. STAT. ANN. § 609.293 (Supp. 1971); N.D. CENTURY CODE ANN. 12-22-07 (1960); PA. STAT. ANN.

18 §4501 (1963); CODE VA. §18.1-212 (1960); REV. CODE WASH. ANN. 9.79.100 (1961); W. VA. CODE § 61-8-13 (1966); WYO. STAT. 1957, §6-98 (1959); V.I. CODE tit. 14, §2061 (1964). Section 3101 of the new Pennsylvania Criminal Code adopted December 5, 1972, defines "deviate sexual intercourse" as "sexual intercourse per os or per anus [sic] between human beings who are not husband and wife, and any form of sexual intercourse with an animal."

103. Franklin v. State, 257 So.2d 21 (Fla. 1971).

104. E.g., Delaney v. State, supra note 32.

105. 257 So.2d at 23.

106. Ibid.

107. See Chapter 3 infra.

108. 257 So.2d at 23. The ferocity of the penalty seems to have weighed heavily in the court's decision. The defendants in the case had been followed by a police officer from a public restroom in St. Petersburg to a spot near the municipal pier. There he saw both get into a car belonging to one of them. Approaching and shining his flashlight into the car's interior, he caught them engaging in a "homosexual act." The court's opinion does not specify what the act was, but it seems likely to have been either fellatio or anal intercourse. At any rate, the opinion refers to those two acts and indicates that the act for which the men were convicted was one that the Florida courts had previously subsumed under "sodomy."

The decision is marred by the action it took on the two convictions. It remanded the cases to the trial court with directions to enter a judgment of guilty under another statute—FLA. STAT. § 800.02—which the court held to be a lesser included offense under an indictment for sodomy. This other statute makes criminal "any unnatural and lascivious act with another person," without further definition, but imposes a penalty of only a $500 fine or six months' imprisonment. It would seem that if the term "crime against nature" is unconstitutionally vague, the term "any unnatural and lascivious act" is equally so. Neither statute is more definite than the other. The court seems to have been concerned to avoid leaving Florida bereft of any sanction at all against homosexual acts, and may have felt that there is less vice in vagueness in a misdemeanor than in a felony statute.

The court's opinion included a dictum that its ruling of unconstitutionality was applicable prospectively only. A federal district court, however, has since then also ruled the felony statute unconstitutional and ordered the release of two prison inmates convicted before the state court decision. Huffman v. Tompkins, No. 72-832-Civ-J-M, and Stone v. Wainwright, No. 72-219-Civ-J-M (M.D. Fla., filed Nov. 6, 1972).

109. See The Advocate, May 10, 1972, at 2.

110. See Florida Legislative Investigation Committee, Homosexuality and Citizenship in Florida (pamphlet published by the Florida Legislature, 1964). This was a piece of sensational journalism verging on official pornography. In the wake of a public uproar over its issuance, the pamphlet was suppressed.

3

The Right-of-Privacy Doctrine

In 1965, in *Griswold v. Connecticut*,[1] the Supreme Court recognized the existence of a constitutional right of privacy within the context of the marital relationship. For the purposes of this discussion, the derivation of that right, whether as a zone of privacy within the penumbras emanating from certain specifics of the Bill of Rights,[2] as an unenumerated right or liberty "retained by the people" as the ninth amendment recognizes,[3] or as a basic value "implicit in the concept of ordered liberty,"[4] is immaterial. It is protected from state infringement by the due process clause of the fourteenth amendment. The Court held that a state cannot prohibit married couples from using contraceptive devices; that such a prohibition invades the intimacy of the marriage bed—a preserve the state may not constitutionally enter.

If the state cannot prohibit the employment of contraceptives by husband and wife in consummating ordinary vaginal intercourse, it cannot prohibit them from engaging in other forms of expression of their love for each other, including the whole gamut of deviate sex acts. The latter issue is not merely a close analogy to the former. The two are applications of the same question—whether the state may validly presume to regulate the sexual intimacies of the marital relationship. It cannot. A sodomy law drawn so broadly as to apply to the consensual relations of husband and wife, as well as others, must thus be unconstitutional.

Despite the emphasis in the *Griswold* opinion upon protecting bedroom activities from the prying eyes of the state, it is possible to see in the decision a rather different import. Instead of cloaking in privacy bedroom activities in general, the decision can be read as establishing the right of a married couple to decide if and when they wish to have children, that decision being an integral part of the marital relationship. If this be the correct reading, it still does not detract from the conclusion just stated. No one can seriously contend that the decisions of husband and wife regarding how they shall physically express their love and affection for each other are a less integral part of their relationship than are family-planning decisions. One could urge, of course, that expression through deviate sex acts has not been part of our traditional ideas about marriage, and thus is not so rooted in our heritage as to be ranked as a fundamental right. But the same is true of family planning. The whole emphasis of the traditional view of marriage handed down to us from our Judeo-Christian origins was on the *procreation* of children, not on limitation of their number. If family planning is now to be viewed as integral to the marriage relationship, so must variety in the physical expression of love. Otherwise, we reduce marriage to a sort of baby factory, in which only the management's decisions on product output are entitled to constitutional respect.

Even if one takes the view that *Griswold* protects only the family-planning decisions of the marital relationship, deviate sex acts are still within its ambit. The state interference struck down in *Griswold* was not an interference with the planning itself, but with the means used to achieve it. The deviate sex acts proscribed by the sodomy laws, together with coitus interruptus, are the oldest means of contraception known to man. If, under *Griswold*, the state cannot prohibit a husband and wife from using artificial means, on what basis can it prohibit them from using these natural means?

A three-judge federal court has declared the Texas sodomy statute void on this basis, in *Buchanan v. Batchelor*.[5] The Texas Court of Criminal Appeals, however, in *Pruett v. State*,[6] disagreed. The latter decision may well have been influenced by the fact that the objection there was being pressed not by a married couple but by a reformatory inmate convicted of forcing the act on a fellow inmate. The opinion in *Pruett* is hardly crystal clear. It seems to be saying that conviction of a husband and wife under the statute is at most a mere possibility, and an unlikely one at that, in view of the obstacles Texas law poses to any effort to convict either spouse on the testimony of the other.[7] But it also implies that the *Griswold* right of privacy should not be extended to protect acts as "offensive" as sodomy. In other words, the Texas state court would apply the right of privacy according to judges' subjective notions of whether or not the acts proscribed are "offensive," sodomy being "offensive" but not contraception.

The *Buchanan-Pruett* standoff illustrates the difficulty of forcing reform of the sodomy laws by means of the privacy doctrine as applied in *Griswold*. Even if one writes off the *Pruett* position as untenable, a court might take several possible stances toward these laws in light of the doctrine:

1. The law is totally void because it is so broadly worded as to apply to consensual acts in private between husband and wife; *no one* may, be convicted thereunder. (This was the *Buchanan* holding.)
2. The law may be void because of such applicability, but a declaration or holding to that effect will be granted only at the instance of one who has standing to raise that objection (*i.e.*, a married couple).
3. The *law* is not void merely because its application to consensual acts between married couples would be unconstitutional, but rather any such attempted *application* will be struck down. (This is invalidity "as applied," in contrast to "facial" invalidity.)
4. The law, despite its breadth of language, should be construed as not intended by the legislature to encompass the consensual private acts of husband and wife, and is therefore entirely valid.

The fourth approach was suggested in the Seventh Circuit case of *Cotner v. Henry*.[8] The petitioner for habeas corpus in that case, after voluntarily entering a plea of guilty, had been convicted of sodomy upon his wife. The record contained no intimation that any force had been used in committing the crime. The Seventh Circuit granted habeas corpus on the ground that the petitioner had been permitted to enter the plea without adequate advice. It noted, however, that in its opinion the Indiana statute could not constitutionally be applied to proscribe consensual sodomy in private between husband and wife. If, then, the state should elect to prosecute Cotner again, the Indiana courts would be afforded an opportunity to construe the statute to exclude acts in such circumstances and thereby avoid the constitutional issue.[9]

This approach seems unsound, because there is no warrant in the language of these statutes for making such an inference about the legislative intent. The statutory language is "Whoever commits. . . . "[10] Such language has always been thought to mean *everyone*. Moreover, until *Griswold,* every case, both in England and America, that touched upon the applicability of the sodomy laws to husband and wife assumed that they *do* apply.[11] The federal court in *Buchanan* was urged to defer passing on the constitutionality of the Texas statute until the Texas courts had had an opportunity to construe it and decide whether it embraced acts between husband and wife. That court declined to do so, stating that the Texas law offered no doubtful question of construction which the Texas courts would be of help in resolving. And in fact thereafter, in the *Pruett* case, Texas's highest appellate court in criminal matters gave no hint of a view that the statute was not intended to apply to husband and wife, though it must have seen that such a holding would obviate the constitutional question. It merely said that successful prosecution of a spouse was highly unlikely in view of Texas's adjective law.

The third approach appears to have been taken in *Towler v. Peyton.*[12] In that case, habeas corpus was denied to a husband who had been convicted of forcing the act on his wife. The court agreed with the *Cotner* dictum that the state could not constitutionally make criminal consensual sodomy in private between husband and wife. It pointed out, however, that the case before it did not involve any such unconstitutional *application* of Virginia's sodomy statute.

This third approach seems likewise unsound, because it is clearly inconsistent with the holding in *Griswold.* The Connecticut anticontraceptive statute attacked in *Griswold* was applicable to everyone, married and unmarried alike, and that case did not hold the latter application to be unconstitutional. Assuming *arguendo* that a state could constitutionally prohibit use of contraceptives by unmarried persons, and that the *Towler* approach is correct, the Supreme Court should have left the Connecticut law intact and merely declared that it could not be enforced against married couples. A fair reading of the opinion, however, shows that the law itself was held void. The task of tailoring such an overbroad law to those situations to which its reach would be constitutional is one for the legislature, not the courts.

Perhaps the *Towler* case should be read to mean that a petitioner whose conduct is not constitutionally privileged will not be heard to challenge the law on the ground of its applicability to other conduct which *is* privileged. This is the second of the four possible approaches mentioned above.[13] Whether this is properly viewed as a question of "standing" or whatever, such an approach would not be inconsistent with *Griswold*, because the challengers in *Griswold* were complaining of a conviction for aiding and abetting conduct which *was* privileged (the use of contraceptives by married couples). Nor would such an approach be inconsistent with the *Buchanan* decision. The ruling in that case was rendered at the behest of a married couple.

Another case that deals briefly with the argument is *Warner v. State*.[14] The acts in question were performed by force by a man and his wife upon an unrelated female victim. They asserted invalidity of the Oklahoma statute under which they had been convicted, on the ground that it was so broad as to cover "consensual acts of married people." The court answered, "We are of the opinion that the United States Supreme Court, in the landmark case of Griswold v. State of Connecticut . . . does not prohibit the state's regulation of sexual promiscuity or misconduct between non-married persons. We, therefore, find this proposition to be without merit."[15]

So far only three states—Kansas, New York, and Pennsylvania[16]—have immunized their sodomy statutes against this obvious point of attack. One would think that all those states which have enacted general penal code revisions since *Griswold* would have done so, but neither Georgia nor Minnesota did, even though, in the case of the latter state, the revision commission had so recommended.[17] Similarly, the matter was apparently overlooked in the substantial change that Utah made in its statute in 1969.[18]

The impediment to effective exploitation of this vulnerability of most sodomy laws is getting the issue properly before the courts. With criminal prosecutions against married couples virtually nonexistent, how can the question of unconstitutional infringement of their right of privacy be raised? Presumably, the only possibility would be a civil action for declaratory judgment. But the absence of any genuine threat of prosecution would open such an action to the objection that it presents no real case or controversy.

Griswold v. Connecticut holds, however, a much broader potential for attack. As the first case to mark off explicitly a sphere of private life into which the state may not constitutionally enter—the private sexual intimacy of husband and wife—it represented the first time that the right of privacy, a rather amorphous concept which had been developing and expanding in civil, mainly tort, law,[19] had been raised to the rank of a constitutionally protected right. Constitutional rights have a tendency to augment with the passage of time. It now appears that this humble beginning presaged the development of a full-blown constitutional right of privacy extending far beyond the marital couch.

One reason for this development is that the notion of privacy itself has a vastly alluring appeal to almost everyone reared in the Anglo-American tradition of personal liberty. This appeal is bound to grow as modern-day Americans crowd closer and closer together in urban agglomerations and big government reaches longer and longer tentacles into their lives. We are presently witnessing a significant growth of interest in limiting the government's power to wiretap telephones, to bug houses and apartments, and to compile and maintain dossiers on political dissidents.

A second reason is that the right of privacy recognized in *Griswold* does not rest on any specific provision of the Constitution whose explicit terms could limit its growth beyond the marital relationship. It is supported by such recognized constitutional rights as the freedom of association, the freedom from self-incrimination, the freedom from unreasonable searches and seizures, and the freedom from having soldiers quartered in private houses. None of these protections is limited in scope to the persons and homes of married couples; thus no basis exists in the words of the Constitution itself for limiting to married couples the constitutional right of privacy first enunciated in *Griswold*. The Court in its opinion applied the right only in that limited context, true, but such a limitation was unlikely to withstand the test of time and logic.

It is worth noting that the Court in its opinion made much of the fact that any enforcement of Connecticut's anticontraceptive laws against married couples would require police invasion of the marital bedroom for telltale signs that contraceptives had been used—an invasion prohibited by the fourth amendment. What the opinion failed to note, however, is that police may enter even the marital bedroom if they possess a warrant validly issued upon probable cause, and that there are other means by which such "private" violations of law can come to the attention of the authorities and be prosecuted, such as revelation by one of the participants who is willing to turn state's witness against the other. All these considerations are present to the same degree in the case of sodomy in private, whether between husband and wife or between unmarried consenting adults. It is therefore difficult to see how a constitutional right of privacy resting on such foundations could be confined to protecting the marital pair and no one else.

The major problem with expanding this constitutional right of privacy is to determine where it stops. As already mentioned, the notion of privacy as developed in tort law is rather ill defined, and gives us little aid in making this determination. Probably all attempts at an a priori delimitation of the right are doomed to failure. Its contours will have to be determined over a period of time on a case-by-case basis. One may venture to predict, however, that the major application of the right is likely to be in the very field with which this book is concerned—sex offenses involving the private acts of consenting adults—and other types of "crimes without victims," such as gambling. Certainly, if the doctrine holds much potential at all for extension beyond the situations to which it has already been applied, it is bound to encompass the private sexual activities of consenting adults, married or unmarried.

The first step in the development of the doctrine since *Griswold* occurred in *Stanley v. Georgia*.[20] In that case the defendant had been convicted by the Georgia courts of the offense of "possession of obscene matter." Police officers had discovered some pornographic films in a bedroom drawer of his home in the course of searching the premises under a warrant for other purposes. The Supreme Court held that mere private possession of obscene matter cannot constitutionally be made a crime.

The opinion for the Court by Mr. Justice Marshall appeared to rely mainly on the first amendment protections of freedom of speech and of the press. He seemed to deny that the exception from such protections carved out for obscenity by prior cases permits the states to deal with it in any way they please. Those cases, he pointed out, involved commercial distribution or possession for that purpose. The Constitution, however, protects the right to receive information and ideas "regardless of their social worth."[21]

Marshall's opinion then proceeded to make a clear allusion to *another* constitutional right—the right of privacy—without any hint that that right is in any sense restricted to married couples or to homes occupied by such couples:

[A]lso fundamental is the right to be free, except in very limited circumstances, from unwarranted governmental intrusions into one's privacy.

> "The makers of our Constitution undertook to secure conditions favorable to the pursuit of happiness. They recognized the significance of a man's spiritual nature, of his feelings and of his intellect. They knew that only a part of the pain, pleasure and satisfactions of life are to be found in material things. They sought to protect Americans in their beliefs, their thoughts, their emotions and their sensations. They conferred, as against the Government, the right to be let alone—the most comprehensive of rights and the right most valued by civilized man." *Olmstead v. United States*, 277 U.S. 438, 478 (1928) (Brandeis, J., dissenting).

See *Griswold v. Connecticut, supra.* . . .

. . . . [Stanley] is asserting the right to read or observe what he pleases—the right to satisfy his intellectual and emotional needs in the privacy of his home. . . . Whatever may be the justifications for other statutes regulating obscenity, we do not think they reach into the privacy of one's own home.[22]

The case is highly significant for purposes of the present inquiry because, like *Griswold,* it appears to be making a leap from the unconstitutionality of various *means* by which the government may invade one's privacy to the unconstitutionality of substantive criminal laws that attempt to prohibit "victimless" behavior occurring in private. It thus constituted an entering wedge for the development of a broader right of privacy than the marital right enunciated in *Griswold.* This reading of the majority opinion is buttressed by the fact that Justices Stewart, Brennan, and White concurred only in the result of the case, on the ground that the evidence to support the conviction had been illegally obtained. They would have had the Court decide only the issue of the constitutionality of the *means* by which Stanley's privacy was invaded, never reaching the issue of the constitutionality of Georgia's substantive criminal law.

It is possible to explain *Stanley* solely by reference to the first amendment freedoms of expression. However, recent Supreme Court allusions to *Stanley* seem to confirm the impression that the Georgia law's infringement of a general constitutional right of privacy constituted its real transgression.

In *United States v. Reidel*,[23] the Supreme Court declined to read *Stanley* as giving people a constitutional right to acquire obscene material from commercial distributors through the mails. In the course of Mr. Justice White's opinion for the majority, he places the following interpretation on *Stanley:*

> The focus of this language was on freedom of mind and thought and on the privacy of one's home. . . . The personal constitutional rights of those like Stanley to possess and read obscenity in their homes and their freedom of mind and thought do not depend on whether the materials are obscene or whether obscenity is constitutionally protected. Their rights to have and view that material in private are independently saved by the Constitution.[24]

This quotation seems to be saying that *Stanley* does not rest on the first amendment freedoms of speech and press at all, because obscenity is simply not within their protection. If, then, these constitutional guarantees were irrelevant to the holding in *Stanley*, that holding can rest only on the alternative ground of a general constitutional right of privacy. No question of *marital* privacy was involved in *Stanley*.

Stanley likewise did not involve any question of family planning or birth control. It involved a person's satisfaction of his mental and emotional needs of a sexual nature. If the right of privacy protects the solitary use of pornography to satisfy those needs, why should it not also protect intercourse?

Justice White's reference in *Reidel* to "freedom of mind and thought," reiterated in Justice Harlan's concurring opinion, may have been meant to denote some other constitutional right independent of the first amendment freedoms of speech and the press. This does not seem very likely, however. Perhaps, in the future, science will make mass manipulation of thought feasible through such direct devices as remote-controlled electrodes implanted in people's brains. At present, though, the only way government can control people's minds and thoughts is by controlling what they hear, read, and see. And these media of communication—speech, the press, films, and so on—are those protected by the first amendment.

Two more recent decisions establish that the right of privacy enunciated in *Griswold* is not strictly limited to married couples but extends to single persons as well. In the first of these—*Eisenstadt v. Baird*[25]—Mr. Justice Brennan's opinion for the Court included a statement explicitly extending the constitutional right of privacy beyond husband and wife:

> If under *Griswold* the distribution of contraceptives to married persons cannot be prohibited, a ban on distribution to unmarried persons would be equally impermissible. It is true that in *Griswold* the right of privacy in question inhered in the marital relationship. Yet the marital couple is not an independent entity with a mind and heart of its own, but an association of two individuals each with a separate intellectual and emotional make-up. If the right of privacy means anything, it is the right of the *individual*, married or single, to be free from unwarranted governmental intrusion into matters so fundamentally affecting a person as the decision whether to bear or beget a child.[26]

His opinion thereupon cites *Stanley v. Georgia* and reproduces in a footnote the portion of that opinion quoted earlier in this chapter. Mr. Justice Stewart is one of the four justices (Brennan, Stewart, Douglas, and Marshall) who joined in this opinion. It thus would appear that at least two of the three justices (Brennan, Stewart, and White) who concurred in the result of *Stanley v. Georgia* but did not join in Mr. Justice Marshall's opinion had now come round to the view that the Constitution does protect a *general* right of privacy.

One can argue that the statement quoted from *Baird* was merely dictum, because that decision rested on the equal-protection clause of the fourteenth amendment, not on the right of privacy (which is applicable to the states through the due process clause of the fourteenth). The decision in the second case, though, is a direct holding on the issue. In this case—*Roe v. Wade*,[27] decided January 22, 1973—the Supreme Court struck down the Texas anti-abortion law on the ground that it violated the right of privacy of an *unmarried* pregnant woman. Although the same result would have been reached had the plaintiff been married, it could not have been reached in this case without the aid of a general right of privacy. *Roe v. Wade* is therefore immensely important, not only for its specific impact on the availability of abortion, but also because it demonstrates that the right of privacy is now a full-fledged member of the family of constitutional rights and extends beyond the marital pair to include single persons as well. It also shows that the right is not inapplicable merely because the forbidden activity involves *two* participants (here the woman and her physician).

Actually, some state appellate opinions involving the sodomy laws already reflect efforts of defense counsel to enlist the aid of a general constitutional right of privacy. None of these efforts has been successful so far, mainly because the cases in question did not involve fact situations appropriate for raising the issue. In the California case of *People v. Roberts*,[28] the defendant was convicted of an act in the public portion of a men's restroom, and in *People v. Hurd*[29] of an act with his own 16-year-old daughter. In these circumstances, one could hardly expect a court to spread over the acts the protection of a general right of privacy. In *State v. White*[30]—a Maine case—the testimony of the complaining witness was to the effect that the act was performed by force, though in private. In the New Mexico case of *Washington v. Rodriguez*,[31] the act took place between two inmates of the state prison, presumably where it could be, and was, viewed by others. In *People v. Frazier*,[32] which involved identical factual circumstances, the court, though conceding that the *Griswold* right of privacy may extend beyond the marital pair to include consenting adults generally, would in no event apply it to acts between prison inmates, who presumably have no privacy or whose right is subordinate to the need for prison order and discipline.

In the Alaska case of *Harris v. State*,[33] the act was performed by force in the presence of a number of witnesses who testified against the defendant at his trial, but the court in that case did plainly intimate that in appropriate circumstances it would countenance an attack upon the sodomy law based on a broad right of privacy. *Raphael v. Hogan*[34] involved a civil action seeking the convening of a three-judge federal court to pass on the constitutionality of New York's consensual sodomy statute. The complaint was dismissed because the plaintiffs had been arrested for supposedly performing the acts as members of the cast of *Che*—an off-off-Broadway play—and hence could hardly raise the issue of a general right of privacy. They were later acquitted of the criminal charge of sodomy, because the state could not prove that the acts were actually completed, rather than merely simulated in the play.[35] In a footnote of the federal court's opinion, however, it said:

> We are not here dealing with private acts of sodomy between unmarried consenting adults, and accordingly, intimate no view as to the constitutionality of the consensual sodomy statute were it sought to be applied to such private conduct.[36]

Substantially the same question—whether the constitutional right of privacy protects sodomy between consenting adults who are not husband and wife—was left unresolved by the Supreme Court of Nevada in *Jones v. State*,[37] and by the Maryland court of appeals in *Hughes v. State*,[38] in which those courts declined to reach such an issue at the behest of a defendant who had been convicted of an act with a minor.

Finally, in *Dixon v. State*,[39] the Supreme Court of Indiana held that the *Griswold* right of privacy should not be extended beyond married couples, so as to invalidate criminal proscription of an act of cunnilingus performed in private between an unmarried man and woman. The woman's testimony was that the act took place without her consent, but this appeared rather improbable in view of the circumstances brought to light by other evidence in the case. The court therefore chose to treat the question as involving an act in private between consenting adults. Two of the judges, however, filed a strong dissent, in which they argued not only that the Indiana statute is void for vagueness but also that the *Griswold* right of privacy cannot logically be confined to husband and wife but must protect the private consensual acts of unmarried adults as well. The subsequent case of *Miller v. State*[40] indicates that these two judges declined to accept the majority's rejection of their views, and continued to dissent on the same grounds. In the wake of *Roe v. Wade* their position now appears vindicated.

Several decisions have raised the issue of extension of the constitutional right of privacy to deviate sexual conduct in the context of civil cases, as contrasted with criminal prosecutions. Here the advocates of extension have been more successful. The first breakthrough in this area occurred in the decision of the United States Court of Appeals for the District of Columbia Circuit in *Norton v. Macy*[41] in 1969. Previously, in *Scott v. Macy*,[42] that court had indicated its uneasiness with the Civil Service Commission's policy of discharging any federal employee discovered to be homosexual. In the *Norton* case, the court overturned such a dismissal, holding that the employee's homosexuality must be shown to impair his effectiveness in his job in order to constitute grounds for dismissal. The opinion referred explicitly to the constitutional right of privacy recognized in *Griswold*.[43]

The same approach was approved by the Supreme Court of California in a case involving a public school teacher whose credentials had been revoked by the state board of education for similar conduct—*Morrison v. State Board of Education*.[44] In *Mindel v. United States Civil Service Commission*,[45] a federal district court held directly that dismissal of a postal clerk for cohabiting with a woman not his wife violated his constitutional right of privacy; however, such conduct was apparently not criminal in the state where it occurred. In *In re Labady*,[46] a federal district court held that discreet homosexuality practiced only in private with other consenting adults could not be a basis for inferring that an immigrant alien lacked "good moral character"—a requirement for naturalization. In that case the court noted that "it is now established that official inquiry into a person's private sexual habits does violence to his constitutionally protected zone of privacy"[47] and "to the extent that these laws [the sodomy statutes] seek to prohibit and punish private homosexual behavior between consenting adults, they are probably unconstitutional in light of *Griswold v. Connecticut*. . . ."[48] (It is also worth noting that the Supreme Court of California has extended the constitutional right of privacy to invalidate a statutory requirement of disclosure of all financial interests by public officials,[49] which obviously has nothing to do with the "intimacy of the marriage bed" so emphasized in *Griswold*.)

Eisenstadt v. Baird raises an additional possibility for invalidating sodomy laws, but under the aegis of the equal protection clause rather than the right of privacy. That case, like *Griswold v. Connecticut*, involved an anticontraceptive law. Before the *Griswold* decision, Massachusetts had forbidden anyone, under pain of felony penalties, to sell, lend, or give away any article for the prevention of conception. In 1966, after *Griswold*, the Massachusetts legislature amended the law to permit licensed physicians to administer or prescribe, and licensed pharmacists to supply on prescription, drugs or articles for the prevention of conception, but only to married persons. Thus, as an accommodation to the *Griswold* ruling, married persons were given access to contraceptives, but not single people. The amended law was struck down in *Eisenstadt v. Baird* as an invidious discrimination against single people, on the following rationale:

If the objective of the law were one of "health"—to protect the public from potentially dangerous substances by requiring dispensation through, or prescription by, a physician—single people were as much in need of such protection as married couples. Thus their exclusion from the category of permissible distributees could not be related to any health objective. Moreover, it was impossible to view the law as a health measure, because a number of contraceptives present no health hazard, and those that do are already regulated by federal and state drug laws. (Significantly, the statute was contained in a chapter dealing with crimes against chastity, morality, decency, and good order.)

On the other hand, the objective could not have been to discourage sexual intercourse outside the marital relationship, because (1) the law permitted married persons to obtain contraceptives whether or not they planned to use them within that relationship; (2) condoms were already legally available in Massachusetts to single and married people alike for *the prevention of disease;* and (3) the crime of fornication in Massachusetts is only a misdemeanor, whereas Baird's crime was a felony carrying a penalty twenty times greater.

The Supreme Court concluded that if, therefore, the evil sought to be reached by the state is the immorality of contraception per se, there is no good reason for distinguishing between the married and the single, so they must both be treated alike. The fact that the favoritism accorded to married people may have been compelled by *Griswold* does not justify the discrimination.[50]

New York's consensual sodomy law[51] would appear to be a prime target for this rationale of *Eisenstadt v. Baird*. Except for a similar provision in Pennsylvania's new criminal code, the New York law is the only one among the fifty states that permits consensual sodomy between husband and wife but not between any other partners. As noted more fully later,[52] this exclusion from the crime of acts between husband and wife was probably an inadvertent result of the intention already built into the new Penal Law to preclude interspousal prosecutions where force was used or one of the spouses was under the age of consent. But whether the result was inadvertent or not, the discrimination against single people looks arbitrary. It is easy enough to see why any sexual activity between husband and wife should not be criminal, even though one of them be an unwilling participant or underage,[53] while the same activity in those circumstances should be criminal if the partners are not married to each other. But it is not easy to see why consensual sodomy should be permitted to husband and wife yet barred to other adults. One cannot reasonably regard the purpose of the New York law as the deterrence of sex outside marriage, any more than one could ascribe that purpose to the Massachusetts anticontraceptive law. Indeed, such an objective is even more incredible in the case of New York because ordinary intercourse between single people—fornication—is not a crime at all in New York. It is hard to resist the conclusion that the "evil" in consensual sodomy is its immorality per se. If so, New York's discrimination between married couples and everyone else bears no relation to the law's objective, and the law is unconstitutional as a violation of the equal protection clause.[54]

It should be noted that the Supreme Court's opinion in *Eisenstadt v. Baird* does not clearly foreclose the validity of a statutory scheme that would outlaw consensual sodomy, as well as contraceptives, for single persons, while permitting both to married couples. If such prohibitions were coordinated into a patterned effort to deter all sexual behavior outside the marital relationship, they *might* at least be consistent with the equal protection clause. Emphasis is on the word "might," because the Supreme Court's opinion made so much of the fact that the Massachusetts objective was *not* to deter premarital sex. The opinion implies that, if such deterrence had been the law's purpose, the requirements of equal protection could have been satisfied, because the classification would then bear a reasonable relation to the objective. On the other hand, it is going too far to assert from either the *Baird* or the *Griswold* decision that the states have "beyond doubt" the right "to enact statutes regulating the private sexual lives of single persons,"[55] because both decisions, and particularly *Baird*, leave open the possibility of a *general* constitutional right of privacy encompassing single people no less than husband and wife. *Roe v. Wade* has now transformed that possibility into a certainty. A patterned scheme to deter all sexual behavior outside marriage is therefore still subject to the *privacy* challenge, even if it be immune to attack on *equal protection* grounds. In the case of New York, at least, the chances seem small that the state will ever attempt such a scheme, because that would entail creating a new victimless crime—fornication—certain to be ignored by all and sundry.

It should now be clear that *Griswold v. Connecticut* has opened a massive breach in the wall of traditional constitutional wisdom surrounding the sodomy laws. If such a law fails to exempt husband and wife from its scope, it is unconstitutional by direct analogy to *Griswold*. If, on the other hand, it does exempt the marital pair, it runs afoul of the equal protection clause by discriminating against single people. A law exempting the marital pair might escape violating the equal protection clause if it formed part of a patterned scheme to deter all sex outside marriage, but many states have no such scheme. Even if a state were to draw up such a scheme, it would still run the risk of invalidity under the broadened right of privacy.

One caveat should be noted before leaving this subject. The constitutional right of privacy is not absolute. Like other individual rights, the state may override it upon the showing of a compelling subordinating interest.[56] What interests a state might put forward in justification of a sodomy law, and whether any such interest is sufficiently compelling to override a fundamental personal liberty, are questions I have deferred to a later chapter.[57] At least one Supreme Court justice has already served notice that he will need a good deal of convincing:

> . . . . I have serious doubts whether the State may constitutionally assert an interest in regulating any sexual act between consenting adults [citing *Griswold v. Connecticut*].[58]

The *Griswold* doctrine as extended by *Stanley v. Georgia* and *Eisenstadt v. Baird* is beginning to bear fruit. On May 24, 1972, in the United States District Court for the District of Columbia, the following stipulation for dismissal was entered in *Schaefers v. Wilson*, a suit in which four male homosexuals had sought a declaratory judgment against the Washington, D.C., chief of police, to invalidate the District of Columbia sodomy statute:

Pursuant to the provisions of Rule 41 (a) (1) of the Federal

Rules of Civil Procedure, it is hereby stipulated by the parties to the above-mentioned action that D.C. Code § 22-3502 (Sodomy), when construed in light of the Constitution (see *Griswold v. Connecticut*, 381 U.S. 479 (1965)), prior decisional law in this jurisdiction (see *Rittenour v. District of Columbia*, 163 A.2d 558 (D.C. Mun. Ct. App. 1960)), and the legislative history of the statute, does not apply, and cannot be applied, to private consensual sexual acts involving adults (persons age 16 and over); and that the above-entitled action is therefore dismissed, each party to bear his own costs. This stipulation shall not be construed as implying that D.C. Code § 22-3502 has been applied in the past by the defendants to private consensual sexual acts involving adults.[59]

On November 3, 1972, Judge Halleck of the D.C. superior court concluded flatly that the statutory proscription "against fornication, sodomy, and adultery engaged in by consenting adults is an unconstitutional invasion of the right of privacy."[60] The case involved a prosecution under section 22-2701 of the D.C. Code, which makes solicitation for prostitution or any other immoral or lewd purpose a crime. The government had contended that criminalizing mere speech of this character did not violate the first amendment freedom of expression because its protection has never extended to speech soliciting the commission of a criminal act. If, however, the statutes criminalizing the sex acts themselves are invalid, this contention fails.

And on September 11, 1972, California superior court judge George Dell of Los Angeles ruled unconstitutional the statute of that state proscribing oral-genital contacts—section 288a of the California Penal Code.[61] This ruling came in a criminal prosecution against the cast—male and female—of a pornographic movie depicting oral-genital contact, both heterosexual and homosexual. Police had watched the filming from a secret vantage point in the studio, having gained admittance under a search warrant without the producer's knowledge. The place was private; only the participants and the film crew (besides the police) were present; and the former were all adults and obviously consenting. The case is thus almost ideal for presenting squarely the issue of the constitutionality of penalizing private consensual adult behavior, heterosexual or homosexual. The state's attorneys have filed notice of appeal.

The sodomy laws of California are unusually vulnerable to a constitutional attack based on the right of privacy. As previously noted, the Supreme Court of California has already applied the right recognized in *Griswold* to situations not involving the private activities of husband and wife. Moreover, on November 7, 1972, the voters of California approved a referendum proposition to add the "right of privacy" to the list of inalienable rights guaranteed by the state constitution. Thus, the right is now enshrined in the specific words of the state constitution so as clearly to protect all citizens of that state, married or single. If, then, one concedes that the California sodomy laws must be invalid in their application to the private consensual activities of husband and wife by direct analogy to *Griswold*, they must be equally invalid as regards the private activities of other consenting adults. The only way apparently available by which a California court might avoid this conclusion is to find some state purpose sufficiently compelling to override the constitutional right. As we shall see in Chapter 5, none of the conceivable justifications a state might offer seems sufficiently compelling, whether the activities in question be heterosexual or homosexual.

NOTES

1. 381 U.S. 479 (1965).

2. This was the rationale set forth in the Court's opinion, written by Mr. Justice Douglas.

3. This notion was added by the concurring opinion of Mr. Justice Goldberg, in which the Chief Justice (Warren) and Mr. Justice Brennan joined. I do not mean to imply that these justices regarded the ninth amendment as itself a *source* of protected liberties. It means simply that the enumeration of specific liberties in the first eight amendments does not disparage the existence of other, unenumerated rights.

4. This was the rationale adopted by Justices Harlan and White in their concurring opinions.

5. Buchanan v. Batchelor, 308 F.Supp. 729 (N.D. Tex. 1970), *vacated and remanded for reconsideration on juris. grounds, sub nom.* Wade v. Buchanan, 401

U.S. 989 (1971). *See also* Wilhelmi v. Beto, 426 F.2d 795 (5th Cir. 1970), and Polk v. Ellington, 309 F.Supp. 1349, at 1353 (W.D. Tenn. 1970). The *Buchanan* case was remanded for reconsideration of the propriety of federal intervention in state criminal proceedings, in the light of Younger v. Harris, 401 U.S. 37 (1971), and its companion cases. Apparently, however, the plaintiffs did not press their suit, so no reconsideration of the jurisdictional question ever occurred. In an almost identical case elsewhere in Texas, a federal court concluded that intervention was inappropriate. *See* Dawson v. Vance, 329 F.Supp. 1320 (S.D. Tex. 1971).

6.   463 S.W.2d 191 (Tex. Crim. App. 1971), *appeal dismissed*, 402 U.S. 902.

7.   That successful prosecution of a married couple seemed equally unlikely in Maryland was cited by a Maryland court in refusing to invalidate that state's sodomy law at the behest of a defendant convicted of an act with a minor. *See* Hughes v. State, note 9 *infra*.

8.   394 F.2d 873 (7th Cir. 1968).

9.   This approach was also suggested in Hughes v. State, 14 Md. App. 497, 287 A.2d 299 (1972), and in Jones v. State, 55 Wis. 2d 742, 200 N.W.2d 587 (1972), but the courts in those cases felt no need to pursue it because the defendant, in their opinion, had no standing to raise the issue.

10.   IND. STAT. ANN. 10-4221 (1956).

11.   *See* Regina v. Jellyman, 173 Eng. Rep. 637 (1838); Smith v. State, 150 Ark. 265, 234 S.W. 32 (1921); Honselman v. People, 168 Ill. 172, 48 N.E. 304 (1897); Hughes v. State, 287 A.2d 299, 304 n.5 (Md. Ct. App. 1972); State v. Nelson, 199 Minn. 86, 94, 271 N.W. 114, 118 (1937); State v. Schmit, 273 Minn. 78, 139 N.W.2d 800 (1965); Cole v. State, 83 Okla. Crim. 254, 259, 175 P.2d 376, 379 (1946); Commonwealth v. Schiff, 29 North. Co. Rep. 283 (Pa. Ct. Quarter Sessions 1944); Commonwealth v. Wiesner, 21 Lehigh Co. L.J. 284 (Pa. Ct. Quarter Sessions 1945); and Lovisi v. Virginia, 40 U.S.L.W. 3459 (Va. Sup. Ct., Sept. 1, 1971) (unreported decision).

12.   303 F.Supp. 581 (W.D. Va. 1969). *Cf.* Mahone v. State, 209 So.2d 435 (Ala. Ct. App. 1968).

13.   This appears to be the position taken in Jones v. State, 85 Nev. 411, 456 P.2d 429 (1969), and in Hughes v. State, *supra* note 9. The defendants in both cases were convicted for an act performed with a minor.

14.   489 P.2d 526 (Okla. Crim. App. 1971).

15.   489 P.2d at 528.

16.   *See* note 21, Chapter 1 *supra*.

17.   The new Georgia provision is GA. CODE ANN. § 26-2002 (Crim. Code 1970 Revision). The new Minnesota provision, MINN. STAT. ANN. §609.293, subd. 5 (Supp. 1971), reads: "Consensual acts. Whoever, in cases not coming within the provisions of subdivisions 2 and 3 [these subdivisions concern sodomy performed without consent], voluntarily engages in or submits to an act of sodomy with another may be sentenced to imprisonment for not more than one year. . . ." The provision recommended by the revision committee was identical but for the insertion of the words "not his spouse" after the word "another." The conclusion seems inescapable that the new law is intended to cover acts between husband and wife, especially since the prior law, in which the definition of sodomy was the same as in the new, had been so interpreted. *See* note 11 *supra*.

18. The change involved reduction of the offense, in its consensual aspect, from a felony to a misdemeanor, but the statute had to be completely rewritten in the process. *See* UTAH CODE ANN. § 76-53-22 (Supp. 1969).

19. Warren & Brandeis, *The Right to Privacy*, 4 HARV. L. REV. 193 (1890), was the first scholarly delineation of the concept, a work which has borne fruit over the years in increasing judicial recognition of this right in many spheres.

20. 394 U.S. 557 (1969).

21. 394 U.S. at 564.

22. 394 U.S. at 564–65.

23. 402 U.S. 351 (1971).

24. 402 U.S. at 356.

25. 405 U.S. 438 (1972).

26. 405 U.S. at 453.

27. 93 S. Ct. 705 (1973). The companion case is Doe v. Bolton, 93 S. Ct. 739 (1973).

28. 256 Cal. App.2d 488, 64 Cal. Rptr. 70 (1967).

29. 5 Cal. App.3d 865, 85 Cal. Rptr. 718 (1970).

30. Note 32, Chapter 2 *supra*.

31. 483 P.2d 309 (N.M. Ct. App. 1971). In a subsequent case that likewise did not involve the "consensual adults in private" issue, one judge urged that the New Mexico statute should be held unconstitutional anyway. *See* State v. Trejo, 83 N.M. 511, 494 P.2d 173 (Ct. App. 1972) (dissenting opinion of Judge Sutin).

32. 256 Cal. App.2d 630, 64 Cal. Rptr. 447 (1967).

33. Note 97, Chapter 2 *supra*.

34. 305 F.Supp. 749 (S.D.N.Y. 1969).

35. People v. Bercowitz, 61 Misc.2d 974, 308 N.Y. Supp.2d 1 (Sup. Ct. 1970).

36. 305 F.Supp. at 755 n. 18.

37. *Supra* note 13.

38. *Supra* note 9. *Accord*, State v. Kasakoff, 503 P.2d 1182 (N.M. Ct. App. 1972) (act performed by force).

39. Note 100, Chapter 2 *supra*.

40. *Ibid.*

41. 417 F.2d 1161 (D.C. Cir. 1969).

42. 402 F.2d 644 (D.C. Cir. 1968).

43. 417 F.2d at 1164. *Accord*, Frank v. Hampton, unpublished decision, No. 69 C 899 (N.D. Ill., filed Oct. 23, 1970), and Richardson v. Hampton, 345 F. Supp. 600 (D.D.C. 1972). *Contra*, Anonymous v. Macy, 398 F.2d 317 (5th Cir. 1968). Two cases since have taken the position that if the employee has access to classified information, the required nexus between his homosexuality and impairment of his job effectiveness has been shown. *See* Schlegel v. United States, 416 F.2d 1372 (Ct. Cl. 1969), and Adams v. Laird, 420 F.2d 230 (D.C. Cir. 1969). But still another case has held that if such an employee is an *openly avowed* homosexual, the required nexus is lacking. *See* Gayer v. Laird, 332 F.Supp. 169 (D.D.C. 1971). The Minnesota case of McConnell v. Anderson, note 35, Chapter 1 *supra*, which involved denial of employment by a state university, followed the same approach as *Norton v. Macy*. But in that case the job applicant denied that he had ever committed any criminal acts in Minnesota and the court deemed

mere surmise to be insufficient. The Eighth Circuit, in reversing that case, did not take the view that McConnell's homosexuality was per se a valid ground for denying him the job, but held instead that he had attempted to foist tacit approval of his "unconventional ideas" on the university. Presumably, if his homosexuality had been more private (or "clandestine," as the court put it) he could not have been denied the job. *See* 451 F.2d at 196.

44. 1 Cal.3d 214, 461 P.2d 375, 82 Cal. Rptr. 175 (1969). The reference to the right of privacy appears in 461 P.2d at 390. The homosexual conduct in question in the case did not, however, fall within the purview of any of California's penal statutes, and appears to have been an isolated incident in the individual's life.

45. 312 F.Supp. 485, 488 (N.D. Cal. 1970). *Accord,* Pope v. Volpe, unpublished decision, Civ. No. 1753-69 (D.D.C., filed Feb. 5, 1970).

46. 326 F.Supp. 924 (S.D.N.Y. 1971). The statutory disqualification of homosexuals to immigrate to America (see note 29, Chapter 1 *supra*) was apparently inapplicable in Labady's case. A report of the decision appears in N.Y. Times, March 25, 1971, at 30, col. 6. *Cf. In re* Edgar, 253 F.Supp. 951 (E.D. Mich. 1966), holding that adultery, though a crime under Michigan law, does not necessarily demonstrate lack of "good moral character."

47. 326 F.Supp. at 927.

48. *Id.* at 929 n. 4.

49. City of Carmel-by-the-Sea v. Young, 2 Cal.3d 259, 466 P.2d 225, 85 Cal. Rptr. 1 (1970). *Cf.* Travers v. Paton, 261 F.Supp. 110 (D. Conn. 1966).

50. The statements in the text present only the analysis contained in the opinion for the Court delivered by Mr. Justice Brennan. Although this was a majority opinion, only four justices subscribed to it (Brennan, Douglas, Stewart, and Marshall). Justices Powell and Rehnquist joined the Court too late to take part. Justices White and Blackmun concurred in the result, but not in the Court's opinion. Chief Justice Burger dissented. Justice Douglas also wrote a separate concurring opinion. The case is historically significant as the first to invalidate a discrimination between married and single people under the equal-protection clause. The Court prefaced its opinion with a quotation from another recent landmark case—Reed v. Reed, 404 U.S. 71 (1971)—which was the first to invalidate a discrimination between men and women under the same clause.

51. Note 12, Chapter 1 *supra.*

52. *See* pp. 101–2, Chapter 5 *infra.*

53. The reasoning is that marriage raises, so to speak, an irrebuttable presumption of consent to sexual contact with the spouse and removes all societal objection to the nonage of either spouse. Even if one were to argue that there should be no presumption of consent to deviate sex acts in marriage, state intervention through the criminal process to protect a nonconsenting spouse is still hardly the way to help preserve or repair an ongoing relationship.

54. In Hughes v. State, *supra* note 9, the Maryland court of appeals rejected the contention that permitting sodomy to husband and wife but denying it to unmarried people would deprive the latter of equal protection. The opinion did not, however, discuss *Eisenstadt v. Baird,* so apparently it was rendered before the latter decision was handed down. In a case subsequent to *Baird,* which denied a homosexual admission to the Bar of New York because of his prior arrest and

conviction in Florida for a consensual act, the two dissenting justices expressed their view that the New York consensual sodomy law "may well be unconstitutional, as unreasonably discriminatory, because it makes it a crime when committed by unmarried persons but not when committed by married persons." *In re* Kimball, 339 N.Y. Supp.2d 302, 309 (App. Div. 1973).

The new Pennsylvania criminal code adopted Dec. 5, 1972, puts Pennsylvania's law in the same vulnerable position as that of New York. It calls the offense "voluntary deviate sexual intercourse" and defines such intercourse so as to exclude conduct between husband and wife. Deviate sex acts are thus forbidden to all other consenting adults, in the heterosexual as well as the homosexual context. Coitus, on the other hand, is not forbidden. The new code has no provision against either fornication or, in contrast to New York, adultery.

55. This assertion was made in Sturgis v. Attorney General, 260 N.E.2d 687, 690 (Mass. 1970). *Accord,* State v. Lutz, 57 N.J. 314, 272 A.2d 753 (1971).

56. *See* Roe v. Wade and Doe v. Bolton, *supra* note 27.

57. *See* text and notes at pp. 98–114, Chapter 5 *infra.*

58. California v. La Rue, 93 S. Ct. 390, 404 n.10 (1972) (dissenting opinion of Mr. Justice Marshall).

59. *See* The Advocate, June 21, 1972, at 1, 24. *Schaefers v. Wilson* was Civil No. 1821–71 (D.D.C., filed May 24, 1972).

60. United States v. Moses, 41 U.S.L.W. 2298 (D.C. Super. Ct., filed Nov. 3, 1972).

61. *See* The Advocate, Oct. 11, 1972, at 1, 8. The style of the case is *People v. Schwartz.* The Advocate, Oct. 25, 1972, at 6.

4

Establishment of Religion

The establishment clause of the first amendment, which is applicable to the states through the fourteenth, does not merely prohibit government from establishing a particular church or religion as the official one. It imposes neutrality on the state where religion is concerned, so that government may not follow a policy either of preferring one religion over another or of aiding all religions at the expense of irreligion.[1] One application of this principle is that the state may not impose a rule of conduct on its citizens for basically religious objectives. If such a law can be shown to have a religious origin, it is immediately suspect and a burden of justification rests upon the state to show that its objective is really secular.

This framework of analysis is well illustrated in *McGowan v. Maryland*,[2] though the law there under attack was sustained. In that case the attack was predicated on the religious inspiration of Maryland's Sunday-closing laws. The Court found, however, that they no longer retained their religious character but served a valid secular purpose—the imposition of a uniform day of rest each week on all working people. That the day chosen happened to be the "Lord's Day" of the Christian religion, thus enabling Christians to observe their particular interpretation of the Fourth Commandment, was deemed no more than a coincidence, just as laws proscribing murder happen to coincide with the Sixth Commandment.

Another, more recent, case that exhibits the same analytical approach but that resulted in invalidation of the law being attacked is *Epperson v. Arkansas*.[3] The law in question was similar to that of Tennessee involved in the Scopes "monkey" trial. It prohibited teaching the Darwinian theory of evolution in the

74

schools. The decision could not be rested on freedom of speech without infringing the states' right to prescribe their schools' curricula. While it might have been rested on "substantive due process" grounds, as in *Meyer v. Nebraska*,[4] the majority, speaking through Mr. Justice Fortas, preferred to rest it on violation of the establishment clause. The obvious purpose of the law was to prevent the teaching of a theory apparently in conflict with the biblical account of creation in Genesis, and no purely secular objective could be found.

The sodomy laws have a demonstrably religious origin. They are directly traceable to Judaism and Christianity. Although one occasionally finds laws bearing some resemblance to them in ancient or modern cultures uninfluenced by Judeo-Christian traditions,[5] generally the posture of such other cultures toward deviate sex acts has been remarkably more relaxed than our own.[6]

Ancient Greek culture extolled homosexual love equally with, if not more than, heterosexual love; however, physical expression of that love through sex acts evoked various attitudes, being approved by many of the intellectual elite but disapproved or ridiculed by others.[7] Significantly, the Greeks believed their gods engaged in such acts, *e.g.*, Zeus with Ganymede. The laws in ancient Greece did not make such acts illegal per se, though there are occasional examples of legislation dealing with particular relationships, for example, laws penalizing prostitution or forbidding slaves to have connection with freeborn youths.[8] Roman civilization before it became Christianized does not differ much in this respect from Greek culture,[9] the Romans being perhaps less idealistic in their attitude toward homosexual affairs. Only in the Zoroastrian religion was "unnatural sin" treated with a severity parallel to that of Judaism and Christianity.[10] It is difficult to determine whether this was an independent development, because the prohibition in the Zoroastrian texts carries the same justification—the association of such "sin" with infidelity and idolatry—as in the Hebrew texts.[11] The ancient Jews may have borrowed from their Persian masters here as in other tenets of their faith, such as the belief in angels and in a cosmic struggle between light and darkness, good and evil.

Islam, the religion that dominates North Africa and the entire Middle East, was heavily influenced by Judaism, and, to a lesser extent, by Christianity. The Koran repeats the story of Sodom and Gomorrah, condemning the "sin" of those cities. Consequently, in

the ancient Muslim religious code, sodomy is, like adultery, a
serious offense punishable by death.[12] Practically speaking, the
offense was a dead letter from the outset, because Muhammad
required for conviction the testimony of more than one witness.
Observers in Muslim countries assert almost unanimously that, in
stark contrast to the formal law, the folk mores have always
tolerated pederasty and homosexual behavior and still do.[13]

On the Indian subcontinent, Sir Richard Burton asserted that
pederasty, though common among the Sikhs and Muslims of the
Punjab, was held in abhorrence by the Hindus.[14] The abhorrence
does not appear to have been particularly virulent, as a class of
male homosexual prostitutes—the Hinjras—flourished openly, and
female homosexuality was not rare.[15] A medical practitioner in
India expresses the view from his experience in examining and
treating patients that homosexual behavior is as prevalent among
the other communities of the subcontinent as among the Muslim
population.[16] Though modern India does have a penal statute
designated "unnatural offenses," this statute bears all the earmarks
of an English origin.[17]

In Japanese culture in the pre-Meiji period (i.e., prior to the
westernization that began in 1868), homosexuality held somewhat
the same position of esteem as it did in ancient Greece. The
warrior caste—Samurai—institutionalized it to much the same
extent as in ancient Sparta. Chinese culture before the advent of
Western influence appears to have taken a neutral stance toward
homosexual behavior. Similarly, the Chinese do not appear to have
disapproved of the common forms of deviate heterosexual sex
acts.[18]

As for the smaller, more primitive cultures of the world, Ford
and Beach summarize the situation as follows:

> Our own society disapproves of any form of homosexual
> behavior for males and females of all ages. In this it differs
> from the majority of human societies. Some people resemble
> us in this respect, but a larger number condone or even
> encourage homosexuality for at least some members of the
> population.[19]
>
> In 49 (64 per cent) of the 76 societies other than our own for
> which information is available, homosexual activities of one
> sort or another are considered normal and socially acceptable

for certain members of the community. The most common form of institutionalized homosexuality is that of the *berdache* or *transvestite*. The berdache is a male who dresses like a woman, performs women's tasks, and adopts some aspects of the feminine role in sexual behavior with male partners. Less frequently a woman dresses like a man and seeks to adopt the male sex role.[20]

For example, among the Indian tribes of North America, most males probably had some homosexual experience during childhood and adolesence. It may have been institutionalized as a stage in sexual growth among certain cultures that maintained bachelor houses. Children who demonstrated a marked preference for the habits of the opposite sex "were watched closely in their development but no effort was made to force them into their natural sex pattern. The emergent transvestite was an amusing oddity for the most part. . . . Indians generally regarded sex deviation as a response to an inner nature or 'call.' Transvestism for a male was considered more acceptable than for a female."[21] Among the Indians of Latin America "sexual deviates and hermaphrodites are recognized without stigma. . . . The supreme Aztec deity . . . and the Quechua earth-mother . . . were ambisexual."[22] In sub-Saharan Africa, homosexual behavior was apparently a matter of disapprobation in society generally and of ridicule within the family, but not a matter for punishment.[23]

The Judeo-Christian attitude toward deviate sex acts begins with the legendary account in Genesis of the destruction of Sodom and Gomorrah by fire and brimstone[24]—hence the generic term "sodomy." The holiness code of Leviticus set up absolute prohibitions against homosexual sodomy and bestiality: "Thou shalt not lie with mankind as with womankind; it is abomination. Neither shalt thou lie with any beast to defile thyself therewith; neither shall any woman stand before a beast to lie down thereto; it is confusion."[25] The wording of the former prohibition, implying that it was aimed at homosexuality between males, but not between females, seems to explain the subsequent exclusion of lesbianism from the crime in English law.[26]

These Judaic commandments had their impetus in the felt need to differentiate the Jewish people and religion from the pagan cultures surrounding them and thereby to create a sense of separateness and distinctiveness in the Jews.[27] Some have suggested that another factor at work here sub silentio may have been the realization that a small and beleaguered nation like the Jews might have a hard time surviving if their sexual energies were diverted into nonprocreative channels.[28] In any event, the attitude of the ancient Hebrews toward sodomy was intimately bound up with their desire to keep the religion of the one true God pure and free from the influence of paganism. This attitude is reflected in the major New Testament reference to homosexuality—Romans 1:26-27—in which Paul, who, we must remember, was a Jew learned in the Mosaic law, equates homosexuality with other evidences of the blindness of the pagan world to the existence and nature of God. But here Paul introduces also the rationale on which Christendom was to fix its attitude—that men who lust after their own gender are perverting the natural order of God's creation, which intended each sex for the other. Unlike the Levitical proscriptions, the passage in Romans may be interpreted to draw within its condemnation lesbians as well, but in this respect it is ambiguous. Besides the passage in Romans, the only other reasonably clear references in the New Testament—1 Corinthians 6:9, 1 Timothy 1:10, and Jude 7—exhibit an equally condemnatory attitude.[29] Oddly, though, the sole reference by Jesus to homosexuality— an oblique one—seems to indicate that he regarded this "sin" as much less significant than others.[30]

The subsequent development of the view of the Christian church toward sexuality is well known. Only the briefest summary will be presented here. The early Church fathers were not Jews but Gentiles immersed in and at the same time confronting the Greco-Roman culture of their time. That culture was characterized by a wide spectrum of views about the sexual side of human nature. Both extremes of this spectrum were alien to Jewish thought and tradition. One—which may be characterized as the licentious attitude—brought sex, both homosexual and heterosexual, into a kind of heedless scramble for all sorts of sensual pleasure or into the worship of idols and the rites of the pagan fertility cults and mystery religions. The other—asceticism—had diverse roots, neoplatonic and stoic philosophy among them. It entailed a virtual renunciation of sexuality, visualizing man as a dichotomy of spirit on the one hand and flesh on the other. Elevation of the spirit could be achieved only at the price of mortifying the flesh.

Ignoring any middle ground between these two extremes, leading figures in the early Christian church, notably Origen, Tertullian, Ambrose, Augustine, and Jerome, opted for asceticism. Probably distorting the intent of Paul's strictures against the flesh and his expressed wish that every Christian could abstain from marriage like himself,[31] they built the scattered passages from the Old and New Testaments already cited, together with those condemning adultery, divorce, and the coveting of a neighbor's wife, into a conception of sexual desire and gratification as *basically evil in themselves,* redeemable only in the context of a permanent union of one man and one woman for the production of children.[32] Celibacy was preferred to marriage as the holier state. This ascetic attitude was reflected in the growth of monasticism and of hermitic withdrawal from the world and in the development of the notion that virginity and sexual continence are, per se, great virtues.[33] Sexual dereliction thus came to be placed almost on a par with the most grievous of sins.

From this point on, it took only the mind of the medieval scholastics to raise sodomy to the position of preeminence among sexual sins, to make it *the* unspeakable crime—the crime not fit even to be named among Christians. It was at this latter stage that sodomy entered Anglo-American law. This development is best epitomized in the *Summa Theologica* of Thomas Aquinas.[34] In his catalogue of the sins of lust, he ranks on one level those directed against mere human beings. Above these, on the highest level, are the sins against God, and there he places bestiality, homosexual sodomy, heterosexual sodomy, and even simple masturbation (though in descending order, as respects their gravity). The theory is simple: God created men and women as sexual beings in order that they might increase and multiply and fill the earth.[35] Since sodomy is nonprocreative sexual gratification, not only is it a pleasure of the flesh and therefore at war with man's spiritual destiny, but even more important, it is against the order of God's creation, diametrically opposed to his purposes, and thus in a very real sense, a sin against God. By comparison, adultery, seduction, and rape, which injure only one's neighbor, are lesser sins.

Although sodomy in English law comprehended only bestiality and anal intercourse, one can see from Saint Thomas's exposition how it later came to comprehend, under the statutes of many American states, other "unnatural" sex acts committed with a human being, whether of the same or the opposite sex. In this connection, it is worth noting that some of the Medieval Church's most prominent campaigns against heresy—those against the Albigenses and the Templars, among others—so commonly yoked the accusation of unnatural sexual practices with that of heresy that the two became synonymous in the popular mind,[36] which used the same word for both—"bugger."[37] The English medieval jurists were agreed that the penalty for this offense should be death and the mode of execution burning, which was the customary mode of execution for heretics and had been prescribed by the Theodosian Code of A.D. 438 for sodomy; however, one authority stated that the offender should be buried alive like those who had dealings with Jews or Jewesses.[38]

During the Middle Ages in England, the offense was within the jurisdiction of the ecclesiastical tribunals of the Church, along with heresy, blasphemy, witchcraft, adultery, and the like.[39] It entered the statute law of England at the time of the Protestant Reformation, when Henry VIII severed the Church of England from Rome and the king's courts began taking over the prerogatives of the courts Christian.[40] The very wording of the original English statute on the subject displays this characteristic medieval equation of sin and crime:

> Forasmuch as there is not yet sufficient and condign punishment appointed and limited by the due course of the Laws of this Realm, for the detestable and abominable vice of Buggery committed with mankind or beast: It may therefore please the King's Highness, with the assent of his Lords spiritual and temporal, and the Commons of this present Parliament assembled, . . . That the same offense be from henceforth adjudged Felony. . . . And that the offenders being hereof convict . . . shall suffer such pains of death, and losses, and penalties of their goods, chattels, debts, lands, tenements and hereditaments, as Felons be accustomed to doe according to the order of the Common-laws of this Realm. And that no person offending in any such offense, shall be admitted to his Clergy, And that Justices of Peace shall have power and authority, within the limits of their Commissions and Jurisdictions, to hear and determine the said offense, as they do use to doe in cases of other Felonies. . . .[41]

The theological underpinnings of this law are made even more manifest in the statute of 5 Eliz. 1, c. 17 (1563), by which Henry's statute, having been repealed by Parliament under Mary, was revived and secured for the next 265 years. The Elizabethan law recited how, since the repeal of Henry's statute, "divers evil disposed persons have been the more bold to commit the said most horrible and detestable vice of buggery aforesaid, *to the high displeasure of Almighty God.*"[42]

The statute of Henry VIII as thus revived by Elizabeth's enactment remained the law of England until 1828, and was in force not only while Blackstone was composing his *Commentaries on the Laws of England* but also during the colonial period and early independence of the American states. By Blackstone's time the notion that the crime was so unspeakable as to be unfit to be named among Christians had become so deeply impressed that he literally refused to name it in his *Commentaries.*[43] He coined instead the phrase "crime against nature," giving rise to that typical eclectic wording of American statutes, which draws both from Blackstone and from Henry's statute—"the abominable and detestable crime against nature, committed with mankind or beast."

This intimate connection between religion and the sodomy laws is again demonstrated by the language of the original statute of North Carolina: "Any person who shall commit the abominable and detestable crime against nature, not to be named among Christians, with either mankind or beast, shall be adjudged guilty of a felony, and shall suffer death without the benefit of clergy."[44]

Sodomy has always been an anomaly among the sex offenses—the black sheep of these criminal laws. It is the only one of the sex offenses that penalizes sexual acts *regardless of relationship and circumstances.* Rape, of course, penalizes coitus when it occurs by force or imposition, or with those under the age of consent (statutory rape). Adultery penalizes the same act when it violates the marital vow of fidelity to one's spouse. Fornication penalizes the same act when it occurs outside the umbrella of marriage, thus being aimed ostensibly at sexual promiscuity. Prostitution usually penalizes sex only when one party pays for it. But sodomy penalizes *certain acts alone,* in any and all circumstances in which they may occur, whether in a "one-night stand" between homosexuals who will never see each other again, or in the most secure and societally sanctioned heterosexual marriage.

The most obvious explanation for this peculiarity of the sodomy laws is that they serve a religious objective—to keep people from engaging in acts that frustrate God's creative purpose and hence from bringing down his wrath on society. Putting the matter in its crudest terms, these laws seek to shield society from fire and brimstone.[45] Though they may appear in the division of the penal code entitled "crimes against the person," they cannot be regarded in any rational sense, at least in their application to the private consensual acts of adults, as a crime against either of the participants.[46] Despite the presence of consent, they might be so regarded if some physical harm resulted. Aiding and abetting suicide, like any intentional infliction of serious physical injury, is considered a crime despite the consent or even invitation of the person committing suicide or being injured. But sodomy is bereft of harmful physical consequences.[47] Plainly, this crime, as the typical statute denominates it, is one against "nature," or, to be even more accurate, is one *against God*.[48]

As already noted, the patently religious origin and even objective of a law will not invalidate it under the establishment clause of the first amendment if it can be found to serve primarily a secular objective as well.[49] The question then is: Can such an objective be unearthed for the sodomy laws, thus rendering the religious objective purely coincidental? This question will be explored in Chapter 5, under the independent rights doctrine. It should be emphasized, however, that the religious derivation of the sodomy laws forces them to bear a heavier burden of justification than legislation of the usual run-of-the-mill kind. They are constitutionally suspect, and any alleged secular justification will be carefully scrutinized to make sure that it is more than just a smoke screen to cover the religious one.

One other point should be made before proceeding to the argument based on the independent rights doctrine. It is no answer to the attack based on the establishment clause that these laws have had a place in the Anglo-American legal tradition for centuries. They could not have been attacked on that ground before adoption of the fourteenth amendment.[50] And only in 1940, in *Cantwell v. Connecticut*,[51] did the Supreme Court definitively state for the first time that the religious freedom clauses of the first amendment were applicable to the states through the fourteenth. In this regard, one may note that the Court has countenanced in recent years more than one such attack on traditional legal positions almost equally hoary.[52]

One case in which a sodomy law was attacked on this basis is *State v. Rhinehart.*[53] The argument was rejected, but the case can hardly be deemed persuasive authority on the question. The court's opinion devoted very little attention to it, so little in fact that the court did not even bother to note that the cases it cited against the contention had to do not with the establishment clause at all, but with the free exercise clause. These were the cases usually cited to the effect that criminal laws which have a valid secular justification are not unconstitutional merely because the peculiar tenets of certain religions urge their adherents to engage in the proscribed conduct (the cases on polygamy and snake handling). Even if the court had perceived the real thrust of the argument—that the law establishes a purely religious view of sexual morality—it would have found the argument irrelevant to the facts before it. Washington's sodomy law is not limited to consensual acts between adults. It also covers acts performed by force and upon minors. The defendant had been convicted of fellatio performed on a 16-year-old boy, and the protection of minors against sexual exploitation by adults is undoubtedly a secular objective, whether the exploitation takes the form of deviate acts or ordinary intercourse. Thus, the question whether the establishment clause is violated by a proscription of deviate sex acts *between consenting adults* is hardly answered by the case. Nevertheless, the case holds a lesson: The argument based on the establishment clause must be kept from confusion with an argument based on the free exercise clause.

Actually, it is difficult to imagine anyone seriously urging invalidity on the basis of the free exercise clause. That basis would require that the religion in question positively enjoin deviate sex acts on its adherents. Perhaps such a sect exists, but even the Metropolitan Community Church[54]—a Christian communion established for the avowed purpose of ministering to the spiritual needs of homosexuals—maintains no such tenet. It asserts only that its interpretation of Christianity does not forbid such acts— a different matter altogether.

NOTES

1. "Neither a state nor the Federal Government can set up a church. Neither can pass laws which aid one religion, aid all religions, or prefer one religion over another." Everson v. Board of Education, 330 U.S. 1, 15 (1947). The clause erects a "wall of separation between church and state." *Id.* at 16. That a particular religious notion is accepted by both Judaism and all branches of Christianity will not keep it from running afoul of the establishment clause. Its offensiveness to the nonreligious person suffices to bar its establishment by law. Engel v. Vitale, 370 U.S. 421, 430 (1962). *See also* Torcaso v. Watkins, 367 U.S. 488 (1961), which, though resting on the free exercise clause rather than the establishment clause, expresses the same idea.

Walz v. Tax Commission, *infra* note 52, makes clear, however, that the state's neutrality may be benevolent. It need not be so strict as positively to hinder the practice of religion. That case refused to require the withdrawal from churches of the tax exemptions allowed to other nonprofit, charitable organizations.

2. 366 U.S. 420 (1961). *See also* Two Guys from Harrison-Allentown, Inc. v. McGinley, 366 U.S. 582 (1961). For an example of the way in which the establishment clause presents issues quite separate and distinct from the free exercise clause, compare the opinions in these two cases with that in Braunfeld v. Brown, 366 U.S. 599 (1961), and particularly with the dissents of Justices Brennan and Stewart in the latter case, 366 U.S. at 610, 616. The fourth companion case to these is Gallagher v. Crown Kosher Super Market, Inc., 366 U.S. 617 (1961).

3. 393 U.S. 97 (1968).

4. 262 U.S. 390 (1923).

5. *See* D. S. BAILEY, HOMOSEXUALITY AND THE WESTERN CHRISTIAN TRADITION 33, 58, 64–69 (1955) [hereinafter cited as BAILEY]. *See also* Bullough, *Attitudes Toward Deviant Sex in Ancient Mesopotamia,* 7 J. SEX RESEARCH 184 (1971); and note 56, Chapter 10 *infra.*

6. *See* W. CHURCHILL, HOMOSEXUAL BEHAVIOR AMONG MALES 75–80 (1967); A. C. KINSEY, W. B. POMEROY, C. E. MARTIN, & P. H. GEBHARD, SEXUAL BEHAVIOR IN THE HUMAN FEMALE 447 (1953). Another secondary though exhaustive source of information on cultural attitudes toward homosexuality is A. KARLEN, SEXUALITY AND HOMOSEXUALITY—A NEW VIEW (1971).

The summary which follows in the text is a reasonably accurate statement of current knowledge on the subject, but is not free from difficulty. Most of our knowledge of advanced non-Western cultures is scanty and comes from anecdotes and unsystematic observations made by Western travelers and sojourners or from the study of literature and art. There have been no large-scale empirical investigations by persons disciplined in the behavioral sciences. As regards primitive cultures, the information is somewhat more reliable, having been gathered largely by trained anthropologists. But even some of their earlier studies are now being questioned, because they tended to read into their observations their own Western stereotypical ideas of sex roles and behavior. In many societies today, both advanced and primitive, it is difficult for Western scientists to gain reliable information about current attitudes and practices, not only because sexual behavior is a more or less private affair everywhere, but also because native respondents are often sensitive to Western reactions and wish to avoid giving the impression that their society tolerates or approves conduct which in Western eyes is regarded as primitive or degenerate. Formal laws may likewise be a poor index of cultural attitudes because the modernization efforts of non-Western societies have often included copying Western laws. For instance, the Indian Penal Code appears to have copied Anglo law on sodomy, and that code has been taken as a model in such other countries as Burma, Ceylon, and Malaya.

7. The best-known examples of this laudatory attitude toward homosexual love are found in Plato's *Symposium*. However, even the *Symposium* illustrates the contrasting attitudes of the Greeks toward physical expression of homosexual love through sex acts. Plato himself, in his later work the *Laws*, advocated making such acts illegal. Nevertheless, that toleration was the general attitude of the Greeks seems rather well demonstrated by Plutarch's discussion of the subject in his *Dialogue on Love*, in volume 9 of his *Moralia* (moral essays) (Harvard Loeb Classics ed. 1961).

8. Homosexuality in ancient Greek culture has been explored exhaustively by modern scholars, yet the treatise by John Addington Symonds remains as good a coverage as any. *See* J. A. SYMONDS, A PROBLEM IN GREEK ETHICS (1908). Other authoritative works are Licht, *Male Homosexuality in Ancient Greece*, in D. W. CORY, HOMOSEXUALITY—A CROSS CULTURAL APPROACH 267–348 (1956); J. Z. EGLINTON, GREEK LOVE (1964); and R. FLACELIÈRE, LOVE IN ANCIENT GREECE 62–100 (J. Cleugh transl. 1962). *See also* M. M. HUNT, THE NATURAL HISTORY OF LOVE 15–51 (1959); A. EDWARDES, THE JEWEL IN THE LOTUS 199–262 (1959); Westermarck, *Homosexual Love*, in Cory, *supra* at 118–19; and ENCYCLOPEDIA OF SEXUAL BEHAVIOR 121–22 (rev. ed. A. Ellis & A. Abarbanel 1967) [hereinafter cited as ENCY. SEX].

9. *See* Westermarck, in Cory, *supra* note 8, at 120-21; ENCY. SEX 124-25.

10. *See* Westermarck, in Cory, *supra* note 8, at 119.

11. *Id.* at 124–27.

12. D. J. WEST, HOMOSEXUALITY 79 (rev. ed. 1968).

13. *See* Sir R. Burton, *Terminal Essay of the Book of the Thousand Nights and a Night*, in Cory, *supra* note 8, at 220–21; Westermarck, in Cory, *supra* note 8, at 116; West, *supra* note 12, at 72, 102; R. DE BECKER, THE OTHER FACE OF LOVE 61–68 (Crosland & Daventry transl. 1969); ENCY. SEX 546; A. EDWARDES & R. E. L. MASTERS, THE CRADLE OF EROTICA 195–226, 227–96, 297–326 (1962).

Raphael Patai gives what is perhaps the most authoritative available summary of Middle Eastern attitudes and practices regarding homosexuality:

> In dealing with homosexuality in the Middle East, careful distinction must be made between the legal position and folk mores. . . . As opposed to the law, in actual practice male homosexuality was rampant in Biblical times and has so remained in the Middle East down to the present day. It may not have been as general as it was in ancient Greece, but the folk mores certainly did not regard it with any measure of disapproval. . . . The Koranic reaffirmation of the . . . [biblical condemnation] (Koran 26:165–66)—made in the context of retelling the story of Lot in Sodom—has

had as little effect on the actual conduct of the folk as the older Biblical law itself.

R. PATAI, SEX AND FAMILY IN THE BIBLE AND THE MIDDLE EAST 168–70 (1959).

> To return once more to the subject of homosexuality, . . . the general statement can be made that neither in the Middle Ages nor in modern times has the practice been opposed by popular opinion. . . . Strictly speaking, . . . these societies or individuals are bisexual rather than homosexual. . . .

Id. at 174.

> The traditional Middle Eastern folk mores countenance homosexual love, as long as it is practiced in secret with no witnesses present. . . .

Id. at 175–76.

14. Sir R. Burton, in Cory, *supra* note 8, at 231–32.

15. *See* Carstairs, *Hinjra and Jiryan: Two Derivatives of Hindu Attitudes to Sexuality*, 29 BRIT. J. MEDICAL PSYCHOLOGY 128 (1956); ENCY. SEX 130–31, 533–34. On India, *see also* de Becker, *supra* note 13, at 71–76.

16. ENCY. SEX 533–34.

17. The statute reads,

> Whoever voluntarily has carnal intercourse against the order of nature with any man, woman, or animal shall be punished with transportation for life, or with imprisonment of either description for a term which may extend to ten years, and shall be liable to a fine.
>
> Explanation:—Penetration is sufficient to constitute the carnal intercourse necessary to the offense described in this section.

Indian Penal Code §377 (1860).

18. On China and Japan, *see* Westermarck, in Cory, *supra* note 8, at 116–17; and de Becker, *supra* note 13, at 76–85.

Probably the most authoritative work on China is that of the Dutch diplomat and art collector, Van Gulik, who has made an exhaustive survey of the art and literature of ancient China dealing with sexuality (up to A.D. 1644, before the advent of Western influence). He explains that the basic underlying view of sexuality held by the Chinese stressed that the male's vital force (or *yang* essence), epitomized by his semen, should be conserved, or compensated by acquiring an equivalent amount of *yin* essence from the woman. He traces out the consequences of this view for deviate sex acts as follows:

> Masturbation [, though forbidden to men, if] practiced by women is viewed with tolerance, since woman's *yin* supply is considered to be unlimited in quantity. . . . A very tolerant attitude is taken also towards sapphism [lesbianism], and for the same reason. It is also recognized that when a number of women are obliged to live in continuous and close proximity, the occurrence of sapphism can hardly be avoided. Homosexuality of men is not mentioned in the handbooks of sex, because those are exclusively concerned with conjugal relations. Literary sources in general adopt a neutral attitude as long as it is engaged in by grown-up persons, it being taken that intimate contact between two *yang* elements can not result in a total loss of vital force for either of them. It is denounced in those cases—according to Chinese historical records not rare in court circles

—where one of the partners abused the emotional tie for obtaining excessive material profit, or for inciting his partner to unjust or criminal deeds. It is praised if such a relationship inspired great artistic achievements. It may be added that while female homosexuality was widely spread, male homosexuality was rare in early times up till the Han dynasty; during that period it was at times deemed fashionable, and it seems to have flourished especially in the early part of the Liu-ch'ao period, and again during the Northern Sung dynasty (960-1127 A.D.). From then onward till the end of the Ming dynasty (1644 A.D.) male homosexuality was of not more frequent occurrence than in most other normal western civilizations.

R. H. VAN GULIK, SEXUAL LIFE IN ANCIENT CHINA 48 (1961). He discounts the observations of foreigners to the effect that male homosexuality was rampant in China in the nineteenth and early twentieth centuries, believing that such relations received undue emphasis because social etiquette of that time was rather tolerant of the public manifestations of homosexuality, while heterosexual relationships were strictly confined to the privacy of the home. *Ibid.* n. 2. He comments on heterosexual fellatio, anal intercourse, and cunnilingus as follows:

> *Penilinctio* was permitted but only as a preliminary or an accessory to . . . [coitus], it must never result in the man having a complete emission. The slight loss in semen and secretions incurred is deemed to be compensated by the *yin* essence the man obtains from the woman's saliva. [Anal intercourse] is also permitted, for similar reasons. Cunnilinctio is approved of, because it prepares the woman for the act and simultaneously procures *yin* essence for the man; it is frequently referred to, especially in texts of Taoist colouring.

Id. at 49.

19. C. S. FORD & F. A. BEACH, PATTERNS OF SEXUAL BEHAVIOR 125 (1951). *See also* Brown, *A Comparative Study of Deviations of Sexual Mores,* 17 AM. SOCIOLOGICAL REV. 135 (1952).

20. Ford & Beach, *supra* note 19, at 130. Opler believes that Ford and Beach give a somewhat misleading picture, because their information is presented out of context and one is therefore uncertain whether it refers to the sexual experimentation of preadolescents or to homosexuality among adults. Opler, *Anthropological and Cross-Cultural Aspects of Homosexuality,* in SEXUAL INVERSION 112 (J. Marmor ed. 1965). Homosexual behavior in the former context may be looked upon with indifference, as among the Cubeo Indians of the Amazon. *Id.* at 116–17. But that may tell us little about the society's attitude toward adult homosexuality. He asserts that

> Actually, no society save perhaps ancient Greece, pre-Meiji Japan, certain top echelons in Nazi Germany, and the scattered examples of such special status groups as the berdaches, Nata slaves, and one category of Chukchee shamans, has lent sanction in any real sense to homosexuality.

Id. at 114. It seems to me from the works I have cited in other footnotes that Opler's statement is misleading in the opposite direction. He may be correct if his intention is that positive approval of homosexuality is largely limited to the instances he cites. Toleration, on the other hand, seems more the rule than the exception, to the extent it is possible to generalize from the present limited state of our knowledge. *See also* text and notes at pp. 293–94, Chapter 10 *infra.*

21. ENCY. SEX 100.

22. *Id.* at 605.

23. *Id.* at 73. On the general subject of sexuality in black Africa, *see* B. DE RACHEWILTZ, BLACK EROS (1965).

24. *Genesis* 18:16 to 19:29. *Cf. Judges* 19:22–25. BAILEY at 1–8 attacks as unfounded the interpretation of the story as referring to homosexual practices. His opposing interpretation of the story is supported by *Ezekiel* 16:49–50; *Isaiah* 1:10, 3:3; and *Jeremiah* 23:14. Whether or not one finds Bailey's exegesis persuasive, the homosexual interpretation rightly or wrongly has held sway throughout Christendom for almost 2,000 years and its influence upon the law is unmistakable.

25. *Leviticus* 18:22–23 (King James).

26. The offense of sodomy, as already noted, was held in England to be limited to bestiality and anal intercourse. *See* note 10, Chapter 1 *supra,* and notes 17–19, Chapter 2 *supra.* Thus, two lesbians could not commit the crime. The offense of "acts of gross indecency," created in 1885, was explicitly limited to males. *See* note 19, Chapter 2 *supra.* This same clear implication of the Judaic law is repeated, again unmistakably, in *Leviticus* 20:13. The latter verse, together with verses 15–16, which repeat the injunction against bestiality, also furnishes the penalty which Christendom later adopted—death. That the penalty was specified for both participants, *and even for the beast* (where bestiality was involved), plainly shows this to be a religious taboo and not, like much of the rest of the Hebrew law, a rule that would be perfectly at home in a secular code. Sodomy is not the only "crime" for which we would find the Old Testament's prescription of the death penalty odd today. *Cf. Exodus* 22:18: "Thou shalt not suffer a witch to live."

It is a curious fact that, even though almost all the American statutes are susceptible of being interpreted to cover lesbian acts, prosecutions of lesbians have been extremely rare in America. *See* Kinsey *et al., supra* note 6, at 484–85.

27. This conclusion is derived from the context of the passage in *Leviticus,* which associates the proscribed practices with the doings of the Egyptians and the Canaanites. Likewise, the pejorative appellation "abomination" is one traditionally applied by the ancient Hebrews to idolatry. *See* BAILEY at 43–44, and 30–37, where he argues, however, that there is rather slender evidence of the prevalence of homosexuality in the cultures that surrounded ancient Israel. *See* also Westermarck, in Cory, *supra* note 8, at 124–27.

28. This possibility is suggested by W. G. COLE, SEX AND LOVE IN THE BIBLE 343 (1959), and before him by Sir Richard Burton in his *Terminal Essay of the Book of the Thousand Nights and a Night,* in Cory, *supra* note 8, at 224–25. Burton's *Terminal Essay* is also reproduced in SIR R. BURTON, THE EROTIC TRAVELER 26–72 (E. Leigh ed. 1967).

29. Like the Sodom legend, some of these passages may have been misinterpreted, but the error, if any, in the translation of the Greek words has been so ancient and universal in the English-speaking world that it is immaterial to the present inquiry.

30. He is reported to have said that if the miracles he performed had been done in Sodom, it would be standing to that very day, and that it would be more

tolerable for Sodom and Gomorrah on the day of judgment than for the towns that rejected his message and his disciples. *Matthew* 10:15, 11:23–24; *Luke* 10:10–12. *Cf. Luke* 17:29–30. This interpolation of Jesus' attitude from these references assumes, of course, that the homosexual interpretation of the Sodom legend in Genesis had become accepted among the Jews by his time—an assumption that has considerable warrant in the evidence of the Pseudepigrapha, of Philo of Alexandria, and of Josephus. *See* BAILEY 11–26.

31. *See, e.g., Romans* 6:12, 19; 7:14–25; and 13:14; 1 *Corinthians* 6:13–20; and 7:1–9, 25–40; and *Galatians* 5:16–24. Paul's counsel not to marry may have been intended to mean *remarriage,* and in any event was prompted by his belief in the imminence of Christ's second coming. It is unlikely that he himself had never been married, since all Jews of his day were expected to marry and betrothals were arranged early in life. The same could be said of Jesus. Alongside Paul's counsel to remain single (or un-remarried), one should mention the curious passage in *Matthew* in which Jesus is apparently depicted as urging those of his disciples who can to follow the example of men "who have made themselves eunuchs for the sake of the kingdom of heaven." *Matthew* 19:10–12. This cryptic, puzzling dialogue, which is not reported in any of the other gospels and which the Church seized upon to justify its adulation of celibacy over marriage, led some early Christians even to castrate themselves.

32. *See* Churchill, *supra* note 6, at 17–26.

33. *See* BAILEY 82–91; Hunt, *supra* note 8, at 93–127; W. E. PHIPPS, WAS JESUS MARRIED?—THE DISTORTION OF SEXUALITY IN THE CHRISTIAN TRADITION (1970); J. CLEUGH, LOVE LOCKED OUT (1964); and W. G. COLE, SEX AND LOVE IN THE BIBLE (1959). Karlen, *supra* note 6, also presents a full description of the historical development of the Christian attitude toward sexuality. Lars Ullerstam is not far off the mark when he says, "According to traditional Christian ethics one should forego one's own needs, if they are not of a religious nature, and satisfy those of others, as long as they are not sexual." L. ULLERSTAM, THE EROTIC MINORITIES 9 (A. Hollo transl. 1966).

34. Saint Thomas Aquinas, Summa Theologica, II-II, Q. *cliv,* 1, 11, and particularly 12.

35. *Genesis* 1:27–28. The ascetic tradition of the Church seems inconsistent with this command.

36. *See* BAILEY 135–41.

37. The term is a corruption of the word "Bulgar." *See* BAILEY 141, 148–9. It refers to the most important of the heresies with which the Medieval Church had to contend—the Manicheeism of the Albigensian Cathari—which spread into Western Europe from Bulgaria and whose adherents were alleged to engage in "unnatural" sex acts. *See* J. C. S. RUNCIMAN, THE MEDIEVAL MANICHEE (1947), and especially at 176–77.

38. *See* BAILEY 145–47, 71–72; and The Theodosian Code IX.vii. 6, at 232 (C. Pharr transl. 1952). *See* also 3 E. COKE, INSTITUTES °58; 4 W. BLACKSTONE, COMMENTARIES °215–16. The passage from Blackstone again clearly signals the religious character of the crime. He declares it to be condemned by "the express law of God"—presumably a reference to the proscriptions in *Leviticus.* He also states that it has been demonstrated to deserve capital punishment by the "destruction of two cities by fire from heaven"—plainly a reference to the biblical account of Sodom and Gomorrah. Of course, these penalties as contrasted with

penances, could not have been imposed or executed by the ecclesiastical authorities, but only by the secular power—the state. Evidence appears totally lacking of the extent to which they were actually carried out in practice. The medieval jurists may merely have been stating what they thought the law *ought* to be. Thus, in England sodomy may never have been punished by the temporal power before 1533, but only dealt with as a sin by the Church. The statute enacted that year would seem to indicate as much. *See* note 40 *infra;* and 2 F. POLLOCK & F. MAITLAND, HISTORY OF ENGLISH LAW 554–55 (1895).

In this connection, it is interesting to note that

> Paradoxically, . . . Christian lawgivers who adopted the Jewish code against intercourse with beasts . . . enlarged it to include the Jews themselves. Cohabitation of a Christian with a Jewess was held to be equivalent to "buggery" with animals. Some authorities included Turks and Saracens in the same category, "inasmuch as such persons in the eyes of the law and our holy faith differ in no wise from beasts." Men and women convicted of copulating with a human being who was not a Christian were put to death, together with their partners.

Ford & Beach, *supra* note 19, at 145, quoting from E. P. EVANS, THE CRIMINAL PROSECUTION AND CAPITAL PUNISHMENT OF ANIMALS 153 (1906).

39. *See* BAILEY 146–47. The penitentials that Bailey discusses elsewhere in his book give us some idea of the penances that the Church courts might have assigned for sodomy. These documents recommend penances for sodomy ranging from 40 days to 14 years.

40. The first English statute, 25 Hen. 8, c. 6 (1533), was enacted in the very year of Henry's famous divorce from his first wife, Catherine of Aragon. This event had precipitated his battle with Papal authority and led the next year—1534—to passage of the Act of Supremacy, which declared Henry head of the Church of England and thus sealed the schism. As the preamble of the statute indicates, it may have been inspired as much by the reluctance of the Church courts to convict offenders or to turn those convicted over to the temporal authorities for punishment, as by a desire to take over their jurisdiction generally. *See* BAILEY 147–48; H. M. HYDE, THE LOVE THAT DARED NOT SPEAK ITS NAME—A CANDID HISTORY OF HOMOSEXUALITY IN BRITAIN 38–39 (1970) [hereinafter cited as HYDE].

41. The quotation is from the original statute cited in the immediately preceding note.

42. (Emphasis added.) Henry's enactment, which, though temporary at first, was made permanent a few years later, was repealed in the reign of his successor, Edward VI, and reinstated in somewhat modified terms. Repealed again by Parliament under Mary Tudor, it was finally reinstated in its original terms by the Elizabethan enactment cited in the text. It then remained the law of England until 1828, when it was replaced by an act consolidating a number of offenses "against the person." But the death penalty was not abolished for the crime in England until 1861. Even then, the maximum punishment remained life imprisonment until the crime, in its application to consenting adults in private, was abolished in 1967. *See* BAILEY 147–51; HYDE 39–40, 92–93.

The first reported trial under the statute, that of the Earl of Castlehaven in 1631 (described at pp. 31–32, Chapter 2 *supra*), is replete with fulminations about the sinfulness of the act and the judgment of God. This trial probably served a purpose of discrediting Catholics, because Castlehaven was a "papist" and Charles I, who is said to have taken a personal interest in the proceedings, was not known for his tolerance of nonconformity, whether of the Puritan or Catholic varieties. The King turned down Castlehaven's appeal for clemency, but consented that the hapless lord be beheaded rather than hanged. *See* HYDE 47–51.

An early Maryland case discloses that sodomy indictments at that time charged the defendant with "not having the fear of God before his eyes, but being moved and seduced by the instigation of the Devil," and characterized the crime as "that sodomitical, detestable, and abominable sin (among Christians not to be named)" which was committed "against the order of nature" and "to the high displeasure of Almighty God." *See* Davis v. State, 3 H. & J. 154 (Md. Ct. App. 1810).

43. 4 W. BLACKSTONE, COMMENTARIES °215. Following in Blackstone's tradition, American appellate opinions are full of deprecatory words about these "perversions" and of other expressions to demonstrate to the world how much the judges detest these acts and how loath they are even to discuss them.

44. N.C. REV. CODE c. 34, § 6 (1837).

45. This purpose is explicit in the two edicts of the Christian emperor, Justinian, of A.D. 538 and 544, which greatly influenced the attitude of juristic thought throughout medieval Christendom. *See* Justinian, Novellae 77, 141. It was not, however, Justinian who made homosexual intercourse a capital offense in the later Roman Empire, but his imperial Christian predecessors. Though the crime had a few ambiguous antecedents in Roman law, it definitively entered Roman jurisprudence as a capital offense by the Theodosian law of A.D. 390. *See* BAILEY 71–72.

46. Under the American statutes the crime is not treated as one against either of the participants. Both are deemed equally guilty and hence are equally subject to prosecution. This stance of the law often forces a prosecutor to choose which of the two he will regard as the "victim." In cases in which one of the participants is a minor, the minor invariably becomes the victim, even though he may have instigated the act. Thus, although he may be of the age of accountability for criminal acts, he is not prosecuted. Where both participants are adults, both are usually prosecuted, unless the testimony of one is necessary to prove commission of the crime. In that case the participant willing to testify is granted immunity from prosecution for turning state's witness and thus assumes the role of "victim." But in both this latter case, and in that of the minor who serves as prosecuting witness, a frequent problem is how to corroborate the witness's testimony, because many states require such corroboration where the witness is himself, in the eyes of the law, a principal or accomplice in the crime.

47. *See* note 22, Chapter 5 *infra*.

48. Some evidence that these laws still rest upon a religious foundation comes from the unsuccessful reform effort in California in 1971. On October 5, 1971, the California state assembly defeated, 41 to 25, a bill that would have removed the criminal sanction from anal-genital and oral-genital contacts between consenting adults in private. Here are some representative arguments from the bill's opponents during the floor debate:

The capital of this state is Sacramento, not Sodom and Gomorrah. . . .

The Bible contains the greatest moral code ever written. [citing *Leviticus* 18:22: "Thou shalt not lie with a man as a woman. It is an abomination"], the words of this Book [have been] a rich heritage. . . . We should be going the other way to improve moral standards upon which this country was built.

[The Bible is a moral code] and people are looking for moral codes on which to base their life-style. . . . It is dangerous for us, in our self-inflated wisdom, to challenge God's wisdom.

[I am] ashamed [of the Assembly for trying to] elevate itself above God. . . . Moral laws are absolute, and man has no business to tamper with them.

The Advocate, October 27, 1971, at 2.

49. *See* notes 1-3 *supra*. *See also* the following quotation from Mr. Justice Clark's opinion for the Court in Abington School District v. Schempp, 347 U.S. 203, 222 (1963):

The test may be stated as follows: what are the purpose and primary effect of the enactment? If either is the advancement or inhibition of religion then the enactment exceeds the scope of legislative power as circumscribed by the Constitution. That is to say that to withstand the strictures of the Establishment Clause there must be a secular legislative purpose and a primary effect that neither advances nor inhibits religion.

50. Reference is, of course, to the argument for invalidity under the *federal* Constitution. Some state constitutions may contain clauses modeled on the first amendment. Since, however, the major delineations of constitutional doctrines usually originate in the United States Supreme Court, decisions in the state courts are rarely rested on these clauses.

51. 310 U.S. 296 (1940). The first case to consider application of the establishment clause to the states through the fourteenth amendment, separately from the free exercise clause, was Everson v. Board of Education, 330 U.S. 1 (1947). It upheld the state law there in question. The first decision holding a state law unconstitutional under the establishment clause was McCollum v. Board of Education, 333 U.S. 203 (1948). That decision appeared to have been undermined by Zorach v. Clauson, 343 U.S. 306 (1952). All these cases dealt with state aid for parochial education or released time from the public schools for religious education. The first case to demonstrate the potential of the establishment clause for attacks on ordinary *criminal* statutes was McGowan v. Maryland, *supra* note 2. Hence this avenue of attack on the sodomy laws has really been visible only since 1961.

52. *See* McGowan v. Maryland, *supra* note 2 (Sunday closing laws); Walz v. Tax Commission, 397 U.S. 664 (1970) (tax exemption of church property held and used for religious purposes); Gillette v. United States, 401 U.S. 437 (1971) (exemption of conscientious objectors from military service). Similarly, the fact that a law has "had history and tradition on its side" has not afforded it any immunity from attack under other constitutional guarantees. *See* Levy v. Louisiana, 391 U.S. 68 (1968).

53. 70 Wash. 2d 649, 424 P.2d 906 (1967), *cert. denied*, 389 U.S. 832 (1967). *But*

see Harris v. State, 457 P.2d 638, 645–47 (Alaska 1969), for intimations that that state's supreme court would view favorably an attack based on the establishment clause; *see also* State v. Trejo, 83 N.M. 511, 494 P.2d 173 (Ct. App. 1972) (dissenting opinion of Sutin, J.).

54. *See* TIME, July 13, 1970, at 46, and August 23, 1971, at 38. L.A. Times, Dec. 8, 1969, Part II, at 1, col. 2, and at 5, col. 1; N.Y. Times, Feb. 15, 1970, sec. 1 at 58, col. 1.

5

The Independent Rights Doctrine

The doctrine that the Constitution imposes restrictions on the substantive law of the states and the federal government, as well as their procedures, independently of the specifics of the Bill of Rights, is a basic bulwark of American freedom. These specific guarantees fall far short of a comprehensive or systematic statement of those rights essential to ensure personal liberty, even in a democracy. The framers of the Bill provided protection against those evils of which they were most immediately aware, as a result of either experience with government in the colonies or fairly recent history in Britain itself (*e.g.*, the English Bill of Rights of 1688). A cursory perusal of the Bill reveals that its guarantees are too particular to provide adequate protection against every arbitrary governmental interference with the liberty of the individual. Yet it would be an intolerable situation, in a society premised on the idea of liberty, if government were able to hamstring and circumscribe the citizen in every way that does not infringe these specifics. For this reason the doctrine has developed in constitutional law that whenever government infringes a fundamental personal liberty, whether or not that liberty is enumerated in the Bill of Rights, it bears a substantial burden of justification. It must not only show that some proper societal objective lies behind the constraint and that the constraint is reasonably related to the accomplishment of the objective; it must also demonstrate that the societal objective is a *compelling* subordinating interest and that the law is *necessary* to its accomplishment.[1] This doctrine, which I prefer to call the independent rights doctrine, has in recent times usually been tied to the due process clauses of the fifth and fourteenth amendments.[2]

The major difficulty in applying the doctrine has been to

determine which personal liberties additional to those of the Bill of Rights are fundamental. Without specific guidance in the words of the Constitution itself, judges might be inclined to set up as fundamental rights their own subjective notions of essential liberty. Precisely such a development occurred in the nineteenth and early twentieth centuries. The Supreme Court overturned a good deal of regulatory legislation, dealing with business practices and working conditions, which the justices deemed contrary to *laissez faire* principles of economics. From *Lochner v. New York*,[3] often cited as the high point of this line of cases, this application of the doctrine has seen a steady decline. It is now in almost total desuetude. Its demise was well deserved. Not only is it clear today that the state generally possesses a legitimate social interest in enacting such legislation; it is equally clear that the ranking of freedom of contract and freedom in the enjoyment and use of property as fundamental human liberties gave, in effect, constitutional endorsement to purely transient social theories that were bound eventually to go out of vogue.

Unfortunately, the bitter taste left by this experience in the economic sphere has cast suspicion on the independent rights doctrine in all its applications. The desire to eliminate the subjective antipathies of judges from their consideration of the validity of any piece of legislation, state or federal, has led some, notably Mr. Justice Black, to the position that "due process" protects only those substantive rights specifically enumerated in the Bill of Rights and no others.[4] This position has never at any time commanded the assent of the rest of the Court.[5]

Admittedly, the independent rights doctrine does give judges considerable leeway for the intrusion of purely personal views on the wisdom or folly of legislation. But discarding it altogether in the presumed interest of "principled" decision would be equivalent to throwing out the baby with the bath water. Retaining the doctrine, even with its attendant risks, seems preferable to limiting American freedoms to the specific clauses of the Bill of Rights.[6]

Since the 1930s, though the Court has declined more and more to apply the independent rights doctrine to regulations of business and economic affairs, it has on a number of occasions applied it to restrictions that impinge on other aspects of human liberty.[7] The doctrine can be traced even in cases decided within the past few years. It was employed by the Court to strike down statutes in the important cases of *Aptheker v. Secretary of State*[8] and *Loving v. Virginia.*[9] In the *Griswold* case, despite the effort of Mr. Justice Douglas to tie, however loosely, the invalidation of Connecticut's anticontraceptive law to the specifics of the Bill of Rights, five of the concurring justices could not be weaned away from the independent rights theory. They must have found its vague contours an equally, if not a more, convenient haven in which to harbor the ruling. Two of them—Justices Harlan and White—without further ado applied to the Connecticut law a typical analysis under the theory and found it wanting. The liberty of men and women to marry and establish a family is a fundamental personal liberty of mankind, and society may interfere with that liberty only upon a showing that its interference is necessary to the furtherance of some appropriate social objective. Three others—Justices Goldberg and Brennan and Chief Justice Warren—while concurring in Justice Douglas's opinion, also found the restrictions of the Constitution to go beyond the specifics of the Bill of Rights and even its penumbras and emanations. Their application of the doctrine differed from that of Justices Harlan and White in seeking to ground the notion of fundamental liberties additional to those of the Bill of Rights in the Constitution's own explicit recognition, in the ninth amendment, that such unenumerated liberties exist in the people and that the Bill of Rights was not intended to disparage them.[10]

Enough has been said to demonstrate that the independent rights theory is still one to be reckoned with. The problem of invalidating the sodomy laws under it is twofold: (1) The liberty which these laws infringe must be shown to rank as fundamental; and (2) the infringement must be shown to be unrelated to *any* proper state purpose, or unnecessary to the achievement of a purpose that *is* proper. Even if the infringement is necessary to the achievement of a proper state purpose, it is still unconstitutional unless that purpose is of compelling importance.

The significance of this inquiry is not limited to the independent rights doctrine. Whatever ultimate fate awaits that theory in future decisions of the Supreme Court, a similar analysis of the rationales a state might offer in justification of the sodomy laws is needed to determine their validity under the first amendment's establishment-of-religion clause. If all the rationales prove specious, that clause should provide a sturdy enough hook for any court to hang its hat on in invalidating them, even if the independent rights doctrine someday becomes completely discredited.

The first problem is easily disposed of. Among the personal liberties ranked as fundamental must be those necessary to satisfy basic needs that every human being experiences. The need for sexual fulfillment is such a basic human need.[11] That fact is now so firmly buttressed by modern science as to be unquestionable; we may be rational animals, but we are animals nonetheless. If the propagation of the species had had to depend on the rational idea that producing offspring is a good thing, we would have been extinct eons ago. This is a key proposition in the revolution generated by Freud in modern man's thought about himself. Sexual fulfillment may not be quite as essential to man's adjustment and happiness as having enough food to eat, and clothing and shelter to protect him from the elements, but it ranks close behind.[12]

The Supreme Court has already implicitly recognized this point. It underlay to some extent the statement made in *Meyer v. Nebraska*[13] and reiterated in *Griswold*[14] that the right to marry, establish a home, and bring up children is a fundamental human right. Marriage and the family fulfill other human needs as well, but marriage is the principal means by which society seeks to regularize the satisfaction of the sexual drive on a continuing basis. In *Skinner v. Oklahoma,* the Court made clear that the right to procreate is one of "the basic civil rights of man."[15]

The *Griswold* decision itself can be read to mean that sexual fulfillment is a fundamental human right. Connecticut's anticontraceptive law certainly did not prevent people from marrying, establishing a home, and raising a family; nor, obviously, did it prevent them from procreating. What it did do was prevent them from attaining sexual fulfillment free from the risk of procreation. Thus, the holding went considerably beyond the language *and intent* of the *Meyer* and *Skinner* cases. The Court in effect told Connecticut that it cannot tie sexual fulfillment to procreation; that sexual fulfillment is a fundamental right independent of the right to produce and bring up children. Although the case dealt with the issue only in the context of marriage and was phrased in the euphemistic language of interference with the intimacies of marriage, its significance as the first judicial recognition of this right cannot be ignored.[16]

In his book *Law, Liberty and Morality,* Oxford's distinguished

professor of jurisprudence, H.L.A. Hart, makes the point in terms
almost parallel to the typical analysis under the independent rights
doctrine:

> [I]nterference with individual liberty may be thought an evil
> requiring justification for simpler, utilitarian reasons; for it is
> itself the infliction of a special form of suffering—often very
> acute—on those whose desires are frustrated by the fear of
> punishment. This is of particular importance in the case of
> laws enforcing a sexual morality. They may create misery of a
> quite special degree. For both the difficulties involved in the
> repression of sexual impulses and the consequences of repres-
> sion are quite different from those involved in the abstention
> from "ordinary" crime. Unlike sexual impulses, the impulse to
> steal or to wound or even kill is not, except in a minority of
> mentally abnormal cases, a recurrent and insistent part of
> daily life. Resistance to the temptation to commit these
> crimes is not often, as the suppression of sexual impulses
> generally is, something which affects the development or
> balance of the individual's emotional life, happiness, and
> personality.[17]

Surely, when it comes to confronting such issues directly, we
Americans do not need the English to teach us lessons. The time
has come for an explicit recognition from the bench that we are *all*
sexual beings, whether we wear mechanics' overalls, hippie beads,
businessmen's suits, academic regalia, or judicial robes.

Assuming, then, that sexual fulfillment is at least as necessary to
"the pursuit of happiness" as travel abroad, so that it can be ranked
as a fundamental liberty, we now proceed to the second part of the
analysis. Is a compelling subordinating interest of society served by
the sodomy laws, and are they reasonably necessary to the
accomplishment of that objective? Here a substantial handicap
must be overcome, because indications exist in prior opinions of the
Supreme Court, particularly in those of justices who have supported the independent rights doctrine, that the constitutionality of
laws like these is beyond doubt.[18]

In the first place, it is necessary to reemphasize that these laws,
excepting only that of Kansas, are not laws against homosexual
behavior. They are not limited by their terms to acts performed
between persons of the same sex, and appellate opinions reflecting

prosecutions for heterosexual activity are not at all lacking. If this objective—deterrence of homosexual acts—were urged as the major purpose behind the statutes, disregarding their express language, it still could not save them. Assuming that no proper societal objective can be found to be served by proscribing heterosexual deviance, the laws would still be unconstitutional for sweeping too broadly and invading unnecessarily an area of protected freedom. Perhaps this overbreadth[19] could be justified if there were any evidence that those who engage in deviate heterosexual acts proceed to homosexual acts as well, but no such evidence has been unearthed by behavioral science.[20] In the absence of such evidence, speculation that this may occur is not enough. (The question of whether a law like Kansas's new statute, which is more narrowly tailored to aim solely at homosexual acts, serves a legitimate social objective will be deferred to the end of this discussion.)

Can a rational justification be discovered for proscribing heterosexual deviance alone? The question involves only acts performed in private between consenting adults. We are not here concerned with the propriety of shielding minors from exploitation by adults, protecting everyone against acts performed without consent, and insulating the populace generally from public affronts. The majority of sodomy laws cover these situations as well as the private acts of consenting adults, and most prosecutions involve them rather than the latter. This probably explains why so little serious attention has been paid to the question of constitutionality. But the legitimate social objectives served by the laws cannot save them if in their application to the private acts of consenting adults they serve no justifiable interest. Again, the invalidating principle is that of unconstitutional overbreadth.

A second obstacle that must be overcome at the outset is the argument that, even if the laws have no legitimate objective in their application to the private acts of consenting adults, they constitute a de minimis invasion of liberty: The infringement is so marginal as to be unworthy of notice. This argument rests on the assumption that as long as ordinary vaginal intercourse is allowed, people possess the principal means of sexual fulfillment, and that taking away these other, subsidiary means is therefore inconsequential.

The expression of love is too variegated a phenomenon to be constrained within such a straitjacket. The act of coitus is in most cases the culmination of a variety of acts by which partners express their love for, and derive pleasure and emotional satisfaction from, one another, none of which is significantly less important. What would love be like if the state could prohibit all kissing, all necking, all petting, and all other forms of foreplay and afterplay? How many husbands have had to resort to manual stimulation to bring their wives to orgasm—an act which, theoretically at least, is within most states' definition of sodomy? Might not this argument permit the state to require everyone to use only the so-called "missionary" position for coitus?[21] Merely to ask such questions should suffice to answer the argument in the minds of most people.

The sodomy laws cannot find justification in protecting the participants from infliction of physical harm. None of the principal acts in question, whether anal intercourse, fellatio, cunnilingus, interfemoral connection, or mutual or solitary masturbation, has any harmful physical consequences unless some pathological condition was already present in the bodily parts concerned.[22]

It is a difficult theoretical question whether the state should prevent people from voluntarily inflicting physical injury upon themselves. In the abortion and contraception cases, the Supreme Court appears to have assumed that the state constitutionally may do so. I see no need to quarrel with that assumption here, because the great majority of deviate sex acts covered by the sodomy laws hold no more potential for physical injury to a willing participant than coitus. Some sadomasochistic sex acts do hold serious potential for physical injury. But even though such practices could be deemed sodomy under some states' definition of the crime, and their proscription could be justified in the interest of preventing physical injury, the law is still unconstitutional. It must be narrowly tailored to aim specifically at the evil in question. Otherwise, it suffers from unconstitutional overbreadth. To proscribe all kinds of deviate sex acts just because one or two are physically injurious invades liberty as unnecessarily as to ban all contraceptives merely because one of them poses a health hazard.

The first rationale that might furnish a plausible warrant for the sodomy laws is the one most commonly thought to underlie repressive sex laws generally: the inhibition of sexual promiscuity. Another way of stating that rationale is that people should confine their sexual activities to one partner, within the commitment and context of monogamous marriage. To some extent, these are different concepts. An individual can eschew promiscuity without undertaking the marital vow. An unmarried person's fidelity to his partner may match or even surpass that of the typical married person, in a society in which the institution of marriage often no longer means lifelong union but only a series of partners one at a time.[23] Nonetheless, the basic idea is that society has a legitimate interest in discouraging fleeting sexual liaisons. Without bothering to question this tenet, one can demonstrate that the sodomy laws have nothing to do with it.

In the first place, in all but three of the states, the sodomy laws make no distinction between acts performed by husband and wife and those performed by unmarried persons. Both are equally illegal. And there is no more cause to think that a husband and wife who engage in deviate sex acts with each other will progress to infidelity than that those spouses who use contraceptives within their own relationship will be encouraged to seek sex outside it—an argument that Mr. Justice White spurned as nonsense in *Griswold*.[24] Even in the three states which are exceptions, inhibition of promiscuity can be shown *not* to be the object of the laws.

In Kansas, where the statute exempts acts between husband and wife, heterosexual acts between unmarried persons are likewise exempted.[25] Moreover, in Kansas, fornication is not against the law. While Kansas law proscribes adultery in the form of vaginal intercourse,[26] adultery in the form of deviate sex acts is not criminal. Although this anomaly may have been the result of an oversight, it tends to confirm the hypothesis that inhibition of promiscuity is not the object of this law.

One might think this was the object of the New York law, since it excludes acts between husband and wife but not acts between unmarried persons, whether heterosexual or homosexual.[27] On the other hand, the New York Penal Law, while proscribing adultery,[28] *does not proscribe fornication*. Surely the New York legislature did not think promiscuity was more likely to be widespread in the case of deviate sex acts than in the case of fornication. Is there, then, an explanation for this exception in the New York statute that has nothing to do with a concern for promiscuity? The answer is yes. The clue lies in the location of the exception for husband and wife, which is found not in the section prohibiting consensual sodomy but in the definition of deviate sexual intercourse found elsewhere in the Penal Law.[29] When the new Penal Law was presented to the legislature, it did not include the offense of consensual sodomy. The revisers had recommended that sodomy, like ordinary intercourse, should be penalized only when the factors of lack of consent or an underage partner were present.[30] In order to ensure that no married person could be prosecuted for an act with his spouse, in either of *these* circumstances, they framed the very definition of the acts in terms that excluded such participants. A similar precaution was observed in the law of rape. All the sections defining gradations of the latter offense use the noun "female" to refer to the victim, but the definitions section of the Penal law defines "female" so as to exclude the actor's wife.[31] The rationale is that marriage raises an irrebuttable presumption of consent to sexual contact with one's spouse and likewise removes all societal objection to the nonage of either spouse. No possibility should exist, therefore, that one spouse will instigate prosecution of the other for either rape or sodomy. When the offense of consensual sodomy was inserted in the new code at the insistence of the legislature, the exclusion of married couples from its scope was thus not the result of any conscious intention to inhibit either premarital or extramarital deviate sex, but resulted from the already inherent objective of the code to preclude interspousal prosecutions under the provisions concerned with force and nonage.

The new Pennsylvania criminal code provision is much like that of New York. It proscribes all "voluntary deviate sexual intercourse," but such intercourse is elsewhere defined so as to exclude acts between husband and wife. On the other hand, the code proscribes neither fornication *nor* adultery.

The inquiry so far has assumed that inhibition of promiscuity is a proper social objective. One may have reservations on this score, however, particularly now that means exist for divorcing coitus from reproduction and thereby for preventing sexual promiscuity from resulting in the birth of children. Few psychologists would question that children can be harmed by the lack of a stable two-parent family.[32] Society would therefore be justified in inhibiting promiscuity *if* there were still, as there used to be in the days before effective contraception, an unavoidable causal connection between the two. But that connection no longer exists. These reservations grow in strength when one asks whether inhibition of promiscuity is a compelling subordinating interest under these new circumstances. Be that as it may, there is no need to explore this thicket, for even if one assumes the legitimacy of this social objective, the sodomy laws do not concern it. Even if a pattern of laws prohibiting all sex, ordinary *and* deviate, outside the marital relationship might satisfy the demands of the independent rights doctrine, none of the present sodomy laws would be saved, because not one of them reflects such a pattern.

Can some justification for the sodomy laws be found in protecting the family structure of American society, apart from any supposed inhibiting effect on premarital or extramarital relations? None comes readily to mind. The notion has been advanced that deviate sex acts are repulsive to many women, as divorce records are alleged to show.[33] I do not know how seriously to take this argument; there is often little correspondence between reality and what women seeking divorce will allege as mental cruelty and their husbands will fail to contest. Many women do find deviate sex acts repulsive, but so do many men. The proposition, even if we assume its truth, has no bearing on the question at bar, which is the constitutionality of prohibiting deviate acts between *consenting* partners. A sodomy statute can be tailored to protect nonconsenting wives or husbands,[34] as well as other nonconsenting persons. One prohibiting all acts, even where both partners are consenting, as supposedly necessary to protect nonconsenting persons, again sweeps too broadly and invades unnecessarily an area of protected freedom.

Another shaky notion is that deviate sex between consenting spouses threatens the stability of the marital relationship. There is no evidence in the scientific literature to support it, and it flies in the face of a good many marriage manuals.[35]

So much for the possible rationales that, in the case of the sodomy laws, can be shown to be absent, irrelevant, or flippant. One other rationale deserves serious scrutiny—the position that society can prohibit harmless acts solely on the ground that the majority finds them repugnant to some philosophical concept, or moralistic notion, of "unnaturalness." This justification deserves close scrutiny because it is the *only* one that can genuinely and honestly be made to fit the sodomy laws as they are presently worded in most states.

Under this rationale, the gravamen of the offense is not the harm it does to anybody or anything, whether to the participants, to someone else, or even to the family structure of society, but the "wrong" it does to "nature." It is doubtful that a vague moral dictum which cannot point to tangible harm of any kind is separable from religion, especially where, as here, its religious origin is unmistakable; but for the sake of argument we will assume that it rests in people's minds no longer on a religious foundation but on either an "instinctive" or a secular-philosophical basis.

The word "instinctive" is used here not in its scientific sense but to denote a deep and powerful feeling of revulsion for which one can give no rational explanation. Behavioral scientists use the word with caution in referring to human beings, because so much of what we once supposed to be instinct in man has turned out to be the result of cultural conditioning. Here again religion is likely to be a major causative factor: The liberal, emancipated citizen of modern India may no longer be conscious of the Hindu religion as a real influence in his life, but he may still feel an "instinctive" revulsion for eating beef. The other most likely source of conditioned "instinct" would appear to be early childhood training. In American culture, children are often trained at a very early age to avoid certain contacts with their genitalia and anus and to regard these parts of the body as "filthy" (as much because of their excretory as because of their sexual functions). The fact that such training occurs very early in life probably explains why the feelings of revulsion are perceived as "instinctive." In any event, neither of these two probable causes of "instinctive" feeling supplies an adequate basis for the law, religion being ineligible because of the establishment clause of the first amendment and the conditioning being irrational.[36]

What of the secular-philosophical basis? Anyone can see that the genital organs serve the function of reproduction; that they can do so without the intervention of artifice only by the coupling of penis with vagina; and that *ergo* any other mode of orgasm is "unnatural" in the sense that it does not serve the reproductive function. Is this philosophical basis an adequate justification for the sodomy laws?

First, such a basis for the laws is only superficially rational. Its fundamental irrationality can be exposed by applying the same analysis to other behavior patterns. To keep from ranging too far afield, let us look at two other types of behavior in the realm of sex:

1. The mammary glands of the female breast produce milk to nourish newborn babies, and the nipples serve to carry it to

the infants' mouths. *Ergo,* for a grown man to engage in manual or oral stimulation of these parts of the female anatomy is "unnatural" because it uses them for some purpose other than the one for which nature designed them. *Ergo,* such behavior is a crime against nature.[37]

2. The mouth enables human beings to consume food and liquid, to speak, and to breathe. *Ergo,* for a person to use it for kissing is "unnatural" because that use is not one of these "natural" functions of the mouth. *Ergo,* kissing is a crime against nature.[38]

From these analogies one can see what is happening in all such progressions based on "natural law." One or a few of the numerous possible functions of a bodily member are selected as the only "natural" functions, based on the selector's personal predilections and prejudices. All the others are labeled "unnatural" and subject to prohibition. It must have been examples like these which prompted Kinsey's famous dictum: "The only kind of abnormal sex acts are those which are impossible to perform."[39] Curiously, the idea that one can criminally offend nature by using his body in a way not "intended" by nature seems limited in our society to the sexual sphere.[40]

Second, to hold that this philosophy is an adequate basis for the laws would violate the requirement that the state point to some compelling subordinating purpose behind its infringement of fundamental liberties. If the state were required only to point to majority philosophy or to majority feeling that has a moralistic tinge, there is no regulation it could not justify.[41] Virginia's miscegenation law and the District of Columbia's segregation law, both of which were voided, at least in part, under the due process clauses as violative of "fundamental rights," would have been justified.[42] Presumably, majorities in both instances honestly felt racial mixing "unnatural," even immoral, but the Supreme Court held that separation of the races was not adequately justified in these cases, despite the feeling or philosophy. Arkansas' anti-evolution law, struck down in the *Epperson* case,[43] also would have been constitutional, because one can raise secular philosophical objections to the idea that man ascended (or descended) from other species.

The anticontraceptive law struck down in *Griswold* is another that would have been justified on the basis of moral-philosophical opinion. Contraceptives interfere with the natural procreative order of things, and doubtless this was the real reason why the law was enacted. It was not urged on the Court in *Griswold,* however, because it must have been recognized as inadequate. Mr. Justice White was left to knock down a straw man—the argument that the law's purpose was to inhibit promiscuity. Since the separation of sexual intercourse from procreation *can* be viewed as a secular moral issue, it is difficult to see why the state could not prohibit it, even within the marital relationship—assuming that such a philosophical notion of immorality is sufficient justification for a criminal law, apart from discernible harm to anyone. The state prescribes the conditions under which marriage is permitted and under which it continues and can be terminated. Why could these not include the condition of abstaining from the use of contraceptives? No one can claim that the Connecticut law took away some freedom of husband and wife that existed before adoption of the relevant constitutional provisions. Effective contraceptives were largely unavailable then.[44] In other words, although marriage as an institution antedates the constitutional guarantees, marriage with contraception does not.

The decisions striking down the anti-abortion laws likewise would never have been reached if moral-philosophical opinion alone could justify the overriding of fundamental liberties. In those cases—*Roe v. Wade* and *Doe v. Bolton*—the widespread and deeply held conviction that terminating incipient human life is immoral failed to prevent the laws from being held invalid. The Supreme Court apparently considered that the state's interest in protecting incipient human life becomes sufficiently compelling to override the pregnant woman's right of privacy only when the fetus reaches the stage of viability, *i.e.,* is capable of life outside the womb, albeit with artificial aids. The Court specifically held that a nonviable fetus is not a "person" covered by the protections of the Constitution. This all seems virtually equivalent to saying that tangible harm to a person is required to override the right.

Third, it is nonsense to suppose that the sodomy laws in the great majority of states rest on a secular-philosophical notion of "unnaturalness." Surely no one would impose felony prison terms for this reason alone. Some powerful irrational force must be at work here, whether religious taboo, aversions traceable from infancy, or a combination of the two.

Fourth, even jurists who have endorsed the view that society can enforce in the criminal law moral tenets that lack any basis in tangible harm have considered this permissible only if the tenet is backed by virtually unanimous opinion.[45] On these matters, a majority should not have the power to ram its opinions down the throat of a substantial dissenting minority, and here a substantial minority can be shown to exist.[46]

Finally, even if we could believe that the sodomy laws rested on this secular-philosophical ground, their infringement of liberty cannot stand unless the state has shown a "compelling subordinating interest." How can it be plausibly contended that this ground meets that test?

If we can assume, then, that these laws in their coverage of private consensual acts between adults lack adequate justification with respect to heterosexual deviance, would they pass muster if more narrowly tailored to cover only homosexual conduct, like Kansas's new statute? The answer to this question is not so obviously negative. True, many of the same factors making for a negative answer in the case of heterosexual deviance are present here: the absence of any such social interests as the protection of everyone from force or imposition, of the general public from open affront, and of juveniles from exploitation by adults; the harmless nature of the acts; and the absence of any destructive impact upon existing marital relationships. Of course, some marriages may founder if the spouses are free to engage in homosexual acts with others, but infidelity of this kind constitutes a much less generalized threat to existing marriages than does heterosexual adultery. Like the latter, it could be guarded against, if necessary, by a narrow criminal law directed only at married persons, prohibiting them from all sexual contacts with persons other than their spouses, whether ordinary or deviate, heterosexual or homosexual. To proscribe *all* homosexual acts *by everybody* bears no rational relationship to the purpose of discouraging marital infidelity. We also can dismiss as possible justifications for such a law the "instinctive" feelings of revulsion and the secular-philosophical notion of "unnaturalness" that we noted in discussing heterosexual deviance, for the same reasons.

The inhibition of promiscuity seems equally irrelevant. Unless promiscuity is to be regarded as an evil sufficient in itself to justify its inhibition by the state[47] (apart from possible consequences like the production of illegitimate children), homosexual acts are not subject to prohibition on this ground, because they cannot possibly entail such consequences or even lead to other acts which would. If promiscuity is regarded as an evil in itself, homosexual acts have no more a necessary relationship to it than heterosexual deviance, unless by definition "promiscuity" covers all acts of participants not married to each other. Since homosexuals are not permitted to marry each other[48] or otherwise to legitimize a "permanent" relationship, such a definition (concealing the answer within its premise) is patently unfair to them.

There are differences between homosexual behavior and heterosexual deviance that might justify a difference in the stance of the law. Unlike heterosexual deviance, homosexual behavior is often an exclusive way of life for those disposed to engage in it. Analysis of the adequacy of the justifications for prohibiting homosexual acts thus cannot be confined to the consequences of the isolated, individual acts themselves. The question must be asked whether homosexual conduct as a general social phenomenon (*i.e.*, a way of life) poses any threat to American society or to its cherished institutions, such as the family, sufficient to justify criminal proscription of the acts themselves. Instead of prejudging this question, let us take a close look at these supposed threats.

One "threat" that can be dismissed quickly is that homosexuality places the race in danger of extinction. The appeal of heterosexuality does not rest on such flimsy footing as our society's mores against homosexuality. In the culture most noted for its idealization of homosexual love—that of ancient Greece—the race was never in jeopardy. Nor does it seem tenable to assert that if homosexuality were tolerated the institution of the family would be threatened by the diminution in eligible candidates for marriage. The institution of marriage is more likely to be threatened by forcing into it people whose orientation is homosexual and who would thus never be at ease there.[49]

A second threat, often raised by law enforcement officials, is that if adults are permitted to indulge in homosexual acts among themselves, they will also seduce and corrupt the young—those below the age of consent.[50] Scientific evidence to support this proposition is nil. Expert opinion holds that only a fraction of adult homosexuals are attracted to children, just as only a fraction of adult heterosexuals are.[51] This myth probably grew up because some instances of private homosexual conduct that come to the attention of the authorities do involve adult defendants and underage partners, but it is unsound to infer from this that most homosexuals would gravitate toward underage partners if restrictions were relaxed. Common sense tells us that if the restrictions on acts with other adults were removed, leaving those on acts with children in full force, the effect should be to cause adults to shun the latter for the former, in order to avoid the risk of prosecution. With penalties the same for acts with both kinds of partners, as is presently the case in a number of states, the law provides no incentive to leave children alone.[52] Anyway, stiff penalties for acts with children should suffice in themselves to deter conduct with such partners, to the extent the law can deter at all. Penalties on acts with adults can hardly provide additional deterrent effect.

A third argument based on fancy rather than fact is that homosexuality breeds instability, untrustworthiness, cowardice, weakness, and general character debility. This is a folk myth. Some scientific investigators have found that their samples of homosexuals, when given various personality tests, could not be distinguished from a control group of heterosexuals.[53] While their samples were too small and too highly selected to permit reliable generalizations about the entire homosexual population,[54] these studies are at least evidence that homosexuals on the whole may be no different from the usual run of heterosexuals, except in their *sexual* orientation and behavior. A number of the expert works on the subject of homosexuality assert that homosexuals exhibit deficiencies of character and undesirable personality traits no more and no less than other human beings; they present as variable a group of personalities and characters as heterosexuals.[55] The popular myth probably rests on the association of male homosexuality with effeminacy. The "bad" traits which our male chauvinist traditions attribute to the female sex thus get ascribed, en bloc, to all male homosexuals. But the association between homosexuality in males and effeminacy is false, and in any event, the argument lacks solid empirical evidence to back it up. The conclusion of some psychotherapists, from their experience in treating patients, that homosexuals possess unstable personalities is, as we shall see later, of doubtful reliability, because the instability they see may very well be due to the implacably hostile attitude of society toward homosexuality (*i.e.*, it is not really inherent in the condition itself), or to the fact that those who are seeking their help would not be doing so but for some severe adjustment problem (*i.e.*, their sample is not really representative).[56]

Two other arguments are so closely related that they are essentially aspects of the same fear—the fear that a general corruption of morals will ensue from removing the legal barriers to homosexual conduct. One of these arguments usually infers that the general decline of other civilizations is traceable to a relaxation of sexual morals[57] and especially to permissiveness about homosexuality. It is impossible to answer such an argument, because we have no way of proving or disproving the hypothesis. Those civilizations are long since dead, and the information we have about them is scanty.[58] To base the regulation of modern American society on reconstructed "lessons" of history is precarious; as one eminent historian has pointed out, if history teaches us anything at all, it is that there are no simple answers to be learned from it.[59]

The second argument asserts that by opening another door to sexual gratification outside marriage—homosexual relationships not being legally entitled to that status—general societal tendencies toward a relaxation of sexual morality will be encouraged. Not only will premarital and extramarital sex increase, but marriage itself may fall into disuse as people discover they can fulfill their needs without undertaking its vows. Sex for pleasure will devalue sex for love, and casual liaisons will replace sustained commitment. Again, it is impossible to assess in any objective manner the risk of such consequences. They have not occurred in other countries.[60] Homosexuality bears no necessary causal relationship to them, just as heterosexuality in itself does not either. Homosexual relationships can involve love and sustained commitment no less than do heterosexual relationships. The reason that they seem on the whole to be more fleeting than the latter is probably that our society discourages them so ferociously. If homosexuals were offered a means of legitimizing their relationships similar to heterosexual marriage, and were encouraged to form and maintain stable partnerships, we might well see that homosexuality breeds unbridled license no more than heterosexuality.[61]

Several other arguments are sometimes heard. The first is that homosexuals constitute a criminal threat generally, and are rapists in particular. The scientific evidence demonstrates that this is one of the grossest of calumnies.[62] The second is that they favor each other in such matters as hiring and promotion, whenever they are in position to do so, with consequent discrimination against heterosexuals.[63] The only scientific inquiry into the truth of this proposition demonstrates it to be equally false.[64] It seems to be another example of the usual canard that Catholics always favor other Catholics, and Jews other Jews. The third is that homosexuals perpetuate a subculture alienated from the rest of American society—a development that threatens the cohesion of the body politic. But a pluralistic society like ours has thousands of subcultures; subcultures per se are no threat. The alienation, on the other hand, is not intrinsic to homosexuality. It is the response of every victimized minority group to discrimination. The appropriate action to eliminate it is to stamp out not the group but the discrimination.

One might also argue that society is entitled to discourage homosexual behavior through the criminal law in order to decrease the load that counseling and therapy of homosexuals place on the nation's mental health personnel. A similar argument has been made with reference to marijuana and other drugs: Since users consume much of the resources available for treating mental health problems, society has here an adequate warrant for deterring use. In the case of homosexual behavior, the sufficient answer to this argument is that mental health personnel believe just the opposite: that eliminating the repressive laws will improve mental health.[65]

The one really substantial argument concerns the development of sexual orientation. Certainly, homosexual conduct as an exclusive way of life cuts a person off from participation in the basic unit of American society, the heterosexual "nuclear" family, and from the possibility of having children. Many people feel that such a family life with children is more wholesome for the average person than any substitute. They hope their own children will choose such a family life, and would deplore any influence tending to deflect them from that choice.

The problem is that sexual orientation seems to be learned, not innate,[66] and science does not yet know exactly when it becomes fixed. Many experts believe this occurs very early in life; others believe it takes place in adolescence, or at least by the age of 21;

and still others think that in a few cases, at any rate, it might occur even after that age.[67] We cannot yet dispel the possibility that adolescents remain malleable in sexual orientation. They may ultimately be influenced not only by which types of sexual gratification they experience as rewarding and which not, but also by what they perceive as acceptable adult patterns of sexual behavior. Consequently, as long as it remains possible that positive barriers to homosexual conduct may help to turn them away from homosexuality and toward heterosexuality, criminal laws against private adult homosexual acts may possess at least a grounding of bare rationality.[68] If adults are permitted to live freely in a homosexual relationship, criminal sanctions against their bringing adolescents into such a relationship may prove insufficient to discourage the latter. The young may conclude that homosexual behavior is not unacceptable as a life style but is merely one of those activities reserved for adults, like the consumption of alcohol.[69] They might even perceive in it a glamor that ordinary heterosexual behavior does not share.

A slightly different variation of the same argument is to say that societal discouragement of homosexual behavior rescues children, and perhaps adults as well, from sex role confusion. By steering everyone toward heterosexuality, society saves people from having to make still another choice about their roles in life. This way of putting the argument is far less persuasive than the other, because it implies that freedom per se is an evil, that people need to be told what to do to save them from the agony of personal choice. Other nations may be founded on such an authoritarian premise, but not America. If our society is going to direct people toward one of two or more alternatives, it should do so because sound reasons exist for preferring that alternative, rather than merely to offer an escape from freedom.

If one accepts this argument (or any of the others, for that matter) as supplying a rational warrant for society's proscription of homosexual acts, the constitutional question remains to be answered. Presumably, the existence of an interest that can be characterized as secular removes the possibility of invalidating a sodomy law under the establishment clause. (I am assuming that we are dealing with a law that proscribes only homosexual deviance.) It does not, however, necessarily meet the attack based on the independent rights doctrine, or on the right-of-privacy doctrine (whether that doctrine be considered an "independent right" or an emanation from the specifics of the Bill of Rights). The latter doctrines require a determination that the societal interest is a "compelling subordinating interest" and that the law is reasonably necessary to effectuate the proper state purpose.

First, it is questionable that the social objective of encouraging heterosexuality is a "compelling subordinating interest." It might be, in a sparsely populated society that needed greater numbers merely to survive. This social interest seems far from compelling at a time when overpopulation is the problem. The fact that a majority in society regard the elimination of freedom of choice in some sphere as likely to "promote happiness" does not, in itself, seem sufficient.

Second, one may doubt that the laws in question are reasonably *necessary* to effect the objective. Our society inculcates heterosexuality in the growing youngster by making it appear desirable, by omitting to talk about or to give favorable cues toward a homosexual object-choice, and by positive, nonlegal inhibitions upon homosexuality.[70] The last consist primarily of verbal and nonverbal reactions that arouse anxiety and threaten self-esteem by identifying a homosexual object-choice with loss of gender identity: A male who is attracted to other males is not a *real* man; a female attracted to other females is not a *real* woman. These are the derogatory implications of the epithet "queer." Such social mores are so ubiquitous that eliminating the legal prohibitions on homosexual conduct is not likely to have much effect. With the social scales already heavily weighted in favor of heterosexuality, the criminal laws hardly affect the balance. Moreover, we have no real evidence there would be a significant popular shift in sexual orientation if the social, as well as the legal, taboos on homosexuality were lifted. Psychiatrists, in general, do not regard this as likely,[71] and the scientific evidence from other species and from other cultures indicates that heterosexuality will always be by far the majority orientation:

> Most males find heterosexual experience anatomically, physiologically, and psychologically most satisfactory, and there is little doubt that they would continue to find it so, even in a society [with no compulsions]. This is true in most species of mammals, where nothing comparable to human

social pressures exist. . . . Genital anatomy makes a heterosexual relation simpler and on the whole more reward-ing than homosexual relations among most mammals. In a fair number of cases, it is probable that differences in aggres-siveness [between males and females] may contribute to the fact that unions between the sexes occur more often than unions between individuals of the same sex.[72]

The zoological and cross-cultural evidence combine to suggest that within limits man is biologically equipped to respond sexually to a great range of stimuli and potential partners. But as the individual matures, sexual interests come to be focused primarily upon heterosexual activities, principally coitus, with members of his own species.[73]

Finally, determination of the constitutional question requires a balancing of the societal interest against the detriment to individ-ual liberty resulting from the criminal proscription. I will not essay such a balance at this point, but rather beg the reader to withhold judgment until he has read the rest of this book, because the magnitude of the individual detriment will not become fully apparent until later.[74] One must also bear in mind that even if the balance be tipped in favor of the societal interest, the only one of the existing sodomy laws thus immune from attack under all three doctrines[75] would be that of Kansas, because it is the only one directed solely against homosexual acts.

Apparently, only a handful of cases has acknowledged the relevance of the independent rights argument, among them *Buchanan v. Batchelor*[76] and *State v. Rhinehart*.[77] Both these cases refused, in effect, to analyze the possible objectives behind the law to determine whether it served a proper state purpose. The court in *Buchanan* said:

We agree that it is not the function of the Court to determine the policy of the state as it relates to morals. The State has regulated sexual relations by the passage of laws prohibiting what it considers immoral acts, such as adultery and fornica-tion and we believe that it has that right with reference to sodomy. The Court's holding today "in no way interferes with a State's proper regulation of sexual promiscuity or miscon-duct."[78]

The argument was likewise summarily dismissed in *Rhinehart*: "There is no merit to this contention. The legislature has, by this enactment, considered the public interest served by it. The prohibition of the statute is a proper exercise of the police power."[79] The *Rhinehart* case, however, involved prosecution for an act with a 16-year-old boy, and the protection of juveniles from exploitation by adults is concededly a permissible objective for a sodomy law. The *Buchanan* case also involved a party to whom application of the statute served a justifiable state purpose; he was under indictment for acts performed in public restrooms. The *Buchanan* case, though, which was a civil suit in federal court for a declaratory judgment and an injunction, also involved as intervenors three parties who posed the issue of the propriety of regulating consensual adult conduct in private—a heterosexual married couple and a homosexual who engaged only in such conduct. The judges held the statute totally void on the basis of its infringement of the married couple's right of privacy, so their failure to examine closely the possible objectives behind the law may be understandable.

NOTES

1. *See* Kent v. Dulles, 357 U.S. 116, 129 (1958); NAACP v. Alabama *ex rel.* Patterson, 357 U.S. 449, 463 (1958); Bates v. City of Little Rock, 361 U.S. 516, 524 (1960); McLaughlin v. Florida, 379 U.S. 184, 196 (1964); Griswold v. Connecticut, 381 U.S. 479, 496-98 (1965) (concurring opinion of Mr. Justice Goldberg).

2. The doctrine was formerly termed "substantive due process." I have avoided use of that label because it no longer fits the doctrine. It arose at a time when the issue of whether the fifth and fourteenth amendment guarantees of "due process" required only procedural fairness was still unsettled. The doctrine was controversial because it held that a guarantee of due *process* could be violated by purely *substantive* laws. The Supreme Court has since incorporated, one by one, the guarantees of the Bill of Rights into the due process clause of the fourteenth amendment. In consequence, almost all the clauses of the first eight amendments are now applicable to state law, though they were written originally to apply only to the federal government. The amendments incorporated include substantive as well as procedural guarantees, so there is no longer any question that "due process" is substantive as well as procedural. The major remaining controversy is whether "due process" covers only the guarantees of the Bill of Rights, or covers also fundamental rights not specified anywhere in the Constitution, and, if such independent rights are also covered, how one goes about identifying them. Thus,

"independent rights" is currently a more descriptive appellation for the doctrine than "substantive due process."

3. 198 U.S. 45 (1905).

4. Mr. Justice Black was probably the most forceful exponent of the idea that the due process clause of the fourteenth amendment incorporates all the rights specified in the Bill of Rights, *but only those. See* his dissent in *Griswold,* 381 U.S. at 507–27, in which he reaffirmed the position he had taken in Adamson v. California, 332 U.S. 46 (1947) and reiterated in Ferguson v. Skrupa, 372 U.S. 726 (1963). If a substantive law does not violate these specifics, it could not, in his view, be declared a violation of due process unless it was wholly arbitrary and capricious.

5. Of course, Mr. Justice Black's view that the due process clause of the fourteenth amendment imposes on the states *all* the specifics of the Bill of Rights, substantive as well as procedural, does now seem finally to have carried the day. Virtually all the clauses of the first eight amendments have now been held incorporated in the fourteenth. But his view that "due process" covers *only* those specifics has not made similar headway.

6. For a recent plea to retain the doctrine, from one whose expertise in the criminal law places him in a unique position to judge the need, *see* Packer, *The Aims of the Criminal Law Revisited: A Plea for a New Look at "Substantive Due Process,"* 44 S. CAL. L. REV. 490 (1971). Professor Packer finds it difficult to draw a distinction between "economic" legislation and legislation affecting other personal freedoms and therefore urges that we must accept some judicial scrutiny of all legislation under the doctrine. Undoubtedly, in some cases it would be impossible to classify a statute as being wholly in only one of the two categories.

7. The beginning of this differentiation can perhaps be traced to Harlan Fiske Stone's famous footnote to his opinion in the *Carolene Products* case. United States v. Carolene Products Co., 304 U.S. 144, 152-53 n. 4 (1938).

8. 378 U.S. 500 (1964). In the *Aptheker* case, the Court confirmed, by a direct holding, that the right to travel abroad is a fundamental personal liberty protected by the due process clause. This idea had previously been enunciated by the Court in Kent v. Dulles, 357 U.S. 116 (1958), but the result in that case had not depended on it.

9. 388 U.S. 1, 12 (1967). *Loving* struck down Virginia's antimiscegenation law. The decision was rested on two doctrines: (1) the equal protection clause; and (2) the notion that the freedom to marry is a fundamental personal liberty protected by the due process clause, which can be restricted only upon a showing that the limitation is reasonably related to the accomplishment of a proper state purpose. The contours of the independent rights theory can also be detected in the cases dealing with infringement of the freedom of association, such as Bates v. City of Little Rock, 361 U.S. 516, 524 (1960). But freedom of association is much more clearly an "emanation" of the first amendment freedoms of speech, press, and assembly, than the freedoms to marry or to travel abroad can be made to appear emanations of *any* of the specific clauses of the Bill of Rights. When, however, such an "emanated" right is itself held to spread a penumbra, as freedom of association was held to protect a group legal services program in Brotherhood of Railway Trainmen v. Virginia *ex rel.* Virginia State Bar, 377 U.S. 1 (1964), the

assertion that the Court is only applying the specifics of the Bill of Rights begins to lose its credibility.

10. The *Griswold* opinions give further support to the continued life of the independent rights theory in that they cite two earlier cases which clearly rested on that theory, without the slightest hint of an inclination to overrule them—Meyer v. Nebraska, 262 U.S. 390 (1923) (right to marry, establish a home, and bring up children), and Pierce v. Society of Sisters, 268 U.S. 510 (1925) (right of modern language teachers to pursue their calling, of pupils to acquire knowledge, and of parents to control the education of their own children). *See* 381 U.S. at 482-83, 495, 502. Beyond these indications, it taxes one's credulity to believe that the Supreme Court is likely ever to overrule such other important decisions resting on the theory as Wieman v. Updegraff, 344 U.S. 183 (1952) (right of public employees to be free from arbitrary dismissal), Schware v. Board of Bar Examiners, 353 U.S. 232 (1957) (right of applicants for the bar to be free from arbitrary restrictions on admission), and Bolling v. Sharpe, 347 U.S. 497 (1954) (right of Negro children not to be subjected to segregated education in the District of Columbia). And surely the assumption made in Jacobson v. Massachusetts, 197 U.S. 11 (1905), and Buck v. Bell, 274 U.S. 200 (1927), that the due process clause protects against arbitrary or unreasonable invasion of bodily integrity, is just as safe today as it was when those cases were decided.

11. If the liberty to wear one's hair a desired length is to be ranked as fundamental, as the Seventh Circuit held in Breen v. Kahl, 419 F.2d 1034 (1969), *cert. denied*, 398 U.S. 937 (1970), then the right to sexual fulfillment must be ranked as fundamental. It cannot be contended that the former is more vital to personal happiness than the latter. For a view opposed to *Breen v. Kahl, see* Freeman v. Flake, 448 F.2d 258 (10th Cir. 1971). The different Circuits have divided about equally on the long-hair issue. Massie v. Henry, 455 F.2d 779 (4th Cir. 1972), which supports *Breen v. Kahl*, reviews these conflicting decisions.

12. Drs. William H. Masters and Virginia Johnson Masters believe that the partners in half of all marriages are troubled with a clinically significant inability to function sexually. They trace this handicap to our culture's failure to regard sex as a "natural function" of human beings, like eating. The fact that sexual expression is the function most responsive to voluntary control has allowed it to be considered as separate from these other natural functions. If one does not eat, he will die, but one *can survive* without sex. But the sexual appetite is as healthy, as honest, and as natural as the appetite for food. This was the theme of their talk to a meeting of the A.M.A.'s Committee on Medicine and Religion in June 1972. *See* S.F. Chronicle, June 19, 1972, at 4, col. 3.

13. *See* note 10 *supra*.

14. 381 U.S. at 495 and 502.

15. 316 U.S. 535, 536, 541 (1942).

16. As noted in Chapter 3, one might argue that *Griswold* means only that the state cannot interfere with the married couple's decisions on family planning. The interference in *Griswold*, however, was not with the *decisions*, but with the *means* by which the couple sought to effectuate them. If some state-imposed limitations on abortion are constitutional, not every interference with the means of achieving family limitation is invalid. We have also noted previously that

cunnilingus, anal intercourse, and all the other acts commonly subsumed under the sodomy laws are no less a means of contraception than that involved in *Griswold.* Like coitus interruptus, they have been used from time immemorial by husbands and wives to avoid further children, as well as to add variety to their sexual relationship. The justices may thus have struck down the state interference in *Griswold* because they perceived that its effect, when conjoined with the sodomy and abortion laws, was to leave a couple with only *one* sure licit means of preventing the birth of children—abstention. The strict Catholic view is precisely this: that the only means of family planning a couple may morally use is abstention from intercourse during those periods when the wife could become pregnant. The *Griswold* decision can therefore justifiably be viewed as holding that it is unconstitutional to limit a couple to abstention, in their choice of a means, because such a limitation interferes with their right to sexual fulfilment.

17. H.L.A. HART, LAW, LIBERTY AND MORALITY 22 (1963). Perhaps psychiatrists would disagree with Hart's statement that "the impulse to steal or to wound or even kill is not . . . a recurrent and insistent part of daily life." They might say, rather, that most people learn early to suppress such impulses, and this learning may be due in part to knowledge that the laws against such acts are clear and strictly enforced. Nevertheless, his point remains valid that the sexual impulse is qualitatively different from these other impulses in its importance for human happiness. Sexuality is built into human beings in a way these other impulses are not. *See* note 12 *supra.*

18. These indications rest on the basic rationale underlying the independent rights theory—that only those rights are so protected which are "implicit in the concept of ordered liberty." Palko v. Connecticut, 302 U.S. 319, 325 (1937). In other words, in determining whether a right is so fundamental as to deserve protection, judges cannot look to their own notions, but must look to "the traditions and [collective] conscience of our people" to determine whether a principle is "so rooted there as to be ranked as fundamental." Griswold v. Connecticut, 381 U.S. at 493 (1965) [concurring opinion of Mr. Justice Goldberg, quoting from Snyder v. Massachusetts, 291 U.S. 97, 105 (1934)]. It thus would seem that statutes like the sodomy laws, which are pretty firmly rooted in Anglo-American legal tradition, can hardly be seen as violating such a fundamental principle. Here are some examples of this type of dictum:

> The laws regarding marriage which provide both when the sexual powers may be used and the legal and societal context in which children are born and brought up, as well as laws forbidding adultery, fornication and homosexual practices which express the negative of the proposition, confining sexuality to lawful marriage, form a pattern so deeply pressed into the substance of our social life that any Constitutional doctrine in this area must build upon that basis.

Poe v. Ullman, 367 U.S. 497, 546 (1961) (dissenting opinion of Mr. Justice Harlan).

> Thus, I would not suggest that adultery, homosexuality, fornication and incest are immune from criminal enquiry, however privately practiced.

Id. at 552.

> The State of Connecticut does have statutes, the constitutionality of which is beyond doubt, which prohibit adultery and fornication. . . . Finally, it

should be said of the Court's holding today that it in no way interferes with a State's proper regulation of sexual promiscuity or misconduct.

Griswold v. Connecticut, 381 U.S. 479, 498–99 (1965) (concurring opinion of Mr. Justice Goldberg).

[T]he statute is said to serve the State's policy against all forms of promiscuous or illicit sexual relationships, be they premarital or extramarital, concededly a permissible and legitimate legislative goal.

Id. at 505 (concurring opinion of Mr. Justice White).

See also McLaughlin v. Florida, 379 U.S. 184, 193, 196 (1964), and King v. Smith, 392 U.S. 309, 320, 334 (1968).

19. In this discussion, the idea of unconstitutional overbreadth is the same idea applied in *Griswold,* namely, that a law proscribing certain behavior under any and all circumstances is invalid if the Constitution permits such behavior to be proscribed only under certain limited circumstances. It is assumed that the law's challengers are themselves within the privileged circumstances. We thus are not here discussing use of the overbreadth doctrine as a kind of "roving commission" to find and cure unconstitutionality. *See* A. Cox, THE WARREN COURT 18 (1968). In other words, we are not asserting the propriety of allowing attacks on these laws by those whose own conduct is not constitutionally privileged, based on the unconstitutional applicability of the law to other conduct. It has been argued that the latter use of the doctrine ought to be limited to cases involving the first amendment freedoms of expression. *See* Note, *The First Amendment Overbreadth Doctrine,* 83 HARV. L. REV. 844 (1970).

20. To the effect that there is no connection between oral-genital sex acts in the heterosexual context and tendencies toward homosexuality, *see* J. L. MCCARY, HUMAN SEXUALITY 315 (1967). According to the Kinsey group, "Some people have considered heterosexual mouth-genital contact a form of behavior indicative of homosexuality, but it is clear that this belief is erroneous." P. H. GEBHARD, J. H. GAGNON, W. B. POMEROY, & C. V. CHRISTENSEN, SEX OFFENDERS—AN ANALYSIS OF TYPES 307 (1965) [hereinafter cited as SEX OFFENDERS]. This statement was preceded by their analysis of data indicating that among homosexual offenders who had had considerable opportunity to engage in heterosexual mouth-genital contact, as, *e.g.,* those who had been married, far fewer had done so than among the heterosexual offenders and the heterosexual control group.

21. *See* note 38, Chapter 2 *supra.*

22. This proposition should be self-evident with respect to all the acts cited, with the possible exception of anal intercourse. On the latter, *see* Masters & Johnson, *Ten Sex Myths Exploded,* PLAYBOY, December 1970, 124 at 126–28.

23. Marriage in our culture has been characterized as "serial monogamy."

24. 381 U.S. at 506–7.

25. KAN. STAT. ANN. 21-3505 (Supp. 1970).

26. KAN. STAT. ANN. 21-3507 (Supp. 1970).

27. N.Y. PENAL LAW § 130.38 (McKinney 1967) contains the proscription of consensual sodomy. The term "deviate sexual intercourse" as employed in that section is defined in section 130.00(2) so as to exclude acts between husband and wife.

28. N.Y. PENAL LAW § 255.17 (McKinney 1967).

29. *See* note 27 *supra.*

30. *See* N.Y. PENAL LAW §§ 130.20(2), 130.40, 130.45, and 130.50 (McKinney 1967), and Commission Staff Notes to § 130.50. Of course, the Penal Law would punish public lewdness even if the participants were husband and wife.

31. The various degrees of rape are covered in N.Y. PENAL LAW §§ 130.25, 130.30, and 130.35 (McKinney 1967). The definition of "female" is found in § 130.00(4). *See also* N.Y. PENAL LAW § 130.20(1) (McKinney 1967), which, though denominated "Sexual Misconduct," covers a "statutory rape" type of situation. It also uses the term "female," thus incorporating that term's restrictive definition.

32. Actually, the presence of both parents in the home is less important than the quality of their relationship with each other and with the children. Studies have shown that the child most likely to develop severe personality problems comes from an "empty shell" family—one in which the parents, though living together formally in the same house, provide no emotional support either to each other or to the children. *See* W. J. GOODE, THE FAMILY 101–2 (1964).

33. This notion was advanced in the jurisdictional statement filed by the State of Texas in the Supreme Court in *Wade v. Buchanan*, note 5, chapter 3 *supra.*

34. I do not mean to imply that this would be wise policy. There is no more reason to make deviate sex acts imposed by force on a spouse grounds for a criminal prosecution than ordinary intercourse likewise so imposed. One could, of course, argue that marriage constitutes, in itself, a consent to ordinary intercourse, but not necessarily to deviate acts, because our traditional ideas of marriage have always included a "union of bodies" for the procreation of children, as well as a union of minds and lives. But such an argument overlooks the realities of maintaining an ongoing relationship. Consent, though legally given, may be later withdrawn in fact. And husbands and wives often have serious differences over the frequency and occasions for ordinary intercourse, which are just as much a threat to the stability of their marriage as any differences over engaging in deviate acts. The best social policy in this area of potential marital discord as in others, in my opinion, is to require the pair either to compromise their differences or to divorce or separate. In any event, interjection of the criminal process will hardly save the marriage. Of course, this is not to say that the criminal process should be unavailable to protect from force a nonconsenting spouse after the marriage has already broken down. Some states do provide that a husband can be prosecuted for raping his wife if the rape takes place after they have ceased to live together.

One might argue that the policy here advocated could prevent a nonconsenting spouse from obtaining a divorce. I disagree. It can hardly be contended that a wife who is raped by her husband would be denied a divorce for "cruelty" merely because the act is not a crime under the laws of that jurisdiction, or because in marrying him she "irrevocably consented" to intercourse. Similarly, deviate sex acts imposed on a wife against her will would constitute cruelty regardless of whether they are criminal or not.

One could also argue that making deviate acts legal between consenting adults may make it more difficult for spouses who find such acts repulsive to refuse to engage in them. A partner's importuning may be harder to resist in a general social climate that approves all acts lovingly done. Thus consent, though apparently given, is lacking in fact. But I see no reason why deviate sexual conduct should here be singled out for special treatment. On many matters, nonsexual as well as sexual, a spouse may go along with a request that he or she would really prefer to deny, simply because resistance would threaten the relationship. Moreover, I find it incredible that any spouse has ever considered the criminal law an aid to resistance. Surely, those who find deviate sex acts repulsive will not cease to resist merely because those acts have become legal.

35. *See, e.g.,* T. H. VAN DE VELDE, IDEAL MARRIAGE, ITS PHYSIOLOGY AND TECHNIQUE 169–71 (Browne transl. 1957); H. M. STONE & A. STONE, A MARRIAGE MANUAL, A PRACTICAL GUIDEBOOK TO SEX AND MARRIAGE 183 (rev. ed. 1952); J. E. EICHENLAUB, THE MARRIAGE ART 47–59 (1961). *See also* Masters & Johnson, note 22 *supra;* and Mandell, *The Value of Variety in Sexual Behavior in the Marital Relationship,* in SEXUAL PROBLEMS 62 (C. W. Wahl ed. 1967). Other quite respectable books on human sexuality also recommend cunnilingus and fellatio as techniques of sexual arousal or orgasm. *See* J. L. MCCARY, HUMAN SEXUALITY 156–59 (1967); P. & E. KRONHAUSEN, THE SEXUALLY RESPONSIVE WOMAN 178–94 (Ballantine ed. 1965); J. D. FOLKMAN & N. M. CLATWORTHY, MARRIAGE HAS MANY FACES 304 (1970); H. A. KATCHADOURIAN & D. T. LUNDE, FUNDAMENTALS OF HUMAN SEXUALITY 239 (1972). Even books by and for Catholics, which contain similar counsels, have received the Nihil Obstat and Imprimatur. *See* J. W. BIRD & L. F. BIRD, THE FREEDOM OF SEXUAL LOVE 112 (1967): "oral-genital stimulation *in the pre-coital love-making of husband and wife* is not immoral. Nor is it unnatural or perverted." To the same effect is J. R. CAVANAGH, COUNSELLING THE INVERT 17 (1966), a book by a Catholic psychiatrist for pastoral and other counsellors. See also THE NEW CANA MANUAL, 1957, at 84 (W. Imbiorski ed. 1957): "What is morally right and wrong in marriage? We start from this idea that your love is a good thing and that you belong to each other. Any part of your body may touch any part of your husband's or wife's body, provided that the act of intercourse itself is completed normally."

36. West's comments about the effect of early childhood toilet training, though referring to the English, are equally applicable to many if not most Americans:

> "Brought up as we are to think of latrines, excrement and all their associations with disgust, the thought of buggery seems to many persons exquisitely horrible, and the way dogs sniff uninhibitedly at each other's anus and excrement they find most revolting. Admittedly, faeces carry germs, but the disgust is acquired, and scarcely proceeds from rational considerations. The mental process is not dissimilar from that of the hysterical girl who finds intercourse impossible because the penis passes urine."

D. J. WEST, HOMOSEXUALITY 204 (rev. ed. 1968) [hereinafter cited as WEST].

37. Manual stimulation of the female breast by the male as a precoital technique, common among humans, is rare in other species of mammals. C. S. FORD & F. A. BEACH, PATTERNS OF SEXUAL BEHAVIOR 46 (1951) [hereinafter cited as FORD & BEACH]. Male mouth on the female breast, though common in the United States among the sexually experienced, is not universal in other cultures. *See* A. C. KINSEY, W. B. POMEROY, C. E. MARTIN, & P. H. GEBHARD, SEXUAL

BEHAVIOR IN THE HUMAN FEMALE 254–55 (1953); Gebhard, *Human Sexual Behavior: A Summary Statement,* in HUMAN SEXUAL BEHAVIOR 209 (D. S. Marshall & R. C. Suggs eds. 1971). Even in the United States, there have existed, and may still exist, extremely divergent attitudes about the naturalness of this technique:

> Mouth-breast contact does occur at all social levels, but it is most elaborately developed again in the upper social level. . . .

> The upper level male considers it natural that the female breast should interest him, and that he should want to manipulate it, both by hand and mouth. The biologic origin of this interest is, however, open to question, because many lower level males do not find the female breast similarly interesting and have little inclination to manipulate it, either by hand or by mouth. Many lower level males rate such mouth-breast contacts as perversions, and some of them dismiss the idea with considerable disgust, as something that only a baby does when nursing from the mother's breast. Considering these opposite reactions to a single type of situation, it must be apparent that a considerable psychic element is involved in the development of individual patterns on this point. The concentration of these patterns in whole social levels indicates that the mores, the long-time customs of the groups, are the fundamental factors in the picture.

A. C. KINSEY, W. B. POMEROY, & C. E. MARTIN, SEXUAL BEHAVIOR IN THE HUMAN MALE 369-71 (1948).

38. Kissing on the mouth, though universal in European and American societies, is rare or absent in a substantial minority of other societies. Gebhard, *supra* note 37, at 209.

> . . . . [T]here are some peoples among whom kissing is unknown. When the Thonga first saw Europeans kissing they laughed, expressing this sentiment: "Look at them—they eat each other's saliva and dirt." The Siriono never kiss, although they have no regulation against such behavior. The Tinguian, instead of kissing, place the lips near the partner's face and suddenly inhale. Concerning the Balinese, Covarrubias writes as follows: "The love technique of the Balinese is natural and simple; kissing, as we understand it, as a self-sufficient act, is unknown and the caress that substitutes for our mode of kissing consists in bringing the faces close enough to catch each other's perfume and feel the warmth of the skin, with slight movements of the head . . . in the manner which has been wrongly called by Europeans 'rubbing noses.'"

FORD & BEACH 49.

39. The quotation appears in W. CHURCHILL, HOMOSEXUAL BEHAVIOR AMONG MALES 69 (1967) [hereinafter cited as CHURCHILL].

40. In all the criminal law, there is practically no other behavior which is forbidden on the ground that nature may be offended, and that nature must be protected from such offense. This is the unique aspect of our sex codes.

Kinsey, Pomeroy, Martin, & Gebhard, *Concepts of Normality and Abnormality in Sexual Behavior,* in PSYCHOSEXUAL DEVELOPMENT IN HEALTH AND DISEASE 12 (P. H. Hoch & J. Zubin eds. 1949). As the Whiteleys put it:

> It is not sinful to use one's teeth for untying knots, one's breath for cooling

one's porridge, or one's intelligence for solving crossword puzzles, though it cannot be maintained that these are the purposes for which these gifts were conferred upon us.

C. H. & W. M. WHITELEY, SEX AND MORALS 85 (1967). Why, then, has our culture singled out the sexual organs and powers for special treatment, prohibiting their use for the mere giving and receiving of sensual pleasure when divorced from the possibility of procreation? The Whiteleys suggest that it is simply the antihedonistic bias of traditional Christianity:

> [T]he obtaining of sensual pleasure is not counted as a legitimate end for which we may use these organs and capacities. That is not what they are for; we were not put into the world just to enjoy ourselves.

Id. at 83. Yet the obtaining of sensual pleasure from eating is not interdicted in modern America, and has been only feebly combatted, if at all, throughout Christian history. No one would think of prohibiting the smoking of tobacco, or the chewing of gum, just because they confer oral pleasure without making any contribution to the obtaining of nutrition, which we could regard as a "natural" function of the mouth. Antihedonism thus does not sufficiently explain the matter. The best explanation of why "sin" and "crimes against nature" have come to have an almost exclusively sexual connotation is that our culture's critical anxieties center on sex. By contrast, the Siriono Indians of Bolivia, whose primary anxieties are about food and eating, seem to have practically no restrictions on sexual behavior. *See* Murdock, *The Social Regulation of Sexual Behavior,* in PSYCHOSEXUAL DEVELOPMENT IN HEALTH AND DISEASE 264–65 (P. H. Hoch & J. Zubin eds. 1949).

Of course, virtually all human progress has consisted of crimes against nature, in the sense of diverting natural functions and processes, through human artifice, from whichever of their usual consequences we don't like to those we do like. Science continually interferes with nature, in order to make human life easier, happier, and more pleasurable. If we followed consistently, in every aspect of existence, the so-called Christian philosophy of not offending against the natural order of things, we would end up like St. Simeon Stylites, who, when the maggots feeding in the festering sores on his body fell to the ground, is reported to have picked them up and replaced them, saying, "Eat what God has given you!"

41. Lord Devlin has argued that the state is justified in criminally prohibiting any act that the great majority of people in the society believe to be "immoral," even though it is harmless in its tangible, observable consequences. Basically, his argument is that otherwise the "common morality" of the society might wither away, thus bringing about either social disintegration or at least a change for the worse. P. DEVLIN, THE ENFORCEMENT OF MORALS (1965). I have not dealt with his arguments here because he, as an Englishman, is not speaking in the context of American constitutional law. Even if one were to concede that his argument supplies some warrant for a state to prohibit "immoral" but harmless acts, it can hardly be contended that this warrant is "a compelling subordinating interest" allowing the state to override fundamental human liberties. Leaving constitutional issues aside, I have endeavored to show elsewhere that Devlin's arguments are based on questionable assumptions. *See* Barnett, *Corruption of Morals: The Underlying Issue of the Pornography Commission Report,* 1971 LAW & THE SOCIAL

ORDER 189. Any reader who wishes to pursue the purely jurisprudential question (as opposed to the constitutional one) is directed to that article.

42. Loving v. Virginia, *supra* note 9; Bolling v. Sharpe, *supra* note 10.

43. Note 3, Chapter 4 *supra.*

44. Attempts to find effective contraceptive devices are about as old as the human race. Various kinds of objects and substances have been placed in the vagina, to serve either as obstructions between the semen and the cervix or as more or less effective spermicidal agents. Crude sheaths for the penis, made of paper, silk, or other substances, have been devised at various times and in various cultures. Of the devices we know today to be reasonably effective, only the condom antedates the last quarter of the nineteenth century. This sheath, made of animal bladders or intestines, was supposed to have been invented by a Colonel or Dr. Condom at the court of Charles II of England, around 1660 to 1680. It did not, however, begin to be manufactured for general sale in England until the last decade or two of the eighteenth century. And it must be remembered that the birth control movement, which sought for the first time to educate ordinary people about contraception and to make contraceptives widely available to all who want them, is a phenomenon of the twentieth century. *See* B. E. FINCH & H. GREEN, CONTRACEPTION THROUGH THE AGES (1964).

45. *See, e.g.,* Schwartz, *Morals Offenses and the Model Penal Code,* 63 COLUM. L. REV. 669, 672 (1963); and P. DEVLIN, THE ENFORCEMENT OF MORALS *passim* (1965). Though Schwartz implies that this limitation on the majority should be a constitutional one, he cites no case authority holding that it is. Devlin, as an Englishman, is not of course speaking about American constitutional law.

46. To show the existence of such a minority, I will limit my discussion primarily to homosexual acts. A fortiori, anyone who does not find deviate acts immoral in the homosexual context is unlikely to find them immoral in a heterosexual context.

Most of the public opinion polls dealing with homosexuality have not asked this kind of question. Usually they ask only whether the respondents think homosexual acts should be a crime. Responses to the latter question may be an unreliable index to moral attitudes, because one may believe certain acts immoral without holding that they also should be criminal. This was the position taken by the special committee of Roman Catholics appointed by the Cardinal Archbishop of Westminster (the English Roman Catholic primate) to advise him what recommendation to make to the Wolfenden Committee on the question of legalizing homosexual acts in Britain. *See* the Catholic committee's report entitled *Homosexuality, Prostitution and the Law,* in 230 DUBLIN REVIEW 57 (No. 471, summer 1956).

Similarly, in America, the Council for Christian Social Action of the United Church of Christ (in 1969), the Council of Church and Society of the United Presbyterian Church in the U.S.A. (in 1970), the Lutheran Church in America (in 1970), and the General Assembly of the Unitarian Universalist Association (in 1970) approved statements opposing criminalization of private homosexual acts between consenting adults, but without asserting that such conduct is sinless. Although the 182nd General Assembly of the United Presbyterian Church in the U.S.A., meeting in May 1970, approved a resolution to the effect that homosexual behavior (along with adultery, prostitution, and fornication) should still be regarded as sin, the vote was almost equally divided, 356 to 347. The Assembly called upon its member churches to support and give leadership in movements toward the elimination of laws governing the private sexual behavior of consenting adults, but without any specific reference to homosexual behavior. *See* L. Williams, *The Churches—Lutherans, Presbyterians, Episcopalians, Unitarians —Where They Stand Today,* VECTOR, Aug. 1971, at 24; W. H. Genné, A Synoptic of Recent Denominational Statements on Sexuality 3 (pamphlet published by the Department of Educational Development, National Council of Churches, n.d.).

The General Conference of the United Methodist Church, meeting in April 1972, after affirming homosexuals as "persons of sacred worth" and calling for the extension of human and civil rights to all persons, including homosexuals, approved the following statement: "We do not condone the practice of homosexuality, and consider this practice incompatible with Christian teaching." SIECUS Report, Sept. 1972, at 4; TIME, May 8, 1972, at 67.

A poll taken from a representative cross-section of Episcopalians (laymen, women, urban and rural clergy, bishops, chaplains, seminary professors, and seminary students) disclosed widely varying attitudes toward homosexuals and homosexual behavior. *See* R. R. Hansel, The Homosexual Problem . . . Theirs or Ours (pamphlet published by the Section for Experimental and Specialized Services, Executive Council of the Episcopal Church, 1970).

On June 25, 1972, the United Church of Christ became the first major American denomination to ordain an avowed homosexual to its clergy. The Ecclesiastical Council of the Golden Gate Association of the Northern California Conference of UCC Churches had voted 62 to 34 on May 1 to approve the Rev. William Johnson for ordination. The denomination's Council for Church and Ministry, a national body responsible for the professional standards of the clergy, reversed the previous denominational policy and adopted an advisory to all UCC churches that each such request for ordination should be considered on its individual merits. SIECUS Report, Sept. 1972, at 4; and S.F. Chronicle, May 1, 1972, at 1, col. 2, and at 22, col. 5. In the churches, change is plainly blowing in the wind.

A Harris poll taken in 1969 discovered that 30 per cent of its respondents found nothing wrong with homosexual acts between consenting adults. TIME, June 6, 1969, at 26. Similarly, a Kinsey Institute survey made in 1971 found that only two-thirds of the population have some negative feelings about homosexual behavior. They found that fewer than 10 percent of those under the age of 25 deemed homosexual behavior "wrong." Gillette, *What the 1972 Kinsey Report Says About You,* SEXUALITY, Nov. 1971, at 68. This noncondemnatory attitude of many of the younger generation is also reflected in the action of the 1970 White House Conference on Youth, held in Colorado, which voted 439 to 127 that "any sexual behavior between consenting, responsible adults must be recognized and tolerated by society as an acceptable life-style." TIME, May 3, 1971, at 39. In the poll that *Psychology Today* took of its readers in July 1969, to which more than 20,000 responded, 60 per cent (in addition to the 4 per cent who were exclusive homosexuals) thought that homosexuality is a matter of individual choice. Another 14 per cent said "there is nothing wrong with it—there is an element of homosexuality in everyone." The readers were overwhelmingly opposed to the idea that homosexuals should be considered criminal and punished accordingly. Athanasiou, Shaver, & Tavris, *Sex*, PSYCHOLOGY TODAY, July 1970, at 52.

Counting heads does not, of course, give the full picture. A number of books by individual writers on the subject of sex ethics have questioned the immorality of homosexual acts. Some of these are by British, Dutch and German authors, but I have included them here because they have had wide circulation and influence in America. I will discuss the American authors first.

Mazur takes the position that homosexual acts and relationships are not immoral per se, but may be immoral in particular circumstances, *e.g.*, with a minor. R. M. MAZUR, COMMONSENSE SEX 69–77 (1968).

Wood urges complete acceptance of homosexuality as a morally permissible alternative to heterosexuality. He advocates that churches should hold social functions for homosexuals, such as dances, and should marry homosexual couples who have built their relationship upon mutual love and devotion. R. W. WOOD, CHRIST AND THE HOMOSEXUAL (1960).

Jones, in his book written for the Young Men's Christian Association, adheres to the view that heterosexual monogamy is the only way in which God's purposes for human sexuality can be completely fulfilled, but he regards the homosexual merely as a handicapped person, who should be encouraged to approximate such a relationship with another person of the same sex, such an approximation being the best of which he is capable. H. K. JONES, TOWARD A CHRISTIAN UNDERSTANDING OF THE HOMOSEXUAL 107–10 (1966).

> Homosexuality can be a relatively creative and fulfilling way of life for the responsible homosexual, and often it can reach a height of fulfillment equal to that of many heterosexual relationships. However, the homosexual relationship is doomed, by its very nature, to never pass beyond a certain point [because only a male and a female can really complement one another, and only they can have children].

Id. at 109.

Rustum and Della Roy take a forthright stance in opposition to the traditional attitude toward homosexuality, and urge that Christians should accept homosexuals and work to make it possible for them to develop deeper and more permanent relationships. R. & D. ROY, HONEST SEX 159–66 (1968). They took a survey of 150 men and women they regarded as "creative Christians":

> Nearly half the men and one-third of the women had been involved in some close way with some homosexual activity (a surprisingly large percentage). Only a quarter of the respondents regarded homosexual acts as abnormal, unnatural, or inherently destructive, while over 60 per cent were open to the possibility that such relationships may be fitted into some framework in society.

Id. at 36.

W. Norman Pittenger, a distinguished American Episcopal theologian now residing in England, is equally, if not more, forthright in asserting that homosexual conduct is not, per se, any more immoral than heterosexual conduct. *See* W. N. PITTENGER, MAKING SEXUALITY HUMAN (1970), and TIME FOR CONSENT:

A Christian Approach to Homosexuality (rev. ed. 1970). In general accord is M. F. Valente, Sex: The Radical View of a Catholic Theologian (1970).

Other works that demonstrate the reappraisal of attitudes toward homosexuality currently under way in religious circles are Shinn, *Homosexuality: Christian Conviction & Inquiry*, Weltge, *The Paradox of Man & Woman*, and Secor, *A Brief for a New Homosexual Ethic*, all essays collected in The Same Sex: An Appraisal of Homosexuality at 43, 55, and 67 (R. W. Weltge ed. 1969); the thirteen essays by different authors collected in Is Gay Good? Ethics, Theology, and Homosexuality (W. D. Oberholtzer ed. 1971); J. A. McCaffrey, Homosexuality: Toward a Moral Synthesis (1969); The Homosexual Dialectic (J. A. McCaffrey ed. 1972); and C. R. Jones, What About Homosexuality? (1972). In addition to these books, articles attacking the traditional moral position are beginning to proliferate in religious journals. *See, e.g.,* the editorial, *To Accept Homosexuals,* and Wright, *The Church and Gay Liberation,* in The Christian Century, March 3, 1971, at 281.

Another set of views that contrast strongly with the traditional Christian stance toward homosexual behavior is presented in *Playboy Panel: Religion and the New Morality,* Playboy, June 1967, at 148–50. The panelists, nine leading liberal clergymen from Judaism, Catholicism, and the various Protestant denominations, also found that deviate sex acts in a heterosexual context presented hardly any moral issue at all. The Catholic spokesman asserted they were immoral for his coreligionists, but only if indulged to the point of orgasm. They are not immoral as foreplay leading to coitus. *Id.* at 72–74. Among secular spokesmen defending private homosexual behavior among consenting adults are R. O. D. Benson, In Defense of Homosexuality (1965); H. M. Hefner, The Playboy Philosophy 128 (1965); A. Ellis, Homosexuality—Its Causes and Cure 88 (1965); and Ellis, *A Rational Sexual Morality,* in The New Sexual Revolution 61 (L. A. Kirkendall & R. N. Whitehurst eds. 1971).

Turning to Europe, one may note that in 1963, a committee of England's Society of Friends stated that homosexuality as a condition is no more to be deplored than left-handedness and is not necessarily morally worse than heterosexuality. Friends Home Service Committee, Towards a Quaker View of Sex—An Essay by a Group of Friends 26–42 (rev. ed. A. Heron 1964). The Roman Catholic Church of the Netherlands, in its new catechism, states that homosexuals are not at fault for their condition and are often hard-working and honorable people, and that the biblical injunctions against homosexuality must be read in the context of the ancient world in which they were formulated. A New Catechism: Catholic Faith for Adults 384–85 (K. Smith transl. Herder & Herder ed. 1967).

D. S. Bailey, an Anglican theologian, takes the position that, while homosexual acts are intrinsically sinful because in opposition to God's purpose for human sexuality, a homosexual is not necessarily morally blameworthy for engaging in them. Bailey, *The Homosexual and Christian Morals,* in They Stand Apart 46–56 (J. T. Rees & H. V. Usill eds. 1955).

The German Lutheran theologian, Helmut Thielicke, likewise acknowledges that homosexuality is against the order of God's creation, which intended each sex for the other. But he says it is merely one of the many symptoms of the disorder among men that flows from the disorder of man's relationship to God. It is not to be singled out as particularly heinous. Even then, the condition of being homosexual is not morally blameworthy because it is involuntarily acquired. In those cases where it is not "curable," the person is making the best of the situation into which he has been thrown if he orders his sexual life according to the same norms that should govern heterosexual relationships. Abstinence, or celibacy, is something no one would think of demanding of all "normal" persons. He does, however, end up counseling sublimation to the homosexual, apparently because the structure and mores of the homosexual subculture and the hostility of society make it unusually difficult to order a homosexual life-style in accordance with the ethical norms applicable to heterosexuality. H. THIELICKE, THE ETHICS OF SEX 277–88 (J. W. Doberstein transl. 1964).

Atkinson, a professor of moral philosophy, takes up, one by one, the various reasons homosexuality is deemed immoral and finds them wanting. R. T. ATKINSON, SEXUAL MORALITY 145–51 (1965). The Whiteleys undertake a similar analysis, with the same result, except that they believe society may assert some moral right to discourage homosexuality, derived from the adjustment difficulties homosexuals experience in Western culture. Society thus perhaps may seek to protect those whose orientation is still malleable from being influenced toward homosexuality. This right should not in their opinion extend to *punishing* homosexual acts. C. H. & W. M. WHITELEY, SEX AND MORALS 89–94 (1967). Still another book dealing with the moral issue of homosexuality is A. DAVIDSON, THE RETURN OF LOVE: LETTERS OF A CHRISTIAN HOMOSEXUAL (1970).

In short, the present situation in America is accurately summarized by the Task Force on Homosexuality of the National Institute of Mental Health:

> Although many people continue to regard homosexual activities with repugnance, there is evidence that public attitudes are changing. Discreet homosexuality, together with many other aspects of human sexual behavior, is being recognized more and more as the private business of the individual rather than a subject for public regulation through statute. Many homosexuals are good citizens, holding regular jobs and leading productive lives.

National Institute of Mental Health, Final Report of the Task Force on Homosexuality, October 10, 1969, at 18.

Of course not everybody takes the issue of sexual morals seriously. The following advertisement appeared in a northern California newspaper in the spring of 1972:

> Couple into sadism, masochism, fetishism, pederasty, fellatio, cunnilingus, bondage, onanism, necrophilia, bestiality, dope, masturbation, incest, macrame, homosexuality, cannibalism and transvestitism, dirty pictures, French kissing and lollipops wants to meet like couples. 751-4462. No weirdos please.

47. One might argue that promiscuity is an evil because it increases the likelihood of the spread of venereal disease. Homosexual contacts do not, however, appear to make any greater contribution to the spread of VD than heterosexual ones. *See* Ketterer, *Homosexuality and Venereal Disease*, 5 MEDICAL ASPECTS OF HUMAN SEXUALITY 114–18 (No. 3, March 1971).

48. An English case, Corbett v. Corbett (otherwise Ashley), [1970] 2 All E.R. 33 (P.D. & Adm.), is perhaps the first authority that marriages between persons of the same sex are not valid. That case did not, however, involve a homosexual marriage but one between a man and a male-to-female transsexual. This court's determination that the transsexual remained a member of the male sex is at least questionable.

Newspapers have reported a number of instances in which homosexual couples—both male and female—have sought marriage licenses in America, none so far with unquestioned success. The basis for rejection of the applications is that the tradition of civil marriage and the context of the laws permitting and regulating it (if not their precise words) limit it to persons of opposite sexes. One such case is that of Jack Baker and James Michael McConnell, of Minneapolis, Minnesota, whose application for a marriage license on May 18, 1970, provoked the public controversy over the latter's offer of employment with the University of Minnesota described in Chapter 1. The denial of their application was upheld by a lower state court November 18, 1970, and again, on rehearing, January 11, 1971. The Supreme Court of Minnesota affirmed this decision on October 15. Baker v. Nelson, 191 N.W.2d 185 (Minn. 1971), *appeal dismissed*, 93 S. Ct. 37 (1972). Meanwhile, Baker and McConnell had succeeded in obtaining a license in Mankato, Minnesota, and were "married" by a Methodist minister on September 3, 1971. Another reported judicial decision denying the validity of same-sex marriage is Anonymous v. Anonymous, 67 Misc.2d 982, 325 N.Y. Supp.2d 499 (Sup. Ct. 1971).

49. The Kinsey group demolishes this argument thus:

It is contended that the general spread of homosexuality would threaten the existence of the human species, and that the integrity of the home and of the social organization could not be maintained if homosexual activity were not condemned by moral codes and public opinion and made punishable under the statute law. The argument ignores the fact that the existent mammalian species have managed to survive in spite of their widespread homosexual activity, and that sexual relations between males seem to be widespread in certain cultures (for instance, Moslem and Buddhist cultures) which are more seriously concerned with problems of overpopulation than they are with any threat of underpopulation. Interestingly enough these are also cultures in which the institution of the family is very strong.

A. C. KINSEY, W. B. POMEROY, C. E. MARTIN, & P. H. GEBHARD, SEXUAL BEHAVIOR IN THE HUMAN FEMALE 483 (1953).

50. *See, e.g.,* Viscount Hailsham, *Homosexuality and Society,* in THEY STAND APART 22–23, 27, 28–29 (J. T. Rees & H. V. Usill eds. 1955).

51. SEX INFORMATION AND EDUCATION COUNCIL OF THE UNITED STATES, SEXUALITY AND MAN 88 (1970); WEST 117–19; J. JERSILD, THE NORMAL HOMOSEXUAL MALE VERSUS THE BOY MOLESTER (1967); E. M. SCHUR, CRIMES WITHOUT VICTIMS 74 (1965); Marmor, *Introduction,* in SEXUAL INVERSION 18-19 (J. Marmor ed. 1965); Pomeroy, *Homosexuality,* in THE SAME SEX—AN APPRAISAL OF HOMOSEXUALITY 11 (R. W. Weltge ed. 1969).

The British study by Schofield found that, actually, the pedophile is more often a heterosexual, in terms of interests and experience, who turns to children—often indiscriminately between boys and girls—in middle age or later (ages 35 to 50) when his heterosexual experiences with other adults have ceased. The pedophiles in his study "did not mix with homosexuals and did not know any." M. SCHOFIELD, SOCIOLOGICAL ASPECTS OF HOMOSEXUALITY 147-55, 212 (1965) [hereinafter cited as SCHOFIELD]. "Very few were interested in adult men." *Id.* at 208. In comparing the homosexual and heterosexual nonconvict nonpatient groups with respect to the ages at which they found potential partners most attractive sexually, he found:

> More . . . [heterosexual] men found girls of under sixteen to be sexually attractive than . . . [homosexual] men found boys under sixteen to be sexually attractive. The . . . [heterosexual] men usually thought that girls were most attractive before they were twenty-one, whereas . . . [homosexual] men thought that the most attractive age for their partners was between twenty-one and thirty.

Id. at 137.

The Kinsey group, in their study of sex offenders of all types, found that, as one moves down the three categories of homosexual offenses from "offenses against adults" to "offenses against minors" to "offenses against children," the offenders became more characterized by heterosexual interests and less exclusively or predominantly homosexual in their fantasies, dreams, and conscious sexual arousal. SEX OFFENDERS 277-79, 303-4, 332-34, 667. Thus, the more exclusively homosexual a person is, the less likely he is to be an offender against youngsters and children. They also found that the typical homosexual offender against minors (age 12 to 15) is an individual who has retreated from competition with adult homosexuals or is a situational offender, and that the homosexual offender against adults is typically not interested in prepubescent boys, prefers (76 per cent) partners over 18, and especially partners of his own age bracket (25–34). *Id.* at 285, 323, 345.

Psychiatrist Irving Bieber says:

> I find that homosexuals as a group are not sexually oriented toward children. Some individual men may be, but very few. . . . [P]edophilia is usually heterosexual. I try to get the point across to parents that they need not be afraid that their children will be seduced or misled if they're in contact with a homosexual. I have analyzed several men whose fathers were homosexual, but the sons didn't become homosexual. The idea that homosexuals are dangerous and that you have to keep them away and worry about them doesn't accord with my clinical experience.

Playboy Panel: Homosexuality, PLAYBOY, April 1971, at 88.

Other enquiries have also confirmed that the typical adult homosexual constitutes no threat to youngsters below the age of consent. See WOLFENDEN REPORT, REPORT OF THE COMMITTEE ON HOMOSEXUAL OFFENCES AND PROSTITUTION para. 57 (authorized Amer. ed. 1963); Note, *The Consenting Adult Homosexual and the Law: An Empirical Study of Enforcement and Administration in Los Angeles County,* 13 U.C.L.A. L. REV. 664, at 738 n. 315, 787 (1966); Slovenko & Phillips, *Psychosexuality and the Criminal Law,* 15 VAND. L. REV. 823–24 n. 84 (1962), quoting from the Report of the New Jersey Commission on the Habitual Sex Offender (1950). On the general subject of pedophilia see J. W. MOHR ET AL., PAEDOPHILIA AND EXHIBITIONISM (1964).

52. The Kinsey group, sketching the profile of those sex offenders convicted of homosexual acts with minors, makes this point cogently:

> While the heterosexual male who finds equally young girls attractive may restrain himself because of social and legal circumstances, the homosexual male is somewhat less restrained; to reverse an old saying, he feels that since he risks hanging anyway he might as well be hanged for a lamb as for a sheep.

SEX OFFENDERS 298. In accord is E. M. SCHUR, CRIMES WITHOUT VICTIMS 111 (1965).

53. *See, e.g.,* Hooker, *The Adjustment of the Male Overt Homosexual,* 21 J. PROJECTIVE TECHNIQUES 18 (1957), reprinted in THE PROBLEM OF HOMOSEXUALITY IN MODERN SOCIETY 141 (H. M. Ruitenbeek ed. 1963). In this classic study, Dr. Hooker matched 30 homosexual males with 30 heterosexual males of the same age, education, and intelligence, gave both groups Rorschach and other projective personality tests, and asked two clinical psychologists to distinguish the homosexual in each pair. The judges were unable to distinguish the homosexual from the heterosexual records better than would be expected by chance. A similar study of lesbians is reported in Armon, *Some Personality Variables in Overt Female Homosexuality,* 24 J. PROJECTIVE TECHNIQUES 292 (1960), with the following result: "[I]ndependent judges who rated the responses blindly could not tell to any reliable degree which were the lesbians' records and which the ones from heterosexuals."

54. *See* Hooker, *Sexual Behavior: Homosexuality,* 14 INT'L ENCY. SOCIAL SCIENCES 225–27 (1968). Admittedly, too, personality "tests" are rather crude measures.

55. *See* Hooker, *Male Homosexuals and Their Worlds,* in SEXUAL INVERSION 87–89 (J. Marmor ed. 1965); CHURCHILL 175; WEST 44–45, 48–53, 58–59; M. HOFFMAN, THE GAY WORLD 32–33 (Bantam ed. 1969) [hereinafter cited as HOFFMAN].

56. *See* Marmor, *Homosexuality and Objectivity,* SIECUS Newsletter, Vol VI, No. 2, at 1 (December, 1970); Marmor, *Introduction,* in SEXUAL INVERSION 20 (J. Marmor ed. 1965). *See also* Chapter 7 *infra.*

57. *See, e.g.,* P. DEVLIN, THE ENFORCEMENT OF MORALS 13 (1965); and P. A. SOROKIN, THE AMERICAN SEX REVOLUTION (1965).

58. The civilizations most often discussed are those of ancient Greece and Rome. In the case of Greece, the social "approval" of homosexuality, if we can call it that, coincided with, as well as followed, the golden age of classical Greek culture—the period roughly spanning the years 500-323 B.C. Many, if not most, of the greatest Greeks of that general period whose names have come down to us through history are known to have been "infected" with ambisexuality, if not homosexuality. Perhaps in the case of Sparta, homosexuality contributed to a decline in the power and prestige of the state through the failure to reproduce, but even there other factors were also at work to lower the birth rate. *See* C. BRINTON, A HISTORY OF WESTERN MORALS 83–85 (1959). In the case of Roman civilization, perhaps one should note that it was pagan Rome which conquered

the world; Christian Rome, which had made homosexual conduct unlawful, fell to
the barbarians. *See* O. KIEFER, SEXUAL LIFE IN ANCIENT ROME 349–64 (1952). One
may doubt whether any reputable historian today would undertake to defend the
proposition that homosexuality contributed to the decay of either civilization.
The only official body ever to inquire into the matter found no evidence of a
connection between homosexual conduct and the decay of any known civilization, ancient or modern. *See* WOLFENDEN, *supra* note 51, at para. 54.

59. The statement is that of the late David M. Potter, William Robertson Coe
Professor of History, first at Yale University and then at Stanford University, who
taught me as an undergraduate at Yale.

60. Some opponents of the policy of tolerance argue that to permit deviant
practices would be to open the floodgates to a great upsurge of immorality,
which would endanger family life and lower the birth rate. Such fears are
grossly exaggerated. No such outcome has arrived in Holland or in other
countries that have long exercised legal tolerance.

WEST 267.

61. Normally when it is impossible to assess risks of this sort the courts
conclude that the matter should be left to legislative judgment. So goes standard
constitutional dogma. It is not fair, however, to apply that dogma in this instance,
because the legislature has already stacked the deck. The criminal laws against
homosexual acts, together with the general stigma of which they are a major
manifestation, have themselves created the social structure and attitudes of the
"gay" world which positively discourage the formation of stable relationships.
Illegality makes many homosexual males feel they must maintain secrecy about
their work, their family relationships, and all aspects of their lives—even their
identity—until they have had enough opportunity to gauge the other's trust-
worthiness. Even a homosexual in the market for a mate thus can advertise
initially only the cosmetic, rather than his genuine, self—a tactic not very
conducive to his objective. On the other hand, many male homosexuals avoid
pairing, because it subjects them to greater chance of discovery. The mere fact of
two members of the male sex living together would raise suspicion. The one-night
stand therefore becomes standard expectation in the "gay" world, because so
many are unwilling to risk themselves beyond it. Even for those who would be
willing, this puts the cart before the horse—sex before love—so that the latter has
less chance of developing. Furthermore, lack of socially approved meeting places
has resulted in commercial institutions like the "gay" bar fulfilling this function,
and these are a rather unwholesome context for any initiation of paired
relationships. *See* Achilles, *Development of the Homosexual Bar as an Institution,*
in SEXUAL DEVIANCE 247 (J. H. Gagnon & W. Simon eds. 1967). Of course, it may
be that the emotional needs of some require a succession of sexual affairs with
different partners, so that promiscuity among homosexuals is not entirely
traceable to sociocultural pressures. Lasting unions seem much more prevalent
among lesbians than among male homosexuals, but even among the latter they
are not as rare as some psychiatrists would lead one to believe. *See* SCHOFIELD
112–16, 136; Hooker, *An Empirical Study of Some Relations Between Sexual
Patterns and Gender Identity in Male Homosexuals,* in SEX RESEARCH—NEW
DEVELOPMENTS 45–49 (J. Money ed. 1965); Hooker, *Male Homosexuals and Their*

Worlds, in SEXUAL INVERSION 97–98 (J. Marmor ed. 1965); WEST 57–58; B. MAGEE, ONE IN TWENTY 82–84 (1966); and HOFFMAN 164–77.

62. On the issue of the general criminal threat, the Kinsey group, in their massive study of sex offenders, found that the homosexual offender against adults is generally not involved in any criminal offenses other than sex offenses, and his sex offenses are almost invariably homosexual offenses like solicitation. Even his non-sex offenses, rare as they are, more often consist of vagrancy and disorderly conduct than of any other kind of crime. The "cruising" and loitering so characteristic of "gay" life predisposes male homosexuals to charges of this kind. SEX OFFENDERS 350–51. They concluded that the "homosexual offenders vs. adults, as a group, do not appear particularly criminal or dangerous. They do not damage society, they merely do not fit into it." *Id.* at 357.

On the matter of homosexual "rape," the Kinsey group found the use of force so rare in homosexual offenses that separate categories for forcible offenses of this kind were not warranted. They did, however, have to set up such a separate category for heterosexual offenses against all three types of victims—adults, minors, and children. The following quotations give their conclusions about the incidence of force in each division of homosexual offenses:

> All in all, the great majority of homosexual contacts between adults take place with mutual consent; homosexual rape is rare and usually confined to prisons and hobo jungles.

Id. at 354.

> By and large, it is quite clear that force and threat are infrequent and quite atypical of homosexual offenses against minor males.

Id. at 320.

> We can point out . . . that the use of physical force, and particularly of severe force is so rare in homosexual offenses against children that a separate category for force offenses was not warranted.

Id. at 293. *See also* WEST 223–29. It seems clear that if society should endeavor to stamp out any sexual orientation on the ground that it leads to rape, that orientation is heterosexuality.

63. This is the justification sometimes given for disqualifying them from military service. *See* C. J. WILLIAMS & M. S. WEINBERG, HOMOSEXUALS AND THE MILITARY 25 (1971).

64. Michael Schofield found that his British subjects showed no tendency to congregate in particular occupations or firms, or to prefer co-workers who were homosexual. They tended, rather, to avoid mixing work relationships with sexual ones. SCHOFIELD 107–8. There is no reason to believe that American homosexuals are any different.

65. The National Association for Mental Health has endorsed the legalization of homosexual behavior in private between consenting adults, asserting

> . . . . it appears to be as deeply motivated as normal heterosexual behavior; it has not been prevented or cured by the harshest punishment. . . . There is no evidence either in empirical research or in the experience of other countries that homosexual behavior in itself endangers the health of the individual or of society.

National Association for Mental Health, Position Statement on Homosexuality and Mental Illness, October 17, 1970.

In similar vein was the recommendation of the thirty-seventh American Assembly which met at Arden House, Harriman, New York, in April 1970, to discuss "The Health of Americans." This conference was composed of professional representatives from "the field of health (practice and administration), the legal profession (bench and bar), the communications media, the academic and business worlds, several professional and public affairs organizations, and government." Among the twenty "recommendations for national action" which that gathering made was an itemizing of the concrete steps which need to be taken by government "to diminish mental anguish and improve mental health of segments of society." Heading this list was a recommendation for the "abolition of all existing laws concerning sexual behavior between consenting adults, without sacrificing protection for minors or public decorum." American Assembly, The Health of Americans 3, 7 (Final Report of the 37th American Assembly, held at Arden House, Harriman, New York, April 23–26, 1970).

Finally, the Task Force on Homosexuality of the National Institute of Mental Health states

> Homosexuality presents a major problem for our society largely because of the amount of injustice and suffering entailed in it not only for the homosexual but also for those concerned about him. . . . Individual homosexuals suffer in being isolated from much of society and from the fact that they live in a culture in which homosexuality is considered maladaptive and opprobrious. Their families suffer in feeling responsible and in adjusting to the problem. Society at large inevitably loses in a number of ways—loss of manpower, economic costs, human costs, etc.
>
> The existence of legal penalties relating to homosexual acts means that the mental health problems of homosexuals are exacerbated by the need for concealment and the emotional stresses arising from this need and from the opprobrium of being in violation of the law. On the other hand, there is no evidence suggesting that legal penalties are effective in preventing or reducing the incidence of homosexual acts in private between consenting adults. . . .
>
> We believe that [repeal of such penalties] would reduce the emotional stresses upon the parties involved and thereby contribute to an improvement in their mental health. Furthermore, such a change in the law would also encourage revisions in certain governmental regulations which now make homosexual acts a bar to employment or a cause for dismissal. By helping thereby to remove a source of anxiety over being discovered, this would make an indirect contribution to the mental health of the homosexual population. It would also serve to reduce the possibilities of blackmail, which are a constant hazard to the homosexual under present conditions.

National Institute of Mental Health, Final Report of the Task Force on Homosexuality, October 10, 1969, at 4, 18–20.

66. *See* Chapter 6 *infra.*

67. *See* WEST 244–45; HOFFMAN 126–27; Romm, *Sexuality and Homosexuality*

in Women, in SEXUAL INVERSION 292 (J. Marmor ed. 1965); Kinsey *et al., supra* note 40, at 21; SEX OFFENDERS 626.

68. In other words, the argument here is that if sexual orientation is determined by one's environment, rather than inborn—a conclusion to which most of the scientific evidence points—then criminal laws against homosexual acts may exert an influence tending to depress the incidence of homosexual orientation. The more deterministic one is, the more plausible the argument sounds, because the law can then be seen as one of the relevant determining factors. The scientific literature does not, however, support this contention. The reader can better judge its plausibility after he has read the summary of scientific knowledge presented in Chapters 6 and 7 *infra.*

69. *Cf.* the following statement of Viscount Hailsham:

> . . . . I can see the gravest objection to a provision of the law which would inevitably give rise to the belief, however erroneous, that homosexual practices were fully permissible for an adult, and therefore in the class of vice to which smoking and drinking belong, or even comparable to a fortune which a young man inherits when he is of age to dispose of it prudently.

Hailsham, *supra* note 50, at 30.

70. *See* HOFFMAN 130–32.

71. *See, e.g.,* Thompson, *Changing Concepts of Homosexuality in Psychoanalysis,* in THE PROBLEM OF HOMOSEXUALITY IN MODERN SOCIETY 43 (H. M. Ruitenbeek ed. 1963).

72. Kinsey *et al., supra* note 40, at 25–26. *See also* A. C. KINSEY, W. B. POMEROY, C. E. MARTIN, & P. H. GEBHARD, SEXUAL BEHAVIOR IN THE HUMAN FEMALE 449 (1953).

73. FORD & BEACH 152.

74. *I.e.,* until after Chapters 6 and 7. My own judgment is given in Chapter 8.

75. I am referring to (1) establishment of religion, (2) the right-of-privacy doctrine, and (3) the independent rights doctrine.

76. Note 5, Chapter 3 *supra.*

77. Note 53, Chapter 4 *supra.*

78. 308 F.Supp. at 733.

79. 70 Wash.2d at 655, 424 P.2d at 909. *Contra,* State v. Trejo, 83 N.M. 511, 494 P.2d 173 (Ct. App. 1972) (dissenting opinion of Sutin, J.).

6

The Scientific View of
Psychosexual Deviation

Two possible lines of argument for the unconstitutionality of the sodomy laws depend uniquely on the knowledge of human sexuality supplied by modern science: psychology, psychiatry, sociology, and anthropology.[1] One of these lines calls into play the equal protection clause of the fourteenth amendment; the other, the cruel and unusual punishment clause of the eighth (which is applicable to the states through the due process clause of the fourteenth). These arguments are somewhat more difficult to establish than those previously discussed not only for this reason (their dependence on scientific data, as opposed to common sense), but also because they are dependent for support upon reasoning by more remote analogy from decided cases in other areas.

A preliminary comment is in order about the use of scientific data to support constitutional arguments. Although it is impossible to measure the influence of such data in shaping Supreme Court decisions, the Court has welcomed its presentation in many cases, from *Brown v. Board of Education*[2] to *Robinson v. California*[3] and *Powell v. Texas*.[4] It clearly played a significant role in the abortion decisions—*Roe v. Wade* and *Doe v. Bolton*. Even if the contours of constitutional doctrine should be relatively timeless, immune from the distortions that might result from being subjected to every wind of change in the behavioral sciences, still it is hardly possible, or even desirable, to immunize judges' minds from the influence of scientific knowledge. In the twenty-first century the American Constitution could not be read through the mind of a judge of the eighteenth century, or even of the nineteenth. Science colors our perception, whether we like it or not. Is it not then preferable to make sure that knowledge is fully available to judges, rather than partially and imperfectly? Without the full spectrum of such knowledge on a subject like the one under consideration here, the decisions of judges may reflect a factual perception that is only partly scientific and, in the other part, myth and superstition.

We have already noted that the sodomy laws entered our jurisprudence in an age that knew nothing of modern behavioral science, and they have remained unchanged ever since. In that age, men believed, largely through the influence of the Church's teaching, that human sexuality was a unitary phenomenon: God had made us male and female in order to procreate, and endowed each of us with an instinct to cleave to a member of the opposite sex in order to fulfill this divine plan. All deviance was a perversion of this native instinct and a transgression of the divine plan, and hence immoral, sinful, and finally criminal. We are only now beginning to realize what an inadequate and distorted view of human sexuality this was. Let us now turn to the modern scientific view of how differences in human sexual behavior develop, and homosexuality in particular.

This summary of the scientific view is undertaken with some trepidation, because science never stands still.[5] Scientific concepts undergo continual revision, as observation and experimentation add to the storehouse of data requiring explanation, and as new ideas are put forth which appear more compatible with the data. Often, differing views contend with each other for acceptance, and, at any one time, it may be hard to predict which one eventually will win more or less unanimous assent. In the field of sexuality, the picture is further complicated by the involvement of a number of distinct major disciplines—biology, psychology, psychiatry, sociology, and anthropology—to say nothing of other specialties like biochemistry and neurology. Researchers in one discipline sometimes seem to be unaware of, or to ignore, the findings of those in others. Moreover, one must candidly acknowledge at the outset that scientific understanding of human sexuality is still in its infancy.[6] The powerful taboos of our society have inhibited research and publication in the area of deviant sexuality, and ordinary heterosexual behavior was ignored by science because it was taken for granted. A reliable understanding of deviant phenomena like homosexuality is difficult to obtain when we know so little about ordinary heterosexual development.[7] The general outlines of the scientific view seem already fairly well fixed, however, and unlikely to be radically altered. At whatever points considerable uncertainty or widely differing views remain, these will be noted and discussed.

Human beings, like all other animals, possess sexual organs differentiated into male and female, and the physical processes that accompany their functioning. The generality of humankind also experiences the impulse or drive toward sexual gratification. The extent to which this sex drive is a built-in component of every human being and the extent to which it is a product of conditioning are unknown; undoubtedly, its intensity varies from individual to individual.[8] The problem is why this more or less insistent drive results in such a variety of behaviors in human beings.

One hypothesis suggested early in the era of scientific exploration of human sexuality was that deviant sexuality, such as homosexuality, has a genetic origin.[9] It was thought to be, literally, "degeneracy."[10] A few scientific studies sought to test this assumption. For instance, in a 1952 study, F. J. Kallman investigated homosexuality in identical and fraternal twins, expecting identical twins to show a higher concordance of homosexual orientation if the genetic theory were true.[11] He did find a perfect concordance in the identical twins he studied, but scientists since have discounted the implication of this finding because investigations of other subjects failed to corroborate it.[12] The concordance in his sample could be explained by nearly identical rearing patterns, parental attitudes, and childhood and adolescent experiences.[13] Moreover, if the genetic theory held true, one would expect to find a greater incidence of homosexuality among the parents, siblings, and other relatives of homosexual individuals, but there is no reliable evidence that homosexuality runs in families.[14] Indeed, with heterosexual conjunction necessary for reproduction, homosexuality, if genetically acquired, would be expected to breed out in the long run.

Discovery of the chromosomal basis for physical sex differentiation offered another avenue of investigation. Since the normal pattern of sex chromosomes for females is XX and that for males XY, perhaps deviant sexuality resulted from freaks of nature such as the XO pattern (Turner's syndrome), the XXY pattern (Klinefelter's syndrome), or the XYY pattern. Although the behavior of individuals with such anomalies may show abnormal tendencies (as, *e.g.*, XXY males being more passive and XYY males more violently aggressive than normal males), these chromosome patterns did not show up more often in homosexuals than in heterosexuals.[15]

In short, very few scientists today believe that homosexuality and other forms of deviant sexual behavior have a genetic origin, although it is possible that as the science of genetics progresses, genetic variations will be shown to be directly relevant. Scientists even now do not discount genetic factors completely, but the influence accorded them is an indirect one, as Marmor indicates:

> This reservation does not mean, however, that biological factors are of no importance at all in the genesis of homosexuality. Insofar as a particular kind of bodily appearance, bodily build, or physical incoordination may affect parental or sibling reaction to a child or his ability to participate in peer activities, it may at times play a significant determining part in the gender-role assigned to him by people in his environment or in his inability to identify with his own sexual group. It may thus facilitate an ultimate homosexual object-choice.[16]

The second hypothesis is that hormonal imbalance occurring either throughout the lifetime of the individual or at some critical point in his development may be a determining factor.[17] Males and females both excrete some of the same hormones, but the normally functioning male will produce a preponderance of male sex hormones and the female a preponderance of female hormones. Endocrine malfunction can occur even in individuals who possess the normal complement of sex chromosomes. If it occurs before birth, it may result in various degrees of physical intersexuality, or pseudohermaphroditism.[18] The reproductive apparatus of the human embryo, in its initial stages, is the same in both male and female. Differentiation occurs largely in response to androgenic hormone, the excretion of which is probably triggered in some unknown way by the male, or Y, sex chromosome. This substance causes the undifferentiated apparatus to develop into that which is characteristic of the male; in its absence, female development, at least of the external genitalia, will occur. Thus it is said that the tendency of nature is to produce a female. The hypothesis is that homosexuality in males might be traced to a deficiency of male hormones (androgens), homosexuality in males being thought to have some connection with female-ness. (This idea, as we shall see later, is a myth.) The levels of androgenic substances in the urine or plasma samples of male homosexuals have been compared with those of a heterosexual control group. In some studies, a difference has been found; in others, even ones using the same techniques, none was found.[19] Reports in the popular press of a finding of differences as a significant scientific breakthrough[20] should therefore be discounted. Such a finding, even assuming carefully controlled and accurate testing procedures, may result from an unrepresentative group of individuals having been chosen for the tests or from the fact that hormone levels in the same individual may differ from time to time.[21] Even if such findings were invariably replicated by other investigators with other groups of subjects, the riddle would remain: whether and how the difference is causally relevant. The most plausible explanation would seem to be that lower androgen levels, by reducing the strength of the sex drive, might produce indirectly a change in the individual's self-image (as being somehow less male than his fellows)[22] or put him at a disadvantage in competing for female favors with his more highly sexed peers. Such a causal connection would be hardly more direct than that indicated above for genetically determined factors like body build. At the present time, therefore, claims that homosexuality is "caused" by hormonal imbalance must be viewed with great skepticism.[23]

This skepticism is reinforced by other data. One is that medical science has signally failed in its efforts to "cure" male homosexuality by artificial injections of sex hormones. Injection of large amounts of male hormones, though it may result in physical virilization depending on the subject (e.g., an increase in coarse facial hair), does not alter the direction of the sex drive. It merely increases the frequency and intensity of the drive.[24] Injection of female hormones appears only to depress the drive, again without altering its direction. Similarly, castration of the adult male, though depriving him of the major source of his body's androgen production, does not affect the direction of his sex drive, and, depending on his age and other factors, may have little immediate effect on its frequency and intensity. John Money says,

. . . . [T]he hormones that bring about sexual maturation [at puberty] do not, according to all the evidence available, have any differential determining influence on the psychosexual, male-female direction and content of perceptual, memory, or dream imagery that may trigger or be associated with erotic arousal. On the contrary, there is strong clinical and presumptive evidence . . . that the libido hormone is the same for men and women and is androgen. Psychosexually, the androgenic function is limited to partial regulation of the intensity and frequency of sexual desire and arousal, but not to the cognitive patterns of arousal.[25]

Another fact long known is that the primates, including humans, are far less dependent on gonadal hormones for sexual behavior overall than are lower mammals. In lower species the female's willingness to copulate is restricted to periods of estrus or "heat" and terminates immediately and completely upon spaying. Male copulation with females thus is limited to certain times during the year, or to a single mating season. In humans and other primates, the female's receptivity is not limited by hormonal control to the times during which she could become pregnant, so that male-female sexual behavior can occur at any time.[26] Moreover, in lower species, the sex hormones appear to release innate (or instinctive) sexual behavior, whereas for the primates, including humans, there is evidence that sexual behavior—even ordinary heterosexual copulation—is not innate, but learned.[27]

Some recent data indicate that male sex hormones (androgens) do play a role in the differentiation of sexual behavior into male and female patterns in lower mammals very early in life (in the prenatal or early postnatal period) but not thereafter. In experiments with one species of lower mammals, female behavior in the form of nest building and retrieving could be produced in adult males by injection of female hormones if gonadectomy had been performed immediately after birth. Similarly, male patterns of behavior—mounting, pelvic thrusting, and general aggressiveness—could be produced in adult females by performing an ovariectomy and injecting male hormones at the same critical early period. If these operations were carried out at a later stage of the animal's life, they had no such effect. This evidence supports the idea that the role of the male sex hormone in adulthood is merely to activate pre-established patterns of sexual behavior, but in some critical early period (which varies with the species) its role is organizational; that is, it will differentiate in both males and females a prepotency for the male pattern of sexual behavior.[28]

The extent to which these findings may be applicable to human beings can only be speculated. If they are, they do not necessarily mean that hormones at this critical early stage have any effect on psychosexual object-choice. All we can say from the evidence is that androgen may serve to organize the neural "circuits" so that in adulthood certain stimuli will call forth physical responses and movements characteristic of males, and its absence at the early critical stage will cause the "circuits" to be organized toward producing the responses characteristic of females. But all possible combinations of sexual behaviors and roles are represented in human homosexuality. Most male homosexuals will engage in *both* "masculine" and "feminine" behaviors, and adopt both "insertor" and "insertee" roles, depending on the situation and the partner (though they may, of course, have preferences).[29] Even if these findings might help to explain the effeminate male homosexual and the masculine lesbian who invariably or usually assume the sexual role of the opposite sex with their partners, they seem to be of no help in understanding the masculine male homosexual and the feminine lesbian who play only the traditional role of their own gender in bed, but always with a partner of the same sex. (Although less visible as homosexuals, these may be no less numerous than the others.) Finally, a development commonly seen among male homosexuals is that the same individual changes his pattern of sexual behavior over the span of his lifetime. One who started out taking an insertor role only (supposedly the "masculine" role) when he was young and attractive will switch to the insertee role as he grows older and finds it more and more difficult to get partners.[30]

Human homosexuality, therefore, does not seem to result from physiological promptings to play the sexual role of the opposite sex. Such promptings might exert an indirect or predisposing influence, rendering one individual more susceptible than another to environmental factors favoring homosexual development, but it seems unlikely that such a contrary organization of the neural circuits through hormonal imbalance in fetal life plays a role in the development of homosexuality in a significant number of people. There is no reason to suspect that hormonal imbalance at the neural organizing stage of fetal life would be more frequent than at the stage of genital differentiation, and pseudohermaphroditism is a rarity by comparison with homosexuality.[31]

Most scientists consider it unlikely that endocrine imbalance will prove to be a direct cause of the complex psychic and behavioral phenomenon of homosexuality. D. J. West expresses a general viewpoint: "[A]lthough physical and hereditary factors play a large part in governing the strength of sexual urges, psychological factors are more decisive in channeling these urges into either hetero-sexual or homosexual directions."[32] According to Wardell Pomeroy, "Most workers in this area now lean toward a conditioning theory, although they acknowledge that physical characteristics or other predisposing factors *indirectly* play a part in the development of a homosexual pattern."[33]

This viewpoint has received considerable reinforcement from the research of John Money, the Hampsons, and others with pseudohermaphrodites. They demonstrated the overpowering influ-ence of conditioning and learning in the development of both gender identity—the sense of being male or female—and gender roles. The gender identity, behavior patterns, and orientation of these physically intersexed individuals were found to depend almost entirely on their assignment to and rearing in a particular sex as children. Psychosexual differentiation generally took place in keeping with the assigned sex, even in cases in which the genetic, gonadal, and hormonal sex were at variance with the assigned sex.[34] When such individuals become aware of their biological gender, they still insist on remaining in the sex classification in which they were reared.[35] The point is not that homosexuality develops always or even usually in conjunction with a confusion of gender identity fostered by parental, sibling, and peer-group attitudes toward the growing child. That, as we shall note in a moment, is untrue. The point is that if both the perceived gender identity and the entire complex of behavioral roles and psychic attitudes associated with it can develop in contradiction to biological gender, then it is unlikely that aberration in a single aspect of the whole—sexual attraction or object-choice—will be found to have a physical origin.

In summary, then, the idea that sexual deviance, and homosex-uality in particular, is traceable to constitutional factors is almost certainly false.[36] Homosexuals are not born that way, nor are they the product of glandular malfunction. If, then, they become that way, how and why does this occur? The answer lies in the individual's life experiences.

As one ascends the scale of comparative animal intelligence in the direction of humankind, the organs and glands of the body associated with the sex drive appear to become increasingly subject to interaction with the control centers of the brain.[37] Although our knowledge of precisely how this interaction takes place is increasing, it is still scanty. For the most part, all we can do is to verify the general consequences of this interaction. In the more intelligent species of mammals, and particularly in human beings, it enables the individual to subject his sex drive to a far greater measure of conscious inhibition and control than in other species. At the same time, that drive becomes increasingly subject to conditioning.[38] Even in lower mammals, sexual behavior is subject to modification by conditioning.[39] (When we say that *conditioning* has occurred, we mean that the memory of previous experiences causes a person to respond to certain stimuli and not to others, or to respond in a different way than he might have responded without the previous experience.[40])

Both psychoanalytic theory[41] and behavioral psychology[42] stress conditioning. The former is likely to emphasize early parent-child experiences which the adult can no longer consciously remember (though some of them may, during treatment, be eventually recalled), while the latter emphasizes conscious learning associated with the receipt of rewards and punishments. Both portray, in effect, different facets of the same phenomenon. Sociologists and anthropologists do not disagree with the theory that sexual behavior in humankind is largely the product of conditioning. They add that conditioning can result from general societal structure and influences, as well as from the immediate interaction of the subject with his family and others.[43]

In human beings, the greater measure of conscious control and the accumulated memories stored in the brain lead to more and more variations from the majority pattern of sexual behavior. Greater conscious control has the same consequence here as in other areas of behavior—an increase in experimentation. That such experimentation should produce greater variations in behavior patterns than is found among other mammals is not surprising.[44] The influence of memory in producing variations from the norm is equally if not more important. Since each person's environment and experience are unique, he possesses a complex of memories that are also unique.

Sigmund Freud's extraordinary contribution to human knowledge was his discovery that many of these memories possessing the most powerful and enduring influence on one's behavior are implanted very early in life and progressively if not immediately forgotten. These memories affect sectors of life other than love and sex; but in this sector their interplay with the development of the emotions and of motor reactions and responses may lead to the greatest diversity of desires and behavior,[45] and excessive repression may have the most upsetting and harmful consequences, resulting not only in a general state of unhappiness but also in emotional and physical exhaustion, neurosis, and even psychosis.

Learning and experience affect sexuality in several ways. They contribute to the formation of personal preferences and tastes in sexual partners. They determine the kinds of stimulation and the types of situations that become capable of evoking sexual excitement. Finally, the overt behavior through which this excitement is expressed depends largely on the individual's previous experience.[46]

It should not be assumed that conditioning takes place only or primarily through the individual's own sexual activities. Human beings also become conditioned through vicarious sharing of experience: hearing, viewing, or reading about the activities and responses of others. "Many individuals become strongly conditioned toward or against having particular types of sexual activity, before they have ever had any actual experience of the sort."[47] The role of association is also important: "[S]exual stimulation by things that one sees, hears, smells, or tastes often depends upon the associations which they evoke, rather than upon the direct physical stimulation of the sense organs through which those things are perceived."[48]

A few examples will indicate how these memories could affect patterns of sexual behavior. One person, as the result of pleasurable oral contact with his mother's breasts in infancy, may experience great emotional satisfaction from using his mouth in oral-genital sex play; another may get nothing from it at all. Someone (male or female) whose tendencies toward aggression were early and vigorously suppressed by stern parental controls may discover in later life that passivity in sexual encounters is more satisfying than aggression, or that just the reverse is true. A fear of pregnancy early instilled in a child, or a childhood fascination with feces and elimination whose manifestations were quickly suppressed, may result in a later preference for anal stimulation over vaginal intercourse. Similar examples could be multiplied many times over.

Conscious and subconscious memories affect the direction of a person's sexual desire, the objects that attract him sexually. No one is sexually attracted to everybody of the opposite sex. That some people prefer blondes, others brunettes, is the result of conscious or subconscious memory influence. One may be attracted to a certain personality or set of physical characteristics because some admired or pleasurably remembered figure in his earlier life possessed it. He may feel aversion to other personalities or sets of physical characteristics because of earlier unpleasant experiences with people who possessed them. Sexual likes and dislikes are consequently as various as people. All this is plain enough within the realm of heterosexuality. What often goes unperceived is that the same causative elements are responsible for and generally operative in homosexuality.[49]

In speaking technically of homosexuality and of homosexuals, we must make clear what we are talking about. In this book, the terms are used to denote a definite preferential erotic attraction to members of the same sex, and persons who experience that attraction, respectively.[50] Confusion has arisen in the use of the terms because some have insisted on employing them to cover the entire phenomenon of homosexual behavior.[51] Many people engage in homosexual behavior, however, even to a considerable degree, without feeling a "definite preferential erotic" attraction for their own sex. They may do so for purely opportunistic reasons, such as the unavailability of the opposite sex (in prisons, for instance). Some adolescent males and young men allow older males to fellate them for money or for status in their own peer groups.[52] Other males fantasy and may conceivably act out homosexual behavior, not because of erotic attraction, but in order to relieve certain nonsexual anxieties about their relationships with other males. Those who engage in homosexual behavior because their preferred partners—the opposite sex—are unavailable are often called "facultative homosexuals." Lionel Ovesey has coined the term "pseudo-homosexuals" for those who fantasy homosexual behavior in order to handle certain anxiety-arousing nonsexual feelings, such as feelings involving power and dependency.[53] As we shall see more fully in a moment, nonsexual anxieties can also be at work in producing true, or preferential erotic, homosexuality.[54] On the other hand, there are probably some genuine homosexuals who never engage in homosexual behavior. The psychic phenomenon and the behavioral phenomenon are not coextensive.[55]

Before getting very far into the subject of the development of homosexuality, we must also dispose of some common misconceptions. One is that homosexuals are attracted to everybody of their own sex, and would solicit any and every person of that gender who walks down the street if they dared. This is not true.[56] Homosexuals exhibit the same degrees of selectivity and nonselectivity as the general range of heterosexuals. Many are extremely choosy about sexual partners, others less so.

A second popular belief is that the male homosexual is a person of delicate physique, high-pitched voice, and effeminate mannerisms, who enjoys dressing in the clothes of the opposite sex and prefers the sexual as well as the nonsexual roles of the opposite sex. A stereotype of the female homosexual, or lesbian, is just the converse of this. These stereotypes have caused laymen in general, and much of the scientific literature, to suppose that homosexuality resulted from a confusion of gender identity, or even from a positive identification with the opposite sex.[57]

Both stereotypes are, generally speaking, false. Most male and female homosexuals feel at home in the traditional roles of their biological gender, apart from psychosexual object-choice, and are indistinguishable from their heterosexual counterparts of the same gender in physical appearance, dress, and personality characteristics. Those who resemble or mimic the opposite sex are a comparatively small minority.[58] Most homosexuals do not feel themselves to be, nor do they wish to become, members of the opposite sex.[59] They are happy to be and remain in the gender group to which their physical endowment has assigned them.[60] As we have noted from the studies of pseudohermaphrodites, even gender identity appears to be learned, so it is not surprising to find that gender identity and sexual orientation can be at variance with each other. Learning that one is a male does not necessarily convey the lesson that one must desire females. There are people who do perceive of themselves as members of the opposite sex trapped in an alien body, but experts now classify this as a distinct phenomenon—transsexualism. Transsexuals are people who some-how learned a gender identity in complete contradiction to their actual *and* apparent biological gender. But for a male to say "I feel I am a woman" and to say "I want a man [sexually]" are quite different things.[61] It is perhaps even more difficult to understand that transvestism—dressing in the clothes of the opposite sex—is also distinct from both transsexualism and homosexuality.[62] A number of male homosexuals enjoy dressing as women but identify them-selves as males and would abhor sex-change surgery; and some lesbians prefer to dress in male attire but identify themselves as women. Quite a few male transvestites not only identify themselves as males but also are definitely heterosexual.[63] Various aspects of traditional gender role, such as dress and psychosexual object-choice, may thus be independent of gender identity (the sense of being male or female) and of each other.

Persons whose gender identity is in contradiction to their genetic and anatomical sex—transsexuals—are rare,[64] probably because extraordinary circumstances are required to develop the gender identity of the opposite sex when one's anatomy is unambiguous. Adult transsexuals suffer tremendous inner conflict because of this incongruence between their self-perception and the appearance of their bodies. Gender identity is apparently learned too early in life[65] to permit them to change through psychotherapy. The contemplation of such a change is mind-shattering: "Me" would become "Not Me."[66] Medical science now seems to be coming around to the viewpoint that the only way to help transsexuals is by changing the body to fit the mind. Through sex-reassignment surgery and the administration of hormones, outward physical appearance can be made to approximate the patient's gender identity. The case of Christine Jorgensen is perhaps the most famous instance of such a treatment. None of the cadre of experts working in this new application of psychiatry, surgery, and endocrinology would even consider such a treatment for people who have merely a homosexual orientation. The procedure is deemed appropriate only for applicants whose gender identity is so clearly fixed as the opposite sex that there is no likelihood he or she will ever regret the operation.[67]

If homosexuality has nothing to do with a confusion of gender identity, how and why does it develop? In any attempt to explain the development of homosexuality, three caveats must first be noted.

First, most of the discussion will have to be of male homosexuality because, by comparison, little is known of female homosexuality. The latter has been the object of much less study than has male homosexuality.[68]

Second, the discussion may be valid for our own culture only—European or Western culture, of which America is a part. Homosexuality in non-Western civilizations and among primitive peoples has been observed, but not studied in depth.

Third, we must speak with reservation of the "causes" of homosexuality.[69] Most information on the life experiences that appear to bring about a homosexual orientation has been developed in the course of treatment of patients. Psychotherapists have found that, in the backgrounds of these individuals, certain experiences appear to be more common than in the backgrounds of their heterosexual patients.[70] The causal relationship then inferred, the explanation of how these experiences resulted in a homosexual orientation, is largely the result of intuitive insight on the part of therapist or patient. Cause and effect has not been demonstrated by any reliable scientific method.[71] Many of these life experiences are common and occur in the histories of heterosexuals as well.[72] Since our ethos does not permit experimentation with the development of human beings, we cannot control the variables, and thus may never know with certainty why a particular life experience or configuration of experiences results in homosexuality in one individual but not in another. Finally, all generalization here is hazardous at best. Any one therapist can treat only a relatively small number of cases in a lifetime of work; to generalize about all homosexual patients from the few he sees may be presumptuous. It is probable that most homosexuals never seek psychotherapy, so generalizing from the patient population to the nonpatient population is still more questionable. It is therefore difficult to be confident that the life experiences thought to be common to homosexual patients are equally common among the homosexual population as a whole.[73] Nonetheless, the therapists' intuitive conclusions can be expected to possess some measure of truth, because they ring true to many patients. The factors they have identified can be taken as illustrative but not exhaustive. No single factor can be considered determinative; a wide spectrum of such factors is likely to be present in any one case, and the factors present may vary greatly from case to case.[74]

Some early explanations, which seem now to have been largely discarded, still cloud discussions of the subject. Some of these derive from Freud himself. In the stages of development of the growing infant, he noticed what seemed to him a progression in the centering of erotic feelings, first upon the mouth, then upon the anus, and finally upon the genitals. If development was fixated at, or regressed to, either of the two earlier levels, Freud believed, deviant sexuality might become the characteristic pattern of adulthood.[75] This theory does not, however, explain a homosexual object-choice. Oral and anal stimulation can take place with a heterosexual object-choice as well as with a homosexual one.[76] If the "orally fixated" male homosexual were merely seeking a substitute for the maternal breast, he would come nearer to finding it in the breasts of another female than in the penis of a male.[77]

Freud was also impressed by his observation that most children, between the ages of approximately 6 and 10 or 12, go through a stage of associating almost exclusively with peers of their own sex. This stage, which has been termed the latency period, Freud thought to be an inevitable homoerotic phase in the child's development toward heterosexuality. He postulated a universal bisexual predisposition in human beings, of which this phase was an expression. If the child's development became fixated at this stage, the final, or heterosexual, stage would never be reached.[78] Adult homosexuality was thus seen as merely an immature sexual pattern—the consequence of an arrested development.

Two difficulties stand in the way of this explanation. One is that Freud's postulation of a universal bisexual predisposition rested on a view of the biological nature and physical development of human beings which has since been seriously questioned.[79] The second difficulty is that the so-called latency period appears to be peculiar to our own culture and to a few others. It is not universal. Even in our culture, there is reason to doubt that such a specifically "homoerotic" phase precedes the "heterosexual." Kinsey's investigations showed that heterosexual sex play among children began even earlier than homosexual sex play.[80]

Still another Freudian notion was that when the male child discovered females lacked penises, he might surmise that theirs had been cut off, and his could be, too. The ensuing "castration anxiety" could result in a homosexual orientation, either because of fear that a female whose vagina was penetrated by his own organ might not give it back, or simply because the presence of a penis on one's sexual partner gave reassurance against the anxiety.[81] This explanation, which seems a bit far-fetched, assumes that the "castration anxiety" arises concurrently with the child's first comprehension of sexual intercourse, whereas in our culture the latter is likely to come at a time when he has already acquired a better understanding of why male and female anatomies are different. The explanation also assumes that children have some concept of castration, but this seems less and less likely in our postrural and post-Spock culture, in which children are neither exposed to the sight of it nor threatened with it. Yet this theory caught the imagination of so many people that one still hears it bandied about. It may hold some truth in the case of certain individuals, especially in view of the massive ignorance of human sexuality in which American children are kept, but it can hardly explain homosexuality in the majority of cases.[82]

Other theories and explanations seem more solidly based.[83] In brief, these theories all reduce to the idea that homosexuality is caused by the growing child's perception of himself, of sexuality, and of both sexes in general, inculcated by significant figures in his environment. The following picture is drawn in starkly contrasting lines to help dramatize these psychodynamics for the reader, but the true picture in most cases is much fuzzier. The conditioning that takes place is usually not even explicit. It consists mainly of subtle, nonverbal messages communicated to the child by, for example, facial expressions, gestures, and the ways in which others touch, hold, and otherwise react to or ignore him. The feelings and attitudes that predispose one to a homosexual orientation may therefore be the result of a long process of conditioning which hardly seems to involve stress and conflict at all. (In any event, efforts to speak precisely about human emotions and interactions must perforce be oversimplified, because the human mind cannot be mapped with the precision of a cartographer.[84])

Therapists have noted, in the family backgrounds of their male homosexual patients, an unusually high proportion of overpossessive mothers.[85] Typically, the mother binds the child close to herself, severely restricting his contacts with other children and particularly his freedom to engage in rough-and-tumble play. Although mothers are supposed to be physically affectionate toward their children, her intimacy with the child is excessive, taking on almost the quality of seduction. They may share the same bed. She may dress and undress in front of him in a provocative manner. She may share confidences with him that adults do not usually divulge to children. All in all, she gives him the impression that he is her favorite in all the world, by according him preferential treatment over other siblings and also over her husband. She discourages masculine attitudes and behavior, such as assertiveness, aggression, exploration, experimentation, and, above all, the development of any interest in other females in adolescence. She may also give the boy to understand that she wanted a girl when he was born.[86] Realizing that his birth was a disappointment to her, he may try to make up for it by assuming roles and behavior that are generally considered more appropriate for daughters.

Although in infancy children *are* dependent primarily on the love, nurture, and support of their mothers, the process of growing up consists of learning that one's survival and happiness are progressively less dependent on mother. The son of such a mother as we have described cannot establish, or discover, his independence. By continuing to foster the feeling that he cannot live without her—a feeling realistic enough in infancy but increasingly false as the child grows bigger and stronger—she keeps him tied to her apron strings. Two principal consequences may follow, both of which are inauspicious for heterosexual development. The first is that the boy acquires an image of himself as weak and helpless, needing a protector or protectress. He can envision himself only as the passive, dependent partner in any relationship, especially any relationship with a woman.[87] The second is that the mother's excessive intimacy with him is almost bound to give rise to strong erotic feelings and responses on his part. When these responses are blocked by the mother's adverse reactions, by fear of retaliation by the father, or by realization of the strength of incest taboos, the repression which results may be so severe that it is generalized to all females. In other words, the Oedipal conflict through which most, if not all, children pass is so heightened and magnified that it is never satisfactorily resolved. On the other hand, the son may avoid all erotic involvement with girls, even in fantasy, because he fears losing or betraying his mother's love for him, which, as we have noted, he forever continues to see as all-important to his survival and happiness.[88] Another possibility is that the relationship with his mother was so satisfying that he never again senses the need for deep emotional involvement with any female.

Often such a mother's overt attitudes are decidedly antisexual. She is puritanical and frigid, and conveys to her son clearly that sex is evil and shameful.[89] She makes plain that she wants him to be a "nice" boy, and that girls are of two types—"nice" or "good" girls, and "bad" girls. He draws the conclusion that with "good" girls emotional intimacy is possible, but not sex, because they are sexually frigid like his mother. With "bad" girls, genital contact is possible, but not an emotional relationship.[90] The sensitive boy who has been thus indoctrinated is at a loss when the sex drive becomes powerful in puberty and adolescence. Sex with "bad" girls seems forbidden because there can be no loving relationship to redeem the evil inherent in the act alone; and who could contemplate with any excitement the prospect of going to bed with a "nice" girl? Or he may regard sex with a "nice" girl as being just as tabooed as sex with mother. The thought of heterosexuality thus either evokes shame and guilt or is devoid of interest, giving rise to furtive, substitute outlets like masturbation and homosexual fantasies and behavior. Knowing from himself that even "nice" boys have powerful sexual urges and responses, no such erroneous dichotomy arises in his mind with respect to other males.

The mother may have such an obsession with cleanliness and propriety that she punishes the child for playing with his own organs (something which probably all children naturally do), and convinces him that genitalia are somehow "dirty" and repulsive. Toilet-training controls already internalized in the child's mind are thus extended to all fondling and playing with his genitals, so that erection and orgasm seem as forbidden as bed wetting and accidental bowel movements. The youngster may come to feel fearful and disgusted about sex altogether—terrorized out of his own instincts.[91] Since virtually all the representations of human sexuality that come to his attention in growing up will be of heterosexuality, he may come to label heterosexual behavior as "dirty" and repulsive. Homosexual behavior, as the less conscious alternative, may escape this labeling by default; or homosexuality, even though similarly labeled, may develop in the youngster because he can hide it from the parent much more easily than heterosexuality, thus minimizing the anxiety of getting caught. Few parents recognize homosexual responsiveness and situations as "sexual." The boy's sexuality is, in effect, forced underground, working itself out in ways that give no outward indication of its presence. From a general prohibition on all forms of sexuality, he salvages an inconspicuous part.[92] It is also possible that engaging in genital activity becomes tolerable only in the presence of a person who is not of the same gender as the parent who imposed these prohibitions—mother.[93]

In our culture, prudish parental attitudes have one other consequence that should be considered in discussing the development of homosexuality. It is an almost total lack of information available to children about sex. Whatever information most children get about sex they get from their peers, not their parents, and much of it is misinformation. If they get anything at all from their parents, it is likely to consist of warnings against and prohibitions on heterosexual contacts. Other than perhaps some minimal knowledge that such contacts produce babies, there is seldom any instruction in what sexuality is all about—how both male and female gain and give maximum pleasure from and to each other—much less any opportunities provided for learning and experimentation. If, as we have noted, even simple heterosexual copulation must be learned, it is not surprising that many fail to learn.[94] In such a culture, there are bound to be deviations from a "norm" that is kept so carefully under wraps.[95] Especially is this true of males. How are "nice" boys supposed to learn, if "nice" girls are supposed to be virgins? Of course, the old double standard used to hold sway: Boys were supposed to learn with prostitutes and other "bad" girls, then marry virgins. A boy whose scruples would not permit him to accept that standard felt excluded from heterosexuality, unless he happened to discover through chance that "nice" girls were not necessarily as cold and prudish as he had been led to believe. Actually, the problem is not so much a deficit in learning about the physical techniques of mating behavior as it is a deficit in learning about their emotional accompaniments.[96] Human intelligence and capacity for experimentation can quickly overcome the former type of ignorance, given a cooperative partner, but the damage done by a misunderstanding of the emotional component of sexuality is likely to be irrevocable.

With heterosexuality so fraught with ignorance, mystery, inhibitions, and taboos—particularly the horrifying possibility of the
unwanted pregnancy—homosexuality may appear to be a far less
fearful alternative. Although it is doubtful that any children in our
culture grow up completely without knowledge of the social taboo
on homosexual behavior, this taboo may be much less influential at
the formative stages of their sexual development than later. While
they are still living at home under parental domination, parental
prohibitions are more strongly felt than those emanating from the
larger society.[97] Parents, it seems, never think to counsel their
children against homosexuality, perhaps because they regard this as
a development too abominable to contemplate, but more likely
because it never occurs to them that this is one of the possible
directions in which their child may develop. Unknown to them, the
child may be getting the covert message that homosexuality is less
undesirable than heterosexuality.[98]

Parental warnings against heterosexual contacts are undoubtedly
reinforced to some degree by antisexual attitudes deeply embedded
in the American cultural background. Despite all the permissiveness thought to be presently characteristic of American culture,
one must always remember that it is at best just that. In books,
sermons, magazine articles, and even in movies and on television,
coitus between single persons is still often either condemned, or
considered an unavoidable evil, or thought to be justified only in
the narrow circumstance of a couple who are seriously in love and
contemplating marriage. A casual toss on the hay is still depicted as
morally deviant. The ideal articulated by many, at least for girls
and often for boys as well, is virginity until marriage and lifelong
fidelity thereafter. And since marriage is something to be
postponed as far into the future as possible, to make sure that it
represents a "mature" choice of the lifelong partner and to afford
opportunity for the acquisition of a good education (getting ahead
in the world being of primary importance), youngsters can hardly
avoid the impression that heterosexuality is largely interdicted.[99]
Coitus is free from the taint of "wrong" only within marriage, so
lust must be equally wrong except in that circumstance.[100]

This fear and guilt about sex is reflected in our society's paranoid
attitude toward obscenity and pornography. Any movie that
depicts a bedroom scene is prohibited to children, but we let them
witness huge amounts of murder and violence. The word "sin" in

popular usage has come to have no connotation other than a sexual one. Other cultures in the world take a much more positive view of human sexuality than ours does. In them, no moral taint attaches to lust; on the contrary, sexuality is looked upon as one of the greatest joys in life. Young people of both sexes are encouraged to learn to be good sexual partners before marriage. Not only are they encouraged to experiment with one another; they are even *taught* sexual expertise by their elders. Commitment may come into being, but is reserved to a time when the individual, having experienced a variety of partners, is better equipped to know what kind of person will suit him best over the long run. In some of these sex-positive cultures homosexuality seems literally unheard of.[101] It therefore may be one of the overhead costs of our generally sex-negative culture.[102]

In the words of Stanley Willis,

> It seems a paradox that there are countless numbers of people whose overzealous childhood morality has resulted in a psychosexual state which will allow their sole adult sexual outlet to be one considered immoral by the very same society which conditioned the earlier excessive pressures toward morality. This childhood "morality" has created, in effect, an inhibiting prohibition of a choice of sex object which otherwise would have been made during the normal course of sexual maturation.[103]

A critical figure in the boy's sexual development is the father. If the father's attitude toward the son is characterized by detachment, aloofness, and lack of sympathy, or, even worse, by open hostility and rejection, the child will respond with fear and hatred. If the father is weak and submissive, the son may learn to regard him with contempt.[104] Either response precludes identification with the father,[105] and thus interferes with the child's assimilation of those roles usually associated with masculinity in our culture, including sexual interest in females.

In his desire to be as little like his father as possible, the boy may identify with his mother, absorbing the roles and attitudes associated with femininity. Or, in flight from the all-enveloping feminine influence of his mother, he may seek to salvage his masculinity by looking outside the home for one or more super-males upon whom to model himself. The result in both cases may be a homosexual orientation, because the boy who has missed the experience of love, warmth, and physical affection in his own father is likely to be set on a lifelong search to fulfill his yearnings for it through reparative relationships with other males.[106] And, at least in our culture, he is unlikely to find other males willing to fulfill these needs of his without sexual involvement. In the one case, his personality may take on a feminine cast;[107] and in the other, it may be hypermasculine. The latter type of personality is hardly more conducive to heterosexual adjustment than the former, because the contempt for women's ways and the overall devaluation of females engendered by a hypermasculine identification interfere just as seriously with the development of heterosexual interests.[108] Companionship between males and females requires some measure of mutual empathy and respect. Moreover, an individual with such a hypermasculine identification is unlikely to feel comfortable with it. Engaged in a never-ending struggle to prevent its erosion, he shuns all contact with females for fear of being engulfed by their feminizing influence. There is indeed some evidence that male homosexuals tend to cluster at both extreme ends of the spectrum in tests for masculine and feminine attitudes, with heterosexuals falling more in the middle.[109] This evidence would seem to confirm that they generally followed more divergent paths to an adult self-image than the heterosexuals, for lack of the usual and easier route of identification with one's father. These consequences of a boy's failure to identify with his father, can, of course, also occur in case the father is deceased or simply absent from the home for a variety of reasons.[110]

Some psychiatrists are firmly convinced that the emotion which lies at the root of a homosexual orientation in males is anxiety over one's own sense of masculinity. If one's masculine identity is seriously deficient, as in the case of the effeminate homosexual, or is precarious, as in the case of even the hypermasculine type, sexual contact with another of the same sex may be viewed as providing needed booster shots of extra manliness.[111] This conviction gains support from several observations: (1) Many American male homosexuals obtain great satisfaction from fellating other males to orgasm and swallowing the semen—behavior which appears to seek a magical incorporation of the other's masculine essence.[112] (2) The desirability of a sexual partner is often measured in terms of the size of his genitalia—what Donald Webster Cory has characterized as the "mystique of the gigantic penis."[113] (3) The need for contact that some homosexuals experience seems far in excess of what one would expect in terms of sexual drive, even granting allowance for variation among individuals in its frequency and intensity. In other words, some homosexuals appear to need and seek far more sexual outlets than "normal." This phenomenon may be more understandable if sexual contact serves primarily to bolster the individual's fading masculine self-esteem, because its effectiveness in this respect is likely to be fleeting. (4) Often male homosexual relationships seem extraordinarily unstable and impermanent, even granting allowance for the undermining effect of social stigma and the greater tendency of the male toward promiscuity. The instability may in part be due to the fact that repeated sexual contact with the same partner provides diminishing returns in making up a felt deficiency within oneself, compared with perpetually new sexual conquests. Of course, fear of being deficiently male is not peculiar to homosexuals; it may equally lie at the root of heterosexual Don Juanism.

Paternal attitudes of aloofness, or rejection, can have any number of roots. The father may just not like the child's looks. Or the boy may not fit the man's image of what his son should be like. This is especially likely if the boy shows signs of being weak, passive, timid, fearful, and uninterested in sports. Many fathers in our society are so taken with the ideal of the virile he-man that they are constantly on watch to make sure that their sons are developing in accordance with these expectations. If the boy does not, the father may reject him. It may also be that many fathers in our society avoid being physically affectionate with their sons, because their own anxieties about homosexuality make them fearful that such contacts will breed it in their sons.[114] By pushing the child away, they succeed only in fostering the very condition they are most concerned to prevent.

Another frequent shortcoming is the failure of fathers to realize that a successful heterosexual adjustment in a society in which females have been largely forbidden to take the initiative depends on the development of a good measure of masculine assertiveness. Yet such assertiveness can hardly develop unless the father gives the growing boy considerable leeway, some independence of action. Indeed, he must tolerate rebellion to a degree. The rigid authoritarian who will brook no assertiveness in his son is unconsciously depriving the boy of the preconditions for heterosexual development. His excessive discipline of the child reinforces the latter's dependence on Mother and his attitudes and feelings of fearfulness, timidity, and weakness. Anyone who has observed the scene in "gay" bars is struck by the fact that so many of the patrons seem to stand around for hours waiting for someone else to make the first move—so much so that the place takes on almost the appearance of a wax museum. Although some observers feel that the explanation lies in the fact that the individuals involved are waiting for their perfect masculine ideal to walk through the door (and he never does), or in an inordinate fear of rejection,[115] it may equally be attributable to simple lack of initiative.

Some psychiatrists believe that the father's influence on the boy's sexual development is far more important than the mother's. They assert that, regardless of the mother's attitudes and behavior, homosexuality will not develop in the child if he has a warm, loving, and supportive father. Not one of their homosexual patients had a good relationship with his father. Many positively hated their fathers.[116] These assertions gain support from psychological interview data, which give clear evidence that a father's sex anxiety is far more influential in feminizing his son than the mother's. On the other hand, these data seem also to indicate that it is the mother's severity of aggression control which is influential, not the father's.[117]

Quite often, the parent-child relationships just described are at least in part the consequence of a bad relationship between the parents themselves. A woman locked into a marriage with a man she does not love and may even actively despise is quite likely to turn to her son for the love and affection she cannot get from her husband, especially if her own strict attitudes to sex preclude divorce or adultery or she feels her attractions are not sufficient to win the kind of man she really wants. Not surprisingly, too, many women who feel hostility toward men in general nevertheless marry one of them in order to have a family of their own and avoid the stigma of spinsterhood. Thus, lacking any emotional satisfaction from her husband, the mother develops the close-binding intimate relationship with her boy so likely to produce in him a homosexual orientation, and subtly discourages his interest in girls because, having no other source of love herself, she dreads being replaced in his affections by another female. Or she may "emasculate" him as a sort of revenge upon the male sex in general, or as a defense against anxiety aroused by male sexual assertiveness.

The father may become jealous of the love and attention she showers on the boy, and this jealousy poisons his own relationship with the child. The mother may convey to the child her feelings of contempt for the father, by dominating him and openly minimizing him.[118] Or she may foster feelings of fear and revulsion in the child by depicting the father as a brute, a clod, and a victimizer. The father may react with anger or infidelity, or by withdrawing into his shell—becoming a cipher in the household—thus confirming the negative picture the mother has planted in the child's mind. Or, especially if he is an immature and emotionally unstable person himself, he may vent his frustrations in physical brutality against the child. (In no level of our society, sad to say, is it taboo for a man to strike his child, but at least in the middle and upper levels it is taboo for him to strike his wife. One is supposed to have some disciplinary reason before striking a child, but even slight pretexts can be used by a father for taking out his own frustrations—sexual or otherwise—on his children. The battered child syndrome is only the worst manifestation of this phenomenon.) Many homosexuals seen in therapy have been found to be veterans of such intense parental warfare and harsh paternal punitiveness.[119]

One should not assume that either parent involved in these relationships with the child is aware of the harm being done to the child's sexual development. The parent does not conceive of these interactions as having any effect on the child's adult sexual adjustment.[120] The mother honestly believes that her protectiveness is needed because the child is weak and sickly.[121] Her excessive affection and intimacy are just part of being an unusually dedicated mother. And many a mother inhibits identification with the father for the very good reason that he does not represent her ideal of masculinity. She may have failed in her efforts to make him over again in the image she prefers, but she can do much to prevent the child from growing up to be like him.

Physical timidity, lack of assertiveness, and other personality traits fostered by the factors just discussed make it difficult for the child to cope with his peers. Children as a group are notorious for their cruelty to other children. The boy who is excessively fearful and therefore avoids fights and all forms of rough-and-tumble play is mistreated and humiliated by the gang. Ostracized by other boys, he becomes a "lone wolf" or plays predominantly with girls.[122]

In some people homosexuality may serve as a reparative device for "chronically insufficient self-love and poorly defined self-image, that has persisted since childhood."[123] In other words, it may be essentially narcissistic. Impairment of self-love in childhood results in the individual's preference in adulthood for a sex-love object anatomically like himself—hence unconsciously identical with himself. Sexual interaction with another male thus becomes a means of bolstering one's own self-love—a necessity for psychological survival and not simply an outlet for erotic pleasure.[124]

A pattern of unsatisfactory relations with peers, once established in childhood, may produce effects extending into puberty and adolescence. Falling far short of the group's standards for an "all-American" boy, the particular youngster may be shunned by girls when dating patterns begin.[125] Rebuffed in his first tentative advances toward girls on a sexual level, he may decide that the game is not worth the candle, rationalize that he is not really interested in the opposite sex anyway, and retreat into homosexual fantasies.[126] Rejection is so painful and embarrassing that he dare not risk it. It evokes the memory of those humiliating rejections by his peers in childhood, because, like them, it takes place in the context of a competitive peer-group "game"—the dating and mating game. Already convinced that he is lacking in prowess, masculinity, or just plain attractiveness, because he never learned in earlier peer-group activities that he could compete successfully, such a youngster chooses to sit it out.[127] His sexual urges, however, refuse to be quelled, and so turn almost unavoidably toward members of his own sex, because homosexuality does not put him so conspicuously to the test.[128]

Peer-group rejection may promote a homosexual orientation in other ways. The boy who is excluded from the gang is hurt by the rejection, no matter how much he may pretend to disdain the others. Wanting to be accepted, he envies those who are and wants to be like them. These feelings of envy and emulation, directed particularly at those boys who come closest to the group's masculine ideal, can easily become sexual.[129] A powerful longing to be like another can give rise to a yearning to possess the other sexually, especially if the former desire appears to be forever incapable of fulfillment.[130] Or the mere presence of other males who exemplify the masculine ideal may arouse anxieties akin to those the youngster felt when he saw other boys accepted and extolled and himself rejected and humiliated. He manages to neutralize these anxieties through homosexual fantasies or contact with such males, either through the feelings of superiority which a sexual "conquest" engenders or through the feelings of acceptance which the other's consent to erotic contact provides.[131] Incongruous though it may seem, even fear of other males resulting from mistreatment and humiliation by one's peers or the brutality of one's father can promote a homosexual orientation itself. By conceiving of other males as love objects, a boy can counter the threat of aggression and neutralize his fear.[132] Such a psychological feat is not so surprising. A similar behavioral phenomenon has been observed among other mammals. Male monkeys defeated in a fight have been known to assume the female coital posture to forestall further attacks by the victor.[133] Of course, the "peers" who evoke these feelings of jealousy, emulation, or fear may often be siblings rather than unrelated individuals.

Harry Stack Sullivan suggested still another possible explanation of the way in which homosexual orientation can develop from a youngster's being out of step with his peers before puberty.[134] The latency period in which boys congregate almost exclusively with boys and girls with girls seems to serve a generally felt need of children at this age for intimacy with their peers of the same sex. This is particularly evident in the chum relationships so characteristic of the period before puberty. In the normal sequence of events, this need for intimacy arises and is satisfied before the lust dynamism sets in (that is, before sexual desires become urgent and specific). The boy satisfies his need for intimacy with his peers prepubertally, and is then ready to direct his attention to the opposite sex when his sexual urges become powerful. But in a number of cases early sexual maturation brings in the lust dynamism before this need is satisfied,[135] or, for many of the reasons already noted, sexual maturation may arrive normally while the need still remains unfulfilled. This simultaneous coincidence of the lust dynamism and the need for intimacy may result in the boy's sexual desires and fantasies becoming attached to his own gender.

Perhaps a good many homosexuals were also late bloomers as far as physical maturation is concerned. If a youngster's development of the more bulky musculature, body hair, low-pitched voice, and mature facial appearance characteristic of adult males occurs later in time than in his age-mates, he is under a handicap in social maturation.[136]

Throughout this discussion it should be evident that much of the difficulty in the achievement of a heterosexual adjustment comes from our society's definition of gender attributes as strongly contrasting. In our culture, the ideal adult male and the ideal adult female are at opposite poles in both physical characteristics and personality traits. Moreover, our extreme competitiveness in sexual matters places a high premium on masculine attractiveness in men and on feminine attractiveness in women, that is, on each individual's coming close to the culture's gender ideal. Yet natural variation makes it inevitable that many men's bodies and personalities will diverge far from the ideal, and many women's as well. So it is not too surprising that those unable or unwilling to live up to these cultural expectations will tend to take refuge in homosexuality. Cultures lacking such a stark contrast between their "ideals" of the male and the female probably have a much lower incidence.[137]

Another cultural factor that probably contributes to the development of a homosexual orientation on the part of many is the segregation of males from females beginning with the approach of puberty. In many if not most situations (particularly sleeping arrangements), girls are kept separate from boys. Such a temporary purdah almost ensures that boys' first experience of interpersonal sexuality to the point of orgasm will be with each other—usually consisting of mutual masturbation.[138] Moreover, in gymnasium locker rooms, dormitories, and the like, boys have far greater opportunities to view each others' nude bodies than they have to view those of girls. Not only do most boys evince a great deal of interest in male genitalia; they also commonly engage in considerable admiration and comparison of each other's bodies.[139] "This admiration can take the form of being sexually aroused by the others, and out of this comes the desire to have sex with the body of another person."[140] Deprivation of free and easy contacts between the sexes at this formative stage of sexual development—probably dictated by our society's preoccupation with safeguarding female virginity—can thus result in youngsters' fixing their sexual fantasies and responses upon the only available objects—their own gender group.[141]

This "accidental" attachment of lust to the boy's own sex through his being thrown continually together with other males may be more common than psychiatric theory has been ready to admit. The role of association in the development of fetishism is well recognized. A chance occurrence linking the first erection and orgasm with some physical object or unrelated event (such as a nearby automobile crash) may cause the individual to associate that object or event with sexual excitement and pleasure.[142] Young boys experience spontaneous erection in a great many nonsexual situations, particularly those evoking a strong emotional response, such as anger, fright, and pain.[143] In the innumerable contacts, particularly physical contacts, that occur between boys in the period from prepuberty on through adolescence, as in games, sports, playful wrestling, fights, and so on, spontaneous erections are bound to occur often. Eventually, the situations or objects—other boys—with which these erections were associated become independently capable of provoking sexual arousal.

Another factor not to be overlooked is simply love. Strong affectional bonds can develop between two males (or between two females) just as they can develop between any two human beings. Yet the model of adult behavior in our society bans all expression of this affection between males in the ways we came to accept as natural in childhood—embracing and kissing. Indeed, beyond the handshake and a clap on the back, our society permits no physical expression of love or affection between males. It even inhibits verbal expression.[144] By contrast, females are permitted to express their feelings for each other openly in embraces and kisses, as well as in words. A boy, then, who experiences these emotions toward another boy may conclude that he must be "queer," that it is abnormal or wrong even to *feel* love for another male. Perceiving himself as some sort of pariah, his experimentation with females becomes even more inhibited. He fears to test his feelings toward either sex by acting upon them, and finds his anxiety building until he becomes obsessed with this conviction, eventually entering the "gay" world a self-proclaimed homosexual. He thus misses the discovery that love and sex, though often intertwined,[145] need not necessarily be so. Had he felt freer to express himself physically with both sexes, he might have learned that it is possible to love both, but that sexual activity is more rewarding with females.[146]

From this discussion of certain factors believed to be significant in the development of homosexuality, it should be clear that the conditioning of the sexual drive toward one's own gender need not involve overt sexual acts at all. A boy may become homosexual without ever having had a homosexual experience in the sense of being intentionally stimulated physically by another male. If and when he does eventually engage in an explicitly sexual act with another male, it is usually because he experiences an intense desire to do so from having already fantasied such contact many times over. Conditioning in terms of psychosexual object-choice is a far cry from simple Pavlovian conditioning of physical stimulus and pleasurable response. It is also a far cry from the simple aversive conditioning which occasionally results from a single traumatic experience. It is more often a pervasive and complex condition-ing—both affirmative toward the one gender and aversive toward the other—resulting from a multitude of influences operating over the whole period of growing up.

The idea that homosexuality results from seduction of children and adolescents by older homosexuals is conspicuous by its absence from the scientific literature. Therapists do indicate that some of their patients report having been thus seduced, but seduction is clearly a much rarer phenomenon than many police officials and moralists would lead one to believe.[147] If homosexuality is the product of conditioning, such an experience could have, theoret-ically, a favorable effect upon its development. But psychiatrists and psychologists believe that, even in those cases where seduction does occur, the normally developing youngster either would never have responded to the advances initially or, if he did allow the act, would look back on it as an occurrence of no significance—a pure lark. It acquires significance only if the boy's prior life experiences have already predisposed him to a homosexual orientation, if the act satisfies some emotional needs in addition to giving mere physical pleasure and release of tension.[148] Their view of the relative insignificance of such an experience would appear confirmed by the evidence that young men who genuinely feel their interests to be heterosexual but who make their living off homosexuals by hustling, even for a period of years, eventually give it up and settle down to the usual pattern of heterosexual marriage, apparently none the worse for wear.[149]

Finally, it should be noted that the operative factors may not be entirely confined to childhood, puberty, and adolescence. Some factors more likely to be felt in an adult setting could exert an influence.[150] Moreover, once one enters the "gay" world, whatever his reasons, he is inevitably pulled into homosexual sex acts, simply because that is what everyone there expects of him. A certain amount of positive conditioning toward homosexuality may then result, especially if the individual lacks prior extensive heterosexual experience. And a fair number of males in our antisexual society reach adulthood without such experience. In this regard, it is important to note that both the "gay" subcultures and the larger society tend to label anyone "homosexual" who has had even one homosexual experience. If he is fearful and uncertain of himself generally where sex is concerned—and a great many Americans are—this labeling by others may cause him to label himself the same way, even though there is very little justification for it. Aware of the psychoanalytic theory that people possess repressed, unconscious urges, he may accept uncritically this societal assessment of himself, and then feel even more guilty and inhibited about seeking relationships with the opposite sex. Such a person may end up a committed homosexual because he never really permitted himself the chance to resolve his uncertainty about sex through extensive heterosexual experience.[151] In other words, he might have discovered that his own preference was for the opposite sex but for having been locked into homosexuality through society's simplistic efforts to label everybody either "queer" or "straight."[152]

It is also important to note that any single male who enters the "gay" world, especially if he is young and handsome, is likely to find that opportunities for sexual gratification are much more plentiful and easy to come by than in the "straight" world. Though sexual frequencies for male homosexuals are not as high as they are for married men, they probably surpass those of unmarried heterosexual males, at least in large urban communities with homosexual meeting places and social institutions. So one whose sex drive is especially high and persistent may stick with homosexual outlets in preference to the rather uncertain chance of finding girls to go to bed with him. Moreover, aside from prostitutes, getting an unattached female into bed usually takes considerable investment of time and energy. Not many women will go to bed with a stranger without at least some social preliminaries. Yet homosexual contacts are frequently made without either partner having spoken a word. Those, therefore, who for various reasons have little time to invest in the search for sexual gratification may become habituated to homosexual outlets because they are quick and cheap. And habits once established are difficult to break.[153]

No discussion of psychosexual development would be complete without mention of the phenomenon of bisexuality. A number of people engage concurrently or alternately in heterosexual *and* homosexual behavior, either during some particular period in life or even throughout their lives. (In order to avoid confusion with the old Freudian notion of physical bisexuality, this behavioral manifestation could better be termed "ambisexuality.") It is quite misleading to attempt to classify all persons as either heterosexual or homosexual. If human sexuality is not a unitary phenomenon, it is equally plainly not even a dual one. Kinsey's pioneering investigation demolished that oversimplification. His group discovered they had to place their subjects along a continuum ranging from those at one end whose experience had been completely homosexual to those at the other whose experience had been completely heterosexual. The experience of those in between fell at different points along the scale, representing varying mixtures of homosexual and heterosexual experience. Doubtless, the same variations exist in feelings and emotions—some people experiencing homosexual attraction more frequently or of greater intensity, others less, and many none at all.[154]

Two points of clarification should be made about this matter. The first is that treating early experiences in life as being on a par with later experiences can give an inaccurate picture.[155] The homosexual experiences of most people with both types of experience consist of a few experiments in prepuberty, puberty, or adolescence.[156] Their adult pattern is exclusively heterosexual because they developed fairly early a definite preference for the opposite gender as sexual partners. It is therefore wrong to classify such persons as ambisexual. The true ambisexual is one who engages in sexual activities with both kinds of partners as a habitual pattern, not an experiment.

The second point is that one should not assume that these

individuals have no preferences between males and females. They are not some kind of singularly undiscriminating Don Juan. They can and do engage in sex with both genders because their sexual feelings toward the two are different.[157] For instance, a man may prefer to make love to a woman when he feels tender, gentle, and protective. But when he feels aggressive, dominating, and powerful, he may find sexual excitement and satisfaction only through "raping" another male.[158] Conversely, many men often enjoy the experience of sexual submission, allowing the other partner to take over and possess them. Such alternation of roles can and does take place in a heterosexual context, but if a man is unable to experience this sensation with his wife or with females in general, he may seek other males for it. Various other emotions and feelings that a man for some reason cannot satisfy with women—some of which he may find impossible to explain—can impel him toward homosexual contact. Many homosexuals report that married men not infrequently have contacts of these sorts with them.[159] Martin Hoffman reports this kind of behavior in his description of "Tom" in *The Gay World*.[160]

Some psychiatrists such as Bieber dogmatically classify all these men as homosexuals,[161] but it stretches one's credulity to believe that all of them are either sexually inactive with their wives or engage in intercourse with them perfunctorily and without enjoyment, and would really prefer to have another male at all times. What is amazing is that such individuals cross back and forth over the rigid line between homosexuality and heterosexuality in violation of the mores both of the "gay" world and of the "straight" world.[162] So far the phenomenon has been very little studied, because such people—particularly the married ones—are rather inaccessible to research.[163] (Of course, women as well as men may be ambisexual.)

What is known of lesbianism tends to confirm that the life experiences which predispose one to it are somewhat comparable to those of male homosexuals.[164] Among lesbians, the mother-father-child triangle again seems highly relevant. The young girl may be unable to identify with her mother, and come to view the female roles in our society with great aversion.[165] She may experience such intense hostility to the father that she comes to view all men in the same light.[166] Or she may become and remain so deeply attached to the father that all men represent him to some extent and are therefore incestuous objects. Desertion or rejection by, or loss of the father, may interfere with her development of a close and intimate relationship with another man.[167] It was such a painful experience that she avoids the risk of its repetition with other males. Family and societal taboos upon hetero- sexuality—particularly fear of pregnancy—play their part.[168] And often the same deficient relationships with one's peers of the same sex in childhood appear in case histories of lesbians as appear in the histories of male homosexuals.[169]

The difference in the incidence of male and female homosexual- ity in our culture, assuming Kinsey's estimates do present the true picture,[170] may be attributable in part to two factors: (1) In our culture, women need not take the initiative in establishing heterosexual relationships, this being the male's prerogative. (2) Women do not have to experience psychic arousal in order to have intercourse, whereas for a male coitus is impossible unless he can get an erection. Moreover, women can remain passive throughout the entire sequence, because it is simply assumed that males will take the active role. Both factors may decrease in females the effect that fears and inhibitions have in preventing the development of heterosexual relationships and the occurrence of heterosexual experimentation.[171] Women who possess such inhibitions may thereby lose them through finding that they do not really reflect reality, or may tolerate them in order to gain the nonsexual rewards of a heterosexual adjustment.[172] Males possessed of such fears find it much more difficult to do either.[173]

All the preceding discussion indicates, if nothing else, that human sexuality, including homosexuality, is an extremely complex and variable thing, and that one must, above all, beware of oversimplification and dogmatism. Before leaving this subject of how psychosexual differences develop, it is necessary to undertake an extensive digression in order to examine a much disputed issue: whether homosexuality ought to be regarded as pathological, and whether it can be "cured" or changed by "treatment." As will be noted later, the resolution of this issue may be of significance for certain lines of argumentation about the constitutionality of the sodomy laws. This book cannot, of course, resolve the issue, but clarification and critique of the various competing notions should serve to enhance understanding of the entire phenomenon of homosexuality and make possible a clearer picture of the various alternative stances that society might realistically take toward it. Without such an appraisal it is difficult to see the constitutional issues in proper perspective.

NOTES

1. An outstanding up-to-date exposition of scientific knowledge about human sexuality in general is found in H. A. KATCHADOURIAN & D. T. LUNDE, FUNDAMENTALS OF HUMAN SEXUALITY (1972). This book should be required reading for all, including the legal profession, who have occasion to deal with problems in this area.

2. 347 U.S. 483 (1954).

3. Note 2, Chapter 9 *infra.*

4. Note 12, Chapter 9 *infra.*

5. And also because I am not an expert in any of the disciplines in question. I have endeavored, however, to present as full and accurate a summary as I can. It might have been preferable to refer the reader to a single book by an expert, but the information presented here has had to be culled from many diverse sources.

6. The fact of the matter is that we really don't know so much as we think we do about sex. The amount of solid research data on sex behavior is so meager that we can truly say we are still in the Dark Ages. There are fewer than a hundred research projects in this field that could be said to meet the requirements of being statistically adequate, theoretically sound and pragmatically important. No other area of human behavior remains so unexplored.

W. B. POMEROY, GIRLS AND SEX 18 (1969). *See also* M.S. WEINBERG & A. P. BELL, HOMOSEXUALITY: AN ANNOTATED BIBLIOGRAPHY ix–xiii (1972), where they emphasize how inadequate and unscientific most "research" on homosexuality has been. Our knowledge of general human physiology is extensive, but we did not know precisely what physical changes occurred in the male or the female body during sexual arousal and orgasm until the work of Masters and Johnson, published in W. H. MASTERS & V. E. JOHNSON, HUMAN SEXUAL RESPONSE (1966) and HUMAN SEXUAL INADEQUACY (1970).

7. Virtually all the literature on homosexuality is marred by the failure of its authors to take account of the fact that heterosexuality is just as much a problematic situation for the student of human behavior as is homosexuality. The only reason it does not seem to us a problem is because we take its existence for granted. However, we should know enough about science by now to realize that it is just those questions we take for granted that are the ones, when properly asked, which would open up new areas of scientific exploration. The question should really be put as follows: "Why

does a person become sexually excited . . . when confronted with a particular kind of stimulus?"
M. HOFFMAN, THE GAY WORLD 30 (Bantam ed. 1969) [hereinafter cited as HOFFMAN].

8. Beach, *Experimental Studies of Mating Behavior in Animals*, in SEX RESEARCH—NEW DEVELOPMENTS 120–23 (J. Money ed. 1965), alludes to experiments with rats and mice, which tend to show that they can be *bred* to have different levels of sex drive. Young, Goy, & Phoenix, *Hormones and Sexual Behavior, id.* at 180–81, indicate other experiments show that different strains of guinea pigs can be bred to exhibit different facilities and frequencies of specific characteristics of sexual behavior. *See also* Phoenix, *Sexual Behavior: Animal Sexual Behavior*, in 14 INT'L ENCY. SOCIAL SCIENCES 194, at 196 (1968).

9. A good discussion of the genetic and chromosomal research here alluded to is found in Pare, *Etiology of Homosexuality: Genetic and Chromosomal Aspects*, in SEXUAL INVERSION 70 (J. Marmor ed. 1965) [hereinafter cited as SEXUAL INVERSION].

10. This was the hypothesis of what was probably the most influential work on the subject in the nineteenth century: R. VON KRAFFT-EBING, PSYCHOPATHIA SEXUALIS—A MEDICO-FORENSIC STUDY (1887).

11. *See* Kallman, *Comparative Twin Study on the Genetic Aspects of Male Homosexuality*, 115 J. NERVOUS & MENTAL DISEASE 283 (1952); Kallman, *Twin and Sibship Study of Overt Male Homosexuality*, 4 AM. J. HUMAN GENETICS 136 (1952). Actually, it is possible for monozygous twins to be cytogenetically discordant. *See* Money, *Sexual Dimorphism and Homosexual Gender Identity*, 74 PSYCHOLOGICAL BULL. 428 (1970).

12. *See* Rainer *et al., Homosexuality and Heterosexuality in Identical Twins*, 21 PSYCHO-SOMATIC MEDICINE 251 (1960); Parker, *Homosexuality in Twins: A Report on Three Discordant Pairs*, 40 BRIT. J. PSYCHIATRY 489 (1964). *See also* Heston & Shields, *Homosexuality in Twins: A Family Study and a Registry Study*, 18(2) ARCHIVES OF GENERAL PSYCHIATRY 149 (1968).

13. *See* Marmor, *Introduction*, in SEXUAL INVERSION 6–8.

14. "There is no convincing evidence . . . that female homosexuality arises from a genetic predisposition. The female homosexuals that have been studied and reported in the literature do not come from families in which there have been significant numbers of other homosexual individuals." Wilbur, *Clinical Aspects of Female Homosexuality*, in SEXUAL INVERSION 272.

15. *See* Money, *Sexual Dimorphism and Homosexual Gender Identity*, 74 PSYCHOLOGICAL BULL. 427 (1970). This statement should perhaps be qualified by noting the existence of some evidence that individuals with Klinefelter's syndrome tend to show a higher incidence of homosexuality than genetically normal males.

16. Marmor, *Introduction*, in SEXUAL INVERSION 7–8. *See also* Pritchard, *Homosexuality and Genetic Sex*, 108 J. MENTAL SCI. 616–23 (1962). The same view is echoed by Albert Ellis:

Thus, a given male may be born with a tendency to be highly sexed, to be physically small and weak, and to be timid and passive in his social relations. If so, he will tend to desire *some* form of sexuality to a high degree, but may feel that (in our competitive society) he is not quite "manly" enough to achieve the heterosexual conquests that he would like to have. Under *these* conditions, [environmental influences that tend to predispose one to homosexuality may have a more serious and enduring effect on such a person than the same influence would have on another male].

A. ELLIS, HOMOSEXUALITY: ITS CAUSES AND CURE 54–55 (1965) [hereinafter cited as ELLIS]. Kallman himself seems to have come round to much the same view. *See* Kallman, *Genetic Aspects of Sex Determination and Sexual Maturation Potentials in Man*, in DETERMINANTS OF HUMAN SEXUAL BEHAVIOR 15–17 (G. Winokur ed. 1963).

17. A summary of this hypothesis is found in Perloff, *Hormones and Homosexuality*, in SEXUAL INVERSION 44. *See also* D. J. WEST, HOMOSEXUALITY 155–66 (rev. ed. 1968) [hereinafter cited as WEST].

18. Pseudohermaphroditism can also result from other causes, such as the administration of synthetic progestin to the pregnant mother.

19. The most recent studies to have found evidence of a difference in hormone levels between male homosexuals and male heterosexuals are those performed by M. Sydney Margolese, Richard Green, and Oscar Janiger in Los Angeles in 1970–71, by a team headed by Robert C. Kolodny at the Reproductive Biology Research Foundation in St. Louis in 1971, and by a British team headed by J. A. Loraine in 1969. The last-mentioned research is reported in Loraine, Ismail, Adamopoulos, *et al.*, *Endocrine Function in Male and Female Homosexuals*, 115 BRIT. J. PSYCHIATRY 1413 (1969). The Kolodny research is reported in Kolodny, Masters, Hendryx, & Toro, *Plasma Testosterone and Semen Analysis in Male Homosexuals*, 285 NEW ENGLAND J. MEDICINE 1170 (1971). The most recent study finding no significant differences was reported in a paper read by Garfield Tourney and Lon M. Hatfield on April 28, 1972, at the meeting of the Society of Biological Psychiatry preceding the American Psychiatric Association conference in Dallas in May. The paper concluded, "Our findings do not support any of the recent work implying some disturbance in androgen metabolism in homosexual subjects." *See* The Advocate, June 7, 1972, at 1, col. 1, and at 12, col. 3.

The data may show that at least the "passive" male homosexual tends to have low androgen levels, but it is questionable whether this demonstrates any causal relationship even in his case. Impotence is often accompanied by low androgen levels, which increase if potency is recovered. Perhaps a lack of sexual stimulation causes lowered androgen levels. We are thus back to the old puzzle: Which comes first—the chicken or the egg? Letter from Dr. D. J. West to the author, September 6, 1972.

20. *See, e.g.,* S. F. Chronicle, May 23, 1972, at 22, col. 2.

21. Some of the problems in testing androgen levels and determining their effect on behavior are described in Lunde & Hamburg, *Techniques for Assessing the Effects of Sex Hormones on Affect, Arousal, and Aggression in Humans*, 28 RECENT PROGRESS IN HORMONE RESEARCH 627, 646–60 (1972).

22. *See* Federman, *A New Look at Homosexuality*, 285 NEW ENGLAND J. MEDICINE 1197 (1971).

23. *See* Perloff, *Hormones and Homosexuality*, in SEXUAL INVERSION 44.

24. C. S. FORD & F. A. BEACH, PATTERNS OF SEXUAL BEHAVIOR 236–37 (1951) [hereinafter cited as FORD & BEACH].

25. Money, *Psychosexual Differentiation*, in SEX RESEARCH—NEW DEVELOPMENTS 14 (J. Money ed. 1965).

26. Phoenix, *Sexual Behavior: Animal Sexual Behavior*, in 14 INT'L ENCY. SOCIAL SCIENCES 196–98 (1968). *See also* FORD & BEACH 251.

27. *See* WEST 30–32, 154–55. The most striking corroboration of the hypothesis that such behavior cannot be innate, but must be learned, in human beings comes from Harlow's famous experiments with monkeys. He raised infant monkeys under conditions of total deprivation of contact with their mothers and other animals. Some of the cages were supplied with mother surrogates made of uncovered wire mesh; others were supplied with such surrogates covered with cloth. Virtually none of the infants so raised were able to copulate in adulthood, even under the influence of the most gentle and experienced members of the opposite sex. On the other hand, if as infants the monkeys were permitted periods of play with other young monkeys (peers), they developed normal adult sexual behavior. Thus, it "seems that in monkeys early contacts with other animals, especially contact with other young monkeys with whom they can engage in sex play, is an essential element in the learning of normal adult heterosexual responses." *Id.* 32. The same is presumably true of humans. A fuller account of these experiments and their results is found in Harlow & Harlow, *The Effect of Rearing Conditions on Behavior*, in SEX RESEARCH—NEW DEVELOPMENTS 161 (J. Money ed. 1965). *See also* Harlow, *Sexual Behavior in the Rhesus Monkey*, in SEX AND BEHAVIOR 234 (F. A. Beach ed. 1965); and Beach, *Retrospect and Prospect, id.* 547–49.

28. This research is summarized in Phoenix, *Sexual Behavior: Animal Sexual Behavior*, in 14 INT'L ENCY. SOCIAL SCIENCES 197 (1968). A fuller account is given in Young, Goy, & Phoenix, *Hormones and Sexual Behavior*, in SEX RESEARCH—NEW DEVELOPMENTS 182–91 (J. Money ed. 1965).

29. *See* Hooker, note 60 *infra*.

30. Laud Humphreys describes this as the "crisis of aging." *See* L. HUMPHREYS, TEAROOM TRADE—IMPERSONAL SEX IN PUBLIC PLACES (1970). *See also* Weinberg, *The Aging Male Homosexual*, 3 MEDICAL ASPECTS OF HUMAN SEXUALITY 66–72 (No. 12, Dec. 1969), and *The Male Homosexual: Age-Related Variations in Social and Psychological Characteristics*, 17 SOCIAL PROBLEMS 527–37 (1970).

31. *See* note 79 *infra*.

32. WEST 155. *See also* Wilbur, *Clinical Aspects of Female Homosexuality*, in SEXUAL INVERSION 272; and Romm, *Sexuality and Homosexuality in Women, id.* 291.

33. Pomeroy, *Homosexuality*, in THE SAME SEX: AN APPRAISAL OF HOMOSEXUALITY 12–13 (R. W. Weltge ed. 1969). *See also* HOFFMAN 121–23.

34. *See* Money, *Sexual Behavior: Deviation: Psychological Aspects*, in 14 INT'L ENCY. SOCIAL SCIENCES 210–11 (1968); Money, Hampson, & Hampson, *An Examination of Some Basic Concepts: The Evidence of Human Hermaphroditism*, 97 BULL. JOHNS HOPKINS HOSPITAL 284 (1955). This evidence has led the Hampsons to posit a "psychologic sexual neutrality in humans at birth." Hampson

& Hampson, *The Ontogenesis of Sexual Behavior in Man,* in 2 Sex and Internal Secretions 1406 (3d ed. W. C. Young 1961). It must be conceded that without some degree of ambiguity in the external genitalia of such individuals, it would have been difficult to rear them in the sex classification opposite to their true biological gender. And an individual who is born physically intersexed is likely also to have received whatever abnormal organization of the brain tissues mediating sexual responses that hormonal imbalance might produce at this stage, which could render him more labile in the acquisition of gender identity. *See* text and notes at pp. 139–43 *supra,* and note 79 *infra.* On the general subject of human hermaphroditism, *see* J. Money, Sex Errors of the Body (1968). (Genuine hermaphroditism—as distinguished from pseudohermaphroditism—occurs when the same person possesses both testicular and ovarian tissue, and is extremely rare.)

35. Ford & Beach 134.

36. *See* Ellis, *Constitutional Factors in Homosexuality: A Re-examination of the Evidence,* in Advances in Sex Research 161 (H. G. Beigel ed. 1963).

37. [Gonadal hormones appear to control the sexual functioning of lower animals, but in the primates and particularly in man,] . . . the cerebral cortex has assumed a greater and greater degree of direction over all behavior, including that of a sexual nature. . . . [This] increasing dominance of the cortex in affecting sexual manifestations has resulted in greater lability and modifiability of erotic practices. Human sexual behavior is more variable and more easily affected by learning and social conditioning than is that of any other species, . . . [precisely because of the increased role of the cerebral cortex].

Ford & Beach 249. *See also id.* 254–55.

38. In the evolution of the vertebrates, the forebrain is the portion which has become most highly evolved, reaching its acme of complexity in the primates and some other higher mammals and, of course, particularly in the human animal. The chief contributions which this developed forebrain makes to human sexual behavior are: (1) an increase in the capacity to be psychologically stimulated by a diversity of erotic situations; (2) an increase in the possibilities of conditioning; and (3) an increase in the capacity to develop inhibitions which interfere with the spinal and autonomic controls of sexual behavior. This curious mixture is what many persons identify as "an intelligent control of the sexual instincts."

A. C. Kinsey, W. B. Pomeroy, C. E. Martin, & P. H. Gebhard, Sexual Behavior in the Human Female 708 (1953) [hereinafter cited as Kinsey, Female].

39. *See* W. Churchill, Homosexual Behavior Among Males 61 (1967) [hereinafter cited as Churchill]. In the words of C. H. Phoenix:

What has been demonstrated is that sexual behavior, in general, is subject to modification just as other aspects of behavior can be modified by varying experience. Thus despite heritability of sexual behavior patterns, dependence on hormonal stimulation and the spinal reflex contribution to patterns of sexual behavior, the complete pattern can be blocked, enhanced, or modified by social and situational experience. The extent to which it can be modified by experience varies primarily with the species, sex, and age of the individual.

Phoenix, *Sexual Behavior: Animal Sexual Behavior,* in 14 INT'L ENCY. SOCIAL SCIENCES 200 (1968).

40. The term "memory" is here used in its broadest sense, to denote all those residues left by past experience and learning in the brain and nervous system. For instance, if a person jerks his finger away from the touch of a hot stove, it is usually due to the "memory" of a burn thus received from touching hot objects in the past.

41. *See* Marmor, *Introduction,* in SEXUAL INVERSION 9–10. He posits "psychosexual neutrality in humans at birth—a neutrality that 'permits the development and perpetuation of divers patterns of psychosexual orientation and functioning in accordance with the life experiences each individual may encounter and transact.'" He compares man with lower animals; as one moves up the evolutionary scale, inherited instinctual patterns becomes less complex but more subject to modification by learning. Human beings are born "with relatively unfocused basic biological drives. . . . The direction these drives take in human beings and the objects to which they become attached are subject to enormous modifications by learning."

42. . . . . [A]ppreciation of the fact that the lower mammals are more dependent upon "sex hormones" than are the primates adds considerably to our understanding of human sexual activities. Accompanying this relative lessening of hormonal control is an increase in the importance of the role of the cerebral cortex in the direction and control of sexual behavior. This finding in turn relates to our conclusion that learning and experience are significantly more powerful in controlling the behavior of primates than that of the lower mammals. Particularly in the case of man, the role of learning is paramount. Moreover, human beings learn much of what they know, not by solitary experimentation but by being taught and by observing the behavior of other members of their society.

FORD & BEACH 16.

43. Men and women do not develop their individual patterns of sexual behavior simply as a result of biological heredity. Human sexual responses are not instinctive in the sense of being determined exclusively by the action of genes or chromosomes. On the contrary, from the first years of life every child is taught about sex, either directly or indirectly. . . . As the result of . . . divergent experiences in early life, the adult members of different societies have quite different opinions as to what is proper or normal in sexual relations, and what is immoral or unnatural.

FORD & BEACH 2.

44. *See* CHURCHILL 62–68.

45. Even some of the most extremely variant types of human sexual behavior may need no more explanation than is provided by our understanding of the processes of learning and conditioning. Behavior which may appear bizarre, perverse, or unthinkably unacceptable to some persons, and even

to most persons, may have significance for other individuals because of the way in which they have been conditioned.
KINSEY, FEMALE 645.

46. FORD & BEACH 261–62. *See also* KINSEY, FEMALE 643–45.

47. KINSEY, FEMALE 646. *See also* CHURCHILL 105–9.

48. KINSEY, FEMALE 648; CHURCHILL 109.

49. *See* CHURCHILL 90.

50. CHURCHILL 33–35 has a good discussion of the elusiveness of these terms. The definitions here indicated are those used by most of the best works in the field. Judd Marmor says, "I prefer . . . to define the clinical homosexual as one who is motivated, in adult life, by a definite preferential erotic attraction to members of the same sex and who usually (but not necessarily) engages in overt sexual relations with them." Marmor, *Introduction,* in SEXUAL INVERSION 4. "Homosexuality is defined . . . as a clinical entity in which the individual is motivated toward the preferred or exclusive choice of a member of the same sex for sexual excitement and gratification, even when heterosexual objects are available." Gadpaille, *Homosexual Activity and Homosexuality in Adolescence,* in SCIENTIFIC PROCEEDINGS OF THE AMERICAN ACADEMY OF PSYCHOANALYSIS, SCIENCE AND PSYCHOANALYSIS, Vol. XV, DYNAMICS OF DEVIANT SEXUALITY 61 (J. H. Masserman ed. 1969) [hereinafter cited as PROCEEDINGS]. *See also* S. E. WILLIS, UNDERSTANDING AND COUNSELLING THE MALE HOMOSEXUAL 28 (1967) [hereinafter cited as WILLIS]; Lindner, *Homosexuality and the Contemporary Scene,* in THE PROBLEM OF HOMOSEXUALITY IN MODERN SOCIETY 55–56 (H. M. Ruitenbeek ed. 1963) [hereinafter cited as RUITENBEEK]; and B. MAGEE, ONE IN TWENTY 19 (1966) [hereinafter cited as MAGEE] (Magee's book, though by a journalist rather than a scientist, is a worthwhile overview of the subject based on extensive inquiry).

Others' definitions, while emphasizing the element of preference, would also appear to require overt behavior. *See, e.g.,* Romm, *Sexuality and Homosexuality in Women,* in SEXUAL INVERSION 284: "An individual should be considered homosexual only when erotic activity with the same sex is practiced repeatedly and preferentially after adolescence." Still others would seem to include any experience of being erotically attracted to a member of the same sex. "Millions of men in contemporary American society at some point in their lives have homosexual fantasies and impulses which may or may not lead to overt homosexual behavior. . . . [A]ny definition of male homosexuality must include one common denominator: that the male experiences active or passive sexual arousal by another male at some level of consciousness—in dream, in fantasy, in impulse, or in act." L. J. HATTERER, CHANGING HOMOSEXUALITY IN THE MALE 1 (1970). *See also* WEST 10. Such a definition would appear too broad, as it would net, in all likelihood, the majority of American males. Kinsey's survey noted that 50 per cent of his sample of American males admitted to having experienced sexual arousal by, or fantasy of, other males at some point in life. *See* A. C. KINSEY, W. B. POMEROY, & C. E. MARTIN, SEXUAL BEHAVIOR IN THE HUMAN MALE 623, 650, 656 (1948) [hereinafter cited as KINSEY, MALE]; KINSEY, FEMALE 474–75.

Some experts appear to use the words "inversion" and "invert" as synonymous with homosexuality and homosexual. Others would confine those terms to cases in which heterosexual erotic attraction is totally or virtually absent—the so-called obligatory homosexuals. *See* WEST 10. Kinsey's group felt that the use of such terms was confusing and should be avoided. *See* KINSEY, MALE 614–15.

51. Irving Bieber appears to be one of these. In a Playboy Forum symposium, he responded as follows to the observation of another participant that the key was whether a person *thinks* of himself as a homosexual: "A man is homosexual if his behavior is homosexual. Self-identification is not relevant. . . . An isolated homosexual experience doesn't define a man as homosexual; but if he has one such experience every year, he would have to be considered homosexual. . . . Fully heterosexual adult males cannot be aroused sexually by other men and they have no desire for homosexual activity." *Playboy Panel: Homosexuality*, PLAYBOY, April 1971, at 67.

52. *See* Reiss, *The Social Integration of Queers and Peers*, in RUITENBEEK 249.

53. Ovesey's essays propounding this distinction are collected in L. OVESEY, HOMOSEXUALITY AND PSEUDOHOMOSEXUALITY (1969).

54. *See, e.g.*, HOFFMAN 136–38. Since power and dependency needs are also served in true erotic homosexuality, it may prove difficult to keep these various classifications distinct—for instance, Hoffman's example, at 139–41, of the male who believes he can somehow incorporate another male's strength and masculinity by sucking his penis, thereby hoping to repair his own low sense of masculine self-esteem. *See also* WILLIS 119–30. Sexual behavior, both heterosexual and homosexual, may be used to express dominance and aggression, as well as erotic attraction, in lower animals too. *See* FORD & BEACH 57–65.

55. *See* M. SCHOFIELD, SOCIOLOGICAL ASPECTS OF HOMOSEXUALITY 147–48 (1965) [hereinafter cited as SCHOFIELD]:

> Homosexuality is not a type of conduct; it is a condition characterized by a psychosexual propensity towards others of the same sex. Some homosexuals do not commit homosexual acts because they exercise a rigorous control over their physical urges . . . But a man may engage in homosexual practices without being a homosexual. . . . It should also be realized that there are many married men who commit homosexual acts.

> Probably the clearest distinction between a true homosexual and a facultative homosexual is that the former requires more than a homosexual act. His desires are psychosexual and he seeks an emotional attachment with another man, including love and close friendship. But the facultative homosexual requires only physical release and so has little regard for his sexual partner and may actively despise him.

56. For one thing, homosexuals are very unlikely to approach anybody—even another homosexual—without getting first a clear indication of sexual interest on his part. Otherwise, they risk rejection. *See* HOFFMAN 44–46, 54–56.

57. *See* Simon & Gagnon, *Homosexuality: The Formulation of a Sociological Perspective*, in THE SAME SEX—AN APPRAISAL OF HOMOSEXUALITY 157 n. 1 (R. W. Weltge ed. 1969).

58. Michael Schofield, in his comparison of a group of British homosexual psychiatric patients with a matching group of heterosexual patients, found no difference between them on the Robust/Delicate scale or the Masculine/Feminine scale, other than a slight tendency for the homosexual men to be more

robust. In comparing two nonpatient groups of homosexuals and heterosexuals, he likewise found no difference. SCHOFIELD 100, 108–9, 130–31. He concluded:

> It is clear, therefore that the appearance of the . . . [nonpatient, noncon-victed] homosexuals is not noticeably different in any way. Those who claim that they can recognize a homosexual instantly must be using some other clue besides appearance. More probably their claim means that they have no difficulty in recognizing some homosexuals, while they remain unaware of the number of homosexuals that they have failed to identify.

Id. 108–9.

The Kinsey group, in their interviewing for the survey *Sexual Behavior in the Human Male,* found that only a small fraction of the males with homosexual histories displayed the affectations, mannerisms, and dress thought to be typical of the homosexual. Indeed, they found that homosexual contact among adult males in Western rural areas was not uncommon. These were outdoor men, virile and physically active. KINSEY, MALE 457–59.

The Bieber group said, in their study of homosexual psychiatric patients:

> In the *Three Contributions to the Theory of Sexuality* Freud stated: "In men, the most perfect psychic manliness may be united with the inversion (homosexuality)." In our . . . [homosexual sample], no manifestations of effeminacy were apparent in 65 per cent of the cases.

I. BIEBER *et al.,* HOMOSEXUALITY 188 (1962) [hereinafter cited as BIEBER].

Mayerson and Lief found that only 3 of the 14 males and 2 of the 5 females in their sample displayed mannerisms of the opposite sex. Mayerson & Lief, *Psychotherapy of Homosexuals,* in SEXUAL INVERSION 318. A British study found such characteristics in only 5 per cent of a group of 64 men in prison for homosexual offenses. Hemphill, Leitch, & Stuart, *A Factual Study of Male Homosexuality,* 1 BRIT. MEDICAL J. 1317 (1958).

The Kinsey group, in their massive study of sex offenders, estimated that, of the homosexuals outside prison, only about 10 to 15 per cent show obvious feminine mannerisms and dress. P. H. GEBHARD, J. H. GAGNON, W. B. POMEROY, & C. V. CHRISTENSEN, SEX OFFENDERS—AN ANALYSIS OF TYPES 642–43 (1965) [hereinafter cited as SEX OFFENDERS]. It is estimated that only 5 per cent of lesbians are recognizable by virtue of mannish characteristics. *See* SEX INFORMATION AND EDUCATION COUNCIL OF THE UNITED STATES, SEXUALITY AND MAN 75–76 (1970); Pomeroy, *Homosexuality,* in THE SAME SEX—AN APPRAISAL OF HOMOSEXUALITY 10–11 (R. W. Weltge ed. 1969).

The same amazement at how few homosexuals are visible has been registered by others who have made independent investigations. *See* HOFFMAN 17–22, 48–50; MAGEE 47–50.

D. J. West summarizes the evidence thus:

> In practice the majority of homosexuals possess no . . . obvious signs. The affectedly effeminate group is a minority which attracts undue public attention and gives rise to a stereotyped idea of the male homosexual that is about as unfair as the stereotype of the beak-nosed, money-grabbing Jew. Those who imagine that they can invariably pick out "one of them" at a glance are certainly mistaken. Homosexuals are to be found anywhere and

everywhere, in all types of occupation and in every social class, but as most of them possess no obvious distinguishing features, either of appearance or manner, the unsophisticated remain in ignorance of their existence.

WEST 44. *See also id.* 69–70, where he makes a similar statement about lesbians.

Among male homosexuals, effeminacy is a great drawback in finding a sexual partner, because, in general, they are most attracted by masculine partners, *not* by feminine ones. HOFFMAN 143. *See also* Lindner, *Homosexuality and the Contemporary Scene,* in RUITENBEEK 53–54, and particularly at 54, where he says:

> Apart from the fact that, as a member of a severely oppressed minority, the invert who adopts such behavior is exposing himself to ridicule, opprobrium, social and even economic ruin, this is the surest way for him to defeat his aims and fail in his perpetual search for sexual gratification. In the "gay" world it is exactly those qualities usually associated with masculinity that are found attractive and hence to be cultivated. Femininity, as such, is to be avoided in these circles, and the "queen" . . . is ordinarily an object of contempt among bona fide inverts.

Thus to be "propositioned" by a homosexual is more likely to be a compliment to the masculinity of the recipient of the invitation, rather than, as most heterosexual males take it in our culture, an insult.

The growing visibility of the masculine majority of male homosexuals is described in Humphreys, *New Styles in Homosexual Manliness,* TRANS-ACTION, March/April, 1971, at 41.

59. WEST 62–63; ELLIS 55–56.

60. Evelyn Hooker, in her research with 30 male homosexuals, found that they all perceived themselves as biological males, preferred to be males, and would not surrender their gender. Apart from their sexual orientation, they otherwise willingly assumed the culturally determined roles of the male sex in our society. There was, of course, a high degree of variation in which of these roles they did accept, and, though they identified themselves as males, some placed themselves toward the feminine end of a masculine-feminine homosexual personality continuum. Even one's place on such a continuum had no significance in determining his preferences for particular types of, or roles in, sexual activity. Hooker, *An Empirical Study of Some Relations Between Sexual Patterns and Gender Identity in Male Homosexuals,* in SEX RESEARCH—NEW DEVELOPMENTS 24–51 (J. Money ed. 1965).

61. *See* R. J. STOLLER, SEX AND GENDER 144–46 (1968) [hereinafter cited as STOLLER]. Besides Stoller's book, the main works on transsexualism are TRANSSEXUALISM AND SEX REASSIGNMENT (R. Green & J. Money eds. 1969); THE PSYCHODYNAMICS OF CHANGE OF SEX THROUGH SURGERY (1969) [a collection of articles reprinted from 147 J. NERVOUS & MENTAL DISEASE (Nov. 1968)]; H. BENJAMIN, THE TRANSSEXUAL PHENOMENON (1966); and J. Wålinder, TRANSSEXUALISM (1967). *See also* G. TURTLE, OVER THE SEX BORDER (1963).

62. *See* WEST 62–63.

63. " . . . [T]ransvestism and homosexuality are different phenomena, and our data show that only a portion of the transvestites have homosexual histories. . . ." KINSEY, FEMALE 451. *See also id.* 679-81.

64. Harry Benjamin estimates that the total number of transsexuals in the United States does not exceed 10,000. TRANSSEXUALISM AND SEX REASSIGNMENT 10 (R. Green & J. Money eds. 1969).

65. The establishment of gender identity roughly parallels the learning of the native language. It is ended probably by the kindergarten age. Money, *Sexual Behavior: Deviation: Psychological Aspects*, in 14 INT'L ENCY. SOCIAL SCIENCES 211 (1968).

66. "It is generally accepted that at 18 months to two years, or about the time of development of meaningful language, the individual's concept of himself or herself as male or female is firmly fixed and that efforts to alter this conviction of maleness or femaleness are productive of severe psychologic trauma." Gendel, *Chromosomes and Sex*, in PROCEEDINGS 1.

67. Transsexuals do not regard themselves as homosexual, but as heterosexual. Their bodies make their orientation appear homosexual, but their feelings cry out, "I am not this body!"

68. *See* Socarides, *Female Homosexuality*, in SEXUAL BEHAVIOR AND THE LAW 462–77 (R. Slovenko ed. 1965).

69. *See* WEST 9–10:

> Unfortunately, though strongly held opinions abound, hard facts about homosexuality and its possible causes are difficult to obtain. Scientific research of necessity progresses slowly, and it will take many years to make up for past neglect.

70. One problem with using psychotherapeutic "findings" about the relationship of homosexuality to an individual's life experiences is that such findings must rely on the patient's memory. But we now know that people constantly edit their recollection of the past, so that the picture they reconstruct may bear little resemblance to what actually happened. This editing could be influenced by what the patient *thinks* the therapist would consider relevant. Simon & Gagnon, *Homosexuality: The Formulation of a Sociological Perspective*, in THE SAME SEX—AN APPRAISAL OF HOMOSEXUALITY 158 (R. W. Weltge ed. 1969).

71. L. J. HATTERER, CHANGING HOMOSEXUALITY IN THE MALE (1970) presents, at 34–47, a long and exhaustive list of the multitude of "causal" factors of homosexuality identified by psychiatric and other investigators. At 42, he observes:

> This long list—which does not even include such other factors as age, family background, social class, and financial status—makes plain why no single cause-and-effect theory can satisfactorily explain what causes homosexuality. Nor has it even been established that some causal factors are more important than others. The literature is confusing on this subject, and recent research by investigators in several disciplines has not necessarily clarified matters, though there is some agreement on the causes of certain specific patterns.

Cf. WEST 206:

> This confusing proliferation of psycho-analytic interpretations casts doubt upon all theories based upon unsupported clinical intuitions.

72. SIECUS makes the following observation about the supposed key factor of a seductive or overattached mother and an absent, weak, or rejecting father:

[N]o studies have been made that could establish how far these findings could be applicable to the total homosexual population, which must certainly include an unknown number who have not been sufficiently disturbed ever to seek psychiatric help. Also the many individuals who have had seductive or overattached mothers and absent, weak, or rejecting fathers and who have *not* become homosexuals should be taken account of.

SEX INFORMATION AND EDUCATION COUNCIL OF THE UNITED STATES, SEXUALITY AND MAN 79–80 (1970). *See also* ELLIS 55–61; and Simon & Gagnon, *The Lesbians*, in SEXUAL DEVIANCE 258 (J. H. Gagnon & W. Simon eds. 1967). A recent study which found the close-binding-mother-and-detached-father relationship more common among a sample of nonpatient homosexuals than among a sample of nonpatient heterosexuals nevertheless questions the causal relation between homosexuality and disturbed parent-child relationships. *See* Evans, *Parental Relations and Homosexuality*, 5 MEDICAL ASPECTS OF HUMAN SEXUALITY 164 (No. 4, April 1971).

73. *See* Hooker, *Parental Relations and Male Homosexuality in Patient and Nonpatient Samples*, 33 J. CONSULTING & CLINICAL PSYCHOLOGY 140 (1969). WEST 187–88 concludes that, to date, clear scientific evidence of the causative factors is just not available, because no systematic research involving deliberate sampling of a wide range of homosexual types has been done, carefully comparing specific features of their upbringing with those of a control group of heterosexuals of similar social and cultural background.

74. Hooker, *Sexual Behavior: Homosexuality*, in 14 INT'L ENCY. SOCIAL SCIENCES 225 (1968):

From the limited evidence currently available, it is clear that the diverse forms of adult homosexuality are produced by many combinations of variables. . . . No single class of determinants, whether psychodynamic, cultural, or biological, accounts for all or even one of these diverse forms. The relative importance of each kind of determinant appears to vary greatly from one individual to another.

See also HOFFMAN 143–45.

75. *See* WEST 204–5.

76. *See* WILLIS 136.

77. The idea here under criticism is one recurrent throughout much of the psychoanalytic literature—that the male homosexual who brings another male to orgasm by using his mouth on the other's penis is making the unconscious equation "penis = fictive breast."

78. *See* Marmor, *Introduction*, in SEXUAL INVERSION 2. This theory also recognizes that unhappy experiences in heterosexual encounters in adult life might cause a *regression* to this homoerotic stage.

79. The most influential attack on Freud's postulation of bisexuality has been that of Rado, *A Critical Examination of the Concept of Bisexuality*, in SEXUAL INVERSION 175. Rado's basic criticism, which seems to have gained wide acceptance among psychiatrists, is that, with few exceptions, human beings are either male or female from the instant of conception. (We now know that this depends on whether they possess a male, or Y, sex chromosome.) They are never really physically bisexual in the sense of possessing dual reproductive capacity.

The trouble with Rado's view is that actual reproductive capacity as male or female can no longer be viewed as the sole determinant of one's sex. A number of variables go to make up the "sex" of an individual. The genetic factor may be only the initial triggering mechanism. Additional variables are the gonads, the sex hormones, the internal accessory reproductive organs, the external genital morphology, the sex of assignment and rearing, and the gender identity and gender role, one or more of which may be in contradiction to the others. As already noted, the human embryo has an undifferentiated reproductive tract in the first stages. The embryonic gonad, for instance, can develop in the direction of either a testis or an ovary; it is the *anlage* of both. The genital tubercle can become a penis or a clitoris. Likewise, the embryo possesses both Wolffian and Müllerian duct systems, which develop, respectively, into the male and the female accessory reproductive organs (epididymis, vas deferens, and prostate in the male, and Fallopian tubes, uterus, and vagina in the female). Admittedly, this reproductive tract will not develop in *both* male *and* female directions. Normally, in a genetic male, the gonads will develop into testes and the Wolffian duct system will grow and mature while the Müllerian duct system deteriorates; and in normal females, the opposite development occurs. But this normal development can be interfered with. In experiments with lower animals, complete sex reversals have been obtained, so that a genetic male is born with a complete, anatomically normal, female reproductive system, and can become pregnant and give birth to young. Some recent research indicates that a similar undifferentiated potential may exist in the brain structures—probably located in the hypothalamus—which control sexual behavior, or that separate "male" *and* "female" brain centers exist in every individual, and that differentiation into the male and female patterns of behavior occurs in response to differing hormonal stimulation of these parts of the embryonic or fetal brain in much the same way as genital differentiation occurs. *See* text and notes at pp. 139–43 *supra;* also Beach, *Retrospect and Prospect,* in SEX AND BEHAVIOR 565–66 (F. A. Beach ed. 1965). If hormonal imbalance occurs at this early stage of development, it seems likely that both brain and genital differentiation would be equally affected. If, however, in some cases it could happen that the brain structures are affected though genital differentiation has proceeded normally, we would have found a constitutional factor that would go far to explain why some anatomically normal males behave more like females and some anatomically normal females behave more like males. Such a contradictory development of the brain and the genitalia is conceivable because the brain apparently may remain temporarily subject to the differentiating effect of hormones even *after* genital differentiation is complete. *See* Money, *Sexual Dimorphism and Homosexual Gender Identity,* 74 PSYCHOLOGICAL BULL. 431–32 (1970). Michael, *Biological Factors in the Organization and Expression of Sexual Behavior,* in THE PATHOLOGY AND TREATMENT OF SEXUAL DEVIATION 26–38 and 47–49 (I. Rosen ed. 1964). Thus, Freud's postulate may ultimately be shown to have more validity than his critics, such as Rado, have been willing to concede. STOLLER 6 n.

Of course, it is not necessary to the notion of the psychic bisexuality of human beings to postulate a physical foundation for it. Since most humans have both a father and a mother, or at least are subjected to the influence of persons of both sexes throughout infancy and childhood, it seems likely that males will have some psychic component of feminine attitudes and feelings, and vice versa with females. C. G. Jung's psychoanalytic theory thus postulates an *animus* and an *anima* in everyone. To think that "normal" little boys will pick up only "masculine" attitudes and feelings and "normal" little girls only "feminine" attitudes and feelings presupposes in them a rather fantastic capacity for always discriminating the ones from the others and consistently rejecting those associated with the opposite sex.

80. *See* KINSEY, MALE 173.

81. This theory was elaborated primarily by Otto Fenichel. *See* O. FENICHEL, THE PSYCHOANALYTIC THEORY OF NEUROSIS 328–41 (1945). A counterpart of this theory—"penis envy"—was similarly postulated for females.

82. For a good critique of this explanation, *see* WILLIS 88–91.

83. The most enlightening psychiatric discussions of homosexuality are found in I. BIEBER *et al.*, HOMOSEXUALITY (1962); SEXUAL INVERSION (J. Marmor ed. 1965); THE PROBLEM OF HOMOSEXUALITY IN MODERN SOCIETY (H. M. Ruitenbeek ed. 1963); A. STORR, SEXUAL DEVIATION (1964); S. E. WILLIS, UNDERSTANDING AND COUNSELLING THE MALE HOMOSEXUAL (1967); and D. J. WEST, HOMOSEXUALITY (rev. ed. 1968). West's book is probably the single most comprehensive review of scientific knowledge yet available on the subject. The Bieber work contains, at 3–18, a summary of the previous psychiatric opinion concerning the development of homosexuality. The discussion in the text relies fairly heavily on this summary, and on other portions of the Bieber book. Where other sources have been used, these are indicated in footnotes at the appropriate points.

A word of warning is in order to the reader who lacks any previous acquaintance with the scientific literature on this subject. Some books in print can only be described as worthless chaff. Others possess some merit, but must still be read with a grain of salt. Publishers and the lay reading public seem to assume that the initials M.D. after anyone's name automatically qualify him or her to tell people everything they need to know about sex, including homosexuality. It is not so.

84. Psychoanalytic theory often seems to assume that it can be, and that the map does not vary much from one individual to another. Thus it has often assumed that what is found to have "caused" homosexuality in one person must also be the "cause" in every other homosexual.

85. The description of the mother-son relationship which follows is largely taken from BIEBER 44–84, 119–25. *See also* WEST 188–96.

86. A very important determining influence in the development of homosexuality is the child's awareness that his sex was a disappointment to his parents or to the more important parent, especially if this disappointment leads them to treat the child as if he were of the opposite sex.

Thompson, *Changing Concepts of Homosexuality in Psychoanalysis,* in RUITENBEEK 47.

87. *See* A. STORR, SEXUAL DEVIATION 84–85 (1964) [hereinafter cited as STORR].

88. *See* WEST 176–81; Knight, *Overt Male Homosexuality,* in SEXUAL BEHAVIOR AND THE LAW (R. Slovenko ed. 1965). Anthony Storr makes the important point that it is harder to rebel against love than against mere authority. STORR 23.

89. *See* West 202.

90. *See* Storr 25.

91. *See* Bieber 181; Storr 21–22. In discussing the effect of early child-rearing practices upon adult male-female roles, Margaret Mead describes the Manus tribe of the Admiralty Islands, in which the most emphasized communication between parent and child is on control of elimination:

> The later transfer to the genitals of attitudes focussed on elimination makes for prudery, haste, lack of pleasure and foreplay in intercourse. . . . [T]he Manus . . . [are] a group of efficient puritans where . . . all love, even the affection between brother and sister, is measured in goods. . . . Between husbands and wives sex is a hasty, covert, shameful matter; and otherwise it is adultery, heavily punished by vigilant, puritanical, ghostly guardians. . . . The sex act becomes a sort of shared excretion, . . . the man to a degree . . . continuing an enjoined activity. . . . A certain amount of sodomy among the young men is a natural concomitant of such a learning system.

M. Mead, Male and Female, A Study of the Sexes in a Changing World 71–72 (1949).

92. *See* Willis 44–45, 76.

93. *Id.* 101.

94. Ford and Beach say the zoological evidence indicates that, among the higher mammals, the role of inherited or innate sexual patterns grows less and the role of individual learning grows correspondingly greater. Individuals reared in a society that denies them all opportunity for experimentation and practice during childhood and adolescence will be forced to go through the essential learning processes after adulthood is attained.

> This type of adjustment may be exceedingly difficult for young adults of either sex, particularly if they belong to a society that inculcates manifold sexual inhibitions in the developing individual. The man or woman who learned during childhood and adolescence that it was "wrong" to examine or stimulate his or her own genitals, that it was even "worse" to have any contact with those of another person, and, particularly, that attempts at heterosexual relations were immoral, is expected to reverse completely at least some of these attitudes on the wedding night or shortly thereafter. This expectation is difficult to fulfill. If the initial lessons have been well learned, the unlearning is bound to take a long time and may never be completed.

Ford & Beach 194–96.

95. The following are some representative comments on this situation:

> The general situation of sexuality in this society may be best described as that of pluralistic ignorance, a condition of non-information and misinformation that serves to direct (or misdirect) a powerful drive.

Gagnon, *Sexual Behavior: Deviation: Social Aspects,* in 14 Int'l Ency. Social Sciences 220 (1968).

> Sociocultural deprivation and ignorance of sexual physiology, rather than psychiatric or medical illness, constitute the etiologic background for most sexual dysfunction.

W. H. MASTERS & V. E. JOHNSON, HUMAN SEXUAL INADEQUACY 21 (1970).

The more society obscures these relationships [male-female], muffles the human body in clothes, surrounds elimination with prudery, shrouds copulation in shame and mystery, camouflages pregnancy, banishes men and children from child-birth, and hides breast-feeding, the more individual and bizarre will be the child's attempts to understand, to piece together a very imperfect knowledge of the life-cycle of the two sexes and an understanding of the particular state of maturity of his or her own body.

M. MEAD, MALE AND FEMALE, A STUDY OF THE SEXES IN A CHANGING WORLD 146 (1949). *See also* Gadpaille, *Homosexual Activity and Homosexuality in Adolescence,* in PROCEEDINGS 64–66.

96. *See* Carstairs, *Cultural Differences in Sexual Deviation,* in THE PATHOLOGY AND TREATMENT OF SEXUAL DEVIATION 424–26 (I. Rosen ed. 1964).

97. In middle-class American culture, because of the absence of free and open discussion between parents and children and the lacing of whatever talks do occur with warnings and prohibitions, the growing child's ego is not given the opportunities to prepare for a reproductively ready body and high levels of sexual desire. The child is

also given clearly to understand that heterosexual intercourse should be postponed indefinitely into the future, while at the same time being sexually stimulated from every side by the sex-preoccupation of the culture. . . . It is noteworthy that tabus against homosexuality have not been much stressed in most youngsters' experience. It is unlikely that any normally perceptive adolescent would be unaware of this cultural tabu, but with a superego still predominantly composed of parental prohibitions, the fears of transgressing heterosexual tabus are infinitely greater.

Gadpaille, *Homosexual Activity and Homosexuality in Adolescence,* in PROCEEDINGS 65–66. Gadpaille sees transient homosexual practices in adolescence as peculiarly likely to occur in cultures with sexually repressive child-rearing, and in which guilt-free heterosexual experimentation post-puberty is denied, because sexual experimentation with one's own sex is more comforting and less threatening in such a culture. Nevertheless, he believes the "healthy" youngster will weather these cultural obstacles to ultimate heterosexuality while the ego-crippled child is likely to "regress" to permanent homosexuality.

98. *See* Harper, *Psychological Aspects of Homosexuality,* in ADVANCES IN SEX RESEARCH 188–91 (H. G. Beigel ed. 1963). Albert Ellis is convinced that our society's antisexuality and puritanism do influence youngsters toward homosexuality, particularly the teachings of religion that it is wicked to lust after the opposite sex and to engage in any form of premarital sex relations. "But they are not equally warned against homosexuality, since *that* kind of behavior is considered to be so abominable by their parents and teachers that it is never even mentioned. In consequence, they fear heterosexuality enormously, are less fearful of homosexuality, and find themselves intensely lusting after members of their own sex, and eventually giving in to this lust." ELLIS 67–69.

Martin Hoffman says:

In some families . . . *heterosexual* feelings are explicitly discouraged as being wicked, while nothing is said about homosexual impulses, so that the child gets the message, even if covertly, that homosexual behavior may be less undesirable than heterosexual behavior.

HOFFMAN 132. *See also id.* 134; and WILLIS 20.

99. For many persons, the most important determinants of behavior are the opportunities which are immediately available—or, conversely, unavailable, although this latter fact is not so often comprehended. Parents and teachers for instance, frequently consider it important to steer children away from certain companions and places, but rarely (as far as sex is concerned) see the necessity for providing opportunities for socially approved patterns of behavior. By its failure to approve of the heterosexual, society becomes responsible for a certain portion of the homosexual activity which occurs in our culture. In fact, the record from our many thousands of specific histories suggests that moral objections to the heterosexual may be more important than personality defects, fixations at adolescent levels, or inherent sin as a source of exclusively homosexual patterns of behavior.

Kinsey *et al., Concepts of Normality and Abnormality in Sexual Behavior,* in PSYCHOSEXUAL DEVELOPMENT IN HEALTH AND DISEASE 20 (P. H. Hoch & J. Zubin eds. 1949).

100. In order to win a desirable mate, the man must arrive at a socially acceptable compromise between the moral dicta regarding continence and chastity and the need to prove his worth as a lover. The young man with too many scruples finds himself at a disadvantage. For some temperaments the task is far from easy.

WEST 200.

101. To get a picture of sexual development in such sex-positive cultures, one should read some of the descriptions in the later chapters of HUMAN SEXUAL BEHAVIOR (D. S. Marshall & R. C. Suggs eds. 1971), and then compare them with J. C. Messenger's description of *Sex and Repression in an Irish Folk Community,* which is the first chapter of the book. See also Carstairs, *Cultural Differences in Sexual Deviation,* in THE PATHOLOGY AND TREATMENT OF SEXUAL DEVIATION 422–31 (I. Rosen ed. 1964).

102. The Kinsey group, in discussing the American cultural condemnation of premarital coitus, points out how this negates, "to a greater extent than most persons ordinarily comprehend," all of the claims extolling heterosexual coitus as the most desirable, mature, and socially acceptable type of sexual activity. The perceived conflict in these appraisals is a source of considerable disturbance for American youth. "Our case histories show that this disapproval of heterosexual coitus and of nearly every other type of heterosexual activity before marriage is often an important factor in the development of homosexual activity." KINSEY, FEMALE 285. *See also* Lindner, *Homosexuality and the Contemporary Scene,* in RUITENBEEK 53; WILLIS 34–35.

103. WILLIS 77.

104. The typical father-son relationship is discussed at length in BIEBER 85–117, and in WEST 188–96.

105. *See* WEST 198.

106. *See* BIEBER 114–15.

107. West reports that in one research study,

. . . . [S]exually maladjusted boys came from parental homes characterized by sexual anxiety and prudishness, maternal authoritarianism, quarrels between parents, and paternal punitiveness. . . . These findings suggest that sexually repressive homes are particularly liable to generate homosexual or "feminized" sons if the father is absent or is a rejecting, aggressive disordered person who forces the child to view masculinity as an unattractive role.

WEST 196.

108. *See id.* 210.

109. *See* Hooker, *Sexual Behavior: Homosexuality,* in 14 INT'L ENCY. SOCIAL SCIENCES 225–26 (1968). Of course, not too much stock should be put in such studies, because gauging a person's overall masculinity or femininity by his attitudes to various activities is not very reliable, considering that masculinity and femininity are culturally determined concepts and that a great diversity of opinion exists even within American culture on what are masculine and what are feminine attitudes and traits.

110. Although most of the evidence of the critical role of the father in the child's sexual development comes from psychiatric treatment of homosexual patients, there is some corroboration from nonpatient populations. For instance, the Kinsey group, in their study of sex offenders, found that all categories of homosexual offenders (against children, against minors, and against adults), tended to show a pattern of not getting along with their fathers and of preferring their mothers over their fathers. *See* SEX OFFENDERS 273–74, 299–300, 327.

111. *See* Socarides, *Homosexuality and Medicine,* 212 J.A.M.A. 1199 (1970).

112. One need not, of course, delve so deeply into the mysteries of the subconscious for an explanation of this behavior. Given a desire for sexual contact with the partner and a desire to give him pleasure (which usually go hand in hand), the male homosexual has only limited options. Mutual masturbation is not very satisfying, and anal intercourse may be uncomfortable or inconvenient, which leaves only fellatio.

One may wonder, moreover, whether these same psychiatrists would explain the propensity of heterosexual males to perform cunnilingus by a desire to incorporate magically the *feminine* essence of *their* partners.

113. See Cory's essay at the end of ELLIS. On the other hand, a similar phenomenon among heterosexual males—worship of the buxom breast—is not invested with any sinister significance.

114. *See* CHURCHILL 160–63.

115. *See* HOFFMAN 54–56.

116. Here again, a caution against too facile generalization is in order. Given the extraordinary range of natural human variation, homosexuals who did have a good relationship with their fathers are almost bound to exist somewhere— probably in the world *outside* the therapists' offices.

117. The data are analyzed in Sears, *Development of Gender Role,* in SEX AND BEHAVIOR 153–59 (F. A. Beach ed. 1965).

118. *See* BIEBER 148–49.

119. Bieber and others emphasize that it is quite often the *combination* of a

detached, hostile father and an intimate, close-binding mother that produces a homosexual son. It is the interaction of the two parents, particularly in the sexual sphere, that arouses overwhelming anxieties which block the path to heterosexual development.

> . . . . [T]he parental constellation most likely to produce a homosexual son . . . is a detached, hostile father and a close-binding, intimate, seductive mother who is a dominating, minimizing wife. . . .

> But . . . it is their sexual attitudes and disciplines that specifically direct themselves toward inhibiting manifestations of assertive, masculine behavior, and they unconsciously attempt to extinguish the son's heterosexuality.

Bieber, *Clinical Aspects of Male Homosexuality*, in SEXUAL INVERSION 250–51.

> Adaptationally, homosexuality is a deviant form of sexual behavior into which a person is driven by the intrusion of fear into the normal heterosexual function. The fear originates in excessive parental discipline in the developmental years of childhood. . . . [T]he child views heterosexuality as a dangerous transgression for which the fantasied punishments are castration and death.

Ovesey, *Pseudohomosexuality and Homosexuality in Men, id.* 220–21.

120. *See* Gagnon, *Sexual Behavior: Deviation: Social Aspects*, in 14 INT'L ENCY. SOCIAL SCIENCES 216–17 (1968).

121. The Institute for Sex Research found that males convicted of homosexual offenses had the poorest childhood health of any sex offenders and worse than that of the control groups. Gebhard, *Situational Factors Affecting Human Sexual Behavior*, in SEX AND BEHAVIOR 484 (F. A. Beach ed. 1965).

122. *See* BIEBER 184, 204.

123. Knight, *Overt Male Homosexuality*, in SEXUAL BEHAVIOR AND THE LAW 441–42 (R. Slovenko ed. 1965).

124. *Ibid.*

125. *See, e.g.,* the illustrative example given in HOFFMAN 148–49.

126. WEST 200–201, 206–7.

127. *Id.* 199. The same may prove true for the "masculine" girl or tomboy. *See id.* 212–13.

128. If his homosexuality is confined to fantasy, it does not put him to the test at all. And reliance on fantasy appears to follow from a sense of sexual inferiority in deviations of all kinds. *See* STORR 34–35.

129. W. B. POMEROY, BOYS AND SEX 68 (1968); WILLIS 104.

130. *See* STORR 85–87.

131. *See* HOFFMAN 136–38.

132. *See, e.g.,* WILLIS 131–33.

133. *See* S. ZUCKERMAN, THE SOCIAL LIFE OF MONKEYS AND APES (1932); also Maslow, Rand, & Neuman, *Some Parallels Between Sexual Dominance Behavior of Infra-Human Primates and the Fantasies of Patients in Psychotherapy*, 131 J. NERVOUS & MENTAL DISEASE 202–12 (1960).

134. H. S. SULLIVAN, THE INTERPERSONAL THEORY OF PSYCHIATRY 277 (1953).

135. The Kinsey group, in their study of sex offenders, noted that the men in

all three of their categories of homosexual offenders had an unusually high incidence of masturbation and sex play before the normal time for puberty. This hypersexuality at an early age, when society has made no provision at all for heterosexual activity, may account to some extent for their homosexuality. *See* SEX OFFENDERS 276, 301–2, 329–30.

136. Discussing the effect that late physical maturation (*i.e.*, a temporary delay in the onset of puberty) may have on psychosexual development, John Money says:

> A few . . . are able to overcome the handicap of a sexually unappealing, prepubertal body morphology and to keep up socially with their age-mates. But the task is difficult and the competition harsh, so that the majority lag in social maturation. . . . If this waiting is too protracted, there may be a permanent scar in social development.

Money, *Sexual Behavior: Deviation: Psychological Aspects*, in 14 INT'L ENCY. SOCIAL SCIENCES 212 (1968). *See also* ELLIS 35–39.

Admittedly, though, the evidence is inconclusive that early *or* late maturers are more frequently found among those who grow up homosexually than among those who grow up heterosexually.

137. Cultural anthropology has established that maleness and femaleness are culturally defined in different ways in different societies. They are not merely statements of genital differentiation but reflect a definite sex stereotype.

> For the children who do not belong to these preferred types, only the primary sex characters will be definitive in helping them to classify themselves. Their impulses, their preferences, and later much of their physique will be aberrant. They will be doomed throughout life to sit among the other members of their sex feeling less a man, or less a woman, simply because the cultural ideal is based on a different set of clues, a set of clues no less valid, but different. . . . [T]he little rabbity man who would have been so gently fierce and definitely masculine if he had been bred in a culture that recognized him as fully male, and quite able to take a mate and fight for her and keep her, may give up altogether and dub himself a female and become a true invert, attaching himself to some male who possesses the magnificent qualities that have been denied him.

M. MEAD, MALE AND FEMALE, A STUDY OF THE SEXES IN A CHANGING WORLD 137–38 (1949).

Even when a male's physique approximates the culture's stereotype, he may find it more and more difficult to feel comfortable about his masculinity in a culture in which the stereotype was developed under frontier conditions but which is now characterized by nine-to-five suits and ties. Kardiner, *The Flight from Masculinity*, in RUITENBEEK 17 is an interesting essay on the possible contribution to homosexuality made by the increasing difficulty males in American society experience in living up to the culture's masculine role expectations.

138. *See* WEST 120.

139. On the whole, the homosexual child play is found in more histories, occurs more frequently, and becomes more specific than the preadolescent heterosexual play. This depends, as so much of the adult homosexual

activity depends, on the greater accessibility of the boy's own sex. In the younger boy, it is also fostered by his socially encouraged disdain for girls' ways, by his admiration for masculine prowess, and by his desire to emulate older boys. The anatomy and functional capacities of male genitalia interest the younger boy to a degree that is not appreciated by older males who have become heterosexually conditioned and who are continuously on the defensive against reactions which might be interpreted as homosexual.

KINSEY, MALE 168.

140. W. B. POMEROY, BOYS AND SEX 67 (1968).

141. From their study of sex offenders, the Kinsey group felt that this segregation and isolation of the two sexes at puberty definitely encouraged a homosexual orientation in boys. *See* SEX OFFENDERS 314–15. "In societies where this temporary purdah is not imposed upon girls the incidence of predominantly homosexual males is much less than in ours." *Id.* 315. Westermarck also concluded from his anthropological and cross-cultural survey that homosexuality is more widespread in those cultures that segregate the sexes and place a premium on chastity, thus isolating unmarried males from unmarried females. The suggestion is that its incidence would diminish with freer relations between males and females from infancy up. *See* E. WESTERMARCK, THE ORIGIN AND DEVELOPMENT OF THE MORAL IDEAS (2d ed. 1917), particularly the chapter "Homosexual Love."

142. Two dramatic illustrative examples from the heterosexual world are described in Gebhard, *Situational Factors Affecting Human Sexual Behavior,* in SEX AND BEHAVIOR 489–90 (F. A. Beach ed. 1965).

143. See KINSEY, MALE 163–65:

The record suggests that the physiologic mechanism of any emotional response (anger, fright, pain, etc.) may be the mechanism of sexual response. Originally the pre-adolescent boy erects indiscriminately to the whole array of emotional situations, whether they be sexual or non-sexual in nature. By his late teens the male has been so conditioned that he rarely responds to anything except a direct physical stimulation of genitalia, or to psychic situations that are specifically sexual. In the still older male even physical stimulation is rarely effective unless accompanied by such a psychologic atmosphere. The picture is that of the psychosexual emerging from a much more generalized and basic physiologic capacity which becomes sexual, as an adult knows it, through experience and conditioning.

See also id. 190–91.

144. *See* Ferenczi, *The Nosology of Male Homosexuality,* in RUITENBEEK 12–15.

145. People . . . think of sexuality as an isolated thing, without realizing that it runs like a scarlet thread intimately interwoven into the pattern of all our affections. . . . But it is in truth an artificiality to separate sex and affection; and the fact that there is a physical element in all emotional relationships, whether recognized or not, and whether acted upon or not,

is surely nothing about which to be alarmed or of which to be ashamed. We may dichotomize ourselves into mind and body; but, especially in our affections, this division cannot be maintained.

STORR 71.

146. Some observers of the sexual scene in other countries assert that homosexuality is far less prevalent in such lands as Italy, where physical expressions of affection between males have traditionally been much freer than in our own. *See. e.g.,* CHURCHILL 167–69, 233–34. Of course, without some survey such as Kinsey's for these other countries, we have no way of knowing whether less homosexual *behavior* occurs there than here, but they may well have a lower incidence of *homosexuality* (in the sense of a definite preferential erotic attraction to the same sex).

147. Schofield found that only 18 per cent of his subjects had had their first homosexual experience with an adult. SCHOFIELD 31–32, 81–82, 109–11. The Bieber group found that 60 per cent of their patient population had their first homosexual experience with a partner approximately the same age (that is, within 2 years of their own age). BIEBER 191–92. Proselytization of boys by adult males thus seems far from being a major factor in introducing youngsters to homosexual experience. The same statement can be made for women as well. *See* Simon & Gagnon, *The Lesbians: A Preliminary Overview,* in SEXUAL DEVIANCE 255 (J. H. Gagnon & W. Simon eds. 1967). *See also* note 51, Chapter 5 *supra.*

148. SEX INFORMATION AND EDUCATION COUNCIL OF THE UNITED States, SEXUALITY AND MAN 80, 91 (1970); WEST 120–24; CHURCHILL 108; Wilbur, *Clinical Aspects of Female Homosexuality,* in SEXUAL INVERSION 269–70.

149. WEST 138. Doshay's survey of boys who had had such experience also confirms this view. *See* L. J. DOSHAY, THE BOY OFFENDER AND HIS LATER CAREER (1943).

150. Several such factors are described in ELLIS 61–66.

151. The Kinsey group points out that exclusiveness in adult sexual patterns is produced not merely by a tendency to repeat the behavior that an individual has found more satisfactory in the past, but also by the fact that our society rewards the heterosexual and ostracizes the homosexual:

> Thus the exclusively heterosexual end of our curve becomes higher than it would be without social compulsions in that direction. But social ostracism is also responsible for some of the completely homosexual histories which are located at the right end of the curve. Because society makes the heterosexual less available to persons who are once discovered to have had homosexual experience, it forces many of them into exclusively homosexual patterns.

Kinsey *et al., Concepts of Normality and Abnormality in Sexual Behavior,* in PSYCHOSEXUAL DEVELOPMENT IN HEALTH AND DISEASE 25–26 (P. H. Hoch & J. Zubin eds. 1949).

152. This process of self-labeling which results from and reinforces the stigmatization of the larger society is a phenomenon observed among all varieties of deviants. *See* OUTSIDERS: STUDIES IN THE SOCIOLOGY OF DEVIANCE (H. S. Becker ed. 1963); J. L. FRIEDMAN & A. N. DOOB, DEVIANCY: THE PSYCHOLOGY OF BEING

DIFFERENT (1968); THE OTHER SIDE: PERSPECTIVES ON DEVIANCE (H. S. Becker ed. 1964); J. LOFLAND, DEVIANCE AND IDENTITY (1969); and D. MATZA, BECOMING DEVIANT (1969).

153. John Rechy, in his novel about a hustler's life in the "gay" world, indicates that some, at any rate, of these young men who think of themselves as heterosexual get trapped in the sexual pattern they developed as hustlers, thus giving rise to the homosexuals' proverb, "This year's trade is next year's competition." J. RECHY, CITY OF NIGHT (1963).

154. See KINSEY, MALE 636–59; KINSEY, FEMALE 468–74. Cf. MAGEE 23–24.

155. In terms of overt experience to the point of orgasm, Kinsey's group found that 37 per cent of the male subjects in their interviews had had some homosexual experience between the beginning of adolescence and old age. KINSEY, MALE 623, 650. They felt this figure was, if anything, conservative, and that the actual incidence might be as much as 5 per cent higher, or still higher. Id. 626. They also found that approximately 13 per cent of their male subjects admitted to erotic reactions toward other males but without overt contacts after the onset of adolescence. Id. 650. On the other hand, 4 per cent were exclusively homosexual throughout life. Id. 651. Thus, they concluded,

> since only 50 per cent of the population is exclusively heterosexual throughout its adult life, and since only 4 per cent of the population is exclusively homosexual throughout its life, it appears that nearly half (46%) of the population engages in both heterosexual and homosexual activities, or reacts to persons of both sexes, in the course of their adult lives.

Id. 656.

But their 37 and 13 per cent figures which go to make up this 50 per cent figure for people who are either ambisexual or exclusively homosexual refer to experience or reaction *since the onset of adolescence*. Many individuals thus were lumped into these categories whose only homosexual experience may have consisted of occasional and isolated youthful experimentation.

156. John Gagnon corrects the wrong impression left by the Kinsey figures cited in the preceding note by his assertion that although one in three American males will have had a homosexual experience to the point of orgasm during their lives, 85 per cent of those who do will have had it only during puberty or adolescence. Gagnon, *Sexual Behavior: Deviation: Social Aspects*, in 14 INT'L ENCY. SOCIAL SCIENCES 219 (1968).

157. HOFFMAN 28–30.

158. The word "rape" is here used in a figurative sense. Actually, nonconsensual homosexual acts are rare, being mainly confined to prisons and hobo jungles. *See* note 62, Chapter 5 *supra*.

159. *See, e.g.*, Pittman, *The Male House of Prostitution*, in TRANS-ACTION, March/April 1971, at 26.

160. *See* HOFFMAN 28–30. *See also id.* 13–22.

161. *See* note 51 *supra*. The Kinsey group dismisses as totally unscientific all such insistence upon classifying as homosexual anybody with more than one exploratory experience. "It would be as reasonable to rate all individuals heterosexual if they have any heterosexual experience, and irrespective of the

amount of homosexual experience which they may be having." KINSEY, FEMALE 469. *See also* WILLIS 27. But Bieber is in good company. Voltaire is reported to have engaged in an "exploratory" homosexual act with an acquaintance. Surprised to learn later that the acquaintance had proceeded to additional acts with others, he is supposed to have exclaimed, "Once, a philosopher; twice, a sodomite!"

162. The Kinsey group found that homosexual outlets among married males reach a maximum incidence of 10.6 per cent of the total number of married males in the 21-to-25-year age group, dropping to 2 per cent of the 45-year-old married males. They believe, however, that the actual incidence is probably higher than this reported incidence. *See* KINSEY, MALE 285–89.

163. One such piece of research which uncovered the phenomenon of married men engaging furtively in homosexual contacts is L. HUMPHREYS, TEAROOM TRADE—IMPERSONAL SEX IN PUBLIC PLACES 41, 105–7, 117–22 (1970). This project raised quite a furor in sociological circles because it involved methods that invaded the subjects' very "private" lives without their knowledge or consent, but it obviously would have been nearly impossible to pursue without using such methods.

164. The rather cursory treatment here given to female homosexuality is not intended to slight the female sex. Even if lesbianism had been as much studied as male homosexuality, a comparably full discussion of it would not be warranted, as the objective has been to present an illustrative, rather than exhaustive, description of how deviant sexuality develops. With such an objective, either male homosexuality or lesbianism could serve equally well as the focal point. The only book by a professional published within the last 18 years and devoted solely to lesbianism would appear to be C. WOLFF, LOVE BETWEEN WOMEN (1971). A good recent panel is presented in *When Women Love Other Women: A Frank Discussion of Female Homosexuality*, in REDBOOK, November 1971, at 84. A review of the scientific literature is found in Kenyon, *Homosexuality in the Female*, 3 BRIT. J. HOSPITAL MEDICINE 183 (1970).

> 165. The female child destined to be a homosexual looks upon her mother with hostility and rebellion. . . . Identification with the mother is impaired by her own hostility.

Wilbur, *Clinical Aspects of Female Homosexuality*, in SEXUAL INVERSION 275. *See also id.* 270–71.

> Disturbance in the relationship with the mother, whom the girl may see as rejecting, as a dominating and controlling figure toward a beloved father, or as a masochistic, compliant, long-suffering creature at the mercy of the males in the household, may produce in the girl intense ambivalence in her feminine identification and in her reactions to men. . . . The mother becomes a symbol of identification that is fraught with anxiety.

Romm, *Sexuality and Homosexuality in Women, id.* 287.

166. *See* WEST 210–11.

> 167. We know that an insufficiently resolved Oedipal phase carrying with it the incest taboo can be a focal deterrent to heterosexuality. When the potential love object represents a parent, a sibling, or an individual who is

identified with an incestuous object, the sexual act becomes imbued with anxiety and frequently cannot be consummated.

Romm, *Sexuality and Homosexuality in Women,* in SEXUAL INVERSION 284.

. . . . [U]nresolved Oedipal feelings with consequent identification of each eligible man as a father figure may create an insurmountable incest taboo, or rejection by the father during puberty may cause the girl to identify with him and to seek a love object representing her mother. . . .

Id. 287.

168. The case histories of many female homosexuals reveal severe cautions, warnings, and even threats by mothers or other adult females in the family about the sexual dangers implicit in the boy-girl relationship. "Conversely, never a word is spoken about any sexual dangers implicit in a girl-girl relationship." Wilbur, *Clinical Aspects of Female Homosexuality,* in SEXUAL INVERSION 274–75. *See also id.* 272.

169. Isolation, the inability to make affectional peer relationships, and play behavior that is predominantly "tomboy" appear distinguishing factors for the homosexual group.

Id. 277.

170. The Kinsey group found that, of the females in their study, 28 per cent had recognized erotic response in themselves to other females, 19 per cent had had specifically sexual physical contact with other females, and 13 per cent had reached orgasm in such contact. KINSEY, FEMALE 452–53. But because of the difficulty in obtaining greater representation of lower-class females in their sample, they surmised that these reported incidences were higher than for the population as a whole, their data having shown greater incidences at each higher educational level. *Id.* 459. By way of comparison, 50 per cent of the males had experienced psychic response to other males, and 37 per cent had had sexual physical contact to the point of orgasm. While 4 per cent of the males appeared to be exclusively homosexual throughout life, the Kinsey group estimated that only 1–2 per cent of females were in this category. *Id.* 474–75. Charles Socarides believes that Kinsey's estimates of the incidence of female homosexuality are too low, at least for today's population. Socarides, *Female Homosexuality,* in SEXUAL BEHAVIOR AND THE LAW 464 (R. Slovenko ed. 1965).

171. Because the female is not dependent on physiological function (the capacity to have an erection) to act as a sexual partner in any situation, it is not uncommon for the female homosexual to have had heterosexual experience.

Wilbur, *Clinical Aspects of Female Homosexuality,* in SEXUAL INVERSION 273.

172. Every physician who has treated female homosexuality or who has seen a number of female homosexuals has had the opportunity to observe that female homosexuals often express desires for children and sometimes have them with or without benefit of marriage. In the author's experience, there have been several female homosexuals who have had children out of wedlock and have insisted on keeping and raising them.

Ibid.

Simon and Gagnon indicate that a majority of the lesbians they interviewed had experimented with the possibility of heterosexual relations, and a good proportion of these had seriously considered marriage:

> The temptation is clearly to sacrifice the sexual gratification for significant gains in the availability of conventional rewards and statuses, such as the approval of friends and family, a recognized position in the general community, a family of one's own, and so on.

Simon & Gagnon, *The Lesbians,* in Sexual Deviance 278–79 (J. H. Gagnon & W. Simon eds. 1967).

173. *See* C. W. Socarides, The Overt Homosexual 47–48 (1968).

7

The "Sickness Theory" of Homosexuality and the Prospects for "Cure"

Laymen generally assume that the scientific community uniformly regards homosexuality as pathological—a mental or emotional illness. Great diversity of opinion exists, however, among scientific investigators. The lay assumption probably derives from the traditional stance of psychiatrists toward the phenomenon. Our society has largely delegated questions of illness and health to the medical profession, so it is not surprising to find such uncritical deference to that branch of medicine concerned with mental and emotional illness—psychiatry. But we must not make the mistake of endowing this medical specialty with omniscience merely because we have assigned to psychiatrists the general task of dealing with mental and emotional illness. Major insights and a large body of knowledge with profound implications for the question may be supplied by other scientific disciplines, such as psychology, sociology, and anthropology.

Several general considerations need to be borne in mind to put the traditional psychiatric position into proper perspective. In the first place, the profession itself has no very exact criteria for drawing the line between health and illness, when no question of physical damage to, or disease of, the brain is involved. When no physical basis, such as a brain tumor, can be found, probably the most one can say is that the patient is experiencing problems in living. Since we all have such problems, the difference between illness and health appears more a matter of degree than a precise line.

Many such problems derive from a conflict between one's

impulses, which Freud termed the "id," and the internal controls over his behavior, which Freud termed the "superego." These controls, originally imposed by external figures such as parents, are internalized by the person in order to keep himself from giving way to the impulses and thereby incurring the risk of punishment. If the controls are so harsh and extensive as to preclude reasonable satisfaction of his impulses, he may experience severe anxiety and even break down under the strain. But we all possess a superego, so the questions of what controls are too harsh and extensive, and of what impulses should reasonably be satisfied, are largely incapable of objective determination.

In making the determination, psychiatrists may be as culture-bound as any one else in our society. They may uncritically, even unthinkingly, import into their theory the Western cultural notion of the unnaturalness of certain types of sexual behavior. When some of them employ the terms "disorder" and "dysfunction" in reference to homosexuality, it is difficult to believe they are wholly emancipated from the old idea that homosexuality is contrary to the order of creation, and to the intentions of God, who made males to fit females and vice versa. The idea may be secularized in their minds, but it is virtually the same idea nonetheless.

Psychiatry may be peculiarly prone to take such a cultural framework of thought into account, because it is a *medically* oriented approach to human behavior. Its purpose is not to study such behavior dispassionately, solely in order to enlarge human knowledge and understanding. Rather, its objective is to "cure." Since problems in living are usually diminished to the extent that one can be brought to live comfortably within society's expectations, the profession has an understandable tendency to define health as whatever the community considers good and virtuous, and pathology as whatever it regards as bad and sinful. Heterosexuality and even monogamy are seen as healthy, and those who cannot find happiness within these limits are labeled sick, immature, or disordered. The very terms "adjustment" and "maladjustment" may mean little else than conformity and nonconformity, respectively.[1]

In the second place, a number of homosexuals are unhappy with their orientation and need help in trying to change to heterosexuality. Whether one regards their condition as pathological or not, it is impossible to ignore their pleas for assistance. As in the case of alcoholism and drug addiction, labeling the phenomenon as illness helps to justify the psychiatrists' proffer of aid. Our society, for the most part, has developed no other profession or organization whose service function is to facilitate behavior modification or merely to help people with their problems in living.[2] Yet psychiatrists probably feel uncomfortable about spending their time and charging their fees for "treating" homosexuals unless they can bring the condition within a specifically medical theoretical framework. Ovesey asserts, moreover, that the sickness theory is itself an indispensable tool of therapy in these cases.[3]

The most influential psychiatric viewpoint is probably that expounded in the study published by Irving Bieber and his co-workers.[4] Basically, their thesis is that all persons are biologically predisposed to heterosexuality and can only be diverted from this path by irrational fear. Having found in the histories of their homosexual patients childhood experiences that apparently promoted an unrealistic fear of the opposite sex, they conclude that homosexuality is caused by such fear. Since any behavior pattern rooted in unrealistic fear is ipso facto pathological, homosexuality is necessarily pathological.[5] Putting the theory into its logical progression may make the assumptions on which it is based easier to see:

1. There is an inherent biological tendency in every human being toward heterosexuality.
2. Natural impulses can only be blocked or inhibited through fear.
3. Therefore, homosexuality must always result from fear.
4. Therefore, homosexuality always coexists with unhappiness and inner conflict, because the individual is fighting against his own innate tendencies.
5. Therefore, homosexuality is always pathological.
6. Therefore, homosexuality must be curable by removal of the fear through psychotherapy, because the individual's natural innate drive toward heterosexuality will then be left free to express itself.

The first and perhaps most critical assumption of the theory is that every human being possesses an inherent biological tendency toward heterosexuality. Yet this is just that—an assumption. Nowhere in the Bieber book or in any other psychiatric work is there any attempt to prove it. The fact that psychoanalytic theories have usually started from that premise hardly establishes it.

One suggested proof is the observation that the great majority of people are heterosexual, but this is what Martin Hoffman calls a pseudo-explanation. It does not really explain anything, but merely restates the observation in the form of an explanation. To say that the two sexes are attracted to each other because all people possess an inherited constitutional drive toward heterosexuality is no more enlightening than to say that a physical body will remain at rest unless acted on by an external force because all bodies possess an inherent quality of inertia.[6] In effect, both statements constitute an admission of ignorance that we do not really know why the thing acts in the way it does. Neither statement is true of the entire population about which it speaks. There are physical bodies, such as animals and other living bodies, which will move even without being acted on by any external force, just as there are members of both sexes who are not attracted to the other sex.

Moreover, in attempting to explain a *majority* pattern of behavior in a population by positing in every individual of that population some innate drive or tendency to engage in the behavior, we may be overlooking some other explanation more consistent with the facts. For instance, it is true that the great majority of humankind wears clothes, but we know better than to postulate some innate attraction to clothing in every human being. The physical discomfort of exposing a comparatively hairless skin surface to cold temperatures is a better explanation, since we know that humans exposed only to warm temperatures often do not wear clothes. But if the majority pattern of clothes-wearing is explainable by conditioning factors, it may be equally plausible to explain the majority pattern of heterosexuality by conditioning.[7] In many other areas of science, we have seen the inherent-quality explanation wither away when it was no longer needed to explain the data.

In the same way, species propagation does not require the positing of an innate attraction between the sexes. Some psychiatrists seem to think that it does.[8] Heterosexual conjunction is necessary to the propagation of the species, but we know from reflecting on our own inner feelings and from human experience that the incentive to reproduce hardly accounts for heterosexual attraction. As Klausner says, "The procreative function loses its centrality for a social psychology of human sexual behavior in view of the empirical fact that less than one in a thousand human coital acts results in pregnancy and fewer are intended to do so."[9] Certainly, there is an observable "tendency" in the human species as a whole, as in other species, to propagate itself. But to infer from this general species tendency some impulse, tendency, or predisposition innate in every member of that species is to engage in a *non sequitur.* Laymen may think it insulting to God or to Nature to imply that he or it lacked the foresight to install in every animal some urge or mechanism to guarantee heterosexual arousal, but scientists surely must regard this possibility as conceivable. To discount it completely is to fall back into the trap of viewing nature as purposive. We recognize that the sun gives light and heat to the earth, but we no longer say that this is the purpose of sunshine. We can admit that animals, including human beings, reproduce themselves through the act of copulation between male and female, without having to insist that the purpose of sex is procreation and therefore every individual must be emotionally wired toward heterosexual attraction. Such an insistence is teleological philosophy, not science.[10]

The Bieber group does attempt to refute the concept of a universal latent homosexual attraction, and in the process they bring together some observations of their own patients to demonstrate that heterosexual tendencies are innate in everyone, but not homosexual tendencies. The demonstration is unconvincing. They state that half the homosexuals studied showed some heterosexual dream content, while only 25 per cent of the heterosexual control group had homosexual dream content. That many of the homosexuals had attempted heterosexual intercourse is also adduced to support the inference.[11] This seems unscientific, because the book notes that 28 per cent of the so-called homosexual sample were in fact ambisexual. They had had more than an experimental acquaintance with heterosexual intercourse.[12] By lumping the ambisexuals with the exclusive or near-exclusive homosexuals, and consequently freeing the heterosexual comparison group of any overt homosexual behavior, the two groups were already biased toward the conclusion to be established. Even then, the book admits that 40 per cent of the heterosexual comparison group had homosexual problems, that is, some psychic responsiveness to homosexual stimuli against which the patient struggled.[13] On the other hand, since 40 per cent of the comparison group indicated no homosexual responsiveness despite extensive probing, Bieber and his collaborators triumphantly conclude that there is no such thing as the "universal perverse impulse" known as latent homosexuality.[14] One suspects that they might have come up with a similar conclusion if they had set out just as energetically to disprove the theory of a universal latent heterosexuality.

Bieber has suggested elsewhere that perhaps the inborn mechanism to guarantee heterosexual arousal in all human beings resides in the sense of smell.[15] Although smell plays a large role in sexual arousal in lower mammals, its significance in humans, while of interest, is debatable.[16] Even in lower mammals, the sexual arousal produced by the odor of the opposite sex may be a result of conditioning.[17] Assuming one could establish that in humans the olfactory sense of males is innately (rather than through conditioning) attracted by the odor of females, and vice versa, homosexuality would not necessarily be demonstrated to be pathological. Instead, we might be set to seeking the cause of homosexuality in our culture not in childhood fear of the opposite sex but in the American craze for deodorants. Be this as it may, it appears that tactile stimuli account for most mammalian sexual responses,[18] and either sex can provide them.

Contrary to the psychoanalytic assumption, rather strong evidence can be marshalled that no biological substratum exists for sexual object-choice. In many species of lower mammals,[19] animals of one sex have been observed to mount others of the same sex and engage in the kind of pelvic thrusting typical of heterosexual copulation. While in many cases this may be merely the consequence of failure to identify the sex of the partner, it apparently also occurs simply because no partners of the opposite sex are available at the time.[20] In species of high intelligence, such as other primates and the dolphin, such behavior or its like has been known to occur even when a partner of the opposite sex was available and receptive.[21] In primates, but rarely in lower animals, the "homosexual" partner has been seen to exhibit the receptive posture and responses typical of the opposite sex. Often, this receptive individual appears to be a young, weakened, or senile male without easy access to food. He will offer himself "homosexually to a strong and protective male who may prefer him despite the fact that both males have noncompetitive access to a harem of importunate females in heat. Later, this male partnership may continue as a strong homosexual 'friendship,' even though food and females both remain plentiful."[22]

We do not, of course, know what the animals are feeling in any of the cases of homosexual behavior in animals. Although the mounting partner sometimes ejaculates upon the back of the other, actual intromission *per anum* probably occurs rarely if at all.[23] Further-more, an *exclusive* pattern of homosexual behavior apparently never occurs spontaneously in any species, whether in the wild or in captivity, though it seems possible to condition an animal to such a pattern by carefully controlled laboratory methods. Thus the parallels to human homosexual behavior and emotions are far from exact. "Homosexuality" in the sense in which it is used in this book (a definite preferential erotic attraction to the same sex) probably does not exist in the animal kingdom. Other animals than humans exhibit both heterosexual and homosexual behavior, but the former always predominates.[24] The fact, though, that what appears to be sexual behavior does occur in other species between individuals of the same sex is rather persuasive evidence that the mammalian heritage is a sexual drive which is "polymorphous" in character, rather than biologically directed toward procreation with the opposite sex.

This conclusion is also supported by the cross-cultural evidence. Homosexual behavior is not uncommon in other cultures, both advanced and primitive.[25] Nothing comparable to the Kinsey surveys exists for the other advanced cultures of the world, so we have no way of estimating its incidence there. Virtually the only information we have on homosexual behavior in advanced non-Western cultures is anecdotal in nature, but it would indicate that the phenomenon is no rarity in any of them.[26] Primitive cultures have been studied far more systematically by Western anthropologists. In certain of the latter, homosexual intercourse *between* adolescents *and* older males is institutionalized as a ritual phase of growing up, so that all males in the society are expected to participate; in these cultures as well as in others, homosexual behavior *among* adolescents or young, unmarried men is considered perfectly normal.[27] Again, however, one rarely finds in any of these cultures a pattern of exclusive homosexuality in adulthood.[28] Often anthropological observers have reported what they thought to be exclusively homosexual adults, but the reliability of many of these reports is now in question because they failed to take into account the context of culture patterns and social structures.[29] For instance, the *berdache*—a male who dresses as a female and does women's work—is commonly found in many cultures,[30] but he may be heterosexual in orientation and behavior. The belief that he was invariably homosexual likely resulted from the common Western confusion of transvestism with homosexuality. Similarly, the institution of the *shaman* in some cultures—usually a male transvestite with whom other men engage in homosexual intercourse as a part of religious ritual, and who is often endowed with magical powers—is an entirely different phenomenon from the ordinary male homosexual of American culture. Even granting allowance for such basic cultural differences, one is struck by the ubiquity of homosexual attraction among other peoples of the world who do not share our patterns of child rearing and sexual attitudes; this attraction does not seem to preclude extensive heterosexual attraction and behavior. The fact that adult males of the Keraki tribe of New Guinea perform buggery on younger males entering adulthood and still assume the usual roles of husband and father in Keraki society[31] casts serious doubt on the psychoanalytic theory that exclusive heterosexuality is the biological norm and homosexual attraction and behavior are invariably the product of an irrational fear of heterosexuality.

Even in Western societies, too many people experience homosexual attraction to make the theory believable.[32] If 50 per cent of the males in American society experience erotic reaction to or behavior with other males, and 28 per cent of the females admit to erotic attraction by other females,[33] the idea that heterosexuality is innate and homosexual attraction always the result of pathological fear appears increasingly incredible.[34] The theory that seems much more consistent with all the factual data, both from our own and other cultures and from the animal world, is, as Freud himself suggested, that "the sexual instinct is in the first instance independent of its object."[35]

The idea that fear of heterosexuality fully explains homosexual attraction is itself open to very telling objections. In the first place, it ignores the multitude of possibilities for a positive conditioning toward homosexuality that exist in our culture.[36] Some of these have already been described in the preceding chapter. In addition, we must always bear in mind that our culture has two ideals of beauty, one masculine, the other feminine. Those who assert that our cultural ideal of beauty is feminine are looking at only half the picture, or at the picture only from a male standpoint. Otherwise, any male actor, no matter what he looked like, would have an equal chance with any other of becoming a star in romantic screen roles. This is plainly not the case. If, then, we have a conception of male beauty as well as one of female beauty, what is there to decree that only females shall become attracted by the former and only males by the latter? Cross-sex imitation occurs in children in matters of behavior, without regard to the social inappropriateness of that behavior to the child's own gender,[37] so we should not be surprised that children can pick up a preference for the beauty ideal of their own sex rather than that of the opposite sex, to which sexual feelings and fantasies attach. This may be particularly likely if a child has been taught or has become convinced that his own sex is more noble and lovable than, and is superior to, the opposite sex.

Many other possibilities exist for a conditioning of one's sexual drive toward the same sex that do not involve fear of the opposite sex.[38] Indeed, fear of heterosexuality often exists in persons who do not experience homosexual attraction. If sexual frigidity toward the opposite sex does not necessarily imply homosexuality, then why should homosexual attraction necessarily imply fear of the opposite sex or of heterosexuality?[39]

The existence of ambisexuals in our own culture further belies the psychoanalytic theory.[40] Many such people have had considerable experience with heterosexual intercourse, though, it often seems, rarely with more than one partner. Yet they still engage in homosexual behavior as well. Moreover, in the ranks of exclusively homosexual adults will be found a number of men who in earlier life had been married and had sired a number of children over the years. Williams and Weinberg, in their study of homosexuals and the military, found that 13 to 23 per cent of the men in their various samples had been married. More than half the men in each of their samples had had sexual intercourse with a female, and in two of their four samples this figure rose to 81 per cent.[41] In such cases, to posit fear of heterosexuality as the cause of the homosexual attraction seems a bit farfetched.[42]

What we know about the sexual orientation of pseudohermaphrodites is also inconsistent with the psychoanalytic theory. The researches of Money and the Hampsons with these physically intersexed individuals have already been noted. The child's gender is often assigned at birth purely on the basis of the appearance of the external genitalia, and may be in flat contradiction to the actual biological sex as determined by the sex chromosomes and internal reproductive organs. Nevertheless, these children generally develop the sexual orientation appropriate to the assigned sex when no question is ever raised about its correctness, even in cases later diagnosed as identical, some of which had been assigned to the one sex and some to the other.[43] Although this orientation is biologically homosexual when the assignment was incorrect, no one suggests that such a development must have resulted from the intrusion of fear. The child, though "she" may be, biologically, a male, doubtless becomes attracted to males through the same process that most females do, because "she" has always been reared unequivocally as a female.[44] Since "her" gender identity and outward appearance are female, "her" sexual orientation toward males can arise just as easily (*i.e.*, without conflict) and seem as natural and comfortable as in the case of ordinary females. If, then, in such a person, homosexuality is not a product of fear of heterosexuality, it is clearly not *invariably* so rooted.[45]

Probably the most devastating evidence against the traditional psychoanalytic stance is provided by Lorenz's work with greylag geese. In their natural state the goslings attach themselves to their mother and follow her around. By substituting himself for the mother during these critical times in the birds' infancy when they would normally have been with her, Lorenz discovered that they would attach themselves to him and then throughout their growing period follow and respond to him as if he were their mother. On reaching sexual maturity, their sexual drives were directed exclusively toward him and other humans and not toward their own species.[46] Significantly, the birds became conditioned to regard humans as sexual objects not through any aversive conditioning toward, or fear of, the opposite sex of their own species, but simply through the "accident" of having been raised by a human "mother." This seems rather good evidence that they possessed no innate biological drive toward the opposite sex which could only be diverted to some other object through fear. The point is not that humans and greylag geese are in all respects comparable. It is rather that if geese lack any inborn mechanism to guarantee heterosexual attraction, other species, such as humans, may lack it too. Again, the datum seems to point to the sexual drive as being something free-floating and unattached in its unconditioned state. If it can attach accidentally to another species, then it certainly could attach just as accidentally to the same sex of one's own species.

There are, of course, fallback positions one can take that seem more defensible than the Bieber stance. One could posit in every human being some innate prepotency or tendency for heterosexual object-choice, which, however, is relatively weak and easily overridden by conditioning.[47] The implications of this view are not greatly different from conceding that no such prepotency or tendency exists. If the tendency were so weak, it could hardly produce inner conflict, and thus pathology, once it had been overridden by conditioning.

A number of psychiatrists and other experts concede that the sex drive is undifferentiated as to objects, so that homosexual attraction is inherently no more unnatural or pathological than heterosexual attraction. Exclusive heterosexuality is not a biological norm but a social convention. Their argument is that a fixed and exclusive pattern of adult homosexual behavior, or even homosexuality in the sense of a definite sexual preference for members of one's own sex, can be adequately explained only by fear of heterosexuality in a culture like our own where every individual has at least some contact with the opposite sex while growing up and the overall societal pressures are toward heterosexual adjustment.[48] In other words, all things being equal, homosexuality could develop in a certain percentage of the population by accidental conditioning. But all things are not equal. Our culture pushes everyone toward heterosexuality. No encouragement is offered to homosexuality. Quite the contrary, a powerful taboo exists against the latter. In such circumstances, the person who gets conditioned to homosexuality without some measure of aversive conditioning toward heterosexuality would likely be rare. Therefore, fear and inhibition of heterosexuality are still at the root of almost all homosexuality, so it must still be regarded as pathological. The argument, it must be admitted, seems formidable. How anyone could become homosexual in our persecuting culture without some kind of negative feelings standing in the path of a heterosexual adaptation is difficult to imagine.

Some of those who hold this position frankly concede its logical implications:

1. Homosexuality is pathological only under certain cultural circumstances, such as our own, not in all cultures at all times. For some few individuals, it may not be pathological even in those circumstances.
2. Exclusive heterosexuality may be equally pathological, because in many cases in our culture it is produced by an

irrational fear of homosexuality. (Few, if any, of the therapists in question, however, have yet started a crusade to
eradicate the latter pathology from American life.)
3. If all cultural controls were removed, ambisexuality, with
heterosexual behavior predominating, might prove to be the
norm for most of the population.

The position's premises may be sound, but its conclusions are
open to serious question. Even if it be conceded that homosexuality
would rarely develop *initially* in our culture without the influence
of some irrational aversion to heterosexuality, the conclusion that
homosexuality must always *remain* based on pathological fear does
not follow. It is quite possible that many homosexuals lose their
fear of heterosexuality yet still remain homosexual. Regardless of
how any particular taste is acquired, it is likely to persist even in
the absence of fear if it allows the individual to obtain adequate
satisfaction of his basic needs. For instance, a person can acquire,
through early traumatic experience, an aversion to eating squash.
Later, he may overcome this aversion through learning that he can
eat squash without gagging. Yet, even then, he may never choose
squash as a food, simply because in the meantime he acquired a
preference for other foods. Since he can satisfy his need for
nutrition without squash, why should he eat it rather than the food
he has learned to prefer?

The same thing may be true of sexual orientation. Many
heterosexuals succeed in overcoming their fear of homosexuality, so
that homosexuality in others does not threaten them. Yet they have
no interest themselves in homosexual behavior, because they find
heterosexuality satisfying enough by itself. Such a state of affairs is
perfectly understandable and accepted when it comes to heterosexuality, but few psychiatrists, even those who adopt the position
just described, are willing to concede as much to people with a
homosexual orientation. Homosexuality, they insist, must continue
to be based on fear of heterosexuality, not on mere preference.

Albert Ellis is one who does make this concession, but then he
withdraws it by saying that one could only base real preference on
extensive experience of both kinds with a variety of partners. He
says he has never heard of a homosexual who has had this calibre of
heterosexual experience.[49] One wonders how many heterosexuals
he knows who have had such extensive homosexual experience. In

fact, a great many heterosexuals have no such extensive *hetero-sexual* experience. Their experience is limited to one partner or a very small number of partners. Ellis at times seems to be implying that everyone, if he were really psychologically healthy, and if there were no cultural controls to skew his behavior in any particular direction, would continue throughout life to engage in heterosexual behavior, say, 80 per cent of the time, homosexual behavior 15 per cent of the time, and autoerotic behavior 5 per cent of the time. But this ignores the tendency of all human beings to establish preferences rather quickly and then to indulge those preferences to the exclusion of all other possibilities.

No one insists that a preference for the opposite sex must be based on extensive experience of homosexual behavior, probably for two reasons: (1) All heterosexuals know that heterosexuality is better anyway (an attitude that "gay" liberationists would term "heterosexual chauvinism"), and (2) human beings can get a pretty good idea vicariously of something outside the range of their own experience. Many people can imagine what homosexual behavior would be like, and they realize they do not want it. Many homosexuals similarly can form a rather accurate impression of heterosexual behavior, since it is so widely depicted and extolled in our culture. The picture holds no attraction for them, not because of fear, but because they do not perceive how it could provide them with any emotional satisfaction. Certainly, the physical pleasure may be as great as or greater than in homosexual behavior, but physical pleasure without emotional satisfaction may seem no better than masturbation.

Even in cases in which the psychiatrist has clearly ascertained that fear of heterosexuality still persists in the adult homosexual, a causal connection between this fear and the behavioral pattern is not necessarily proven. There may be a chicken-and-the-egg paradox in homosexual fear of heterosexual behavior. Instead of the fear of heterosexuality producing a homosexual orientation, a homosexual orientation may produce the fear of heterosexual behavior. For instance, a male homosexual may avoid occasions for getting a girl into bed because he cannot imagine how he could get an erection with her. The thought of girls does not excite him sexually, so he is fairly sure that the reality will not either. On the other hand, he already knows through fantasy that the idea of another male provokes arousal, so he assumes that the reality will do so too. Probably few heterosexual males would go to bed with a girl if they were equally convinced that they would prove impotent. The fear in such case, if we can call it that, seems realistic rather than irrational.

The answer that might be given to these objections is that sexual preferences are not maintained in a cultural vacuum any more than they are formed in one. Society does not insist that everyone eat squash; it permits a wide choice of foods. But when it comes to psychosexual object-choice, only heterosexuality is permitted, though few restrictions are placed on selections within that overall limitation. What therefore demands explanation is why a minority appears unable to conform to the taboo on homosexuality.[50] If it were merely a question of the establishment and maintenance of ordinary preferences, surely the minority would conform, just as people who like squash would consume other foods instead if society forbade them to eat it. A homosexual orientation, so the assertion goes, can only be maintained in the face of such cultural hostility by the operation of fear blocking the path to a heterosexual adaptation.

The problem with this answer is that factors other than fear of heterosexuality are sufficient to explain the failure of the minority to conform. For one thing, many people have a fairly high tolerance for deviance in themselves. Being different from other people does not arouse much anxiety, as long as the chances of being discovered are small. And admittedly, in the case of homosexuality, the chances *are* small, at least in the anonymity of large urban settings. But even those severely disturbed by the incongruence between their feelings and behavior and the demands of society seem incapable of conforming. Why should this be?

A plausible explanation is that the acquisition of sexual orientation involves a kind of learning different from the acquisition of tastes and preferences. Something akin to imprinting may be occurring in human beings. The experience of Lorenz with his geese has already been described. In human beings, there may be a critical period during which sexual orientation is formed. This time is probably when the person first begins to think of others as sexual objects, though this may vary from one to another. For some, it may occur at puberty or in early adolescence. For others, it may occur earlier in life.[51] We do not know exactly when it occurs.[52] In contrast to the majority, a certain portion of both males and females begin to have conscious and explicit sexual fantasies not of the opposite sex, but of their own. Whether this peculiar twist is caused by fear of the opposite sex or of heterosexual behavior, by positive conditioning toward their own sex, by a combination of the two, or even by accident, is less important than the fact that this fantasy life can be focused as exclusively on their own sex as that of the others may be focused on the opposite sex. If nothing intervenes to stop the progression, all the usual dreams and feelings associated with the budding of sexuality—such as love, romance, warm affection, touching, kissing, and, finally, orgasm—get tied in with these images of another person of the same sex. And once the progression is complete, it is as difficult to reverse as the similar progression that takes place in the majority. Often nothing will intervene because the youngster involved never reveals these feelings and fantasies to his parents, a teacher, or any other adult interested in his welfare. He probably realizes that there is something different about him, but he knows less about homosexuality than he understands about heterosexuality. The result is a romantic attachment to his own sex that may be as nearly fixed and irrevocable as the others' romantic attachment to the opposite sex.

Total eradication of this attachment and a rerouting of the individual through the same progression but with the opposite sex in mind seems an almost impossible psychological feat, because one can never go back and relive "the splendor in the grass, the glory in the flower."[53] Even ordinary conditioning is more difficult to reverse than it is to come by initially,[54] and this is not ordinary conditioning. As John Money points out, certain kinds of learning occur at critical points in human life.[55] Once this learning has taken place, it becomes extremely difficult to unlearn, because the thing learned is a component of personality in everyone. Gender identity, for instance, which is learned by about the age of acquisition of meaningful language, is probably the core of these personality components. Sexual orientation is probably learned later, and may therefore be somewhat more susceptible to being unlearned, but the difficulty is still formidable.[56] Psychotherapists may succeed in enabling one who has gone through this progression homosexually to have heterosexual intercourse easily and comfortably and to find it pleasurable. They may equally succeed in bringing him to regard the opposite sex with warm and sympathetic feelings, and even to love one of them as one can come to love any other human being. What is exceedingly more difficult is the re-creation, in respect of the opposite sex, of the same romantic sexual feelings or intensity of feeling he came to experience for his own sex while growing up. For him, the opposite sex may therefore always lack that certain magnetism, that exciting potential, it possesses for the person who grew up heterosexual.

The maintenance of a homosexual orientation in adult life can therefore be explained by the possibility that sexual orientation, once learned, becomes an integral part of one's personality in much the same way and to somewhat the same extent as gender identity. Assuming, then, the absence of any innate drive toward heterosexual attraction, the homosexual can be as comfortable with his orientation as the heterosexual with his.[57] There is no need to posit a continuing fear of heterosexuality. The individual may raise defenses against changing his orientation for the powerful reason that change would mean denying a part of himself that colors his entire being and his perception of the world around him.[58] It would have him turn his back on a profound development of his personality that he sensed, not, as society sees it, as something which is bad and evil, but as something which was good and beautiful. The picture of a new personality that the therapist holds up before him is emphatically, *"Not Me."*[59]

One final question must be raised about both the traditional psychiatric stance and the fallback position just discussed. Even assuming that fear of heterosexual involvement lies at the root of homosexuality, why should this ipso facto mean that the condition is pathological and must be subjected to treatment and cure? A great many people have phobias of one sort or another. Some are afraid of high places; some are afraid of flying; some are afraid of snakes; some are afraid of public speaking. Although the fear in all these cases may be irrational, we do not insist that these people are mentally ill and must all flock to the nearest psychiatrist to be cured. The reason we do not is that we recognize it is perfectly possible for such people to pull their own weight in society and live a reasonably happy life without shedding their phobias, simply by avoiding the situation that arouses their fear. Certainly, their potential in life is commensurately diminished, but no one insists that standing on mountaintops, flying in airplanes, handling snakes, or speaking in public is essential to a happy life and to adequate social functioning. It thus becomes clear that the characterization of homosexuality as pathological by reason of a basis in fear must rest on an additional hidden premise—that personal happiness and adequate social functioning are inseparable from heterosexuality. But no empirical foundation exists for such a premise. The heterosexual psychiatrist, like any other heterosexual, simply takes it for granted, because he cannot imagine how *he* could possibly be happy if deprived of the opposite sex. Many homosexuals, however, insist that they can be quite happy and function quite adequately if society will just stop its harassment. This brings us to another variant of the sickness theory.

Ellis urges that the maintenance of a homosexual orientation in our culture is sick because the individual, by exposing himself to the hostility of society, is defeating his own best interests. He points to the case of a man who continually gets himself into trouble with the police by engaging in sex acts in public restrooms as an example of such self-defeating behavior. This, he insists, must be regarded as sick.[60] One may perhaps agree with his thesis as applied to his example, but the example is atypical. Many overt homosexuals, probably the great majority, manage to engage in homosexual behavior without ever getting into trouble with the law. Their practices are so discreet that they never come to the attention of the police, their employers, or even their families. Their orientation is a secret known only to themselves and other homosexuals. Indeed, it is a fact that even the majority of those who do get into trouble with the law were careful not to be discovered. They just underestimated the chances of being found out.[61] The discreet homosexual who has learned how to avoid discovery therefore would never agree with Ellis's argument. He is likely to admit that being heterosexual would be far easier, but being homosexual does not prevent him from achieving his nonsexual goals in life.

Many homosexuals today are beginning to turn Ellis's argument back on him. They feel it amounts merely to saying that they are in conflict with social attitudes, which can be wrong as often as they are right and just. His argument concedes that homosexuality would not be pathological but for society's attitude. In other words, if the individual psyche could be isolated from its social milieu, it might exhibit no inner conflict and therefore no pathology. The conflict arises only because society demands that everyone conform to a standard of normalcy. We might, of course, call anyone in collision with his society "sociopathic," but this seems a misnomer unless we are to subscribe to the value judgment that conformity is always healthy and nonconformity always sick.

Homosexuals see themselves as in a position no different from that of blacks. Admittedly, in American society, it is easier to be white because most Americans are white and they discriminate against people who are different. But there is nothing intrinsically bad about being black, so the better solution to the difficulties blacks encounter is to challenge the prejudice, rather than bleach their skin color to pass for white. Many homosexuals today feel the same about their condition. Their sexual orientation is as integral a part of their personalities as the black's race is a part of his. So they refuse to be discreet any longer. Instead of "hiding in their closets" they come out on the streets shouting "Gay Is Good!" Not only do they feel no need to go to the therapists for "cure"; they even insist they are not sick and that society must stop labeling them so. The solution, as they see it, is to change society's attitude rather than themselves. Although many categories of emotional illness do exhibit resistance to cure during psychotherapy, it would be amazing to find a "National Coalition of Schizophrenic Liberation Fronts" demonstrating at psychiatric conventions to demand an end to the whole business of their diagnosis, treatment, and cure.[62] This is what we find homosexuals doing today. Changing society's attitudes may be an uphill battle, but if the blacks can do it, maybe they can too. Certainly, theirs is as reasonable a position to take, given Ellis's premises, as the solution of individual treatment and change that he urges.

Of course, "sociopathic" can have an intended meaning other than that the individual is on a collision course with society's mores and prejudices. It can mean that the behavior is, in some way, definitely harmful to man's life in society. It may be a cancer that threatens the body politic, though it does not derogate from the psychic health of the individual himself. This seems to be the notion put forward by Marshall and Suggs in the concluding chapter of the book *Human Sexual Behavior*.[63] The color of one's skin can hardly threaten the social fabric, but homosexuality, it is urged, may. On this issue, however, neither anthropologists such as Marshall and Suggs *nor* the psychiatrists can speak more authoritatively than any social philosopher (using the last term in a broad sense). Indeed, the social harms Marshall and Suggs find inherent in "those more profoundly disturbing activities" of the American homosexual are the same old shibboleths examined earlier in this book and found wanting.[64] If, then, no definite harm to society can be found, homosexuality cannot be classified as an illness under the sociopathology rubric.

Several other arguments that homosexuality is pathological can be found in the literature. The Bieber book implies that if homosexuality is "caused" by husband-wife and parent-child relations full of conflict and strife, it must be pathological. This again seems a *non sequitur*. Under psychoanalytic probing most people might reveal severe wounding from one or the other or both of their parents in childhood. Few children escape such wounding, because few parents are in all respects, or at all times, the ideal parents we think they should be. The critical question is whether the child grows up to be a reasonably happy individual able to function adequately in society.[65] That his adjustment varies in some respect from the average, or usual, norms exemplified by the population as a whole ought not to be taken as indicative of a resulting psychopathology, unless we are prepared to label all idiosyncrasy pathological.

Psychiatrists are beginning to recognize that certain abnormal (in the sense of varying widely from the average) adult patterns may not result from parental wounding or indeed from any conflictual process in childhood at all. For instance, Stoller believes from his research that transsexualism in males results not from any conflict but from the perfectly comfortable continuation of a symbiotic relationship between mother and child like that which existed in the womb.[66] The male childhood transsexuals he has seen are relaxed, happy, creative, and fearless.[67] They do not seem troubled by the incongruence between their anatomy, which is unambiguously male, and their gender identity, which is just as unambiguously female. Society may later bring about inner disturbance by its insistence that the latter must conform to the former; and even without social intolerance, the discrepancy between the two would perhaps inevitably create some problem in attaining a satisfying interpersonal sex life. However, since we now have the means to alter anatomy to conform to or, rather, approximate gender identity, one begins to wonder why psychiatrists should continue to insist that psychic transsexualism is pathological and should be diagnosed and treated early by psychotherapeutic methods, while the person is still in childhood, so that his identity can be made to conform to his anatomy. This seems nothing more than blind adherence to some ideal drawn from our concept of Nature. Matter is somehow more "natural" than Mind.[68] All psychic deviations from this idea of what is "natural" are viewed as pathological and therefore must be corrected. But in fact Nature continually casts up myriads of deviations from every norm we attempt to establish. In the area of human personality, we cannot hope to arrest this process of variation, even if we had more control than we do over the variables that influence it. Unless society is to devote an inordinate proportion of its resources to what may prove a futile battle to correct all such personality deviations and bring them back into line with some ideal norm, it had better change its concepts of illness and health so that we come to tolerate the maximum deviation possible.

Of course, physical deformity, injury, and disease occur naturally too, and no one suggests we equate them with health. The difference is that they generally interfere seriously with individual happiness and functioning in any context. But some of the so-called "illnesses" and "disorders" of psychiatry seem not to present any inherent obstacle to personal happiness or to adequate functioning. They pose an obstacle only because of our society's intolerance of being different.

The question then is, why introduce anxiety into a personality where none existed before? Such anxiety is inevitable whenever we label the personality as pathological and try to change it through therapy.[69] Why should not society let people be and do what they want to be and do, if they are happy and cause no serious social disruption, instead of trying to make them all be and do according to some supposed idea of what is natural or normal?[70] To pose these rhetorical questions is not, of course, to answer them, but merely to highlight some of the reexamination of basic assumptions currently going on in the mental health field.

If such a bizarre aberration as transsexualism can result from nonconflictual learning processes in childhood, then a fortiori it would seem that homosexuality could too. Here, as in other areas, psychiatry may have been thrown off base by its early overemphasis on the role of conflict in producing adaptations varying from the norm.[71] But even if a particular aberration was produced by childhood conflicts, to insist that it must continue to be pathological in the adult even when those conflicts no longer trouble him seems highly gratuitous.[72]

Some may insist, however, that the great majority of adult homosexuals really do experience severe inner conflict; that neither are they happy nor do they function adequately in society. They are seen as needing to be "cured" because of the many and varied symptoms of neurosis or perhaps even psychosis they exhibit.[73] In other words, homosexuality, though not necessarily pathological in itself, is associated in our society with neurotic symptoms. Or perhaps this presence of neurotic symptoms proves that homosexuality is in itself pathological in some way yet unknown to us. For instance, many homosexuals exhibit paranoid fears. Others appear to suffer from the "obsessive-compulsive personality" syndrome. Some are even schizophrenic.

In the first place, these supposedly factual generalizations are drawn almost exclusively by psychotherapists from their sessions with individual patients. Presumably, only those homosexuals suffering from severe psychic conflict would be flocking to the therapist's door. His view of the phenomena thus is bound to be distorted by this self-selection of the population sample he sees. In other words, his sample is collecting itself for examination by the very criterion that promotes the sickness theory.[74] Since the homosexuals who do not come to his couch remain *invisible* in the world outside, he has no adequate contact with them which might compensate for and correct the picture he forms from the therapist's chair.

The most sweeping generalizations about homosexuals come from the pens of these "experts." For instance, Albert Ellis states baldly that most homosexuals are "short-term hedonists" and "goofers."[75] Perhaps the ones he has seen are, but at most he can have seen only a few hundred. There must be thousands of homosexuals he has never met, who, like author Merle Miller, have distinguished themselves through hard work and diligent application.[76] Yet Ellis purports to speak from the standpoint of a scientist when he makes such a generalization. Even more sweeping statements occur in other ostensibly scientific works, such as Socarides' book.[77]

Some scientific investigators, such as Hooker and Hoffman, have made an effort to find the type of homosexual who would never darken a therapist's door. Their findings about the adjustment of the people they discovered do not correspond with the therapists' portrait.[78] The view of such investigators is probably best exemplified by Wardell Pomeroy's statement:

> If my concept of homosexuality were developed from my practice, I would probably concur in thinking of it as an illness. I have seen no homosexual man or woman in that practice who was not troubled, emotionally upset, or neurotic. On the other hand, if my concept of marriage in the United States were based on my practice, I would have to conclude that marriages are all fraught with strife and conflict, and that heterosexuality is an illness. In my twenty years of research in the field of sex, I have seen many homosexuals who were happy, who were participating and conscientious members of their community, and who were stable, productive, warm, relaxed, and efficient. Except for the fact that they were homosexual, they would be considered normal by any definition. To insist that they are abnormal, or sick, or neurotic just because they are homosexual is to engage in circular reasoning which smacks of a blind moralism founded in our Judeo-Christian heritage.[79]

Some proponents of the sickness theory object that the subjects of these nontherapeutic investigations were also very highly selected,[80] so that it is not surprising if they seem as well adjusted as a random sample of heterosexuals. The problem, of course, is that since the homosexual population of America must remain largely invisible to avoid incurring the social stigma, it is extremely difficult to collect a random sample or even to figure out how to go about it. The Institute for Sex Research has recently conducted several investigations into the life adjustment of homosexuals on a hitherto unprecedented scale. Although the data are still being analyzed and the reports will not be published for some time yet, the director of the Institute—Paul Gebhard—indicates that the results of these investigations confirm the findings of Hooker, Hoffman, and others that many homosexuals seem as reasonably well adjusted as heterosexuals, and are holding down jobs and living productive lives.[81] Of course, even such evidence as this may not convince therapists like Charles Socarides, who insists that the depth of the disturbance in a homosexual's personality can only be plumbed on the analytic couch.[82] (Therapists who take such a view could probably find disturbance in everybody's personality if they looked as long and hard as they do to find it in every homosexual's.)

Admittedly, only a random sample collected by impeccable methodology from the homosexual population as a whole could show whether neurotic symptoms are more common in homosexuals than in heterosexuals, and such does not seem possible under current conditions. Albert Ellis concedes that even then, the conclusions might be unreliable, because he feels a great many people who are psychological misfits drift into the homosexual camp who would not normally do so. Their neuroses or psychoses make it doubly difficult for them to find and keep heterosexual partners in our culture.[83] Unable to form a stable relationship with anybody of either sex, they find sexual gratification easier to come by homosexually, given the structure and attitudes of the "gay" subculture, which take promiscuity for granted. It might prove an exacting task to weed out these and other "facultative homosexuals" so that the population to be sampled consists only of homosexuals in the sense in which that term is used in this book.

Even lacking such a perfect study, it would seem that one conclusion can already be safely drawn from the imperfect investigations done to date. This conclusion is that homosexuality is not invariably associated with neurosis.[84] Some homosexuals seem psychologically healthy by any standard, as long as their peculiar sexual orientation is not viewed as a symptom per se.[85] If this is the case, then it would seem one ought to look for the origins of the neurotic symptoms seen in many homosexuals not in the condition itself but elsewhere.

Hooker suggests that many of the personality traits of "the homosexual" thought to be a result of the pathological nature of homosexuality, such as lack of dignity and poise, obsessive concern with the characteristic that marks him as peculiar, withdrawal and passivity, self-hatred, protective clowning, and the like, are typical of those found among members of other victimized minority groups, such as blacks, and therefore may be more an ego defense against the prejudice of the dominant culture than symptoms of individual psychopathology.[86] West makes the same point.[87] It certainly seems plausible that if everyone keeps telling a person he is sick, disordered, and neurotic, as well as immoral, a sinner, and a criminal, self-doubt is almost bound to ensue, together with many of the traits associated with the labels.

It is only within living memory that the blacks of America have as a group begun to approximate other Americans in self-assurance, dignity, and pride. Having been told for centuries, by social structure and subtle hint if not always directly, that they were inferior to whites, many acted as if they were inferior. As increasing numbers of whites acknowledged them as equals in fact as well as in theory, and as they saw blacks from other lands treated with dignity and respect, many blacks of America began to shed the personality traits here thought to be innate in their race. With homosexuals, the effect of the derogatory labeling by the larger society may have been even more devastating than in the case of the blacks. To be told one is "sick in the head" may be a greater blow to the ego than to be told one is inferior. A tremendous stigma attaches to mental illness in our society,[88] while almost none attaches any more to physical illness. Perhaps many psychiatrists would disclaim any intention to characterize homosexuals as mentally ill when they call homosexuality a "personality disorder" or "dysfunction," but all such fine distinctions are bound to be lost on the general public, including the homosexuals themselves. These labels inflict just as much social damage on the homosexual as the old sin and crime labels, despite their humanitarian objective.

Even more persuasive explanations of the neurotic symptoms can be found than this. As noted previously, the traditional American attitude toward homosexuality equates it with effeminacy in the case of males and masculinity in the case of females. To say another man is "as queer as a three-dollar bill" is to say that he is not a real man. He is something other than a man. He is, in effect, the equivalent of neuter, or of the opposite sex. Even if our culture had succeeded in shedding its inherited notion that women are basically inferior to men, this would still be a profoundly unsettling label to live with. If gender identity is perhaps the deepest element of most people's personalities, a challenge to that identity can in and of itself alone produce psychosis. Stoller describes the case of a patient who, having been raised as a girl, was told at the age of 14 that she "might be a boy."[89] She had been discovered to have Turner's syndrome—the XO chromosome pattern—which results in neither ovaries nor testes though in female-appearing external genitalia. The situation as bluntly explained to her left her with the quite accurate impression that she was neither a girl nor a boy, but some kind of freak. He asserts unequivocally that by the age of 18 she had developed into a genuine *psychotic,* all as the result of this brutal shattering of her gender identity. A comparable patient, who was told merely that she was sterile due to an unexplained anatomical defect, developed neither psychosis nor any other disturbance beyond the expected disappointment and sadness at the prospect of never having children of her own.[90] Her mental health remained unimpaired because no doubt of her gender was raised. These examples indicate how the threat to a homosexual's gender identity posed by society's attitude toward him could explain why he is neurotic or even on the borderline of psychosis.[91]

This challenge to gender identity inherent in the popular attitude toward "queers" probably also explains the intense fear of, and hatred for, homosexual males manifested by many heterosexual males. Perhaps occasionally sensing glimmerings of a similar attraction within themselves, they find even the very idea of homosexuality too great a threat to their sense of maleness to tolerate.[92] The psychiatric profession itself seems not to have escaped the effects of the popular view. The tendency in psychiatric writings to equate homosexuality in males with a feminine identification is marked. The well adjusted, happy male homosexual may therefore simply be one who has managed to resist all these efforts to dub him a female or a freak. He has discovered that his feelings and behavior do not make him, in any sense, less a male.[93] With such a chorus of voices to the contrary surrounding him, however, it is not surprising that he might prove exceptional.

Finally and most importantly, the neurotic symptoms find abundant explanation in stress resulting from the condemnation to which homosexuals are subjected in our society.[94] One experience of listening to a group of heterosexuals talking about "cocksuckers" and "queers" is enough to convince any male homosexual that he must at all costs conceal his orientation from others. He must present a masked face in all ordinary human contacts, pretend to be something other than what he is. The strain of this continual need for concealment is enormous in itself.[95] The fear of exposure can hardly be called paranoid, because it has a realistic basis. The individual has no way of assessing the magnitude of the threat to which he may be subject from those who do not understand or accept homosexuality. At a minimum, exposure would involve ridicule, humiliation, and ostracism. It would probably also involve loss of employment and the wrecking of an entire career. Beatings and even death have been inflicted on known or suspected homosexuals by gangs of young toughs bent on ridding the world of such "scum."[96] Blackmail too is a possibility. Since the homosexual knows that his sexual behavior is against the criminal law, he dares not call on the police when blackmailed, because it is conceivable they might seek to arrest and prosecute him. Anyway, instigating prosecution of the blackmailer would risk exposure of his deviance, and the consequences of exposure could be almost as devastating as those of being prosecuted. Even when he is subjected to simple assault and robbery, or attempted murder, by a sexual partner, he can hardly feel free to call on the police for protection or assistance in bringing the criminal to justice, for the same reason.[97] If he does call on the authorities and they do seek to protect him, defense attorneys know that one of the surest ploys for getting their clients acquitted by a jury is to show that the victim was a "queer." Realization that one is outside the protective mantle of the criminal law, as well as in continual violation of that law, is almost certain to produce estrangement and alienation from society, which can take the form of withdrawal and apathy or rage and defiance.[98]

Apart from legal condemnation and social ostracism, there are numerous personal disadvantages of being a homosexual,[99] many of them stemming from the social structure and attitudes of the "gay" world, with which the individual must somehow cope. Homosexuality as a way of life is shaped, for everyone, largely by the already existing institutions, mores, and attitudes of the subculture. The individual homosexual may deplore their shallowness and prefer customs and institutions similar to those of the "straight" world. But no matter how much he may dislike these folkways, he can do little personally to change them. If he is to live as a homosexual, he must take them as he finds them and adjust to them as best he can. When to these stresses are added all the usual ones that everybody faces in life, it is surprising that homosexuals as a group manage as well as they do. D. J. West paints graphically the condition into which many homosexuals descend if they allow themselves to dwell on their plight:

> The sense of guilt [induced by society over homosexuality] may grow so acute that the individual feels he can fit in nowhere and do nothing right because the burden of shame

and inferiority paralyzes all initiative and destroys all pleasure in human contacts.[100]

Few people can weather a powerful and pervasive threat to their
self-respect and sense of security without some support from others.
The black child who grows up in an atmosphere of racial prejudice
may be cushioned from the shock, at least to some extent, by the
support of those to whom everyone turns most naturally for
comfort in times of crisis and stress—his parents, his brothers and
sisters, and his other relatives. But often the homosexual who makes
a clean breast of things is condemned and disowned by his family.
From no one else, except other homosexuals, can he get that
reaffirmation of his personal worth so essential to the maintenance
of emotional health and equilibrium. And these others are supposedly infected with the same sin-sick syndrome as himself.[101] It is
small wonder that he becomes neurotic.

Actually, we need not here seek to resolve the dispute about
whether homosexuality is pathological. The most important lesson
to be drawn for our purposes from this brief survey of the state of
knowledge about deviant sexual development is that the types of
behavior in which, and the partners with whom, people prefer to
engage for sexual gratification are largely beyond their own power
to control or to change. In other words, in this area, the terms
"preference" and "psychosexual object-choice" do not denote
deliberate choice, or choice in any meaningful sense of the word.[102]
Rather, people are in the grip of their memories, conscious and
subconscious, both of their past relationships with other people of
both sexes and of the patterns of sexual stimuli and response which
have already proved emotionally satisfying. One does not *choose* to
be attracted to somebody, any more than he *chooses* his likes and
dislikes generally. Whether or not attraction exists depends on how
closely the particular object conforms to some ideal already
ensconced in the mind of the beholder.[103]

It has been aptly said that, in this sphere, people are programmed, much as a computer is, by the information fed into them.
The social system is designed to program heterosexuality and
monogamy, but with many it does not succeed in accomplishing
either objective. They end up programmed in other directions. The
system is not foolproof, because it cannot guarantee that each
person's immediate environment while growing up will be identi-

cal with those of all other people. The inevitable variations in these micro-environments are bound to result in individuals who diverge from the ideal norms of the group. People, of course, are unlike machines in that they can choose not to respond to a stimulus that provokes arousal as a result of this programming. But they *are* like machines in the sense that they cannot choose to respond to a stimulus which, because of such programming, provokes no arousal at all. To return again specifically to the phenomenon of homosexuality, the crucial fact is that a person who is sexually oriented toward his own gender does not respond psychically to heterosexual stimuli, albeit he does possess the same power everyone has to suppress his reactions to those stimuli to which he does respond. And it bears repeating that this condition is the product of a complex of influences and environmental factors over which he had no control, the vast majority of which occurred during childhood and adolescence. As someone has put it, no male homosexual ever woke up one morning to say, "This is my day for boys!"

In Anglo-American law, we have long since retreated from the position that children should be held as responsible for criminal acts as adults. We no longer consider that moral responsibility attaches until one has reached such an age of discretion that he can be deemed in control of his own personality. For the same reasons, it is impossible to regard the homosexual as responsible for the acquisition of a mental and emotional condition the formation of which seems largely brought about by parental and peer-group relations from infancy on. This is not to say that these youngsters are unaware of their burgeoning sexual desires toward their own sex. They are equally aware of the lack of desire toward the opposite sex. In the latter respect, they realize that they seem radically different from the majority of their fellows. But this does not mean they have any idea that they are becoming "homosexuals." At this stage, many of them have never even heard of the word, much less of the criminal laws that prohibit homosexual acts.[104] There can be no doubt that the majority of homosexuals never consciously realize or admit to themselves what is happening to them until the die is already cast. Many assume these feelings and emotions to be a transitory phase, if they worry about it at all. They may be just lagging behind their peers in this aspect of sexual maturation. Expecting heterosexual interest to develop in the normal course of events, just like muscles and beards or breasts and hips, they wait and wait for it to arrive, but it never does. Eventually, many do proceed to join the majority pattern of heterosexual marriage and child-rearing, even though aware of their lack of heterosexual desire. They do this not so much with the idea of effecting a cure, but simply because they have been taught to believe that everyone is basically heterosexual and that marriage to a person of the opposite sex is the thing to do. The consequence is often bitter disappointment and tragedy for both parties to such a misalliance.[105]

The second important lesson to be learned from the scientific knowledge about homosexuality is that the condition is very likely to be with us for a long time to come. The chances of eradicating it seem nil. If its origins lie not in genetic variations but in deeply entrenched cultural attitudes toward sex and mating and in common patterns of child-rearing and gender roles, each new crop of babies is bound to include its usual share of those who will grow up homosexual. Even if America could stomach the idea of shipping all existing homosexuals off to Auschwitz, it would be faced with a new batch of them in the very next generation. Nor would massive new efforts to enforce strictly the laws against homosexual acts be of any avail, because homosexuality is not, like VD, the result of infection by others. Prevention through early detection, diagnosis, and treatment of hormonal imbalance is equally out of the question if homosexuality is not "caused" by glandular malfunction.

Peter and Barbara Wyden, in their book *Growing Up Straight*,[106] advocate that the solution lies in educating parents to avoid the types of relationships with their children which, according to the Bieber study, appear conducive to a homosexual orientation, and to recognize homosexual tendencies in their children and get psychiatric help before those tendencies become fixed. But even if we knew that parent-child relationships were the sole or even major influence in producing homosexuality (and we do not know this),[107] the Wydens' solution looks hopeless.[108] The relationships described earlier in this book seem obviously to presuppose the sort of parents who would never think of reading the Wydens' book, much less any other educational material on human sexuality. They just do not realize that their actions are likely to have any effect at all on their child's future sexual orientation. Even if they were made aware of this likely effect, it is doubtful that they could change, because, as we have seen, the parents' behavior is itself often the product of deepseated emotional conflict. Finally, the Wydens seem to be holding out a false hope in suggesting that incipient homosexuality can be "diagnosed" in children. A pronounced tendency toward effeminacy in males or masculinity in females might be observable in childhood, but effeminacy in males and masculinity in females are not always or even usually correlated with homosexuality.

The only solution to "the homosexual problem," assuming it really is a problem and that some solution does exist, would appear to lie in changing our cultural attitudes and patterns toward a more affirmative view of sex in general and of heterosexuality in particular. Specifically, the change must include a complete reversal in our traditional stance to sex education. Children must be actively *helped* to understand human sexuality and the state of their own bodies at every stage in their development, and to be happy and comfortable with their sexual feelings and physical responses. Letting nature take its course just will not do. If parents cannot or will not provide this help, and it seems clear that a great many of them will not, then society must step in to do so, whether through its public school system or through some other means of education. Such change looks as if it will be long and painfully slow in coming. Unfortunately, even then, its beneficial effects might not manifest themselves for several generations, because the influence of formal teaching is weak in comparison with that of parents, siblings, and peers. I am not suggesting that sex education should include normative judgments on the relative merits of hetero- sexuality and homosexuality. Moral judgmentalism has done enough damage already. The goal should rather be simply to lower the level of sexual anxiety in youngsters overall. From the current state of our knowledge about sexual problems in general, it would appear that anxiety is a primary causal factor, and one which society could take definite steps to alleviate. Although the net effect might be an increase in homosexual behavior in the form of experimentation and ambisexuality, homosexuality in the sense of a fixed and exclusive preference is likely to diminish.

The question then remains: Assuming we cannot prevent homo- sexuality, can we "cure" it? The possibilities that lie within the prospects of "cure" must be grasped in order to complete our perspective on the problem. Perhaps the word "change" is more appropriate than "cure," since there is still such wide disagreement about whether homosexuality is pathological. Theoretically, anything that is the product of learning and conditioning can be unlearned, but theory is not always borne out by practice. Much dubious information seems to be circulating about the ability of the experts to "cure" homosexuality. It must be emphasized to begin with that "cure" does not mean, and cannot reasonably be expected to mean, simple abstention from homosexual intercourse. Since no one but a saint can be expected to abstain from all sexual activity, "cure" can only mean redirection toward heterosexuality.

As already noted, perhaps the most widespread assumption in the psychiatric profession has been that everyone is endowed naturally with the condition of heterosexuality (attraction to the opposite sex), that some experience or experiences in a homosexual's past have obstructed this innate direction of his sexual drive, thereby deflecting it into his current pattern of behavior, and that this pattern is constantly being reinforced by irrational attitudes resulting from these past experiences. A "cure" can be effected through psychoanalytic techniques, which uncover these long-forgotten experiences, dispel the fear they engendered (which nipped his heterosexual development in the bud), and remove all the present irrational props of his behavior, thereby unblocking the current and letting it flow toward its predestined target—a heterosexual object.

The problem is that therapists with the most experience in trying to change homosexuality in the male—such as Lawrence Hatterer and Albert Ellis—have discovered that traditional psychoanalysis does not suffice in these cases.[109] They must go a step further and encourage the individual to develop heterosexual interests. Ellis even assigns homework to his male patients. They must make definite efforts to meet girls, to go out on dates with them, to engage in kissing, necking and petting, and, finally, to seduce them to bed and intercourse. By providing maximum encouragement and praise for all such efforts and maximum discouragement for all relapses into homosexual fantasies and behavior, the therapist exhorts, cajols, pushes, and prods the patient not only into regarding heterosexuality with pleasure and anticipation but also into experiencing it. Thus, in psychotherapy, traditional analysis has been at least partially displaced by, or conjoined with, vigorous efforts at behavioral modification on the part of the therapist.[110] Their approach undoubtedly seems likely to be more effective. As

Wardell Pomeroy puts it, "just as one doesn't learn to like ice cream by giving up pie, so one doesn't learn to like heterosexuality by giving up homosexuality."[111] Curiously, some of these therapists seem oblivious to any ethical problems in the patient's using these unwitting girls to help effect his "cure." Both Ellis's and Hatterer's books are extremely useful for getting an idea of how this kind of therapy works, because both include extensive samples of their sessions with patients, which they had transcribed from tapes.[112] Some therapists have also had a measure of success with group therapy.[113]

The "cure" rate of homosexuals in psychotherapy is nonetheless discouraging. The most optimistic claim of success does not exceed 50 per cent,[114] and many of the more energetic advocates of treatment seem not to have managed better than a 20 to 30 per cent rate.[115] It is difficult even then to judge how much faith to put in these statistics. Some therapists state simply that the patients were "better" or "much improved," without indicating what this means in concrete terms. Even when "cures" are claimed, sometimes the therapists do not make clear whether they are calculating these "cures" in terms of those whose homosexual feelings have been replaced by heterosexual desires, or merely in terms of those whose behavior patterns have changed. Often claims of the latter type have not been backed by continued observation of the subjects over a long period of time to ascertain the true measure of recidivism.[116] What many therapists know, but the public generally does not, is that some whose desires are and remain homosexual can *function* heterosexually for short or even long periods in their lives.[117] Many human beings can respond sexually to physical stimulation in the complete or virtual absence of psychic attraction to their partner, by fantasizing about some other, ideal partner.[118] Such fantasies are commonplace during masturbation.[119] The point is that change to a heterosexual behavior pattern does not necessarily constitute a "cure." One whose emotions remain unchanged but who, by some psychological sleight of hand, can function heterosexually, is hardly a happily adjusted person. He has merely conformed to the outward appearances imposed by society. Ellis affirms that the complete eradication of homosexual desires is an unrealistic goal in treatment. He believes that the best which can be hoped for is the development of a certain amount of heterosexual feeling, so that the person will be psychically ambisexual, but with heterosexual behavior, hopefully, predominating.[120]

Another problem with these statistics of "cures" is that the therapists often seem to fail to distinguish between the person with a definite preferential erotic attraction toward his own sex (the "homosexual" in the sense used in this book) and "facultative homosexuals." For instance, one example of a "cure" offered by Ellis involved a young man who openly admitted throughout the therapy that he was attracted to and wanted to have sex with girls, but used homosexual outlets because they were easier and allowed the other person to take the initiative, thereby eliminating the possibility of his being rejected.[121] This case seems hardly typical of homosexuals in general, unless one posits such attraction in every one of them even in the face of his categorical denials.

Perhaps the greatest problem with these statistics lies in the therapists' failure or refusal to distinguish ambisexuals from homosexuals. As already noted, Bieber insists on defining as homosexual anyone with more than a purely nodding acquaintance with homosexual behavior.[122] The Bieber group claimed a fairly high rate of "cure," but when one looks at those who were "cured," the group appears to consist mainly of ambisexuals.[123] This insistence that all ambisexuals must be categorized as homosexuals is bound to result in distortion when one is trying to form an accurate impression of the chances of "curing" exclusive or near-exclusive homosexuality. To get someone who already experiences some attraction to the opposite sex to give up his homosexual behavior is bound to be an easier task.[124]

The situation is probably somewhat comparable to efforts at changing gender identity in adults through psychotherapy. In a number of cases, such change has proved manageable despite the fact that in most cases it appears impossible. Stoller believes that in some people, contrary to the usual pattern, gender identity does not become fixed as either male or female but remains more or less fluid and hence capable of being shifted in either direction without serious personality disturbance. He categorizes those in whom such shifts are possible as having neither a male nor a female, but a "hermaphroditic," gender identity.[125] If such middle ground really exists in the case of gender identity, it would seem even more likely to exist in the realm of sexual orientation, which is apparently much less a matter of black-or-white. Here as elsewhere, increasing scientific sophistication brings the realization that Nature does not deal in discrete categories.

That psychotherapy has helped some, but not others, to change to a satisfying heterosexual pattern of behavior should not be surprising if the general picture of sexual development portrayed in the preceding chapter holds true. One would expect as many variations in the formative factors even among the more narrow category of genuine homosexuals, and as varying chances of a successful reprogramming of sexual orientation, as in any other human behavioral phenomenon. As already noted, if homosexuality is rarely the product of a single traumatic experience, the uncovering of long-forgotten occurrences through classic psychoanalysis is not likely to help much. Homosexuality in many cases may be the product of a multitude of past experiences and influences, and thus may be no easier to alter than it would be to rebuild an entire personality structure from the ground up. And if, as seems likely, heterosexual attraction is *not* innate in every human being or in any of them, but is itself the product of conditioning, it is quite conceivable that the conditioning of particular individuals has never impelled their sexual drive toward members of the opposite sex, but only toward those of their own sex. In such cases, no attempt to obliterate homosexuality can revive a suppressed heterosexuality, because none is there to revive. Successful redirection of the orientation may be as difficult to achieve as converting a confirmed heterosexual to exclusive homosexuality.[126] Undoubtedly many homosexuals do not seek psychotherapy for their condition, not because of any perverse refusal to be "cured," but because they fear that the only success possible would be to leave them asexual. They are not conscious of sexual attraction to the opposite sex, and cannot perceive how psychotherapy could create feelings and desires they are certain they do not possess.

The matter of sexual attraction, or lust, can be overemphasized. In cases in which an absence of erotic arousal by the opposite sex has been overcome, it still may be difficult for the homosexual to envision his future in terms of heterosexual marriage, because his only experiences of having loved another person very deeply involved his own sex. For him to renounce this and accept in its stead what he must regard as a pale substitute is expecting too much. American homosexuals today generally refuse to employ or acknowledge the term "homosexual" in relation to themselves, because it exaggerates the importance of the *sexual* element in their orientation. They prefer the words "gay" or "homophile," which in their minds carry the emphasis of a total loving relationship with their own sex, instead of a merely sexual one.

Many experts consider that the possibilities of "cure" today, in the sense of complete redirection of one's emotional desires, are no better than they were when Freud wrote his discouraging "Letter to an American Mother"[127] some thirty years ago, and that the most psychotherapy can hope to accomplish in many cases is to help the person adjust to his condition.[128] At any rate, psychiatrists seem generally agreed that the chances of a successful redirection of one's sexual orientation through psychotherapy are heavily dependent on youth and a high level of motivation to change.[129] Where the patient is under 21 and heterosexuality is essential to the achievement of goals he cherishes, such as having children, success is more likely than in the case of older persons who see no advantage from changing other than greater social acceptability.

Other factors are also important in attempting to assess the prognosis for change: How early the homoerotic interest manifested itself and whether it continued unabated through adolescence and into adulthood, and how strongly habituated the person is to homosexual behavior (the quantitative extent of overt practice).[130] In addition, family relationships, nonsexual relationships with the opposite sex, self-image, work identity, social history, and present life situation bear heavily on the prospects for change.[131] Finally, the presence of a strong cross-sex identification is a negative indicator:[132] The very effeminate male homosexual and the very masculine lesbian have the poorest prospects.[133] If the therapist, in order to substitute heterosexual attitudes and behavior patterns, must get the patient aggressively to seek out the opposite sex as sexual partners and take the risk of going to bed with them and failing in the performance, not only must an emotional revolution of the first order be effected but the cooperation of willing individuals of the opposite sex must be obtained in this acquisition of reassuring new experience.[134] The latter may prove quite difficult to the extent that the patient diverges from the masculine or feminine romantic ideal of our society.[135]

No one pretends that psychotherapy in these cases, even if ultimately successful, is short or cheap. This is long-term individual psychotherapy, for which the optimum is probably between 200 and 350 hours.[136] Full-scale psychoanalysis, if indicated, could reach 900 hours. With charges running at the rate of $35 an hour, one can begin to appreciate the extraordinary financial burden of a "treatment" whose prospects for success are dismal. The majority of homosexuals could not afford such "treatment" even if they wanted it.[137] Unless government is willing to subsidize the cost, it can hardly expect them to change. Moreover, if the homosexual proportion of the total population is somewhere between 4 and 10 per cent, or is even as low as 2 per cent,[138] there are not enough trained and experienced personnel around to do the job. With only about 25,000 psychiatrists in a population in excess of 200,000,000,[139] most of whose time must be spent with more serious psychological disorders, the futility of this hope for eradicating homosexuality becomes evident.[140]

Actually, psychotherapy is not the sole conceivable method of "curing" homosexuality. A number of behavioral scientists, primarily in the British Isles and in other Commonwealth countries, such as Australia, have advocated and experimented with what is euphemistically termed behavior therapy.[141] This consists of a series of treatments in which the patient is subjected to painful electric shocks, or to bouts of vomiting induced by emetic drugs, while being shown sexually exciting pictures of his own sex, but not while being shown pictures of the opposite sex. These methods for developing in the patient's mind an association of pain with the provocative homosexual stimuli, even when combined with efforts to overcome his fears and inhibitions through heterosexual experimentation (termed "desensitization"), do not appear to have achieved a much higher rate of success than psychotherapy.[142] Psychotherapists look upon these methods with considerable skepticism, because they do not seek to discover, expose, or modify the underlying motivations for the behavior, but seek only to alter the behavior pattern itself by blocking it through the association with physical pain. Although the method is much cheaper than psychotherapy, it has the disadvantages of being more susceptible to abuse and of possibly producing unforeseen and undesirable side effects in other areas of the patient's behavior. Finally, in many cases, it may only succeed in obliterating the patient's homosexuality without creating any heterosexuality to take its place—a result as inhumane as castration.

Recently, scientists have discovered that they can produce intense sensations of pleasure through stimulation of specific areas of the brain by means of tiny electrodes.[143] Physical sexual responses might be produced by this method; indeed, erection has already been produced in male monkeys. The possibilities for inducing heterosexual attraction in homosexuals in whom it did not previously exist seem, theoretically at least, to be obvious. By applying the stimulation coincidentally with the appearance of heterosexual objects and situations, therapists might be able to recondition a person to heterosexuality by associating it with artificially induced pleasure. Little use has yet been made of this technique in treating homosexuality, so its utility remains largely a matter of speculation. A combination of all three techniques—psychotherapy, aversion therapy, and positive reconditioning—might prove more efficacious than one of them alone.

Both types of physical therapy—positive and aversive—pose a serious moral issue if they are thrust upon the patient without his full and free consent,[144] because they can modify his personality structure against his will. They are brainwashing, pure and simple. Psychotherapy, on the other hand, even when offered to a criminal defendant as the alternative to imprisonment, does not pose such an issue, because it simply cannot work without the patient's active cooperation. It therefore cannot violate a patient's personal integrity as can these methods of artificially induced pain and pleasure. If, however, anyone freely and voluntarily seeks to undergo behavior modification by such methods, fully aware of the risk of failure, the moral objections vanish.[145]

Experimentation in America with aversion therapy for homosexuality has apparently been confined mainly to prisons and state mental hospitals, where the patient's consent, if any, is dubious. Few people not under confinement have volunteered for such techniques. Of course, even the most painful sort of involuntary brainwashing could perhaps be justified in order to eliminate certain types of antisocial behavior, if no other method were effective. But the really soggy swamp, as some psychiatrists such as Stoller recognize, is

> the whole issue of who defines what is antisocial and how much does this behavior endanger society or its individuals. How much pain should be inflicted on a patient to make him

conform? For the homicidal, a great deal. How much for the transvestite? To what extent does society's lenient attitude cause deviant behavior to increase? Does deviant sexual and gender behavior weaken a society? What does "weaken a society" mean? . . . How do we discuss transvestism and its treatment if we haven't the answers to these kinds of questions?[146]

Stoller's puzzlement, though referring specifically to transvestism, is just as applicable to homosexuality and to all forms of sexual deviance that do not pose any direct threat to others.

Finally, it should be noted that some people switch from an apparently exclusive homosexuality to heterosexuality spontaneously, that is, without therapy of any kind. Such a radical change in orientation, though it may take place at any stage of life, is more likely to occur while the individual is relatively young.[147] How and why these changes occur seem largely unknown. This possibility makes it even more difficult to assess the efficacy of all kinds of therapy. "Cured" individuals may include some who would have changed anyway, without therapy.

A word is in order on the scientific attitude toward "unnatural" sex acts in the heterosexual context. The recent literature does not seem to exhibit a single instance in which such acts have been, per se, condemned as pathological. Some marriage manuals assert that oral-genital contact is perfectly normal as long as it occurs as foreplay (*i.e.*, culminates in coitus), thus implying that such contact may take on pathological overtones if indulged in to the point of orgasm, as an end in itself.[148] Since no reason is given why orgasm attained by this means should be deemed pathological, one suspects that our cultural bias toward the procreative function of sex may be at work here. Most such manuals never mention the possibility of anal intercourse, perhaps because the authors doubt that their readers have any interest in this form of sexual activity but perhaps also because it would less often be indulged as foreplay than as a substitute for coitus. Masters and Johnson take the position that anal intercourse is a perfectly good means of orgasmic satisfaction for both male and female, once the female has gotten over the painful sensation that accompanies anal intromission in the uninitiated.[149] Not only is the anal orifice richly supplied with nerve endings capable of giving pleasurable response; the research of Masters and Johnson has established that contractions of the anal sphincter generally occur spontaneously as part of sexual orgasm in both male and female.[150] In other words, the nerve system of the anal area appears to be closely connected with that of the genital area.[151] In the male, too, the proximity of the prostate to the anal orifice makes possible a heightening of sexual excitement through digital stimulation of this organ through the orifice.

Although anal intromission is probably rare in the animal kingdom, if it occurs at all,[152] oral-genital contact is ubiquitous there in the heterosexual context.[153] Kinsey's investigations showed also that in American society, the latter form of behavior is widespread among the upper classes though often regarded as a perversion among lower socioeconomic groups.[154] In this respect, he believed that the upper classes have rediscovered an important part of the mammalian sexual heritage. Recent research involving electrical stimulation of various areas of the brain in mammals seems to prove his point. This research has demonstrated that oral, or "eating," responses, such as sucking and salivation, can be elicited by stimulation of an area of the brain pinpointed as immediately adjacent to that which controls sexual responses. Thus, physiologically speaking, orality and sexuality appear intimately connected in mammals.[155] Interfemoral intercourse and genital apposition are techniques mainly used by African blacks, though they occur sporadically elsewhere.[156] As far as manual stimulation of the genitalia—mutual masturbation—is concerned, it is so commonly a part of foreplay in the primates[157] that no scientist has ever dreamed of considering it unnatural or pathological. Some marriage manuals advocate it as a means of bringing the wife to orgasm if in coitus the husband attained orgasm before she did. In general, they urge that some type of extra stimulation of the mons area in the wife—oral or digital—be effected by the husband before penile intromission in order to bring her to the plateau stage of sexual excitement that precedes orgasm, the woman often experiencing a slower rate of buildup of sexual tension. Otherwise, the husband risks developing a chronic pattern of reaching orgasm before his wife and thus leaving her unsatisfied.

Before leaving the contribution of scientific data to our understanding of deviant sexuality, we must make some effort to grasp the dimensions of the incidence and frequency of the behaviors in question. It is impossible to estimate precisely how many acts of sodomy take place annually in the United States, but in all likelihood the number is staggering. No one has ever attempted to estimate how many "unnatural" sex acts take place annually between members of opposite sexes.[158] The Group for the Advancement of Psychiatry estimated that 6 million homosexual acts take place in this country for every 20 convictions.[159] The Wolfenden Report alludes to estimates in Britain ranging from 2,500 to 1, to 30,000 to 1.[160]

If one limits the question to homosexual acts, the figure still is bound to be astronomical.[161] The Kinsey studies indicated that 4 per cent of the white adult male population of the United States were exclusively homosexual throughout life, and that another 8 per cent were exclusively homosexual during at least a 3-year period between the ages of 16 and 55.[162] Even if the figure for lifelong exclusive homosexuals is as low as 2 per cent of American males,[163] this means well over 1 million adult male homosexuals.[164] And a total of 37 per cent of the subjects of the Kinsey study admitted to having had at least one homosexual contact to the point of orgasm at some period between the onset of puberty and the arrival of old age, mostly in early adolescence.[165] For females, the Kinsey group found that the comparable figure for those in the exclusively homosexual category was 1 to 2 per cent, and for those who had had at least one contact to the point of orgasm, 13 per cent.[166] Other studies have tended, if anything, to confirm these figures.[167] Granting allowance for the objections that can be made to Kinsey's sampling technique, one must nonetheless admit that if his estimates of the percentage of such persons in the total population are even remotely close to the truth,[168] the number of homosexual acts occurring annually in America must be in the millions,[169] and the number of people who have committed the "crime against nature" in homosexual or heterosexual contexts, must also be in the millions.[170] (It is important to note that the figures here quoted from the Kinsey studies dealt with behavior, not merely emotional propensities.) The total criminal detention capacity of this country—prisons, jails, and other types of detention centers—is only about 425,000,[171] so that there is no realistic hope of controlling the phenomenon through the criminal process, even if that were desirable.[172]

Let us summarize the salient features of this information, particularly as they relate to homosexuality:

1. The sex drive is a fundamental impulse common to all animals, including humans. Its satisfaction is intimately bound up with the personal happiness and psychic well-being of the individual.

2. In a sizable percentage of human beings, this impulse, through no fault of their own, is directed toward members of their own sex.

3. In a significant proportion of such cases, redirection of this impulse toward members of the opposite sex is not possible. In the rest, it is not feasible considering the high cost of psychotherapy and the insufficient personnel available for it.

4. The number of "unnatural" sex acts committed annually in America, and the number of people involved in the commission of such "crimes," is so fantastically high that only a tiny fraction of the offenses and the offenders could possibly be subjected to the criminal process, even if the police could discover every case and prove the participants' guilt.

What is the relevance of this information to the issue at hand—the constitutionality of the sodomy laws? Should not these points be more appropriately addressed to the attention of legislators, rather than the courts? On the contrary, they are quite relevant to the constitutional question. It remains only to show how.

NOTES

1. On the general subject of the elusiveness of the concepts of mental health and illness, the most important works are probably T. S. Szasz, THE MYTH OF MENTAL ILLNESS (1961), THE MANUFACTURE OF MADNESS (1970), and IDEOLOGY AND INSANITY—ESSAYS ON THE PSYCHIATRIC DEHUMANIZATION OF MAN (1970); N. O. BROWN, LOVE'S BODY (1966); R. D. LAING, THE POLITICS OF EXPERIENCE (1967); and R. D. LAING AND ANTI-PSYCHIATRY (R. Boyer ed. 1969). On the particular problem of defining normal and deviate sexual behavior, *see* Marmor, *"Normal" and "Deviant" Sexual Behavior,* 217 J.A.M.A. 165 (July 12, 1971); and Johnson & Fretz, *What Is Sexual "Normality"?,* 1 SEXUAL BEHAVIOR 68 (No. 3, June, 1971). For indications that some, at any rate, of the experts in psychiatry and psychology believe that their colleagues are rationalizing their moral disapproval of homosexuality or defending society against nonconformity by labeling homosexuality an illness or personality disorder, *see* Marmor, *Homosexuality and*

Objectivity, SIECUS NEWSLETTER, Vol. VI, No. 2, at 1 (Dec. 1970); T. S. SZASZ, THE MANUFACTURE OF MADNESS 160 (1970); G. WEINBERG, SOCIETY AND THE HEALTHY HOMOSEXUAL (1972); M. FREEDMAN, HOMOSEXUALITY AND PSYCHOLOGICAL FUNCTIONING (1971); Seidenberg, *The Accursed Race,* 8 PSYCHIATRIC OPINION 6 (No. 1, February 1971); Van den Haag, *Notes on Homosexuality and its Cultural Setting,* in THE PROBLEM OF HOMOSEXUALITY IN MODERN SOCIETY 293–94, 297–98 (H. M. Ruitenbeek ed. 1963) [hereinafter cited as RUITENBEEK]; and Lindner, *Homosexuality and the Contemporary Scene, id.* 72–73. A panel discussion at the American Psychiatric Association convention in Dallas, May 1–5, 1972, took the same tack. *See* The Advocate, June 7, 1972, at 12, col. 1. On February 8, 1973, the APA's Committee on Nomenclature, meeting in New York City, began deliberating the removal of homosexuality from the list of diagnostic categories in the Manual of Mental Disorders. The committee agreed that whether a person prefers to have sexual relations with a member of the same or of the opposite sex was, in itself, not an indicator of a mental disorder. N.Y. Times, Feb. 9, 1973, at 24, col. 1. A perceptive discussion of the matter is also found in W. CHURCHILL, HOMOSEXUAL BEHAVIOR AMONG MALES 239–55 (1967) [hereinafter cited as CHURCHILL].

2. Of course, pastoral and marriage counsellors fill the gap to some degree, but they are not generally regarded as qualified to deal with deep-seated emotional issues like homosexuality. Clinical psychologists are beginning to develop this service function, but many of them seem almost indistinguishable from psychiatrists in their urge to fit people's problems into a health-illness dichotomy.

3. The therapist must from the outset establish for the patient three fundamental assumptions on which the therapy is based:

    1. Homosexuality is pathologic. It is not a natural biologic phenomenon.

    2. The homosexual act is an overdetermined symptom with specific unconscious meanings.

    3. Homosexuality is a treatable illness. Through treatment, the normal heterosexual direction of the sexual drive can be reestablished.

These assumptions provide the therapeutic framework within which the therapy is conducted. They must be reiterated again and again throughout the therapy. They are transmitted to the patient not only by the technical maneuvers of the therapist, but also by his attitude. Hope is contagious and is a necessary ingredient in any therapy. Not all psychiatrists, therefore, should treat homosexuality. Those who lack conviction that homosexuality is a treatable illness, but believe instead that it is a natural constitutional variant, should not accept homosexuals as patients.

L. OVESEY, HOMOSEXUALITY AND PSEUDOHOMOSEXUALITY 119 (1969).

4. A good critique of the Bieber study—its assumptions, techniques, and conclusions—is found in CHURCHILL 260–91.

5. Following are some representative statements from the Bieber work which, it should be noted, dealt only with male homosexuality:

We *assumed* that the dominant sexual pattern of the adult is the adaptive consequence of life experiences interpenetrating with a *basic biological tendency toward heterosexuality.*

I. Bieber et al., Homosexuality 20 (1962) (emphasis added) [hereinafter cited as Bieber].

> A homosexual adaptation is a result of hidden but incapacitating fears of the opposite sex.

Id. 303.

> Homosexuality . . . is acquired and discovered as a circumventive adaptation for coping with fear of heterosexuality. . . . At any age, homosexuality is a symptom of fear and inhibition of heterosexual expression.

Id. 305.

> Any adaptation which is basically an accommodation to unrealistic fear is necessarily pathologic. . . .

Id. 303.

> We are committed to Rado's own proposition that homosexuality is an adaptation to fear of heterosexuality, and we extend this proposition to account for all homosexual behavior.

Id. 309.

> We assume that heterosexuality is the biologic norm and that unless interfered with all individuals are heterosexual.

Id. 319.

6. M. Hoffman, The Gay World 119–21 (Bantam ed. 1969) [hereinafter cited as Hoffman].

7. *See* A. C. Kinsey, W. B. Pomeroy, C. E. Martin, & P. H. Gebhard, Sexual Behavior in the Human Female 449 (1953) [hereinafter cited as Kinsey, Female], for a discussion of behavioral factors that provide an adequate explanation of the majority pattern of heterosexuality without resorting to the innate attraction idea.

8. A curious example of such reasoning is found in W. J. Gadpaille's paper, *Homosexual Activity and Homosexuality in Adolescence*, in Scientific Proceedings of the American Academy of Psychoanalysis, Science and Psychoanalysis, Vol XV, Dynamics of Deviant Sexuality 62–63 (J. H. Masserman ed. 1969) [hereinafter cited as Proceedings]. He begins by criticizing the postulation by Ford and Beach (who were following Freud's own theory) of an inherent biological tendency for sexual inversion in all mammals:

> An important biological observation often neglected is that the nerve endings of the genitals capable of being excited to the point of pleasure and orgasm are susceptible to non-specific stimulation. That is, innumerable forms and agents of touch, pressure, friction, etc. can produce a sexual response. Perhaps one is on the surest ground only when postulating that there is a biological tendency for the release of sexual tension or the gratification of sexual desire, and that various modes of release may be utilized under different conditions.
>
> . . . .
>
> We begin with the premise that, because in the normal body there is a biological drive toward sexual excitation and gratification, and because the stimuli capable of gratifying that drive may be non-specific, therefore an individual is not in any way biologically limited to heterosexual gratification of sexual tension.

Then he goes on to say:

> Our second premise is that the individual is biologically predisposed to ultimate heterosexual preference, at least by the time of full reproductive capacity.

But he does not explain where he gets this second premise, except to intimate that there must be some biological tendency toward heterosexuality since most species of living things can propagate only through heterosexual unions. This same uncritical leap of reasoning, from the fact of *species* propagation to the positing of a heterosexual predisposition in each *individual*, seems also evident in Socarides' book, though he begins by denying any innate connection between sexual instinct and the choice of sexual object:

> Homosexuality, the choice of an object of the same sex for orgastic satisfaction is not innate. There is no connection between sexual instinct and the choice of sexual object. Such an object choice is learned, acquired behavior; there is no inevitable genetic or hormonal inborn propensity toward the choice of a partner of either the same or opposite sex. However, the male-female design is taught and exemplified to the child from birth and culturally ingrained through the marital order. This design is anatomically determined as it derives from cells which in the evolutionary scale underwent changes into organ systems and finally into individuals reciprocally adapted to each other. This is the evolutionary development of man. The male-female design is perpetually maintained and only overwhelming fear can disturb or divert it.

C. W. SOCARIDES, THE OVERT HOMOSEXUAL 5–6 (1968). This one paragraph, by the way, comprises Socarides' entire discussion of the assumptions on which his treatise is based.

9. Klausner, *Sexual Behavior: Sociological Aspects*, in INT'L ENCY. SOCIAL SCIENCES 202 (1968). SIECUS asserts that "there is wide agreement today that man does not from birth possess an instinctive desire to achieve any specific goal in regard to sex." SEX INFORMATION AND EDUCATION COUNCIL OF THE UNITED STATES, SEXUALITY AND MAN 74 (1970).

10. *See* HOFFMAN 98–111; C. H. & W. M. WHITELEY, SEX AND MORALS 81–83 (1967).

11. BIEBER 222.

12. *Id.* 220.

13. *Id.* 273–74.

14. *Ibid.*

15. *See Playboy Panel: Homosexuality*, PLAYBOY, April 1971, at 73.

16. *See* Schneider, *The Sense of Smell and Human Sexuality*, 5 MEDICAL ASPECTS OF HUMAN SEXUALITY 157 (No. 5, May 1971). It is reasonably clear that in women the acuity of the olfactory sense is related to sex hormone levels. *See* Money, *Psychosexual Differentiation*, in SEX RESEARCH—NEW DEVELOPMENTS 15–17 (J. Money ed. 1965).

17. Schein and Hale believe the evidence points toward the hypothesis that various sensory cues—including olfactory ones—serve primarily in most species of mammals to identify the sexual situation in terms of the animal's prior

experience. *See* Schein & Hale, *Stimuli Eliciting Sexual Behavior,* in SEX AND
BEHAVIOR 467–71 (F. A. Beach ed. 1965). They state,

> Selectivity seems determined in large part during the early stages of sexual
> activity on the basis of successful achievement of intromission with
> associated animals. Failure to achieve intromission with inappropriate
> objects or animals has the effect of gradually restricting a male's sexual
> responses to receptive females of the same species. Thus, mammals identify
> sexual partners on the basis of negative experiences (inhibiting responses to
> non-receptive animals or objects) rather than through a positive mechanism
> similar to that observed in imprinting. Birds imprinted to biologically
> inappropriate objects continue to prefer these objects over conspecifics,
> despite the fact that normal achievement of the consummatory reward
> usually is impossible.

Id. 470. Heterosexual arousal through smell in lower mammals is likely to be a
result of conditioning because in many species the female will copulate only
when she is in estrous or "heat." Her enhanced odor in that period signifies a
potentially willing, rather than rejecting, partner to the experienced male. In
humans, the situation is not comparable.

18. *See* KINSEY, FEMALE 571, 591.

19. A discussion of homosexual behavior in lower mammals is found in
Denniston, *Ambisexuality in Animals,* in SEXUAL INVERSION 27–43 (J. Marmor ed.
1965) [hereinafter cited as SEXUAL INVERSION], and in D. J. WEST, HOMOSEXUALITY
22–25 (rev. ed. 1968) [hereinafter cited as WEST].

20. CHURCHILL 61.

21. C. S. FORD & F. A. BEACH, PATTERNS OF SEXUAL BEHAVIOR 134, 136, 139–40
(1951) [hereinafter cited as FORD & BEACH].

22. Masserman, *Preface,* in PROCEEDINGS at viii–ix.

23. *See* the interview with Frank Beach in A. KARLEN, SEXUALITY AND
HOMOSEXUALITY—A NEW VIEW 399 (1971).

24. *See* Pomeroy, *Homosexuality,* in THE SAME SEX—AN APPRAISAL OF
HOMOSEXUALITY 3–4 (R. W. Weltge ed. 1969).

25. *See* WEST 17–21; FORD & BEACH 18–19, 143, 257–59.

26. *See* text and notes at pp. 75–77, Chapter 4 *supra.*

27. Hooker, *Sexual Behavior: Homosexuality,* in 14 INT'L ENCY. SOCIAL
SCIENCES 230 (1968); Opler, *Anthropological and Cross Cultural Aspects of
Homosexuality,* in SEXUAL INVERSION 108, and particularly 116–17.

28. For an illuminating report by a careful anthropologist on one such
primitive society in Melanesia, see Davenport, *Sexual Patterns and Their
Regulation in a Society of the Southwest Pacific,* in SEX AND BEHAVIOR 199–203 (F.
A. Beach ed. 1965). This society, which he calls East Bay, not only tolerates, but
approves, homosexual intercourse as well as masturbation as alternatives to
heterosexual intercourse. Very nearly every male engages in extensive homosexual activities, either as young single men of the same age group, or as older
married men with young boys from 7 to 11 years of age. Yet the exclusively
homosexual man is nonexistent in this culture. When told that many Europeans
were exclusively homosexual, the only response from these natives went
something like, "Isn't that a shame!" On the other hand, the members of this

society found nothing peculiar or wrong about some of their men being exclusively heterosexual. In this society, homosexual intercourse usually consists of masturbatory foreplay culminating in anal intercourse. Mouth-genital contact was unknown. Even though exclusive homosexuality seemed unknown, it is of interest to note that at least one of Davenport's native respondents admitted to a *preference* for homosexual intercourse over heterosexual.

29. Hooker, *Sexual Behavior: Homosexuality*, in 14 INT'L ENCY. SOCIAL SCIENCES 230 (1968).

30. Suggs & Marshall, *Anthropological Perspectives on Human Sexual Behavior*, in HUMAN SEXUAL BEHAVIOR 230 (D. S. Marshall & R. C. Suggs eds. 1971).

31. FORD & BEACH 177–78, 265.

32. WEST 42–43.

33. These figures are from the Kinsey surveys. *See* KINSEY, FEMALE 452–53, 474–75. Admittedly, they may not be entirely representative of the American population. They remain, however, the best estimates we possess to date.

34. *See* A. C. KINSEY, W. B. POMEROY, & C. E. MARTIN, SEXUAL BEHAVIOR IN THE HUMAN MALE 659–60 [hereinafter cited as KINSEY, MALE].

35. Freud, *Three Essays on the Theory of Sexuality*, in 7 STANDARD EDITION OF THE COMPLETE PSYCHOLOGICAL WORKS OF SIGMUND FREUD 148 (J. Strachey transl. 1953).

36. *See* Marmor, *Introduction*, in SEXUAL INVERSION 10–11.

37. When boys and girls are exposed to male and female adults who vary drastically in their power or control over resources, they tend to imitate the behaviors of the more powerful adult. . . . In such a situation, if the male adult has greater control over resources than the female, both boys and girls imitate his behavior to a greater degree. Likewise, if the female adult has greater power over rewards than the male, her behavior tends to be imitated more frequently by both boys and girls. This experiment demonstrates that cross-sex imitation occurs, and is facilitated when the opposite-sex model has greater power than the same-sex model.

Mischel, *A Social Learning View of Sex Differences in Behavior*, in THE DEVELOPMENT OF SEX DIFFERENCES 57–59 (E. E. Maccoby ed. 1966).

38. *See* KINSEY, FEMALE 447; CHURCHILL 116–18; A. ELLIS, HOMOSEXUALITY: ITS CAUSES AND CURE 52 (1965) [hereinafter cited as ELLIS].

39. *See* L. ULLERSTAM, THE EROTIC MINORITIES 100 (A. Hollo transl. 1966).

40. CHURCHILL 95–96.

41. C. J. WILLIAMS & M. S. WEINBERG, HOMOSEXUALS AND THE MILITARY 156–57 (1971).

42. In clinical practice, an evenly balanced attraction to both sexes is relatively rarely encountered. . . . [But] the fact that such patterns can develop shows clearly that flight from the physical aspects of heterosexuality cannot be the explanation of all obligatory homosexual behavior.

WEST 214–15. To the same effect is HOFFMAN 163.

. . . . [I]t must be recognized that the homosexual is in many instances, among both single and married males, deliberately chosen as the preferred source of outlet; and it is simply accepted as a different kind of sexual outlet by a fair number of persons, whatever their marital status, who

embrace both heterosexual and homosexual experiences in the same age period. Consequently, the high incidence of the homosexual among single males is not wholly chargeable to the unavailability of heterosexual contacts.
KINSEY, MALE 289.

43. *See* Hampson & Hampson, *The Ontogenesis of Sexual Behavior in Man*, in 2 SEX AND INTERNAL SECRETIONS 1401–30 (3d ed. W. C. Young 1961).

44. *See* Money, *Factors in the Genesis of Homosexuality*, in DETERMINANTS OF HUMAN SEXUAL BEHAVIOR 19 (G. Winokur ed. 1963). In this article, Money concludes that we must alter our definition of homosexuality so that it no longer means sexual attraction and behavior between people who are biologically of the same sex, but between partners both of whom identify themselves as belonging, and *appear* to belong, to the same sex. Gender identity and external body morphology are, in his view, the factors that together should determine whether or not we characterize a relationship as homosexual.

45. Of course, physically intersexed people are a special case, from whom it is unwise to generalize to the physically normal population, because the hormonal imbalance that produced the pseudohermaphroditism could also have weakened whatever innate neurological basis may exist for a polarity of attraction between the sexes. Thus, these unusual people may have, innately, greater lability in the acquisition of sexual orientation than the physically normal person. Nevertheless, it seems that the data from this field of research tend to support the following hypotheses: (1) Gender identity and sexual orientation are both learned, not innate. (2) The only innate factor with much influence on this learning process is external body morphology, because it is the sole criterion by which others—parents, siblings, peers, etc.—distinguish a child as male or female, and therefore treat him as such. (3) Our culture associates attraction to males with being a female and vice versa, so if others have consistently identified a child as female, she will normally grow up to fulfill this gender role imposed by the culture. Thus, there is no puzzle requiring a psychoanalytic explanation when a pseudohermaphrodite always reared and treated as a female becomes sexually oriented toward males, though it is later discovered that "she" is in biological fact a "he." The ordinary homosexual remains a puzzle. What demands explanation under these hypotheses is not that his sexual orientation is in contradiction to his biological gender, but that it is in contradiction to his culture's expectations.

46. *See* K. Z. LORENZ, KING SOLOMON'S RING (1952).

47. *See* Maslow, *Critique and Discussion*, in SEX RESEARCH—NEW DEVELOPMENTS 137–39 (J. Money ed. 1965).

48. This view is expressed in, *e.g.*, Thompson, *Changing Concepts of Homosexuality*, in RUITENBEEK 42–43; CHURCHILL 97–98, 101–2, 104–5; Marmor, *Introduction*, in SEXUAL INVERSION 11; ELLIS 54, 78–80; Socarides, *Female Homosexuality*, in SEXUAL BEHAVIOR AND THE LAW 463 (R. Slovenko ed. 1965); and WEST 15–16, 187–88. The viewpoint is well summarized by SIECUS:

Many psychiatrists feel that, aside from the sexual maladaptation, it is perfectly possible for a homosexual to be happy and to make a good social adjustment. However, they also believe that homosexual behavior could not be maintained in the face of a hostile and punitive environment unless

strong neurotic fears blocked the path to heterosexual adaptation. Therefore, they conclude, homosexual behavior is in itself a form of emotional
illness, at least in our society at this time.
Sex Information and Education Council of the United States, Sexuality
and Man 77 (1970).

Of course, these statements may not represent the present views of their
authors. Marmor, for one, has now come round to the position that homosexuality
should not be regarded as an illness. *See* note 1 *supra.* It is worth remembering
that Freud, after regarding homosexuality as an illness in his earlier writings,
stated categorically toward the end of his life that it could not be classified as an
illness, though he still considered it an immature sexual pattern. *See* note 127
infra.

49. Ellis 78–79.

50. In putting the question thus, West seems clearly to have reached the heart
of the puzzle. West 187–88.

51. Although . . . [a child] may not have begun having sexual relations, no
one is any longer so naive as to believe that children do not have romantic
and sexual fantasies from earliest childhood; we also know that such
fantasies in most cases already point to future heterosexual or homosexual
interests that cannot be shifted by an act of will, or always even by
psychiatric treatment.
R. J. Stoller, Sex and Gender 258 (1968) [hereinafter cited as Stoller].

52. *See* note 67, Chapter 5 *supra.*

53. The reference here is to William Inge's play, *Splendor in the Grass*, in
which he uses the following passage from Wordsworth's poem *Intimations of
Immortality* to parallel the feelings associated with the budding of sexuality and
one's first great romantic love:
What though the radiance which was once so bright
Be now for ever taken from my sight,
Though nothing can bring back the hour
Of splendour in the grass, of glory in the flower;
We will grieve not, rather find
Strength in what remains behind;
. . . .

54. *See* Ellis 44.

55. In his article, *Sexual Behavior: Deviation: Psychological Aspects*, in 14
Int'l Ency. Social Sciences 209, at 209–10 (1968), he discusses this principle of
the critical period:
[It is] that period in the development of some system or function when the
organism passes from a neutral or undifferentiated stage to a differentiated
one. It is during this critical period that development is vulnerable to
interference and deflection, which, if they occur, will leave a permanent
residual in structure or function. . . . In behavioral science, the European
animal ethologists were the first to observe that patterns of behavior,
including sexual behavior, can be experimentally changed during a critical,
developmental learning period, and thenceforth this deviance becomes
relatively fixed. In other words, particular atypical experiences may

interfere or deform the genetic, hormonal, or neural norms of behavioral development otherwise expected.

. . . . In man, perhaps even more so than in lower species, peculiarities and special features of experience during critical periods may change the expected genetic, hormonal, or neural norms of development.

56. *See* the interview with Money reported in A. KARLEN, SEXUALITY AND HOMOSEXUALITY—A NEW VIEW 403 (1971); *see also* Money, *Sex Hormones and Other Variables in Human Eroticism*, in 2 SEX AND INTERNAL SECRETIONS 1397 (3d ed. W. C. Young 1961).

57. In trying to understand the fact that most homosexuals are not in any danger of psychosis, Robert Stoller suggests that

Perhaps homosexual desires are not as threatening to homosexuals because their identity is different from that of "healthy heterosexuals": The homosexual, if he has stronger and more primitive identifications with women, may not so profoundly threaten his sense of masculinity when he loves a man. Having once established his identity—even if by a conflict-laden route—he may be doing what comes naturally, not just doing it defensively. . . . In other words, one can have the rather comfortable identity of being a homosexual (even in the many cases where this is the end-product of a stormy, neurotic personality development), just as one can have the rather comfortable identity of being a heterosexual. . . .

STOLLER 156–57.

58. *Id.* 162.

59. *See* Hooker, note 68 *infra; see also* C. J. WILLIAMS & M. S. WEINBERG, HOMOSEXUALS AND THE MILITARY 134–36 (1971).

60. *See* ELLIS 79.

61. Probably the situation most likely to elicit police activity is homosexual contact in public restrooms. But L. HUMPHREYS, TEAROOM TRADE—IMPERSONAL SEX IN PUBLIC PLACES (1970), demonstrates that the participants in such contacts take elaborate precautions against being discovered by nonparticipants, whether police, teenagers, or "straight" adults. *See also* P. H. GEBHARD, J. H. GAGNON, W. B. POMEROY, & C. V. CHRISTENSEN, SEX OFFENDERS—AN ANALYSIS OF TYPES 354–55 (1965).

62. Actually, an association of former mental patients has recently been organized to combat abuses of the power our society has entrusted to the psychiatric profession. Several members of this group made a rather effective appearance on the David Susskind television show.

63. Suggs & Marshall, *Anthropological Perspectives on Human Sexual Behavior*, in HUMAN SEXUAL BEHAVIOR 218 (D. S. Marshall & R. C. Suggs eds. 1971).

64. These social dangers are (1) the threat to the biological survival of American society through the failure to reproduce; (2) the sexual abuse of children by homosexual adults; (3) homosexual rape; (4) the perpetuation of an alienated subculture within American society; (5) the contagious nature of homosexuality; and (6) the favoritism shown by homosexuals to others of their kind in employment situations, the military, the arts, etc. It is amazing to find two people who lay claim to the objectivity of science trotting out so many allegations

about the deleterious nature of American homosexuality without a shred of scientific data to back them up.

    65. In this post-Freudian world, major psychic wounds are increasingly viewed as par for the human condition and . . . few survive their parents without such wounding. . . . [Thus there] has been a scaling down of the goals set for men; instead of exceedingly vague and somewhat utopian goals we tend to ask more pragmatic questions: Is the individual self-supporting? Does he manage to conduct his affairs without the intervention of the police or the growing number of mental health authorities? . . . Has he learned to accept himself? These are questions we are learning to ask of nearly all men; among the remaining exceptions is found the homosexual. In practically all cases, the presence of homosexuality is seen as prima facie evidence of major psychopathology. When the heterosexual meets these minimal definitions of mental health, he is exculpated; the homosexual—no matter how good his adjustment in nonsexual areas of life is—remains suspect.

Simon & Gagnon, *Homosexuality: The Formulation of a Sociological Perspective,* in THE SAME SEX: AN APPRAISAL OF HOMOSEXUALITY 17 (R. W. Weltge ed. 1969).

    66. STOLLER 89–107.

    67. *Ibid. See id.* 126–30.

    68. To get some idea how cruel this concept can be when put into practice, the reader is referred to a couple of examples from Stoller's book. The first involves a child brought up unquestioningly as a boy, but who in fact was a female with external genitalia resembling a boy's—the result of adrenogenital syndrome. At the age of six, the true biological sex was uncovered by the onset of a precocious puberty, producing physical virilization (deepening of the voice, enlargement of the phallus, and the growth of body and facial hair) along with the beginning of menstruation. Stoller describes the outrageous treatment of this child:

> He could have been managed by removing his ovaries, uterus, and vagina, in which case he would have still needed medical treatment, but his sense of identity would have been left intact. However, sufficient pressure was exerted by medical authorities (for moralistic reasons) that his "penis" was amputated, and his "scrotal sac" was split and recreated as the external lips they were originally meant to be anatomically; then the child was told that he was a she. The subsequent psychiatric treatment that was attempted resulted after several years in a child who was a grotesque caricature of a girl. She is now twelve years old. She says she does not ever want to go out with boys, does not ever want to marry, does not want children, and would like to be a "cowboy or a racer" [of automobiles] when she grows up.
>
> I evaluated but did not treat this child, and could not have treated it because my attitude would have been too inimical to any chance of a child thus successfully switching gender. However, I did have the opportunity to see "her" three times for follow-up over the subsequent six years and thus to witness the failure of this brave attempt.

STOLLER 238.

The other example is a physically normal girl first seen at the clinic at the age of 15. Her gender identity being unquestionably male, she begged for a transsexual operation. Stoller quotes her own words from the transcript of a psychiatric interview:

> Right now I have to have this because I believe I have grown as a boy. And it is about time I start thinking about girls, which isn't right because of my body, but in my mind it is normal. I don't feel I am abnormal as a boy. Nothing about me seems abnormal, except I have the wrong body. In other words, the head is put on the wrong body. That's the way I figure it. I don't know if it is right; I don't have a medical mind. I figure when I get older, I will grow and think from boyhood into a man. I don't know whether I can be one, but I believe that's the way I am going to think. Your body is just something that holds you together; it's part of you; it's an important part—but your mind is strong; it is your will; your mind is everything. I mean as far as everything you want to be. If you had the body, the hands to play baseball, and it just wasn't in your mind, and it wasn't what you enjoyed, you might go and be a doctor. When all this was going on, I thought of God: Am I doing wrong? God created me as a girl, so maybe I should be. But I couldn't be, and which is more important, your mind or your body? God created my mind too, and if my mind is working this way, He created that. I just couldn't figure it out. I went to the priest; he didn't help me any. He got me all confused. I didn't know what to do. So I just sat down and thought. I used to pray a lot. We studied about God dying on the Cross for us, and I think if He did all that suffering, I can do this suffering for Him, but I can't suffer all my life like this; I would go crazy. I have got to have an out, a way to solve my problem, try to face up to it and solve it. . . . And so far I have solved this much of it.

Id. 200.

The agonizing this girl went through over her transsexualism is typical of that which a great many homosexuals undergo. The sense that their orientation is right and normal for them, and unalterable, yet incongruous with their physical sex, and the inability to reconcile their predicament with religious teachings that tie morality to "naturalness," combine to produce an equally intolerable dilemma for them. Evelyn Hooker notes that homosexuals she has interviewed believe their sexual orientation to be "a fate over which they have no control and in which they have no choice. . . . To fight against homosexuality is to fight against the inevitable, they believe, for they would be fighting against their own 'nature' in its essential form as they experience it. They believe that homosexuality is as 'natural' for them as heterosexuality is for others." Hooker, *Male Homosexuals and Their Worlds,* in SEXUAL INVERSION 102–3.

The more one surveys the literature, the more it becomes apparent that the medical profession, and particularly psychiatry, has not so much *found* norms *in* nature as it has *imposed* theological ideals *on* nature: God created them male and female; male and female created He them. The profession's task, like that of a priesthood, is to preserve inviolate this divinely ordained dichotomy between the sexes. Not only is a chasm fixed between the two, so that none may cross from one side to the other, but every blurring of the line must also be stamped out.

69. *See* A. COMFORT, THE ANXIETY MAKERS (1967).

70. A recent impressive broadside in which a legal scholar particularly attacks the unholy alliance of psychiatry with the law is N. N. KITTRIE, THE RIGHT TO BE DIFFERENT: DEVIANCE AND ENFORCED THERAPY (1971).

71. STOLLER 102–3, 262–63.

72. West argues that homosexuality, even though it may result from unresolved neurotic conflicts arising from the Oedipal situation, can represent a workable adaptation to life, allowing release from tension and development of the personality and character in normal ways. In other words, it is not necessarily indicative of chronic neurosis and maladjustment. WEST 183–85.

73. *See* ELLIS 80, 81–84.

74. *See* Marmor, *Introduction*, in SEXUAL INVERSION 16; CHURCHILL 40; HOFFMAN 163.

75. ELLIS 81.

76. Of course, one could cite other distinguished figures from the past whose homosexuality is without question, such as Tchaikovsky. In many, the fact that one is sexually deviant can itself promote a kind of overkill in career endeavors.

> Many sexually deviant people are . . . intensely ambitious, and try to compensate for their inner sense of inferiority by achieving such power and success that they can compel respect and admiration even if they cannot command affection from their fellows.

A. STORR, SEXUAL DEVIATION 34 (1964).

77. Following are quotations from C. W. SOCARIDES, THE OVERT HOMOSEXUAL (1968).

> All homosexuals suffer from a severe degree of psychic masochism.

Id. 97.

> All homosexual acts constitute a masochistic-sadistic transaction between the homosexual and his partner which serves as a defense against regression to early points of fixation (undifferentiated phase).

Id. 216.

> All homosexuals suffer from a sense of inferiority and guilt over their disability due to their infantile fears which have isolated them from the social-sexual relationships of a majority of the population.

Id. 217.

> All homosexuals deeply fear the knowledge that their homosexual behavior constitutes an erotized defense against a threatening masochistic state and in some cases the most severe masochistic state of the undifferentiated phase fusion.

Id. 227.

78. *See* Hooker, *The Adjustment of the Male Overt Homosexual*, in RUITENBEEK 141; HOFFMAN 154–63. *Cf.* Kinsey *et al.*, *Concepts of Normality and Abnormality in Sexual Behavior*, in PSYCHOSEXUAL DEVELOPMENT IN HEALTH AND DISEASE 28–29 (P. H. Hoch & J. Zubin eds. 1949). Michael Schofield, in his British study comparing sample homosexual patient, homosexual convict, and homosexual nonpatient, nonconvict groups with similar sample groups of heterosexuals, found that there were many more similarities between the homosexual patient group and the heterosexual patient group than between the homosexual patient group

and the homosexual nonpatient group. "The only differences [between the former two] are those items specifically connected with their sexual preferences." He concluded that "Homosexual patients are not typical homosexuals and doctors should not generalize from their experience with patients." M. SCHOFIELD, SOCIOLOGICAL ASPECTS OF HOMOSEXUALITY 160–61 (1965). On the other hand, he found that the homosexual nonpatient, nonconvict group had many more similarities to the heterosexual nonpatient group than to any of the other homosexual groups, apart from choice of sexual partner. *Id.* 177–78.

79. Pomeroy, *Homosexuality,* in THE SAME SEX—AN APPRAISAL OF HOMOSEXUALITY 13 (R. W. Weltge ed. 1969). Ernest van den Haag tells of a colleague who kept saying, "All my homosexual patients are sick," to which he finally replied, "so are all my heterosexual patients." Van den Haag, *Notes on Homosexuality and Its Cultural Setting,* in RUITENBEEK 297.

80. The subjects of Hooker's research cited in note 78 *supra* were supplied by a homophile organization.

81. Gebhard describes this research as follows:
The three studies referred to are:
(1) A study of 458 predominately homosexual white males in one area of Chicago.
(2) A comparative study of the social and psychological adjustments of homosexual males in the U.S.A., Copenhagen, and Amsterdam.
(3) A study of over 1000 predominately homosexual males and females in the San Francisco area.
All the studies have some measurements of adjustment, self image, happiness ratings, etc. None have been published, but the U.S.-Copen-hagen-Amsterdam study is now in manuscript and should see print within a year; the authors will be Martin Weinberg and Colin Williams. The other two studies are further from completion. Our policies preclude giving anyone access to our unpublished research findings, but we can reaffirm the statement that most homosexuals in our samples have achieved adequate social and psychological adjustment. Some clinicians, and particularly psychoanalysts, would maintain that an adequate adjustment is impossible because of the stress of living in a hostile society, or because homosexuality is in itself pathological, or because guilt is inescapable, et cetera. We prefer to ask if an individual meets the minimal requirements of adjustment: (1) is he self-supporting in some legitimate occupation?, (2) does he manage to keep out of conflict with society?, and (3) does he make meaningful emotional relationships with other persons? An affirmative answer to all three questions I interpret as an adequate adjustment. Most homosexuals not only meet these minimal standards, but surpass them. It is true that the homosexual is subject to more stress than the average heterosexual, but this does not mean he is maladjusted.
Letter from Paul H. Gebhard, Director, Institute for Sex Research, Inc., Indiana University, to the author, March 21, 1972.

82. "Only in the consultation room does the homosexual reveal himself and his world. No other data, statistics, or statements can be accepted as setting forth the

true nature of homosexuality." Socarides, *Homosexuality and Medicine*, 212 J.A.M.A. 1199 (1970).

83. ELLIS 74–77.

84. Hoffman makes clear how deviance from society's norms and mental illness do not necessarily, or even usually, coexist in an individual. HOFFMAN 116–19.

85. . . . . [M]any mature people with predominantly homosexual proclivities have excellent ego strength and fine character structure which permit them to respond to their life situations with an appropriate mobilization of their intellectual, social, and creative resources. They often constitute an accomplished and highly informed group within their particular subculture. These persons seldom present themselves specifically for treatment of their homosexuality, and generally there exists little reason for their doing so.

S. E. WILLIS, UNDERSTANDING AND COUNSELLING THE MALE HOMOSEXUAL 8 (1967) [hereinafter cited as WILLIS]. *See also id.* 108, 168; and Wolfenden, note 10, Chapter 1 *supra*, paras. 25–30.

86. Hooker, *Male Homosexuals and Their Worlds*, in SEXUAL INVERSION 103–5.

87. WEST 243.

88. This statement received ample substantiation in August 1972 in the withdrawal of Senator Thomas F. Eagleton's candidacy for the Vice-Presidency, forced by disclosure of his psychiatric treatment in the 1960s. Public reaction demonstrated that mental illness in an individual's history, no matter how long ago it occurred or how cured it may have been, renders him unworthy of trust and confidence in the eyes of the public.

89. STOLLER 24–28.

90. *Id.* 17–23.

91. *Id.* 151–53.

92. *See* WILLIS 67–71. Szasz suggests that the intolerance may be due to a perception that homosexuality symbolically undermines the value of these males' favorite game—heterosexual activity. Szasz, *Legal and Moral Aspects of Homosexuality*, in SEXUAL INVERSION 135.

93. STOLLER 153. This conclusion is buttressed by Dickey's study, which found that the sense of personal adequacy was highest in those male homosexuals who mixed freely with "straight" men and were accepted by them, and who felt no conflict over sexual roles, tolerating or preferring a passive sexual role while maintaining a self-image of normal masculinity. Dickey, *Attitudes Towards Sex Roles and Feelings of Adequacy in Homosexual Males*, 25 J. CONSULTING PSYCHOLOGY 116 (1961).

94. The psychologic significance of any type of sexual activity very largely depends on what the individual and his social group choose to make of it. . . . The truth of this thesis is abundantly evidenced by our thousands of histories which, among them, include every conceivable type of sexual behavior without subsequent psychologic disturbance, while the same sort of behavior in other histories may bring shame, remorse, despair, desperation, and attempted suicide. . . . Failing to comprehend that their own

attitudes and the social codes generated these disturbances, most persons identify them as direct evidence of the intrinsic wrongness or abnormality of the sexual act itself.

In one or another of the cultures of the world, nearly every type of sexual behavior has been condemned, while in other cultures the same activities have been considered desirable sources of pleasure and socially valuable. Heterosexual coitus is extolled in most cultures, but forbidden to Buddhist and Catholic priests. Homosexual activity is condemned in some cultures, tacitly accepted in others, honored as a religious rite in others, and allowed to Buddhist priests. Behavior which is accepted by the culture does not generate psychologic conflicts in the individual or unmanageable social problems. The same behavior, censored, condemned, tabooed, or criminally punished in the next culture, may generate guilt and neurotic disturbances in the non-conforming individual and serious conflict with the social organism. This seems to be the source of most of the disturbances which we have found in the histories of American females and males who masturbate, who engage in heterosexual petting, or in homosexual relations, or animal contacts, or utilize sexual techniques which, biologically normal enough in themselves, are taboo in our particular culture.

KINSEY, FEMALE 320. *See also* Kinsey *et al.*, *Concepts of Normality and Abnormality in Sexual Behavior,* in PSYCHOSEXUAL DEVELOPMENT IN HEALTH AND DISEASE 30–32 (P. H. Hoch & J. Zubin eds. 1949); and R. BENEDICT, PATTERNS OF CULTURE 262–65 (1934). WILLIS 25–26 outlines the same view that it may not be homosexuality per se which constitutes the basis of the personality disturbances that homosexuals exhibit, but the individual's anxious response to society's reaction to homosexuality. In his words,

The person with a predominantly homosexual adjustment often feels excluded from the sense of collective strength which is intrinsic to a secure identification with the conforming majority group. A sense of alienation occurs when an individual believes his deviant behavior is considered evil in his society. The effect of such alienation is corrosive to his sense of personal security and often creates a centrifugal force which carries him even further from constructive convergence with the rest of society. The threat to his esteem touches off anxiety reactions, which in turn tend to mobilize whatever coping capacities have in the past proved effective for him. . . . When threatened by exclusion from the social unit, one is forced into a pit of loneliness, frustration, and despair. This despair is deepened when the factors which have resulted in the sense of alienation seem unalterable or outside one's own control. The male homosexual is often in this position.

WILLIS 3–4. *See also id.* 15–16.

95. *See* WEST 107–8; CHURCHILL 188–92; B. MAGEE, ONE IN TWENTY 51–54 (1966).

96. For one example of such an incident, *see* CHURCHILL 194–97.

97. *See* Magee, *supra* note 95, at 89–92; Wolfenden, note 10, Chapter 1 *supra,*

paras. 109–12. These books deal with British, rather than American, experience, but the situation in the two countries is probably comparable.

98. It is evident that an individual's willingness to contribute constructively to his society is likely to be proportional to the degree of acceptance or estrangement he feels from that society. It is improbable that anyone will have respect for, or commitment to, the ideals of a society that consistently makes him its victim. He is more likely to react with either social withdrawal or contemptuous antisocial protest and cynicism.

WILLIS 7.

99. See Magee, supra note 95, at 126–27; CHURCHILL 53–56.

100. WEST 53.

101. See WILLIS 165–68, where he also delineates some additional reasons the reassurance sought from other members of the outcast group fails to provide adequate ego support.

102. See STOLLER 268–71; A. STORR, SEXUAL DEVIATION 118–19 (1964); Bieber, Clinical Aspects of Male Homosexuality, in SEXUAL INVERSION 254.

103. . . . . [F]alling in love implies amongst many other things that a person can relate his inner world of phantasy to a real person in the external world and thus find, at any rate for a time, the greatest happiness known to man. It is only when the inner figure and the outer appear to coincide that the phenomenon of falling in love occurs, and that there is a complete correspondence between the sexual desires which the person has felt in phantasy and the desire which he now feels for an actual person.

A. STORR, SEXUAL DEVIATION 26 (1964). The old saying puts it more succinctly: "Beauty is in the eye of the beholder."

104. Stanley Willis has described poignantly the plight of the male homosexual in our society:

These early prohibitions [on sexuality in general] were most strongly associated with the female. The resultant puritanical sense of guilt colliding with a later unrelenting biological need for sexual expression produces a compromise, i.e., the sexual need is deflected away from the heterosexual object because this carries the most stringent early taboo. In the context of adult life, the homosexual choice is socially unacceptable. But the child has no knowledge that this social aversion will occur. He makes his choice in good faith, so to speak, in an attempt to avoid the pain of shame in childhood, only to find that he has become the victim of later social sanctions against homosexual behavior. His conflict is heightened by the criminal sanctions imposed on homosexual behavior. Hence he is indicted by the pressure of a prohibitive and punitive infantile superego on the one hand, and damned by a sense of social alienation resulting from his homosexual choice on the other. It seems a paradox that his later status as a pariah was compelled by his early willingness to completely acquiesce to his society's norms. He ends up the victim of a cruel double bind.

WILLIS 188.

105. *See* Romm, *Sexuality and Homosexuality in Women,* in SEXUAL INVERSION 291; WEST 239–41; F. BELLIVEAU & L. RICHTER, UNDERSTANDING HUMAN SEXUAL INADEQUACY 138–40 (1970). The Kinsey group, in their study of sex offenders, found a tendency toward at least one brief marriage in all three of their categories of homosexual offenders: 40 per cent of the homosexual offenders against children had one marriage that broke up in two years or less; 41 per cent of the homosexual offenders against adults did; and 37 per cent of the homosexual offenders against minors did. P. H. GEBHARD, J. H. GAGNON, W. B. POMEROY, & C. V. CHRISTENSEN, SEX OFFENDERS—AN ANALYSIS OF TYPES 282 (1965). The portion of the sample groups of homosexuals studied by Williams and Weinberg who had ever been heterosexually married ranged from 13 to 23 per cent. *See* C. J. WILLIAMS & M. S. WEINBERG, HOMOSEXUALS AND THE MILITARY 156–57 (1971).

106. P. & B. WYDEN, GROWING UP STRAIGHT—WHAT EVERY THOUGHTFUL PARENT SHOULD KNOW ABOUT HOMOSEXUALITY (1968).

107. *See* note 72, Chapter 6 *supra.*

108. *See* B. MAGEE, ONE IN TWENTY 34–42 (1966).

109. *See* L. J. HATTERER, CHANGING HOMOSEXUALITY IN THE MALE (1970), and ELLIS. West summarizes the matter:

> Unfortunately, in many cases the discovery of infantile fears of incestuous relationships and suchlike fantasies, which the analysts believe to have been the original cause of the turning away from normal sex, does not in itself bring about a disappearance of homosexual desires.

WEST 254.

110. The therapeutic task is to break up . . . [the vicious] circle, reverse the homosexual pattern, and establish pleasurable heterosexual relations. This can be done by decreasing the intensity of the . . . motivations which propel the patient toward genital contact with male objects, while simultaneously enhancing his sexual interest in women. . . . There is only one way that the homosexual can overcome this . . . [phobic avoidance of the female genital] and learn to have heterosexual inter-course, and that way is in bed with a woman. . . . Sooner or later, the homosexual patient must make the necessary attempts to have inter-course, and he must make them again and again, until he is capable of a sustained erection, penetration and pleasurable intravaginal orgasm. The achievement of these end goals can be facilitated by helping the patient to gain insight into the unconscious fantasies which convert the vagina into a source of danger. We must emphasize, however, that such insights are the means to an end; they are not the end itself.

L. OVESEY, HOMOSEXUALITY AND PSEUDOHOMOSEXUALITY 106–7 (1969). He finally comes to the conclusion that "the ultimate therapeutic goal" is a *successful marriage. Id.* 119–24.

111. W. B. POMEROY, GIRLS AND SEX 141 (1969).

112. *See* note 109 *supra.* Hatterer's book, which includes many case histories and innumerable warnings and counsels to other therapists about techniques likely to help or hinder, furnishes an excellent sense of the difficult and extensive nature of the therapy needed to "cure" homosexuality. It also provides a vivid,

real-life picture of the suffering many men undergo from having internalized our society's phobia of homosexuality. One cannot come away from the book without feeling that the phobia has created more evil than its object.

113. See, e.g., Hadden, *Treatment of Male Homosexuals in Groups*, 16 INT'L J. GROUP PSYCHOTHERAPY 13 (1966), *Group Psychotherapy of Male Homosexuals*, 6 CURRENT PSYCHIATRIC THERAPIES 177 (1966), *Group Psychotherapy for Sexual Maladjustments*, 125 AM. J. PSYCHIATRY 327 (1968), and *Group Therapy for Homosexuals*, 5 MEDICAL ASPECTS OF HUMAN SEXUALITY 116 (No. 1, Jan. 1971).

114. See D. CAPPON, TOWARD AN UNDERSTANDING OF HOMOSEXUALITY 265–66 (1965); Mayerson & Lief, *Psychotherapy of Homosexuals*, in SEXUAL INVERSION 312–14.

115. Mayerson & Lief, *supra* note 114, at 332 report a 22 per cent cure rate. The Bieber study reported a cure rate of 27 per cent. BIEBER 276. Hatterer states that, of his group of patients on whom he made 2-to-15-year follow-ups, 49 recovered, 19 partially recovered, and 76 remained homosexual. L. J. HATTERER, CHANGING HOMOSEXUALITY IN THE MALE viii (1970).

116. WEST 235–36.

117. *Id.* 233–34; Knight, *Overt Male Homosexuality*, in SEXUAL BEHAVIOR AND THE LAW 442–43 (R. Slovenko ed. 1965).

118. The Kinsey group thus explains how a male can have sex with a physically, mentally, and esthetically unattractive, lower level prostitute:

> As far as his psychologic responses are concerned, the male in many instances may not be having coitus with the immediate sexual partner, but with all of the other girls with whom he has ever had coitus, and with the entire genus Female with which he would like to have coitus.

KINSEY, FEMALE 684.

119. See KINSEY, MALE 510–11; KINSEY, FEMALE 667–68, 164–65.

120. ELLIS 42, 112–13.

121. *Id.* 95–108.

122. See note 51, Chapter 6 *supra*.

123. The Bieber group claimed that 29 of their 106 "homosexual" patients (27 per cent) became exclusively heterosexual during the course of psychoanalytic treatment. Their table shows, however, that 15 of the 29 were already ambisexual at the start of treatment. Exclusive homosexuals made up less than half their "cures." Of the exclusive homosexuals they treated, only 19 per cent were exclusively heterosexual at last contact, while 19 per cent were ambisexual, 3 per cent were sexually inactive, and 57 per cent were still exclusively homosexual. BIEBER 276.

124. See WEST 230–37; Mayerson & Lief, *supra* note 114, at 332. But Mayerson and Lief make clear that "actual heterosexual performance is not so important a prognostic factor as is psychological heterosexual orientation. . . . the presence of manifest erotic heterosexual content in dreams is directly correlated with heterosexual improvement." *Id.* 323.

125. STOLLER 29–38.

126. WEST 237.

127. The letter, now in the archives of the Institute for Sex Research, Inc., Indiana University, Bloomington, Indiana, appears in SIECUS NEWSLETTER, Vol.

VI, No. 2, at-5 (Dec. 1970). It also appears in Ruitenbeek 1. It reads as follows:

April 9th, 1935

Prof. Dr. Freud
Wien, IX., Berggase 19.

Dear Mrs. ———

I gather from your letter that your son is a homosexual. I am most impressed by the fact that you do not mention this term yourself in your information about him. May I question you why you avoid it? Homosexuality is assuredly no advantage but it is nothing to be ashamed of, no vice, no degradation, it cannot be classified as an illness; we consider it to be a variation of the sexual function produced by a certain arrest of sexual development. Many highly respectable individuals of ancient and modern times have been homosexuals, several of the greatest men among them (Plato, Michelangelo, Leonardo da Vinci, etc.). It is a great injustice to persecute homosexuality as a crime and a cruelty too. If you do not believe me, read the books of Havelock Ellis.

By asking me if I can help, you mean I suppose if I can abolish homosexuality and make normal heterosexuality take its place. The answer is, in a general way we cannot promise to achieve it. In a certain number of cases we succeed in developing the blighted germs of heterosexual tendencies which are present in every homosexual; in the majority of cases it is no more possible. It is a question of the quality and the age of the individual. The result of treatment cannot be predicted.

What analysis can do for your son runs in a different line. If he is unhappy, neurotic, torn by conflicts, inhibited in his social life, analysis may bring him harmony, peace of mind, full efficiency, whether he remains homosexual or gets changed. If you make up your mind he should have analysis with me—I don't expect you will—he has to come over to Vienna. I have no intention of leaving here. However don't neglect to give me your answer.

Sincerely yours with kind wishes,

Freud

P.S. I did not find it difficult to read your handwriting. Hope you will not find my writing and my English a harder task.

128. West 242–43.

129. *Id.* 241; Bieber, *Clinical Aspects of Male Homosexuality,* in Sexual Inversion 266; L. J. Hatterer, Changing Homosexuality in the Male 57–59 (1970). Mayerson and Lief agree that motivation to change is highly important, but not necessarily age. Mayerson & Lief, *supra* note 114, at 321–22, 316.

130. Hatterer, *supra* note 129, at 60. But one cannot make a safe prediction even in the case of apparently confirmed patterns. West 246.

131. *See* Hatterer, *supra* note 129, at 61–67.

132. *See* West 241.

133. Another good discussion of factors relevant to the prognosis for a successful "treatment" is found in L. OVESEY, HOMOSEXUALITY AND PSEUDOHOMOSEXUALITY 107–17 (1969).

134. WEST 255.

135. But for the laws against prostitution, the difficulty could perhaps be overcome by utilizing sexually experienced volunteers of the opposite sex, who are paid to assist in the therapy, as Masters and Johnson have done for their unmarried heterosexual patients at their clinic in St. Louis. Other therapists also have been utilizing such sex "surrogates." See S. F. Chronicle, Dec. 18, 1972, at 1, col. 2, and at 24, col. 1.

136. SEX INFORMATION AND EDUCATION COUNCIL OF THE UNITED STATES, SEXUALITY AND MAN 80 (1970); BIEBER 275–302; Wilbur, Clinical Aspects of Female Homosexuality, in SEXUAL INVERSION 279–80. In a number of cases, however, less time may be necessary to effect great improvement. See D. CAPPON, TOWARD AN UNDERSTANDING OF HOMOSEXUALITY 261, 264 (1965); Ellis, The Effectiveness of Psychotherapy with Individuals Who Have Severe Homosexual Problems, 20 J. CONSULTING PSYCHOLOGY 192 (No. 3, June 1956).

137. Many homosexuals have no desire to change. See C. J. WILLIAMS & M. S. WEINBERG, HOMOSEXUALS AND THE MILITARY 133–34 (1971).

138. The 4 per cent figure is the Kinsey group's estimate of white American males who are exclusively homosexual throughout life. See text and notes at p. 235 supra. The 2 per cent figure is an estimate apparently arrived at by the armed forces after World War II. See Playboy Panel: Homosexuality, PLAYBOY, April 1971, at 63.

139. There were approximately 23,000 psychiatrists in the United States in 1969. The number is estimated to be 26,700 in 1975. See A. A. ROGOW, THE PSYCHIATRISTS 15, 32 (1970).

140. See HOFFMAN 194–95; WEST 42.

141. See M. P. FELDMAN & M. J. MACCULLOCH, HOMOSEXUAL BEHAVIOR: THERAPY AND ASSESSMENT (1971). See also S. RACHMAN & J. TEASDALE, AVERSION THERAPY AND BEHAVIOR DISORDERS: AN ANALYSIS (1969).

142. WEST 256–60. McConaghy, Aversion Therapy in the Treatment of Male Homosexuals, in BEHAVIOUR THERAPY 45–56 (G. L. Mangan & L. D. Bainbridge eds. 1969), reports:

> . . . . [A]t a year following treatment, homosexual feeling is absent in about 15 per cent of the subjects treated, reduced in another 50 per cent and unchanged in 35 per cent. Heterosexual feeling is not significantly changed.

Feldman & MacCulloch, supra note 141, claimed a 60 per cent "cure" rate, but it appears that their group included a good many ambisexuals. They had little success with what they term "primary" homosexuals.

143. See Beach, Experimental Studies of Mating Behavior in Animals, in SEX RESEARCH—NEW DEVELOPMENTS 128–31 (J. Money ed. 1965); also MacLean, New Findings Relevant to the Evolution of Psychosexual Functions of the Brain, id. 197–217.

144. See Shinn, Homosexuality: Christian Conviction and Inquiry, in THE SAME SEX—AN APPRAISAL OF HOMOSEXUALITY 49 (R. W. Weltge ed. 1969).

145. I do not mean to appear too harsh on behavior therapy. For homosexuals wanting to change and who appear to have good prospects of becoming heterosexual, these techniques may help by relieving them of temptation. For the ambisexual who wants to become heterosexually orthodox, or faithful, they may equally prove to be a boon.

146. STOLLER 243–44.

147. ELLIS 45–46. Shifts in the other direction can also occur. In view of the resistance to change exhibited by most people, these spontaneous shifts are very curious phenomena and deserve more study.

148. See, e.g., J. E. EICHENLAUB, THE MARRIAGE ART 49 (1961).

149. Masters & Johnson, Ten Sex Myths Exploded, PLAYBOY, December 1970, at 126–28.

150. See W. H. MASTERS & V. E. Johnson, HUMAN SEXUAL RESPONSE (1966).

151. On the erotic significance of the anus and mouth in both the male and the female, see KINSEY, FEMALE 585–88. Very little anthropological data exist on the incidence of heterosexual anal intercourse in the rest of the world.

> The dearth of reports and the absence of this technique in myths suggest that it is uncommon (as in the United States); but it is not rare. In a very few societies (prehistoric Peru is one), it seems to have been fairly common.

Gebhard, Human Sexual Behavior: A Summary Statement, in HUMAN SEXUAL BEHAVIOR 210 (D. S. Marshall & R. C. Suggs eds. 1971).

152. See note 23 supra.

153. See FORD & BEACH 66, 259.

154. See KINSEY, MALE 572, 576–77; KINSEY, FEMALE 257–58, 361. See also FORD & BEACH 40. Gebhard summarizes the incidence in humans thus:

> Male mouth on the female genitalia (cunnilingus) seems well established in parts of Oceania and in the higher civilizations of Asia, but, again, anthropological data are scant. In Africa, the technique is mainly used in the north and is said to be an Arabic innovation. In the United States, the technique is common in some subgroups (for example, in the married upper-socioeconomic stratum) and infrequent in others (the lower-socio-economic stratum, the unmarried, among others), where disapproval may be violent. Female mouth on the penis (fellation) exemplifies much the same distribution as cunnilingus. However, the practice of fellation does not imply the practice of cunnilingus; some societies (Mohave, Basongye, prehistoric northern Peruvian) exhibit the former and lack the latter. But the presence of cunnilingus almost always implies the presence of fellation.

Gebhard, supra note 151, at 209–10.

155. Money, Psychosexual Differentiation, in SEX RESEARCH—NEW DEVELOPMENTS 13–14 (J. Money ed. 1965).

156. Gebhard, supra note 151, at 210.

157. See FORD & BEACH 66, 259; KINSEY, MALE 367–69, 575–76; KINSEY, FEMALE 256–57, 361. Gebhard says that "use of the male hand on female genitalia is universal, and use of the female hand on the male penis is common among

sexually experienced individuals almost everywhere." Gebhard, *supra* note 151, at 209.

158. The Kinsey studies give us some idea of the incidence of such acts in a heterosexual context:

> In marital relations, oral stimulation of male or female genitalia occurs in about 60 per cent of the histories of persons who have been to college, although it is in only about 20 per cent of the histories of the high school level and in 11 per cent of the histories of the grade school level. . . . [T]he above figures must . . . represent minimum incidences. In nearly all of the upper level histories which involve oral contacts the males make contacts with the female genitalia. In about 47 per cent of the histories, the females make similar contacts with the male genitalia.

KINSEY, MALE 576–77.

159. *See* M. PLOSCOWE, SEX AND THE LAW 209 (1951), quoting from a report of the Group for the Advancement of Psychiatry (No. 9, *Psychiatrically Deviated Sex Offenders*, 1950).

160. Wolfenden, note 10, Chapter 1 *supra*, para. 40 n.

161. Michael Schofield made the following calculations about the number of homosexual acts committed annually in England and Wales, in his 1965 study: The average number of homosexual acts per year per person committed by the 150 homosexuals in his sample was 52. From this he estimated that if five per cent of the male population in England and Wales were homosexual, there would be 57,951,400 homosexual acts committed each year in that territory. If one takes his calculations and applies them to the United States, this total number of acts would have to be multiplied by four, because the American population is approximately four times that of England and Wales. The object of his arithmetic was to estimate the chances of a homosexual offense being brought to official notice. On the basis of 4,800 homosexual offenses having come to the attention of the police in England and Wales in 1962, he figures that the chances were consequently about one in 11,600. M. SCHOFIELD, SOCIOLOGICAL ASPECTS OF HOMOSEXUALITY 157 (1965).

162. KINSEY, MALE 651.

163. This is an estimate based on Armed Forces statistics published after World War II, in which about 10 million Americans served. Four-tenths of one per cent were rejected at induction centers for homosexuality (presumably these were people who admitted they were homosexual in response to a questionnaire); another four-tenths of one per cent were separated from the services because of it; and the estimate was that perhaps an additional one per cent went undetected. *See Playboy Panel: Homosexuality*, PLAYBOY, April 1971, at 63, cols. 2–3. Bieber thinks the estimate of an additional one per cent who went undetected is extravagant, but it seems rather an underestimate. It is very unlikely that *half* of all the American homosexuals who volunteered or were called up for service in America's most fervently patriotic war of this century either removed their masks willingly on the prompting of a simple official question at induction or else got caught later engaging in homosexual acts.

Several empirical surveys of homosexuals have demonstrated that the majority served and were never discovered. *See* C. J. WILLIAMS & M. S. WEINBERG, HOMOSEXUALS AND THE MILITARY 59–61 (1971).

164. If one takes the Kinsey percentages as coming reasonably close to the truth, the number of males in America today who are exclusively or predominantly homosexual for most of their adult lives would be from 2 million to 4 million. Marmor, *Introduction*, in SEXUAL INVERSION 22 n. 9.

165. KINSEY, MALE 623, 650. The Kinsey group believed the actual incidence in the American male population as a whole might be as much as 5 per cent higher, or still higher. *Id.* 626. However, it appears that 85 per cent of these males with overt homosexual contact in their histories had it only during puberty or adolescence. Gagnon, *Sexual Behavior: Deviation: Social Aspects*, in 14 INT'L ENCY. SOCIAL SCIENCES 219 (1968).

166. KINSEY, FEMALE 452–53, 474–75. Here, in contrast to their study of males, the Kinsey group felt that their figures were probably too high to represent accurately the experience of the total female population of America, mainly because lower-class females were under-represented in their sample and their data showed greater and greater incidences at each higher educational level. *Id.* 459. Socarides, however, thinks Kinsey's estimates of female homosexuality too low, at least for today. Socarides, *Female Homosexuality*, in SEXUAL BEHAVIOR AND THE LAW 464 (R. Slovenko ed. 1965).

167. The most recent collation and comparison of the statistical studies which have been made is found in a working paper, "Incidence of Overt Homosexuality in the United States and Western Europe," prepared in 1968–69 for the National Institute of Mental Health Task Force on Homosexuality by Dr. Paul H. Gebhard, Director of the Institute for Sex Research, Inc., Indiana University. *See also* the poll reported in note 170 *infra.*

168. D. J. West argues that Kinsey's data and percentages are bound to be close to the truth, that is, reasonably reliable. *See* WEST 35–42. At all events, there have not been any similar large-scale studies made either before or since to contradict Kinsey.

169. In the total male population, single and married, between adolescence and old age, . . . 6.3 per cent of the total number of orgasms is derived from homosexual contacts.

KINSEY, MALE 610.

170. Of the entire male population, about 30 per cent have been brought to climax at least once in oral-genital contacts with other males, and 14 per cent have brought other males to climax by the same techniques. KINSEY, MALE 373. Mouth-genital contacts of some sort, with the subject as either the active or the passive partner, in homosexual or heterosexual contexts, occur at some time in the histories of nearly 60 per cent of all males. The incidence of such behavior is 72 per cent of college-level males, 65 per cent of high-school-level males, and 40 per cent of those who have never gone beyond the eighth grade. *Id.* 371. Thus, about 60 million of the approximately 100 million American males will violate the sodomy laws at least once during their lives.

A fascinating recent poll of attitudes and practices in the realm of sexual behavior appears in PSYCHOLOGY TODAY, July 1970, at 39–52. The magazine had included a research questionnaire in its issue of July 1969, inviting its readers to respond. More than 20,000 did so. Although it is impossible to tell how closely the respondents represent a random sample of the population as a whole (they would doubtless fall into the higher strata in terms of education and intelligence), the results are some indication of the attitudes and practices of a sizable group of Americans. Of the total sample, the percentages who engage in oral-genital stimulation (fellatio and cunnilingus) are rather startling. Thirty-eight per cent of the male respondents, and 41 per cent of the female, take the active role in such behavior "frequently"; 34 per cent of the males and 37 per cent of the females take the passive role "frequently." Twenty-eight per cent of both males and females said they had engaged in such conduct in the active role "several times," and the passive role figures for this frequency were 27 per cent for males and 31 per cent for females. For those who had engaged in such behavior "once or twice" the percentages were (1) active role—13 per cent for both sexes, and (2) passive role—16 per cent for both sexes. Only 21–23 per cent of the male respondents and 16–18 per cent of the females said they had never engaged in such behavior, and, of these, a high proportion admitted they had wanted to. *Id.* 43.

Interestingly, 850 of the respondents stated they were homosexuals, 75 per cent of them males. This represented about 4 per cent of the total sample of respondents—a figure that corresponds roughly to Kinsey's estimate of exclusive homosexuals in the male population of the country at large (4 per cent). Likewise, 37 per cent of the male respondents as a whole admitted to having had at least one homosexual experience—a figure that corresponds exactly to Kinsey's data published in 1948. *Id.* 50.

171. PRESIDENT'S COMMISSION ON LAW ENFORCEMENT AND THE AD-MINISTRATION OF JUSTICE, THE CHALLENGE OF CRIME IN A FREE SOCIETY 1 (1967).

172. Of course, this is true of consensual sexual behavior generally, as the Kinsey surveys make clear:

> It will be recalled that 85 per cent of the total male population has pre-marital intercourse . . . , 59 per cent has some experience with mouth-genital contacts . . . , nearly 70 per cent has relations with prostitutes . . . , something between 30 and 45 per cent has extramarital intercourse . . . , 37 per cent has some homosexual experience . . . , 17 per cent of the farm boys have animal intercourse. . . . The persons involved in these activities, taken as a whole, constitute more than 95 per cent of the total male population. . . . [So, if we were to send to jail or prison all "sex offenders," it would be equivalent to proposing that] 5 per cent of the population should support the other 95 per cent in penal institutions.

KINSEY, MALE 392.

8

Equal Protection of the Laws

The fourteenth amendment of the American Constitution provides that no state shall "deny to any person within its jurisdiction the equal protection of the laws." This clause does not merely require the states to *apply* their laws equally to all and sundry; it also prohibits invidious discrimination within the law itself. The critical question is what kinds of discrimination are invidious. Obviously, the law must make distinctions between people. For instance, the law of inheritance generally prefers descendants before ancestors, and both before collateral relatives. Traditional analysis under the equal-protection clause has therefore made the answer depend on whether the discrimination rests on a reasonable classification. In other words, is the characteristic by which the law singles out some for preferential treatment over others a reasonable basis, in light of appropriate social objectives the law seeks to further? One must first identify these social objectives, then determine whether they are reasonable and appropriate for the state to pursue, and finally ascertain whether the discrimination embodied in the law is reasonably related to their furtherance.

One may ask what all this has to do with the sodomy laws. Generally, such laws do not purport to establish any classification, or to discriminate between people on any basis. They simply prohibit various kinds of sex acts deemed to be unnatural, regardless of the characteristics of the participants. Kansas's law is the sole exception; it prohibits such acts only between persons of the same sex. On closer analysis, however, it becomes clear that the sodomy laws of other states as well, although they purport to penalize equally both the heterosexual and the homosexual, contain a built-in discrimination against homosexuals. These laws, except in Illinois, Connecticut, Colorado, Oregon, Hawaii, Delaware, and Ohio,[1] may prohibit all oral-genital and anal-genital contacts.[2] Except where judicial decision has already limited them, such laws in many states are capable of being stretched by interpretation to cover interfemoral contact and mutual masturbation as well; indeed, as already noted, some have already been so construed.[3] In effect, therefore, these laws manage to bar all sexual expression between homosexuals because no alternative means exists for them which is licit. Such an alternative does exist for the heterosexual—namely, coitus. The state, by limiting lawful interpersonal sexuality to a single mode, discriminates against those incapable of it.[4]

To admit that the sodomy laws contain a built-in discrimination against homosexuals hardly answers the question of constitutionality under the equal-protection clause. It is common knowledge that the major enforcement of these laws has always been against homosexuals, rather than heterosexuals.[5] The question is whether such discrimination is rationally related to the furtherance of an appropriate social objective. If, as already noted, society may have a reasonable claim to discourage homosexuality in order to help steer the young and impressionable toward the majority pattern of heterosexuality, then surely such laws meet the test. The answer is not quite so simple.

The United States Supreme Court in recent years has created exceptions to the general principle that the equal-protection clause is satisfied on the mere showing of a rational connection between the discrimination and some appropriate social objective. Apparently, the general principle had proved inadequate to prevent the states from acting in ways fundamentally unfair to one group of human beings within their jurisdiction. In these exceptional cases, a stricter standard is therefore applied. The state must show a *compelling* social objective and that the discrimination is *necessary* to its accomplishment. The detriment to individual citizens is so great that it will counterbalance any ordinary social objective and any merely rational connection. The first of these exceptions can be called the exception for regulations impinging on "fundamental human rights." If the effect of the discrimination is to deny or infringe a fundamental right, it is subject to the stricter standard. The second exception can be called the rule of inherently "suspect" classifications. Among such classifications are those based on race or national origin.[6] Efforts have also been made to include discriminations based on gender, on wealth, and on legitimacy of birth, but the Supreme Court has not yet clearly conceded that these classifications too are inherently suspect.[7] If a suspect classification is involved, the stricter standard will be applied whether or not the regulation impinges on fundamental rights. Often, however, both exceptions may be invoked against the same law because it employs a suspect classification and *also* impinges on a fundamental right.[8]

In the case of racial segregation, for instance, the state could plausibly assert that it had a legitimate interest in minimizing social friction and that segregation of the races was reasonably related to the accomplishment of this purpose. Yet segregation by race was deemed so fundamentally unfair to racial minorities that this justification could not save it.[9] It perpetuated a badge of inferiority no less odious than slavery itself. Similarly, the state obviously has an interest in promoting the institution of marriage, but that does not make valid every distinction in rights it establishes between legitimate and illegitimate children.[10]

In the case of distinctions based on race, gender, or legitimacy, the characteristic is, of course, one acquired involuntarily at birth. But the appeal to one's sense of unfairness does not rest on the fact that people are born into a certain condition. It rests rather on the fact that the person may have acquired involuntarily the characteristic on which the discrimination against him is based and may be powerless to change it. Certainly, in the case of poverty, although many are born into that condition, many also manage to escape it, while others who were born in affluence sometimes descend into poverty. The point is that poverty is often not the fault of the person afflicted with it, and is at all events beyond his power to change overnight. Thus, when the law conditions the availability of, say, divorce, on the ability of a person to pay litigation costs, it denies him equal protection of the laws,[11] although no one has seriously questioned the general legal requirement that civil litigants must pay such costs. The right to terminate an unsatisfactory marriage, being so intimately bound up with the pursuit of happiness, must not be so conditioned on the ability to pay that the poor are denied it.

The sodomy laws deny all sexual expression to those whose

orientation is toward members of their own sex. Many such persons are incapable of heterosexual intercourse, or are at least incapable of it without the assistance of prolonged psychotherapy for which they cannot afford to pay. Sexual orientation, though acquired after birth, may be therefore as indelible a characteristic of personality as race or gender, and ought to be equally regarded as a "suspect" classification. Discriminations on this basis impose a badge of inferiority just as demeaning to human dignity as discriminations based on race, national origin, gender, or legitimacy. To deny to homosexuals all sexual expression with members of their own gender group is also to deny them a fundamental human right. Its effect is to condemn them to a lifetime of sexual continence or autoeroticism. The detriment to the individual here is enormous. Even in the case of persons in the same category who are capable of heterosexual intercourse, the detriment is considerable. Much frustration and unhappiness can result from being confined to a heterosexual object-choice when one's basic emotional attraction is toward members of one's own sex. The point is simply that homosexuals constitute one of this nation's minorities, no less than racial minorities. The sodomy laws inflict great discrimination upon them by depriving them of all licit means of sexual fulfillment, while the majority—heterosexuals—possess in every state at least some such means. We have created a "society of the erotically privileged" in that "erotic enjoyment has become, in our society, the privilege of people with a specific pattern of hetero-sexual needs."[12]

Again, however, neither the magnitude of the detriment to the individual resulting from the discrimination nor the indelibility of the characteristic on which it is based is controlling. Against these must be balanced the legitimate interest the state seeks to further by means of the discrimination. Suppose, for example, that a person's orientation is solely toward children. Pedophiles are no more responsible for their sexual orientation than anyone else, and, like the homosexual, may be incapable of changing, or at least unable to change without prolonged psychotherapy. Does this mean that laws which deny them sexual expression with the objects of their attraction—children—deny them equal protection? Certain-ly not. In such cases the detriment to the individual in being denied such outlets is balanced by the need to protect children from a direct sexual encounter that may prove traumatic or fix prematurely the course of their psychosexual development.[13] Similarly, if one is attracted sexually only to people who are not attracted to him, he is plainly not deprived of equal protection if the law precludes him from imposing his desires by force. The direct protection from imposition which society is justified in affording others adequately balances the denial of sexual expression to the individual.

In the case, however, of a general prohibition against all sexual expression with other willing adults, including even such expression under the aegis of marriage, as is true of homosexual expression, no sufficient justification can be found to balance the detriment to individual happiness that such discrimination entails. This is not a matter on which reasonable men may differ, so as to be properly a question for resolution by a legislature. As already noted, the only justification for this discrimination which is the least bit respectable is the state's interest in discouraging the development of a homosexual orientation on the part of those young and malleable enough to be yet subject to influence. Whatever harm in this respect might result from allowing adult homosexuals to express themselves sexually with each other in private is too remote and indirect when poised against the immediate individual detriment in denying such expression—a lifetime of sexual continence or at least sexual frustration for those whose orientation toward their own sex is already fixed and ineluctable. This judgment is reinforced by the fact that no one in the relevant scientific disciplines—psychology, sociology, and psychiatry—has ever identified the law as an influence in shaping youngsters toward heterosexuality. Homosexuality develops in children and adolescents despite the social sanctions against it, of which the law is only one and probably the one of which they are the least likely to be aware.

Rustum and Della Roy, in speaking of the need for Christians to eradicate the inequity of demanding abstinence for homosexuals, put the issue forcefully:

> Who are we, then, comfortable in our heterosexual affluence, to decree that the sexual Lazarus on our doorstep should volunteer to starve because he doesn't like the food we eat?[14]

Whether or not one regards the consequences of sexual deprivation as a serious matter, it is not the only deprivation involved. If the homosexual is denied the possibility of a relationship with a member of his own sex, where can he be expected to turn for love? Few heterosexuals stop to think where they would be without the emotional relations implicit in the nuclear triangle of husband-wife-children. The ancient Greeks were undoubtedly right in holding that to love and be loved is the food of the soul. Yet the love of husband and wife, parent and child, is denied to the homosexual by the very essence of his being. If society puts beyond the pale for him all same-sex relationships, is it not also condemning him to a lifetime of emotional starvation?

One of America's great judges, in commenting on the necessary imprecision of constitutional guarantees like the equal-protection clause, summed up as follows the process of analysis by which judges must inevitably apply them:

> If a court be really candid, it can only say: "We find that this measure will have this result; it will injure this group in such and such ways, and benefit that group in these other ways. We declare it invalid, because after every conceivable allowance for differences of outlook, we cannot see how a fair person can honestly believe that the benefits balance the losses."[15]

NOTES

1. *See* note 12, Chapter 1 *supra.*
2. *See* notes 20–75, Chapter 2 *supra.*
3. *See* text and notes at note calls 78–79, Chapter 2 *supra.*
4. The situation is somewhat analogous to a law allowing all persons to make a will, subject to certain formal requirements, one of which being that the will be witnessed and the testator see the witnesses sign. Though such a law does not purport to establish any classification between people, it obviously contains a built-in discrimination against the blind. One is also reminded of Anatole France's famous quip that the rich and the poor are equally forbidden to sleep on park benches.
5. Apparently no empirical studies have investigated the question of discriminatory enforcement of the sodomy laws. The impression I have from reading appellate opinions is that more of them involved homosexual than heterosexual acts. If one could show a deliberate pattern of discriminatory enforcement of a law applicable on its face to both heterosexual and homosexual activities (and most American sodomy laws are so applicable), then homosexual defendants could rightly claim a denial of equal protection. The Constitution requires that impartial laws be impartially administered. Their claim would presumably thus

be valid even if one were to concede that a law directed against their activities alone might be constitutional. I believe it would be fairly easy to show that some other laws, such as those making it a crime to solicit for a lewd act, are administered almost solely against homosexuals. Indeed, two law students—Barry Copilow and Thomas Coleman—have demonstrated that from June through September of 1972, the Los Angeles Police Department made 166 arrests for solicitation of lewd conduct under section 647(a) of the California Penal Code, and that all but six of these were for homosexual solicitation. (The six exceptions involved female prostitutes.) Since all the complaints were made by police decoys, and only male officers were assigned to such duty, it becomes obvious that this law is deliberately not enforced against heterosexual solicitation by males. See The Advocate, Feb. 14, 1973, at 2–3. The sodomy laws, however, are a different kettle of fish. They cover acts performed by force or with minors, as well as consensual adult behavior. Since the majority of charges under these laws involve such special circumstances, heterosexual cases are prosecuted as readily as homosexual ones. Discriminatory enforcement against homosexuals thus is unlikely to be demonstrable in the case of these laws.

6. *See* Loving v. Virginia, 388 U.S. 1, 9 (1967); McLaughlin v. Florida, 379 U.S. 184, 191–92 (1964); Korematsu v. United States, 323 U.S. 214, 216 (1944); Takahashi v. Fish & Game Commission, 334 U.S. 410 (1948); and Oyama v. California, 332 U.S. 633 (1948).

7. On the matter of classifications based on gender, see Reed v. Reed, 404 U.S. 71 (1971), Stanley v. Illinois, 405 U.S. 645, 658 (1972), and Eisenstadt v. Baird, 405 U.S. 438, 447 n. 7 (1972); on wealth, see Dandridge v. Williams, 397 U.S. 471, 485–86 (1970), United States v. Kras, 93 S. Ct. 631 (1973), Bastardo v. Warren, 332 F. Supp. 501 (W.D. Wis. 1971), and Doe v. Schmidt, 330 F. Supp. 159 (1971); and on legitimacy, see Levy v. Louisiana, 391 U.S. 68 (1968), Labine v. Vincent, 401 U.S. 532 (1971), Weber v. Aetna Casualty & Surety Co., 406 U.S. 164 (1972), and Gomez v. Perez, 93 S. Ct. 872 (1973).

8. An excellent analysis of these exceptions is found in the opinion of the Supreme Court of California in Sail'er Inn, Inc. v. Kirby, 5 Cal.3d 1, 95 Cal. Rptr. 329, 485 P.2d 529 (1971), in which that court invalidated a sex-based discrimination. It held gender to be a suspect basis of classification and thus applied the stricter standard for justification.

The decline of the simple rationality test under the equal protection clause has been noted by others. *See* Karst, *Invidious Discrimination: Justice Douglas and the Return of the Natural-law-due-process Formula*, 16 U.C.L.A. L. REV. 716 (1969). *See also* Karst & Horowitz, *Reitman v. Mulkey: A Telophase of Substantive Equal Protection*, 1967 SUP. CT. REV. 39; Michelman, *Foreword: On Protecting the Poor Through the Fourteenth Amendment*, 83 HARV. L. REV. 7 (1969); and *Developments in the Law—Equal Protection*, 82 HARV. L. REV. 1065 (1969).

Some of the cases which have overturned state laws under the equal protection clause despite the presence of a rational basis for the discrimination are Harper v. Virginia Board of Elections, 383 U.S. 663 (1966) (Virginia's poll tax held unconstitutional as violative of equal protection, despite such rational bases as the need for tax revenue and the notion that persons who are required to pay such a tax will take greater interest in the processes of government); Levy v. Louisiana,

391 U.S. 68 (1968), and Weber v. Aetna Casualty & Surety Co., 406 U.S. 164 (1972) (holding unconstitutional Louisiana statutes that had allowed recovery for wrongful death, and of workmen's compensation benefits, of the parent only to legitimate or "acknowledged" illegitimate children, thus discriminating against other illegitimate children); Williams v. Rhodes, 393 U.S. 23 (1968) (holding unconstitutional Ohio's electoral laws designed to limit the number of candidates and parties placed on the ballot); and Shapiro v. Thompson, 394 U.S. 618 (1969) (holding unconstitutional the one-year residency requirement for qualifying for welfare payments). While in *Harper, Williams,* and *Shapiro,* the discrimination placed an unequal burden on the exercise of a right already recognized as fundamental (the rights to vote and to participate in the political process, and to travel and move freely from state to state), the discriminations in *Levy* and *Weber* did not. The right to sue for wrongful death or to recover workmen's compensation benefits is everywhere the creature of statute, and is surely not a fundamental right like those involved in the other cases cited. Moreover, the right to travel freely can hardly be regarded as more fundamental than the right to sexual expression.

9. The cases of this sort are legion, but two of the most illustrative are, of course, Brown v. Board of Education, 347 U.S. 483 (1954), and Loving v. Virginia, 388 U.S. 1 (1967).

10. *Compare* Levy v. Louisiana, Weber v. Aetna Casualty & Surety Co., and Gomez v. Perez *with* Labine v. Vincent, all cited note 7 *supra.*

11. *See* Boddie v. Connecticut, 401 U.S. 371, 383–90 (1971) (concurring opinions of Justices Douglas and Brennan). *Cf.* Griffin v. Illinois, 351 U.S. 12 (1956).

12. L. ULLERSTAM, THE EROTIC MINORITIES 12, 13 (A. Hollo transl. 1966). Ullerstam was referring to Swedish society, but his characterization is equally applicable to American society, if not more so. The same point has been made by the late American psychotherapist, Robert M. Lindner:

> Sex, in short, throughout the life of an individual born into the society which you and I inhabit, is under a virtual ban, except for a brief period when, if we manage to satisfy certain requirements of time, place, person, condition, method, manner, intention, and frequency—as well as the additional ceremonial duties imposed by law, religion, and custom—our erotic potential may be executed.

Lindner, *Homosexuality and the Contemporary Scene,* in THE PROBLEM OF HOMOSEXUALITY IN MODERN SOCIETY 57–58 (H. M. Ruitenbeek ed. 1963).

Ullerstam argues that there is little, if any, solid justification for the discrimination and deprivation to which society subjects the erotic minorities, such as the homosexuals, the exhibitionists, the sadists and masochists, the voyeurs, the transvestites, the zoophiles, the incest offenders, the necrophiles, and people who desire group sex. Though his point may seem outrageous or just plain silly at first sight, it becomes less so the more one thinks about it. He urges that society should give consideration to how it might help these people fulfill their unusual sexual proclivities, rather than denying them altogether. For example, one interesting possibility is to facilitate sadists meeting masochists, and voyeurs getting together with exhibitionists.

13. These supposed harms are far from being demonstrated by the scientific data so far available. It may rather be that our denial of sexual experimentation to youngsters growing up is far more productive of adult sexual problems than any uncensored consensual experience they could possibly have, even an experience with an adult. For instance, West says,

> Boys who avoid overt homosexual conduct at adolescence because they are inhibited, probably stand a greater chance of becoming chronically homosexual as adults than the boys who go in for sexual romps and commit "gross indecency" without a second thought. Research does in fact suggest that persistent homosexuals tend to be relatively late starters as regards overt sexual acts.

D. J. WEST, HOMOSEXUALITY 122 (rev. ed. 1968).

SIECUS states that the short-term effect on the child of a consensual sexual encounter with an adult is rather minor, unless the parents blow it up by overreacting and exhibiting irrational anxiety and even aggression against the child. (This overreaction is often the product of the parents' rage at themselves for their helplessness to shield the child from such an experience.) A profound long-term effect, even from violent offenses, is rare; the children usually grow up to be unremarkably normal in their sexual behavior. SEX INFORMATION AND EDUCATION COUNCIL OF THE UNITED STATES, SEXUALITY AND MAN 90 (1970). *See also* note 148, Chapter 6 *supra*.

Perhaps a less vulnerable justification for prohibiting consensual sexual encounters between adults and minors or children is that the latter are so unequal to the normal adult as to make it difficult to tell whether their participation was really consensual or not. Any adult, because he represents authority figures in general, may evoke apparent consent from a particularly obedient child which the child might have withheld if the advance had come from one more nearly his equal or peer. Of course, one must not make the mistake of assuming that the advance always proceeds from the adult. Not a few of the sexual encounters between adults and either minors or children are initiated by the latter.

14. R. & D. ROY, HONEST SEX 160 (1968).

15. L. Hand, *The Contribution of an Independent Judiciary to Civilization*, in THE SPIRIT OF LIBERTY 179 (I. Dilliard ed. 1952).

9

Cruel and Unusual Punishment

Although the Supreme Court, in the 1947 case of *Louisiana ex rel. Francis v. Resweber*,[1] had assumed, without deciding, that the cruel and unusual punishment clause of the eighth amendment was applicable to the states through the fourteenth, its first flat holding to this effect was *Robinson v. California*.[2] The latter case also introduced a novel twist to the meaning of that clause—a twist holding considerable potential for invalidation of convictions under the sodomy laws. The clause had previously been regarded as encompassing only two prohibitions: (1) a prohibition on punishment of a *kind* that is inherently cruel; and (2) a prohibition on punishment that is cruelly excessive in proportion to the gravity of the offense charged.[3]

The new meaning *Robinson* gave to the clause was that it may prohibit a state from defining behavioral phenomena as crime under circumstances in which any infliction of punishment would constitute cruelty. In *Robinson*, the offense was the status of being addicted to narcotics, and the punishment authorized by the statute was a jail term of not less than 90 days nor more than one year. The defendent received the minimum sentence. The Supreme Court held the statute invalid under the eighth amendment, on the ground that a state may not make criminal the *status* or *condition* of narcotics addiction, as opposed to the sale, purchase, or possession of narcotics or the commission of some other antisocial act within the state.

Precisely why punishment of the status of narcotics addiction violates the cruel and unusual punishment clause is not clear from the Court's opinion. Two possible rationales have been suggested for the result in *Robinson*. The first is that all laws penalizing a mere status violate the eighth amendment. That is to say, a state may punish acts but not a status. This rationale seems the one most consonant with Justice Harlan's concurring opinion, in which he characterizes California's law as the punishment of a "bare desire to commit a criminal act"—an action he calls "arbitrary" and hence void.[4] The problem with resting *Robinson* on a pure status-act distinction is that no convincing reason can be offered why the punishment of a status is in itself "cruel and unusual." Status crimes have long been part of the Anglo-American legal tradition, so they are hardly unusual.[5] Likewise, it is impossible to discover any reason why the punishment of a status, as opposed to an act, is inherently cruel.[6] In any event, such an interpretation of *Robinson,* if correct, holds no potential at all for an attack on the sodomy laws, because these laws definitely penalize acts, not a status.

The second possible explanation of *Robinson* is that punishing a person for having an illness—here the "illness" of narcotics addiction—is unconstitutionally cruel. This explanation derives considerable support from Justice Stewart's opinion for the Court and from Justice Douglas's concurring opinion. Yet unless this rationale is to dissolve into the mere status-act distinction, one must adduce some reason that the punishment of an *illness,* as opposed to some other kind of status, is inherently cruel. Their opinions offer two possible reasons:

1. Whenever one has acquired an illness, he is helpless to get rid of it without treatment. In other words, an illness is a status the victim is helpless to change. Thus, a law punishing him for it not only can have no deterrent effect;[7] it also is morally repugnant because it punishes where there is no fault.
2. One may acquire an illness innocently and involuntarily. Here again, the emphasis seems primarily to rest upon the lack of moral responsibility for the condition. Justice Stewart's opinion stressed the fact that narcotics addiction may result from the administration of narcotics in the course of medical treatment for some other condition, or from the fact that the person afflicted with it was born to an addicted mother.[8]

Robinson should probably be read as resting on both these factors: helplessness to change the status, and the possibility of innocent or involuntary acquisition. Without the latter factor, the former would seem insufficient to justify the result, because a law penalizing the status of narcotics addiction would have some deterrent effect and would be based on some degree of moral responsibility if the only way one could become a narcotics addict were through the voluntary ingestion of narcotic drugs for other than medical purposes. However, the true importance of the second factor to the result in *Robinson* can be severely questioned. Only a very small fraction of narcotics addiction results from medical treatment or being born to an addicted mother. Moreover, the Court in *Robinson* showed no inclination to demand proof that the defendent came by *his* addiction involuntarily or innocently.[9]

If, then, the second suggested rationale for *Robinson* is the only one that can pretend to explain the case adequately, it opens up considerable possibilities for constitutional control of substantive criminal law. It may operate as a direct limitation on *what* a state can criminalize, not merely as a limitation on the kind or amount of punishment a state can attach to various crimes. (So, of course, may the first suggested rationale, but the elimination of status crimes altogether would be a pitifully insignificant limitation on the states' power to define crime.) For example, if an illness of which one is helpless to rid himself without treatment and which *may* be acquired innocently or involuntarily cannot be made a crime, plainly any other status that meets these same tests cannot be made criminal, whether or not it is properly classifiable as an illness. Moreover, if the illness cannot be punished as a crime under such circumstances without the punishment being deemed cruel and unusual, how can it be other than cruel and unusual punishment to impose penalties for the symptoms of the illness, though these be acts? To recall Mr. Justice Stewart's example, if "even one day in prison would be a cruel and unusual punishment for the 'crime' of having a common cold,"[10] then one day in prison would be an equally cruel and unusual punishment for the "crime" of sneezing. Finally, if an act merely symptomatic of the illness cannot constitutionally be made criminal, does not the same line of reasoning support the notion that any act "compelled" by a mental condition over which the actor has no control must be excused on constitutional grounds, thus giving rise to a constitutionally imposed and defined requirement of *mens rea*?[11]

All these potential implications of *Robinson* were brought out in the 1968 case of *Powell v. Texas*.[12] In that case the defendant was convicted of being "found in a state of intoxication" in a public place and fined $50. He raised the issue of the constitutionality of his conviction under *Robinson*, introducing evidence to the effect that he was a chronic alcoholic and that the state or condition of intoxication—essential to constitute the crime as defined by the Texas law—was part of the pattern of his disease and occasioned by a compulsion symptomatic of the disease. His effort failed, and the opinions of the justices, far from dispelling the ambiguity of *Robinson*, disclosed deep divisions within the Court over its meaning and potential for application to other situations. What the case reveals is of such great significance for the application to the sodomy laws of the *Robinson* line of attack that it deserves a detailed examination.

Justice Marshall's opinion for the Court, denying Powell's claim, appears to rest on three lines of reasoning:

1. The record in the case was utterly inadequate to support the constitutional argument advanced by Powell. It contained very little about the circumstances of the particular drinking bout that led to his conviction, about the origin and nature of his own drinking problem, and about the condition or "disease" of alcoholism itself. Is alcoholism a disease in fact, or is it called a disease simply because the medical profession has agreed it should attempt to treat it? There seems to be great disagreement concerning when one becomes an alcoholic, *i.e.*, what symptoms manifest the illness. Presumably, at least two elements must be proven—inablility to abstain from taking a first drink, plus loss of control of the amount of intake once drinking has commenced. But in Powell's case neither element was clearly proven.

2. Perfectly valid utilitarian justifications may exist for the type of law here under attack, even as applied to chronic alcoholics. There is no known method of generally effective treatment for alcoholism, and treatment facilities are woefully lacking. Thus, a decision of the sort requested would have the tragic practical consequence of returning great numbers of homeless drunks to the streets, where they endanger both themselves and others, without even the modicum of sobering up provided by a short jail confinement. Moreover, by forcing sole utilization of civil commitment—the only alternative means of isolating such people from society—the Court might be condemning them to long periods of confinement with no more hope of effective treatment than if

criminal incarceration were retained, the latter being generally fixed by law to a very short period. In the present context, therefore, one cannot say "that the criminal process is utterly lacking in social value."[13] Also, criminal sanctions for public drunkenness *may* well deter many from getting drunk in public, causing them to confine their drinking to home.

3. Extension of *Robinson v. California* to this situation, as urged by the dissent, would create, under the aegis of the eighth amendment, a constitutional standard of criminal responsibility. This would violate essential notions of federalism and freeze all experimentation and all dialogue between psychiatry and the law. "The State of Texas . . . has not sought to punish a mere status, as California did in *Robinson;* nor has it attempted to regulate appellant's behavior in the privacy of his own home. Rather, it has imposed upon appellant a criminal sanction for public behavior which may create substantial health and safety hazards, both for appellant and for members of the general public, and which offends the moral and esthetic sensibilities of a large segment of the community."[14]

Justice Black's concurring opinion, in which Justice Harlan joined, besides amplifying some of the utilitarian justifications for jailing those found drunk in public, makes clear that these two justices would restrict *Robinson* to the mere prohibition of status crimes. Powell's crime, though defined in terms of being found drunk in a public place, is not a status crime, but the penalization of overt behavior. They would view any proposal to extend *Robinson* to crimes punishing behavior, as opposed to "bare desires and propensities,"[15] as pregnant with disaster.

The opinion of Justice White, who concurred solely in the result of the case, contrasts sharply with Black's. He regards Black's and Harlan's efforts to restrict *Robinson* to the mere prohibition of status crimes as repudiating the entire thrust of that opinion:

> If it cannot be a crime to have an irresistible compulsion to use narcotics [citing *Robinson*], I do not see how it can constitutionally be a crime to yield to such a compulsion. Punishing an addict for using drugs convicts for addiction under a different name. Distinguishing between the two crimes is like forbidding criminal conviction for being sick with flu or epilepsy but permitting punishment for running a fever or having a convulsion. Unless *Robinson* is to be

abandoned, the use of narcotics by an addict must be beyond
the reach of the criminal law. Similarly, the chronic alcoholic
with an irresistible urge to consume alcohol should not be
punishable for drinking or for being drunk.[16]

He then proceeds to point out, however, that Powell was not
convicted for drinking or being drunk, but for being found drunk in
a public place. No necessary connection was shown either generally or in his particular case between being a chronic alcoholic and
being drunk in public, the trial court's finding of such a connection
being wholly without support in the evidence. The chronic
alcoholic who is homeless would present a different case. He thus
concluded that Powell's case *on the record as presented* did not fall
within the scope of the eighth amendment as interpreted by
Robinson.

The dissenting opinion of Justice Fortas, joined in by Justices
Douglas, Brennan, and Stewart, takes the position that *Robinson*
clearly establishes that the eighth amendment "places some
substantive limitation upon the power of state legislatures to define
crimes for which the imposition of punishment is ordered."[17] That
limitation consists of prohibiting the state from defining as criminal
a status that one cannot change: "Criminal penalties may not be
inflicted upon a person for being in a condition he is powerless to
change."[18] It is immaterial that he may at one time have had
power to avoid getting into that condition. The opinion asserts that
a criminal penalty may not, consistently with the eighth
amendment, be imposed on a person suffering from a disease for a
condition—such as being intoxicated in public—which is a characteristic part of the pattern of his disease and which is not the
consequence of his volition but of a compulsion symptomatic of the
disease. Although the opinion appears to blur the distinction
between *condition* and *act* in characterizing public drunkenness as
a condition rather than an act, it implies that the same view would
be taken of *conduct* which is "a characteristic and involuntary part
of the pattern of the disease as it afflicts him."[19] That is to say, a
state may no more criminalize behavior without running afoul of
the eighth amendment than it may criminalize a status or condition
under the same circumstances. On the other hand, independent
acts to which his disease or condition may contribute, but which
are "not a characteristic and involuntary part of the pattern" of his

disease, such as drunken driving, assault, theft, or robbery, are not to be deemed excused on this constitutional ground.

From this survey of the opinions in *Powell*, it becomes apparent that, of the justices still on the bench who took part in that case, three (Douglas, Brennan, and Stewart) support a view of *Robinson* that holds some potential for a constitutional attack upon sodomy convictions. To this group may be added Justice White, although it is not clear from his opinion in *Powell* that he would be opposed to an outright overruling of *Robinson*. Having dissented in *Robinson*, he may be in favor of abandoning altogether its extension of the meaning of the eighth amendment. Assuming the contrary, however, it is clear that his view of *Robinson* closely parallels that of Douglas, Brennan, and Stewart. Justice Marshall's position is closer to that of Black and Harlan but not quite as rigid. Though he recognizes the dangers of creating a constitutional doctrine of *mens rea* under the aegis of the eighth amendment, his emphasis upon the inadequacy of the record in *Powell* and upon the utilitarian justifications for criminal prohibition of *public* drunkenness may indicate a willingness to extend *Robinson* beyond the mere prohibition of status crimes, provided the extension is limited to "private" behavior, utilitarian justifications for the law under attack are absent, and the record abundantly demonstrates that the behavior is truly an *involuntary* symptom of the disease or condition which the defendant is powerless to change.[20]

The parallels between homosexuality and either narcotics addiction or chronic alcoholism are obvious. All three have traditionally been regarded as matters of moral responsibility, and consequently as appropriate subjects for regulation by the criminal law. The medical profession and the behavioral scientists almost unanimously attack this traditional position as erroneous. There is widespread disagreement among these experts whether any of the three is properly classifiable as an illness, or merely a condition entailing unhappy consequences for the individual in society. Many assert that homosexuality is an illness or at least a "personality disorder," or is symptomatic of some complex underlying, though little understood, psychopathology. But all agree that if any action should be taken by society with respect to those so "afflicted" with any of these conditions, it should take the form of treatment by qualified practitioners in the field of mental health, not incarceration in jail or prison. Their goal of bringing about a shift in society's attitude toward these conditions may largely explain why many such experts would expand the definition of "illness" to cover them. Yet legislators seem reluctant to decriminalize these conditions or their manifestations, doubtless from fear that the lack of criminal sanctions might encourage greater numbers to experiment with alcohol, drugs, and homoerotic sex and thus perhaps acquire the status in question.

All three conditions do not inherently involve any direct harm to others. Homosexuality, unlike drug addiction and alcoholism, poses no danger of physical injury or debilitation to the person himself. As for tangible harm to others that may result indirectly from the condition, homosexuality is the one of the three least likely to produce it. The homosexual, unlike the addict or the alcoholic, is not driven to steal or rob to satisfy his urges. His condition entails no loss of consciousness or of motor control—effects posing physical danger to others as well as himself—nor any diminution in his ability to work. Although crimes of passion do occur in the "gay" world, it is doubtful that their incidence is any higher than among heterosexuals.

All three conditions are generally impossible to change without some form of therapeutic help. Even with it, change is not certain, because no generally effective method of treatment exists for any of them. As for the factor of innocent or involuntary acquisition, homosexuality is probably always acquired innocently and involuntarily. In its case, as contrasted with alcoholism or addiction, the status or condition—the propensity—is generally acquired without any precedent acts. In other words, the propensity is acquired before and independently of the acts associated with the condition; the acts usually then follow. Alcoholics and addicts, on the other hand, do not acquire the propensity except by indulging in the acts. Excessive indulgence habituates the individual, both physically and psychically, to further repetition of the acts.[21] Since, in the great majority of cases, the alcoholic or addict took his first drink or drug voluntarily, there is much more reason for holding him morally responsible for having acquired his status than the homosexual. True, he may have believed, erroneously, that he could indulge without becoming addicted. But surely few people take their first drink or drug without knowledge that many who do so end up addicted. They could never have become an alcoholic or addict without assuming the risk inherent in taking that first drink or drug.

A difference may exist between homosexuality and the other two in the strength of the urge to engage in the acts symptomatic of the condition. Behavioral science as yet has made no attempt to measure such possible differences. The difference, if any, should be immaterial from the standpoint of the law, because it is clear that in the case of homosexuality the urge is too strong for the law's deterrence to repress it completely. The average homosexual can control his propensity to the extent necessary to avoid acts in public or under other circumstances where they would be likely to be detected by the police or otherwise cause him embarrassment,[22] but not to the extent of avoiding them altogether and always. The same is true of many chronic alcoholics and drug addicts. A few homosexuals may even succeed in abstaining altogether, just as some alcoholics and addicts manage to arrest their habit and thereafter avoid alcohol and drugs altogether. True, there is in the case of alcoholism and narcotism the phenomenon of physical addiction—the experience of withdrawal symptoms—which is not present in homosexuality. But we do not yet know to what extent addiction is the product of a physical craving (like hunger) and to what extent it is the product of psychological imbalance or simply an inability to cope with the problems of life, and thus of a purely psychic desire for induced euphoria and escape from reality.[23]

In the case of homosexuality, the urge does have some physical basis in the tension that builds up periodically through the production of the sex glands. This tension, along with generally experienced psychic factors such as the desire for warmth and intimacy with another human being, produces that insistent prompting called the sex drive. By comparison, no universal urge provides the stimulus to drink alcohol or ingest drugs to excess. The physical basis for the latter is peculiar to those afflicted and develops out of the condition itself.

Even a person who has never experienced homosexual desires possesses some capacity to estimate the strength of such impulses. By gauging the strength and frequency of his own impulses toward heterosexual intercourse, he can form some idea of the impossibility of completely deterring the homosexual by law from ever performing the acts symptomatic of his condition. The legal threat is simply too remote in relation to the strength of the impulse. In other words, homosexual acts are as "compulsive," in a general way, for the homosexual as heterosexual intercourse is for the

heterosexual; they are no more nor less deterrable than heterosexual intercourse.[24] If a complete ban on heterosexual intercourse would be "cruel and unusual punishment" in violation of
the eighth amendment, then so is the complete ban on homosexual
intercourse represented by the run-of-the-mill American sodomy
statute.

It is debatable just how vital to the Court's conclusions in
Robinson and *Powell* utilitarian justifications for the criminal law
really were. Even if we assume they were important, none of the
same justifications exists for subjecting homosexual acts per se to
the criminal process. There can be no justification for isolating
homosexuals from the rest of society, because they pose no danger
either to themselves or to others. The detention system is incapable
of holding any but a tiny fraction of them. Furthermore, the
detention imposed by the sodomy laws is no temporary confinement of short duration like that involved in both *Robinson* and
Powell; it is prison detention, measured in years rather than days.
Deterrence is possible only in the same sense and to the same
degree that deterrence of heterosexual acts is possible, *i.e.*,
preventing the molestation of children, the use of force or
imposition, and public displays.[25] As for the utilitarian notions of
reform and rehabilitation, even the meagre boost toward achievement of these objectives that jail provides to the alcoholic or addict
is absent in the case of the homosexual. The provision of food,
shelter, and a chance to sober up may help only insignificantly to
cure alcoholism or narcotism, but at least it constitutes a first step
in that direction. In the case of homosexuality, criminal detention
is a step backward. With jails and prisons universally segregated by
sex, homosexual activity in general is rife in such places.[26] Even
heterosexuals confined there for long periods turn in desperation to
homosexual outlets for release, so how could anyone expect jail or
prison detention to effect anything but a reinforcement of the very
condition—homosexuality—for whose manifestations the individual
is being punished?[27] "Trying to cure a homosexual by sending him
to prison is like trying to cure an alcoholic by locking him up in a
distillery."[28]

This leaves only two of the standard justifications for a criminal
law: community condemnation and retribution. Significantly, none
of the justices in *Robinson* or *Powell* discussed either of these as
independent bases for support of the laws there in question. The

idea of retribution or vengeance is that society must inflict injury in return upon a wrongdoer in order to shore up the moral order, which would otherwise be endangered if his wrongdoing were to go unsanctioned. The idea of community condemnation is somewhat different: It means that the criminal law serves as a formal signpost or warning that the majority considers certain behavior "bad" or undesirable.

The idea of retribution is not applicable in the case of homosexual acts in private between consenting adults. It makes sense only where crimes with victims are concerned, and is in any event inappropriate where the actor is not morally responsible for his act. The mere use of narcotics or alcohol, even addiction to them, does not in itself harm anyone other than the user or addict. The same is true of homosexuality and its manifestations. And, as already noted, the latter are as morally blameless as these other acts and conditions, if not more so. If retribution is no justification for laws penalizing the use of narcotics or alcohol, it is no justification for laws that penalize the manifestations of homosexuality.

Community condemnation is, on the other hand, some justification. Undoubtedly, the majority in society detests all three conditions here discussed, or at least believes that their consequences for the individual are bad and that they should therefore be discouraged. But society can show its disapproval in ways other than branding the conduct criminal.[29] *Robinson* and *Powell* demonstrate that community condemnation alone will not suffice to justify application of the criminal stigma to behavior merely symptomatic of a status or condition that may have been innocently or involuntarily acquired and is impossible to change without help from others. In such cases, the absence of moral responsibility renders application of the criminal stigma unconstitutionally cruel.

In summary, then, the *Robinson-Powell* extension of the eighth amendment, if not overruled or restricted to the mere prohibition of status crimes, holds fair to overturn convictions of consenting adult homosexuals for sodomy in private. Since, however, it is not demonstrable that homosexuals are any more impelled by their condition to engage in public acts than are chronic alcoholics to get drunk in public, the chances of invalidating convictions for sodomy in public places under this authority are remote. With respect to acts in private, on the other hand, the condition of homosexuality seems as much within the rationale of *Robinson-Powell* as narcotism or alcoholism. Like them, it is a condition for which the holder is not morally responsible; and acts of sodomy are nothing more than symptoms of the condition in the same way that drinking alcohol and using drugs are symptomatic of alcoholism and narcotism. To extend the *Robinson-Powell* rationale to invalidate convictions for such acts would hardly open the floodgates to development of a constitutional definition of criminal responsibility generally.[30] It would, on the other hand, remove an injustice as unconscionable as that of stigmatizing drunks and addicts as criminals.

It is important to emphasize that the *Robinson-Powell* line of attack cannot invalidate the sodomy laws themselves. Even a law applicable only to the private consensual acts of adults would not be unconstitutional per se. *Powell* demonstrates that the law itself will not be held void but only its application to a particular class of defendants—namely those afflicted with a condition they are powerless to change and who as a result are subject to an insistent urge to engage in the prohibited acts. In the case of the sodomy laws, presumably only the so-called "obligatory" homosexual could be brought within this protection. *Powell* can also be taken as a portent that the *Robinson* extension of the cruel and unusual punishment clause will be applied to invalidate his conviction only where a proper predicate has been laid by expert testimony about his particular propensities and behavior patterns.[31] There might be a problem in identifying such persons and distinguishing them from the heterosexual or ambisexual whose indulgence in homosexual intercourse is situational and optional, but it would not appear insuperable. Unfortunately, the potential of this line of attack is difficult to assess because it is still uncertain whether or not *Robinson* will be restricted to the mere prohibition of status crimes.

Research has disclosed only three sodomy cases in which the *Robinson* line of argument under the eighth amendment was apparently employed.[32] In *People v. Roberts*,[33] the court simply stated that it did not find *Robinson* reasonably applicable to the case at bar, which involved an act in the public part of a men's restroom. In light of *Powell v. Texas*, that judgment seems sound. In *People v. Frazier*,[34] the act involved two inmates in a prison cell. The defendant contended that the imposition of an additional term for homosexual acts committed in prison was "cruel and unusual punishment." It is impossible to determine from the opinion whether this contention was made with reference to the *Robinson* line of reasoning or how well it was elaborated, because the court brushed it aside with the single comment that it knew of no authority for such a proposition. In *Perkins v. North Carolina*,[35] the *Robinson* argument appears to have been ably presented, but the court chose to read that case as prohibiting only status crimes. The defendant was thus held not within it because his crime consisted of an act. The opinion in *Perkins* unfortunately does not reveal whether the act in question took place in public or in private. Presumably it took place in public because both participants were prosecuted—an unlikely event in the case of private acts, where the testimony of one of the participants is normally needed to establish the crime.

NOTES

1. 329 U.S. 459.
2. 370 U.S. 660 (1962).
3. *See* text and notes at note calls 9–21, Chapter 10 *infra*.
4. 370 U.S. at 678–79.
5. The status crime of vagrancy is the one that comes most readily to mind. Papachristou v. City of Jacksonville, 405 U.S. 157 (1972), invalidated a vagrancy ordinance, but not because it created a crime of status. The Supreme Court held it void for vagueness.
6. The reasons offered by Justice Black for deeming status crimes "particularly obnoxious"—the unreliability of evidence of propensity and the uncertainty that even a proven propensity will manifest itself in actual behavior—do not seem applicable to the situation in *Robinson*. *See* his concurring opinion in Powell v. Texas, 392 U.S. 514, at 543–44 (1968). It is fanciful to assert that the California statute involved in *Robinson* sought to punish for a "bare desire to commit a criminal act." The status involved in *Robinson* was narcotics addiction, which could hardly mean anything other than the *habitual use* of narcotics, and there was adequate evidence in the record that Robinson was an habitual user. Likewise, what is chronic alcoholism (the condition involved in *Powell*) but *habitual drinking* to excess? In both cases, it may be possible to prove the status by evidence other than the overt behavior of the subject, as, for example, by medical testimony based on his blood or urine samples. But even the latter are evidence that the overt behavior—the ingestion of drugs or alcohol—did occur, though they do not prove that it occurred within the prosecuting jurisdiction. It

would seem that Justice Black's objections go rather to the quantum of proof needed to convict for a status *generally*, than to any inherent cruelty or arbitrariness in making Robinson's status a crime. I do not mean to assert that status crimes are unobjectionable. Since, in general, they seek to subject people to control who have not yet engaged in any identifiable harmful conduct but are thought likely to do so, they seriously impair one of our important values—personal liberty. *See* H. L. PACKER, THE LIMITS OF THE CRIMINAL SANCTION (1968). *See also* Papachristou v. City of Jacksonville, 405 U.S. 157 (1972). But the status crime in *Robinson* seems rather to be convicting for actual conduct, under the "status" label.

7. Presumably, what the Court means here by an absence of deterrent effect is that the law cannot force the victim of the condition to shed it forthwith, because he is powerless to do so. However, a law punishing the status of narcotics addiction might have a long-range deterrent effect both in the sense of discouraging others from taking the steps (drug use) that often lead to such status and in the sense of prodding the victims themselves to seek a "cure" through treatment. In the same way, a law making it a crime to have a common cold might impel people to take more precautions against catching cold or to seek medical treatment once they have caught it.

8. 370 U.S. at 667 n. 9.

9. It may be argued that the real thrust of *Robinson* has nothing to do with the cruelty of applying California's statute to Robinson himself or to the great majority of addicts. The constitutional infirmity of the statute lay in its overbreadth: By defining the crime as addiction to the use of narcotics, however such addiction was acquired, the statute netted those whose addiction was acquired innocently and involuntarily as well as those whose addiction was acquired otherwise. Under this rationale, *only* status crimes would be rendered unconstitutional, but *not all* of them. Such crimes would be unconstitutional only if the status is one that cannot be gotten rid of without treatment and *may* have been acquired innocently or involuntarily, *and* if the statute is so broadly drawn as to encompass all persons afflicted with it. Consequently, a statute punishing a status would not run afoul of the eighth amendment if the status were one that the holder could get rid of at will, *or* were one that could only be acquired knowingly and voluntarily, *or* if the statute were narrowly drawn so as to exclude those who came by such status innocently or involuntarily.

10. 370 U.S. at 667.

11. *See* Dubin, *Mens Rea Reconsidered: A Plea for a Due Process Concept of Criminal Responsibility*, 18 STAN. L. REV. 322 (1966). *See also* Note, *The Cruel and Unusual Punishment Clause and the Substantive Criminal Law*, 79 HARV. L. REV. 635 (1966).

12. 392 U.S. 514. Two of the most valuable discussions of this case and its implications are Greenawalt, *"Uncontrollable" Actions and the Eighth Amendment: Implications of Powell v. Texas*, 69 COLUM. L. REV. 927 (1969), and Fingarette, *The Perils of Powell: In Search of a Factual Foundation for the "Disease Concept of Alcoholism,"* 83 HARV. L. REV. 793 (1970).

13. 392 U.S. at 530.

14. *Id.* at 532.

15. *Id.* at 548.

16. *Id.* at 548–49.

17. *Id.* at 566.

18. *Id.* at 567.

19. *Id.* at 559 n. 2.

20. Some indication exists of the attitude of Chief Justice Burger on this issue. Although he joined the Court after its decisions in both *Robinson* and *Powell,* he participated in similar cases while on the bench of the United States Court of Appeals for the District of Columbia Circuit. In Easter v. District of Columbia, 361 F.2d 50 (D.C. Cir. 1966), he concurred in sustaining the defense of chronic alcoholism to a charge of public drunkenness, not on the constitutional ground of the eighth amendment, but on the basis of Congressional recognition of alcoholism as a disease and on the inherent power of the D.C. Circuit to shape the criminal law of the District of Columbia. Since his failure to join the majority opinion in that case on the constitutional issue may be explainable merely as an instance of judicial abstention from constitutional questions whenever an alternative ground for decision is available, he may be willing to join the position of Douglas, Brennan, and Stewart when the constitutional issue is unavoidable. At any rate, his position in Salzman v. United States, 405 F.2d 358 (D.C. Cir. 1968), indicates he does not share the view of Black and Harlan that excusing a chronic alcoholic for public drunkenness would necessarily lead to a general doctrine of *mens rea* requiring exoneration of other criminal acts resulting from drunkenness.

21. It is, of course, possible that many people who become alcoholics and narcotic addicts do so because they already possess a propensity to addiction. In other words, they have an "addictive personality" to begin with. But some such personalities become addicted instead to overeating or even to drinking excessive amounts of water. So the point is still true that almost no one becomes addicted to alcohol or drugs without an initially conscious and deliberate choice to take that drink or drug, while one can become a homosexual without ever having indulged in a homosexual act.

22. Even those persons who have been convicted for engaging in homosexual acts with other adults were found generally to have taken reasonable precautions against being reported by their partners or observed by others. In other words, they obviously chose places and persons they considered safe.

> However, they underestimated the activity of the police, which accounted for over two thirds of the arrests. Slightly over one third of the offenses were seen by the police, not infrequently from some vantage point where they were on watch. Nearly one fifth were discovered by the police in the process of other investigations. Lastly, one fifth of the offenses stemmed from unequivocal entrapment: a plainclothes man or person employed by or persuaded by the police made himself available for homosexual solicitation and in more cases than not encouraged it. When a homosexual male made an approach he was usually permitted to make a physical contact or to become verbally specific about his desires, and at this point he was arrested by the 'bait' or by police or detectives waiting nearby.

P. H. Gebhard, J. H. Gagnon, W. B. Pomeroy, & C. V. Christensen, Sex Offenders—An Analysis of Types 354–55 (1965).

23. Most people can consume alcohol regularly throughout their lives without becoming chronic alcoholics. Both alcoholism and narcotism may be promoted by social influences and psychological problems peculiar to American culture. The Turkish peasants of Anatolia have traditionally and regularly consumed opium in small quantities, without developing massive addiction. It is also common knowledge that the ordinary Frenchman daily consumes rather large amounts of wine without the loss of control and consequent inability to function characteristic of the American alcoholic.

24. Some homosexuals, like some heterosexuals, may be driven by special emotional needs to seek an extraordinary quantity and variety of sexual contacts, or to seek them deliberately under conditions posing physical danger or the risk of arrest or other embarrassment. But this is not characteristic of the condition per se. For such persons, whatever their orientation, the possibilities of deterrence are obviously much less than in the case of the average homosexual or heterosexual.

25. Deterrence can be used in a number of senses, of course. Here it is used in the sense of deterring an exclusive homosexual from ever committing homosexual acts. As for persons who are basically heterosexual or who fall somewhere in the various ranges of ambisexuality, criminal laws directed against homosexual acts may conceivably effect a larger measure of deterrence. Deterrence may also be thought of in the sense of encouraging or impelling an individual afflicted with some disease or condition to seek a cure for it. Even if one may not be morally responsible for having that illness or condition, he could be deemed morally responsible for failure to seek to cure or change it. However, in the case of homosexuality, much more compelling reasons can be given for excluding such considerations from view in the context of the constitutional issue here in question than in the case of narcotism or alcoholism.

For one thing, the end result being sought by "cure" is different. It is not abstention, but rather the redirection of one's sexual impulses. Although society could reasonably demand that people abstain completely from alcohol and drugs, nobody should be expected to become totally asexual. Christian tradition has tended to assert that people *can* abstain from sex, and it is certainly true that sexuality is the natural function of humans most responsive to voluntary inhibition and control. Human beings cannot live long without food and water, but they *can* stay alive for an entire lifespan without sex. Nevertheless, experts such as Masters and Johnson remind us that sexual expression is no less a natural function of the human being than eating and drinking. The sexual appetite is just as natural as the food appetite, and in most people, total suppression of it is incompatible with happiness. This is true for homosexuals as well as heterosexuals. *See* the discussion of Masters and Johnson before the A.M.A.'s Committee on Medicine and Religion, reported in S. F. Chronicle, June 19, 1972, at 4, col. 3.

The other reason concerns the availability of "cure." Of the two techniques with any potential for success, neither has proven successful with more than a minority of "obligatory" homosexuals. One—behavior therapy—has not been tried in the United States nearly as extensively as it has in England, so practitioners trained in it are not widely available in the United States. As previously noted, it is a treatment that not only involves considerable infliction of pain but also poses the problem of potential unforeseen side effects in other areas of the patient's behavior. The other technique, long-term psychotherapy, is so expensive that only the moneyed few can afford it. Unlike alcoholism and narcotism, homosexuality has yet to attract any public funds for treatment and treatment centers. Even for those wealthy enough to pay for psychotherapy themselves, a serious question is posed whether they should be expected to do so, in light of the dismal prospects of success. Surely, deterrence in the sense of encouraging an individual to seek a cure is a reasonable justification for a criminal law only if the "cure" is readily available and either inexpensive or provided at government expense, and if there is some fair chance of success.

    26. The male who is convicted because he has made homosexual advances to other males, may be penalized by being sent to an institution where anywhere from half to three-quarters of the inmates are regularly having homosexual activity within the institution.

A. C. KINSEY, W. B. POMEROY, C. E. MARTIN, & P. H. GEBHARD, SEXUAL BEHAVIOR IN THE HUMAN FEMALE 21 (1953). On the prevalence of homosexual behavior in captive communities segregated by sex, the literature is voluminous. See J. F. FISHMAN, SEX IN PRISON (1934); J. G. WILSON & M. J. PESCOR, PROBLEMS IN PRISON PSYCHIATRY (1939); Karpmann, *Sex Life in Prison*, 38 J. CRIM. L. & CRIMINOLOGY 475–86 (1948); G. M. SYKES, THE SOCIETY OF CAPTIVES: A STUDY OF A MAXIMUM SECURITY PRISON (1958); Huffman, *Sex Deviation in a Prison Community*, 6 J. SOCIAL THERAPY 170–81 (1960); D. A. WARD & G. G. KASSEBAUM, WOMEN'S PRISON: SEX AND SOCIAL STRUCTURE (1965); R. GIALLOMBARDO, SOCIETY OF WOMEN (1966); C. B. VEDDER & P. G. KING, PROBLEMS OF HOMOSEXUALITY IN CORRECTIONS (1967); Gagnon, *The Social Meaning of Prison Homosexuality*, 32 FEDERAL PROBATION No. 1 (March 1968); Kassebaum, *Sex in Prison*, 2 SEXUAL BEHAVIOR 39 (No. 1, January 1972); and P. C. BUFFUM, HOMOSEXUALITY IN PRISONS (1972).

    27. D. J. WEST, HOMOSEXUALITY 124–32, 251–52 (rev. ed. 1968).

    28. B. MAGEE, ONE IN TWENTY 20 (1966).

    29. One way in which society might seek to discourage all three such conditions without resorting to the criminal sanction is through its control of public education. The use of this medium to deal with normative questions in the field of sexuality is currently a matter of considerable controversy. Nevertheless, the possibilities of using such other means for influencing behavior need to be explored, as we become increasingly aware of the inappropriate load we are otherwise placing on the criminal sanction. See, generally, H. L. PACKER, THE LIMITS OF THE CRIMINAL SANCTION (1968). I do not personally favor use of education to spread moral judgments about any form of private consensual adult behavior in the realm of sex.

    30. Limiting the reach of *Robinson* to acts *symptomatic* of the disease or condition in question seems no more a limitation imposed by mere fiat of the Court—unbuttressed by any principled basis for drawing the line at that point—than limiting *Robinson* to the simple prohibition of status crimes. Even if the future should see the eventual development of a constitutional doctrine of *mens rea*, at a point when we know more about human psychology, is that unthinkable?

31. Justice Marshall's reference in *Powell* to the desirability of testimony on the circumstances of the drinking bout that led to Powell's arrest and conviction may be taken as implying that any particular act, even one merely symptomatic of a disease or condition, will not be constitutionally excusable under *Robinson* unless it was so compelled by the disease or condition as to be involuntary. Such a restriction of the *Robinson* principle would raise an impossible problem of proof. Moreover, such a restriction would be needed only if *Robinson* were extended so broadly as to impose a generally applicable constitutional principle of *mens rea*. If *Robinson* is limited to acts that are the usual manifestation of an illness or abnormality, no purpose would be served by requiring that each act be shown to have been "compelled." A showing that the overall behavior pattern is involuntary, even though the defendant might have been capable of abstaining from the particular act for which he was convicted, should suffice.

32. Perhaps a fourth case—Hughes v. State, 14 Md. App. 497, 287 A.2d 299 (1972)—should be included. The defendant, who had been convicted of fellatio with a minor male, apparently urged that any prison term imposed on him would constitute "cruel and unusual punishment" by subjecting him to an environment that could only reinforce homosexual tendencies. The court rejected his contention without mention of the *Robinson* and *Powell* cases.

33. 256 Cal. App. 2d 488, 64 Cal. Rptr. 70 (1967).

34. 256 Cal. App. 2d 630, 64 Cal. Rptr. 447 (1967).

35. 234 F. Supp. 333 (1964).

10

The Ferocious Penalty

The burden of this book so far has been to demonstrate that the laws making sodomy in private between consenting adults a crime are unconstitutional. In this chapter, however, we shall assume *arguendo* that the criminalization of such behavior is not unconstitutional and confine our discussion to whether the punishment meted out is subject to constitutional limitation. Such an inquiry is also relevant to a major category of sodomy prosecutions in which the state's right to criminalize the behavior cannot be seriously questioned—those involving consensual acts between adults in public. Although sodomy in such circumstances can be prosecuted under misdemeanor statutes prohibiting public lewdness, it may also be, and often is, prosecuted under the sodomy statute itself in order to subject the offender to the heavy penalties authorized by the latter. The question is whether those greater penalties may constitutionally be inflicted, although, as noted hereafter, certain considerations may justify a penalty for public acts in excess of that authorized for acts in private.

As already noted, Illinois does not criminalize private adult consensual behavior[1] and it subjects public behavior only to the relatively slight misdemeanor penalty prescribed for public lewdness generally.[2] This same situation now obtains or soon will obtain in Connecticut, Colorado, Oregon, Hawaii, Delaware, and Ohio with the entry into force of their new criminal codes.[3] In New York, adult consensual sodomy, whether in private or in public, is subject only to a maximum penalty of 3 months in jail and a fine of $500;[4] in Utah and Kansas, to a maximum of 6 months in jail and a fine of $299 and $1,000, respectively;[5] and in Minnesota, to a maximum of 1 year of imprisonment and a fine of $1,000.[6] Thus, in these four states, the offense between consenting adults, whether categorized as a petty or simple misdemeanor or a gross misdemeanor, carries relatively minor penalties for acts both in private and in public. In all the remaining states, the District of Columbia, Puerto Rico, and the Virgin Islands, adult consensual sodomy is a felony with maximum prison terms ranging from 3 years to life, except that in New Jersey the offense is denominated a "high misdemeanor" carrying a maximum prison term of 20 years.[7]

It has been firmly established only since 1962 that the eighth amendment's prohibition on the infliction of cruel and unusual punishment is applicable to the states through the fourteenth.[8] At times some have argued that this clause of the eighth prohibits merely the infliction of *kinds* of punishment that are inherently cruel, like the rack and the screw.[9] Before *Robinson v. California*, the Supreme Court's most recent occasion to use the clause to strike down a penalty involved this rather limited meaning. In *Trop v. Dulles*,[10] the Court invalidated a provision of the Immigration and Nationality Act depriving of citizenship any soldier convicted of desertion in time of war. The Court held that denationalization was an inherently cruel and unusual punishment and thus forbidden by the eighth amendment. But *Robinson v. California* itself demonstrates that the meaning of the clause is broader. In that case the Court invalidated a penalty of 90 days in jail while recognizing explicitly that this *kind* of punishment was not in itself cruel and unusual.[11] Indeed, if the clause were limited to prohibiting inherently cruel *modes* of punishment, it would be virtually a dead letter, since, apart from denationalization and, in one state, whipping,[12] almost the sole means of criminal punishment used throughout the United States are fines, imprisonment, and execution, all of which have been traditionally regarded as in no wise inherently cruel or unusual.[13]

The other meaning of the clause more directly relevant to our present inquiry is that it prohibits the infliction of punishments excessive in proportion to the gravity of the offense. In 1892, in *O'Neil v. Vermont*,[14] the Supreme Court had occasion to consider this meaning of the clause in relation to state law. The majority of the Court failed to reach the issue for several reasons, one of which was that the eighth amendment had not been made applicable to the states through the fourteenth. Mr. Justice Field, in a dissent joined by Justices Harlan and Brewer, took the view that it was applicable—a view since vindicated by *Robinson*—and thus reached the question of whether the clause prohibited excessive punishments. They answered that question in the affirmative, holding that sentences against a defendant totaling 54 years in prison for making 307 illegal sales of liquor were cruelly excessive in relation to the gravity of the offenses.[15]

The case that establishes the proposition, however, is *Weems v. United States*,[16] decided in 1910. It involved a provision of the Bill of Rights of the Philippine Constitution identical in substance with the eighth amendment. *Weems*, in holding that the Philippine provision prohibited punishments unusually excessive in relation to the gravity of the offense, clearly was also intended as an authoritative delineation of the meaning of the eighth amendment.[17] A minor official had been convicted of falsifying an official document to conceal a small sum of money of which he had wrongfully disposed. He had been sentenced to a punishment of 15 years of *cadena temporal* under a provision of the old Spanish penal code still in force in the Philippines. *Cadena temporal* involved imprisonment at hard and painful labor, carrying a chain from wrist to ankle at all times, denial of all assistance from outside the prison, denial of all civil rights while in prison, and denial of all political rights and surveillance for life by the authorities after release. Since even the minimum punishment prescribed by law—12 years of *cadena temporal*—would have been excessively cruel, the Court ordered Weems's release.

Although some language in the majority opinion supports the notion that the Court deemed the *kind* of penalties involved in *cadena temporal* to be cruel and unusual, the major thrust of the majority opinion is the excessiveness of the penalty. This interpretation of the case is unmistakable when it is seen that the dissenters—Justices White and Holmes—directed their efforts at buttressing the proposition that the cruel and unusual punishment clause prohibited merely the infliction of punishments of a *kind* inherently cruel.[18] Subsequent Supreme Court statements make clear that this view of the *Weems* holding is established.[19] Indeed, it borders on absurdity to assert that the cruel and unusual punishment clause does not prohibit cruelly excessive punishments. The other two clauses of the eighth amendment read: "Excessive bail shall not be required, nor excessive fines imposed. . . ." Thus, with the rest of the amendment directed at excessiveness, it would be anomalous to interpret the final clause as interdicting only certain *kinds*, and not *quantums*, of punishment.[20] We would have to ascribe to the amendment the intention of precluding government from fining a person $100,000 for stealing a loaf of bread, but not from imposing a prison term of 200 years for the same offense. There are, of course, plenty of state and lower federal cases which state boldly that determining the range of imprisonment for crime is solely a legislative question,[21] but these cases must be dismissed as erroneous.

The really debatable question is not whether the eighth amendment prohibits excessive terms of imprisonment as well as excessive fines, but what standard determines the excessiveness of the punishment. Lack of any standard in the amendment itself is doubtless a major reason why the courts have so frequently shirked their duty to control legislative irresponsibility in this area. A subsidiary question is whether, assuming that the range of punishment authorized by the legislature is permitted by the applicable standard, a punishment meted out by a court within that range can be unconstitutionally excessive under particular circumstances. In other words, does the clause inhibit judicial discretion in the fixing of sentences within the legislatively determined range, as well as that range itself? On the main question, adequate authority exists both for determining the proper standard of excessiveness and for guidance in its application to particular penalties.

The conventional view of the standard to be drawn from *Weems* holds that the punishment must be rationally proportioned to the gravity of the offense. Professor Packer, on the other hand, besides arguing that *Weems* rests more on cruelty in the sense of *mode* than on cruelty in the sense of *excessiveness*, urges that if *Weems* supports any principle on the latter issue, it is that "under appropriate circumstances a proportion of punishment to crime may be so aberrational as to violate 'standards of decency more or less universally accepted.' "[22] Under either standard—rational proportionality or universal decency—the question still persists: How does a court go about determining whether a particular punishment or range of punishments violates this standard?

Two possible approaches suggest themselves. One has been called the legislative ends test. To decide whether a punishment is rationally proportioned to the gravity of the offense, one presumably must isolate the harm caused by the offense and determine how serious it is, weighing the penalty in light of it. Whatever one may think of retribution as a guiding principle for penology, "an eye for an eye, and a tooth for a tooth" does serve usefully as a *limiting* principle of punishment. No one would think it fair or just to exact an eye in recompense for the loss of a toenail. One should also take into account other generally accepted goals of penology in determining whether the penalty is excessive, such as deterrence, isolation, and rehabilitation.

The other approach has been called the comparative law test. If the yardstick is "standards of decency more or less universally accepted," then a comparison of the penalty with those imposed for the offense by other jurisdictions, or for similar offenses even within the same jurisdiction, should give some fair indication of whether it ought to be deemed excessive. Of course, one problem this approach immediately poses is determining the universe to be used for purposes of comparison.

Still a third approach appears feasible at first sight—testing the penalty by the "common conscience" of the community at large—but a perusal of the cases in which it was attempted demonstrates its futility.[23]

Actually, the two genuinely feasible approaches are not mutually exclusive, but complementary. Both are needed even if one agrees with Professor Packer that ultimately the standard is one of decency rather than strict proportionality. No testing of a penalty against the legislative ends can give any precise answers. We will never be able to say, "so much is exactly right, no more and no less." But it hardly makes sense to determine decency purely on the basis of a tabulation of the penalties inflicted by other jurisdictions or for comparable offenses. Cruelty may be more the rule than the exception in the particular universe selected for comparison. Both approaches together provide a far more dependable guide to decency than either alone.

In applying the comparative law test, it may be argued that the universe from which comparisons are to be drawn should be limited to other American jurisdictions, because the majority in *Weems* did limit itself to comparing the Philippine penalty of 15 years of *cadena temporal* with penalties imposed in America or by American legislation in the Philippines for comparable offenses. But the effect of such a limited test would be to overturn only those legislative determinations of punishment that are far out of line with the punishment adopted for the crime by the great majority of

American states. In other words, excessiveness would be determined solely by a headcount of American jurisdictions. Such a
limitation is inappropriate; if one legislature can exhibit ferocity in
fixing the penalty for a crime, many legislatures can do the same,
particularly when they share the same culturally conditioned
aversion to the behavior in question.

In fact, rejection of such a limitation is compelled by the
reasoning in *Trop v. Dulles.*[24] Although that case involved the
mode rather than the excessiveness of punishment, why should
different tests determine whether a mode of punishment violates
the eighth amendment and whether a quantum violates it? In *Trop*
the Court was faced with a punishment authorized by Congress—denationalization—which the individual states have no
authority to inflict. Therefore, no American analogues existed to
guide the Court's judgment in determining whether this punishment was cruel and unusual. Indeed, one could assert that, since
the action was that of the national Congress, the fairness of the
penalty represented the judgment of the American people generally, in the same way that near-universal adoption of a penalty by the
legislatures of the fifty American states would. The Court, however,
reached beyond the confines of this nation and even of those
countries sharing its legal traditions, to compare this practice of
denationalization with the practices of all the other states of the
world. *Trop* thus recognizes that the standard of "decency" or
"civilized treatment" at the heart of the cruel and unusual
punishment clause demands a more extensive inquiry and comparison than *Weems* would lead us to believe. Rightly so; America is a
civilized nation, but not the only one, and even a civilized nation is
capable of barbarity. If the comparative law test is to be used as a
guide in determining excessiveness of punishment, as well as
cruelty in the mode, it must be conceived broadly enough to
include the practices of nations other than the one whose practice
is under scrutiny.

Another important idea contributed to this analysis by *Trop v.
Dulles* is that the standards of decency referred to by the Court are
not those of the dead past, which, by reason of sheer inertia, may
remain locked into our legislation. They are, rather, enlightened
standards that may be at variance with past or present practice.
Chief Justice Warren's emphasis upon "evolving standards of
decency that mark the progress of a maturing society"[25] implies

that what may have seemed perfectly permissible to our forebears in the eighteenth century can *become* cruel and unusual as the society matures. Notions of "decency" are not fixed and immutable; they evolve as the society progresses.

Let us apply the comparative law test as here conceived to the punishments fixed by the sodomy laws. As already noted, there are seven American jurisdictions[26] in which sodomy between consenting adults in private is or soon will be no crime at all. In four others, it is a misdemeanor carrying maximum jail sentences ranging from 3 months to 1 year.[27] In the rest, it is, for all practical purposes, a felony carrying maximum prison terms that range from 3 years to life.[28] Surely something must be seriously amiss when some American states authorize life imprisonment for certain behavior that others feel no need to criminalize at all.

The contrast becomes even starker when the legal stance of foreign countries is brought into the scales.[29] The Code Napoleon, the penal sections of which contain no proscription of deviate sex acts between consenting adults in private, has made such behavior licit in France since 1810;[30] and through its influence, the same situation prevails in Spain,[31] Portugal, Italy,[32] and a number of other countries where the laws were modeled on it. Such behavior has been legal in Belgium since 1867,[33] in the Netherlands since 1886,[34] in Denmark since 1930,[35] in Switzerland since 1937,[36] in Sweden since 1944,[37] in Hungary and Czechoslovakia since 1962,[38] in England and Wales since 1967,[39] in East Germany since 1968,[40] in West Germany[41] and in Canada[42] since 1969, in Finland since 1970,[43] in Austria since 1971,[44] and in Norway since 1972.[45] In Greece,[46] Turkey,[47] Poland,[48] and Iceland, such behavior is not criminal. Only in Ireland[49] and Scotland,[50] among all the countries of Europe outside the communist orbit, does such behavior still constitute a crime, but in Scotland the fact that prosecutions must be approved by the Lord Advocate or his officers has rendered them negligible.[51] Among the communist countries, such behavior remains criminal in Rumania,[52] Bulgaria,[53] Yugoslavia,[54] and the Soviet Union,[55] carrying a maximum prison term of 5 years in the last country. From this survey, however, it is apparent that the United States and the Soviet Union are the only major countries in Europe and North America[56] still criminalizing such conduct. Even the Soviet penalty seems mild by comparison with those authorized by many of the American states.

Almost every expert body passing upon the question has recommended that consensual acts between adults in private should not be criminal at all. Among these are the Wolfenden Committee in Britain[57] and, in the United States, the American Law Institute,[58] the National Association for Mental Health,[59] the Task Force on Homosexuality of the National Institute of Mental Health,[60] the National Commission on Reform of Federal Criminal Laws,[61] and the penal code revision commissions and committees of Alaska, Iowa, Kentucky, Maryland, Massachusetts, Michigan, Nebraska, New Jersey, Vermont, and Washington.[62] The International Congress on Criminal Law, meeting at the Hague in 1965, recommended that all countries decriminalize such behavior.[63] Of the other state penal code revision commissions whose work has reached the stage of formal recommendations,[64] New Hampshire's has recommended a misdemeanor penalty with a maximum of 1 year in jail and a $1,000 fine; the Texas committee is recommending a maximum of 6 months in jail and a $1,000 fine; and in Montana, the commission, after first recommending a maximum of 5 years' imprisonment, finally settled on a maximum of 10 years. (The present penalty in Montana is a minimum of 5 years and a maximum of life.) In California, the revision committee's staff came up with a draft calling for decriminalization of such behavior, but the committee chairman revised it to insert a felony penalty of 5 years for *homosexual* conduct. (The Texas and Montana drafts likewise apply only to homosexual conduct.) What the full committee will recommend remains to be seen. Meanwhile, the California State Bar has passed a resolution recommending the removal of consensual acts between adults in private from the criminal law.[65]

In view of the overwhelming body of enlightened world opinion just described and the rather remote interests a state might claim to justify the criminal sanction for such conduct, the *maximum* imposable penalty consistent with the eighth amendment would appear to be a fine of, at most, a few hundred dollars. No justification exists for isolation or attempted rehabilitation of offenders, and there is little hope of deterring specific individuals, so it is difficult to see how a prison or jail term—even one as short as New York's authorization of three months—could be justified, especially since no one is "harmed" by the conduct in any ordinary acceptation of the word. Even that most minimal of psychic harms is absent—the thrusting of offensive conduct upon the view of unwilling observers. Nor is there any *risk* of harm to others, such as may exist in the case of drunkenness. As previously noted, the only rational basis for such a law is the idea of simple community condemnation of the behavior in order to achieve some measure of general deterrence. This objective can be attained just as readily by a prohibition to which only a moderate fine is attached.

Whether or not the arguments against punishment other than a moderate fine are persuasive, it is cruelly excessive without any doubt to stigmatize such behavior as a felony, with maximum prison terms measured in years or by the offender's life. Nor can felony penalties be justified when the behavior takes place in public, though obviously the factor of psychic harm to involuntary observers justifies a greater penalty than for acts in private. Any use of prison terms as a sanction should be impermissible under the eighth amendment unless the behavior in question inflicts some serious and tangible harm. Deviate sex acts, even in public, have no intrinsic capacity for harm to others, either direct or remote. Psychic harm is their maximum potential. Even then, such harm may not often be realized, because it depends on the susceptibility of the beholder. Many people are merely curious or bemused by such conduct. Even among those genuinely distressed, few seem sufficiently so to be willing to go to the trouble of signing a complaint and appearing in court as a prosecuting witness.[66] Yet this is the minimal amount of cooperation society expects of its citizens in combating crime generally. If the people supposedly harmed by these crimes are unwilling to undergo minor inconvenience to see the criminals brought to justice, then prison terms are an excessively harsh punishment in relation to the gravity of the offense. Consequently, disregarding the comparative law test and turning to the only other practicable test for checking the reasonableness of a court's judgment on "decency," we still find that the penalty imposed by most states is unnecessarily cruel. It greatly exceeds what could be needed to accomplish the permissible ends of the criminal sanction.

Why, then, are these draconian penalties still in force? Much of the explanation lies in the aversion to deviate sex acts to which many Americans, including legislators and judges, are culturally conditioned. But the major impediment to a successful attack on the ferocious punishments for adult consensual sodomy becomes apparent when one realizes that most such laws lump together all deviate sex acts as a single offense, regardless of circumstance. In many statutes, acts with minors, even small children, and acts performed by force are categorized as the same offense as acts performed between consenting adults. They are all the single offense of sodomy and subject to the single range of punishment prescribed by the statute condemning it. A state can constitutionally prescribe life imprisonment for forcible sodomy if it can constitutionally prescribe life imprisonment for forcible rape.

The question therefore seems reduced to the subsidiary one mentioned earlier in this discussion: If the range of punishment authorized by the legislature is not objectionable, can a punishment meted out by a court within that range be attacked as unconstitutionally excessive under particular circumstances? Many appellate courts, called upon to review other judges' sentences, have rejected this contention. If the legislatively authorized range is unobjectionable, they assert that the sentencing judge has complete discretion to impose any penalty within that range,[67] provided his discretion has not been influenced by such invidiously discriminatory factors as race. Only if he has exceeded the punishment authorized by statute will his sentence be declared unconstitutional. Of course, if the reviewing court is a court of the same jurisdiction but superior to the sentencing court, it may see fit to exercise an inherent power to correct abuses of discretion by the inferior tribunal. But this differs materially from determining that the sentence passed by the lower court is *unconstitutional*.[68]

This traditional viewpoint as applied to the sodomy laws is erroneous. It serves only to obscure the real constitutional issue. Even if it represents a correct view of the eighth amendment's reach, generally speaking, which is not conceded, it is not the appropriate analysis to be applied to the sodomy laws. In their case, the real issue is whether the legislature can constitutionally combine into one crime, with the same range of punishment, such disparate behavior as an act in private between consenting adults and an act performed by force by an adult on a small child. Logically, this must be deemed prohibited by the eighth amendment. Otherwise, a legislature could render the amendment completely nugatory by combining trivial offenses with heinous ones and authorizing for the single consolidated offense the greater penalty justified by the more serious crime.

Of course, the extent to which a legislature may distinguish among various circumstances in creating categories of crime does not ordinarily pose a constitutional question. Fine distinctions among the myriad circumstances that accompany crime are not compelled by the eighth amendment. The distinctions sought here are hardly fine distinctions, however. They have existed throughout Anglo-American jurisprudence from time immemorial with respect to ordinary intercourse. In the case of coitus, acts performed by force—categorized as the crime of rape—have always been distinguished from consensual acts. Among the latter, acts with those who are under the age of consent (traditionally called "statutory rape") are distinguished from acts between persons capable of consenting in law (denominated "fornication"). Within the latter group, acts in public ("public lewdness") have traditionally been distinguished from acts in private.

The critical question is whether a legislature could, consistently with the eighth amendment, lump together into one category of crime all these disparate acts of coitus and attach to that crime a maximum penalty of, say, life imprisonment on the justification that such a maximum is not excessive as applied to forcible rape. If the traditional view—that any sentence within the legislatively authorized range is constitutional—is correct, imposing a sentence of life imprisonment for one act of fornication by two consenting adults in private becomes permissible. The absurdity of such a proposition is self-evident, yet this is precisely what has occurred in the case of sodomy. The act or acts themselves are comparable to ordinary intercourse; they are simply various forms of deviate intercourse. No rational basis exists for allowing, in the case of such acts, a categorization of crime that would be constitutionally intolerable in the case of coitus.

It makes relatively little difference from the viewpoint of justice whether the legislative categorization of the crime is declared unconstitutional, or the traditional view of unlimited judicial discretion to sentence within the legislatively authorized range is replaced by a view that the Constitution fetters such discretion. In either event, the eighth amendment's ban on cruelly excessive punishment will have been vindicated. But from an administrative point of view, the alternative chosen makes considerable difference. In the case of the sodomy laws, the preferable approach is to declare the legislative categorization of the crime unconstitutional.

That would force redefinition of the crime along lines comparable to rape, statutory rape, public lewdness, and fornication, and would avoid the necessity of constitutional review of judicial discretion in sentencing in the multitude of individual cases.[69]

A recent decision lending considerable support to the preceding analysis is *Ralph v. Warden, Maryland Penitentiary.*[70] In that case the offender had been convicted of rape and sentenced to death. The Fourth Circuit held that his sentence violated the eighth amendment because death is excessively cruel as a punishment for rape when the victim's life was neither taken nor endangered and no lasting psychic or physical injury was inflicted. Unfortunately, the opinion does not clearly indicate whether it was faulting the statute for categorizing the crime of rape too broadly and authorizing death under all circumstances, or the sentencing court for inappropriately having chosen death in this case out of the range of punishment authorized. Although one may disagree with the court's application of its analysis of the meaning and reach of the eighth amendment to the facts of that case, the analysis itself comports perfectly with that suggested here, even to the extent of using both the comparative law and the legislative ends tests. If the punishment for rape must distinguish between life-endangering and non-life-endangering situations, it stands to reason that the punishment for sodomy must distinguish between cases involving mutually consenting adults and cases involving force or children.

In none of the sodomy cases in which excessive punishment was claimed has the contention been successful. In some, the claim does not appear to have been justifiable or to have been strenuously pressed. In *People v. Hurd,*[71] which involved an act with the defendant's 16-year-old daughter, the court's treatment of the issue consisted of one sentence: "We fail to see, and Defendant does not point out, how or wherein his convictions constitute cruel and unusual punishment. . . ."[72] In *State v. Phillips,*[73] the defendant was convicted on several counts of distinct acts with two girls, 8 and 9 years old. Consecutive sentences totaling 54 years were imposed without the possibility of parole. The reviewing court held that the punishment was not cruel and unusual: "We will not upset the sentences . . . as long as he [the trial judge] stays within the statutory limits and does not abuse his discretion."[74]

In *State v. Stubbs,*[75] the claim would appear to have had more merit. The act in that case took place between two adults and was apparently consensual, although the opinion does not make clear whether it occurred in public or in private. The sentence imposed was 7 to 10 years in prison. The eighth-amendment claim was brushed aside in a statement that reveals an erroneous view of its reach: "When punishment does not exceed the limits fixed by the statute, it cannot be considered cruel and unusual punishment in a constitutional sense."[76] In *Bue v. State*,[77] the defendant was discovered in *flagrante delicto* with a fellow cellmate in the El Paso city jail. The act was obviously one between consenting adults, and could hardly be deemed public except in the sense that a jail cell affords little privacy. The sentence was *15 years* in prison. Again, the eighth-amendment claim was disposed of in one terse line: "The punishment being within the limits authorized by statute was for the jury and is not excessive."[78]

The only two cases in which the claim was clearly meritorious and would appear to have been ably and fully presented to the courts are *Perkins v. North Carolina*[79] and *Washington v. Rodríguez.*[80] The former involved a consensual act between two adult males (whether in public or in private is unclear). Perkins's codefendant had pleaded *nolo contendere* and been sentenced to 5 to 7 years in prison; he had already been released on parole when this case was heard in federal court. Perkins, on the other hand, had demanded a jury trial. Upon conviction, he had been sentenced by the state court to 20 to 30 years—a sentence well within the range of 5 to 60 years then authorized by the North Carolina statute. The federal judge clearly regarded both the sentence imposed and the range authorized by the statute as greatly excessive. His opinion noted that no adult homosexual offenses had been punished by more than a 5-year sentence in North Carolina within the last decade, absent special circumstances. He cited a long list of other crimes, many far more serious than this one, for which the statutory range of punishment was far less. It is also clear that he was aware of *Weems*, having referred to that authority. Nevertheless, he concluded:

> If the usual five year sentence is "right," then twenty to thirty years is "wrong." Certainly twenty to thirty years is unusual. There can be no justification for such disparity of punishment. But the sentence is within the astounding statutory limit of "not less than five nor more than *sixty* years," and it is well

settled that within statutory limits even the harshest sentence, absent special circumstances, is not cruel and unusual within the meaning of the Constitution.[81]

In support of this latter proposition, he cited only state court decisions. Curiously, his opinion never came to grips with the idea that the legislative range could itself be unconstitutional. A fellow human being was thus subjected to potential deprivation of his liberty for 30 years on the basis of this narrow view of the eighth amendment.[82] Though that view is supported by some state cases, it is contrary to both reason and justice and to the clear trend of decision and dicta in the United States Supreme Court. Adverse criticism of the range of punishment authorized by the North Carolina statute, both in the *Perkins* opinion and in later comment upon that case,[83] did, however, prompt the state legislature to reduce the maximum from 60 to 10 years.

In *Washington v. Rodríguez*, the two defendants were tried jointly for committing the offense of sodomy while incarcerated in the state penitentiary for other crimes. Although the opinion does not so state, presumably the act was consensual and both participants were competent adults. At that time, the New Mexico sodomy statute authorized imprisonment for not less than 1 year or a fine of not less than $1,000, or both, in the discretion of the court. Each defendant was sentenced to a term of not less than 1 year, no maximum being specified. Under these circumstances, the maximum term was *life*, according to earlier precedent.[84] The contention that these sentences of potential life imprisonment violated the cruel and unusual punishment clause was rejected by the appellate court. The crutch on which the court leaned for its conclusion was the New Mexico Indeterminate Sentence Act, which was in effect at the time sentence was passed but had been repealed before the appeal was considered. According to the opinion, the objects and purposes of that act precluded a finding that the sentence amounted to cruel and unusual punishment. Quoting from a prior New Mexico case,[85] the court noted that the act was designed to effect

a break from the definite and fixed sentence in favor of an indeterminate period of punishment which would be proportioned to the progress of the prisoner toward rehabilitation. This is accomplished by making incarceration and its duration a matter within the discretion of competent parole authorities. In this manner the "punishment" is made to fit the offender rather than the crime.[86]

It then proceeded to cite a prior New Mexico case[87] in which cruel and unusual punishment was held to imply only "a limitation upon the form and character of punishment that may be prescribed and not a limitation upon the duration."[88] The result of the case thus appears to rest on three propositions, all of which are manifestly indefensible:

1. The eighth amendment prohibits only barbarous modes of punishment, not excessiveness.
2. The legislature may prescribe life imprisonment for even the most trivial of offenses, because parole authorities should have discretion to proportion the term of incarceration to the progress of the offender toward rehabilitation.[89]
3. Sodomists can be expected to make progress toward rehabilitation by being confined in prisons where *nobody* is allowed a chance for "normal" sexual outlets.

If cases like *Perkins* and *Washington* do not demonstrate the need for vigorous application of the eighth amendment, nothing will.

NOTES

1. *See* note 12, Chapter 1 *supra*.
2. *See* ILL. ANN. STAT. 38 §11-9 (1964) (which prescribes a maximum penalty for public indecency of 1 year in jail and a $500 fine).
3. The sodomy provisions of these new codes are cited in note 12, Chapter 1 *supra*. The sections covering public lewdness and the penalties authorized for that offense may be found by reference to the citations given there.
4. For the New York consensual sodomy provision and applicable penalty, *see* note 12, Chapter 1 *supra;* the New York public lewdness provision is N.Y. PENAL LAW §245.00 (McKinney 1967), for which the maximum punishment is the same as for consensual sodomy. Under section 3124 of the new Pennsylvania Criminal Code, consensual sodomy between adults is, like indecent exposure under section 3127, punishable only as a misdemeanor of the second degree, which carries a maximum term of 2 years.
5. *Compare* UTAH CODE § 76-53-22 (1969 Supp.) (sodomy) *with* UTAH CODE §§ 76-39-5(1), 76-1-16, 76-39-13 (1953, Supp. 1971) (lewdness, indecent exposure, and obscene behavior). *Compare* KAN. STAT. ANN. 21-3505 (Supp. 1970) (sodomy)

with KAN. STAT. ANN. 21-3508 (Supp. 1970) (lewd behavior), both being subject to the same penalty prescribed by KAN. STAT. ANN. 21-4502 (1) (b) (Supp. 1970).

6. In Minnesota, the same penalty is prescribed for consensual sodomy and for indecent exposure, lewdness, and public indecency. *See* MINN. STAT. ANN. §§ 609.293, subd. 5, 617.23, 609.03, subd. 2 (1964, Supp. 1971).

7. Under the old Delaware law and in Virginia, the maximum prison term is 3 years. *See* DEL. CODE ANN. 11 § 831 (1953); CODE VA. §18.1-212 (Supp. 1971). Kentucky, Louisiana, New Hampshire, South Carolina, and Wisconsin authorize a maximum of 5 years. *See* KY. REV. STAT. 436.050, 435.105 (1971); LA. REV. STAT. 14:89 (1951); N.H. REV. STAT. 579:9 (1955); CODE LAWS S.C. § 16-412 (1962); WIS. STAT. 944.17 (1958). Five years is apparently also the maximum term imposed under the UNIFORM CODE OF MILITARY JUSTICE, Art. 125, 10 U.S.C. § 925 (1970). Six years is the maximum in Nevada. *See* NEV. REV. STAT. 201.190 (1967). A maximum of 10 years is prescribed in Alabama, Alaska, the Canal Zone, the District of Columbia, Iowa, Maine, Maryland, Mississippi, New Mexico, North Carolina, North Dakota, Oklahoma, Pennsylvania (under the old law), Puerto Rico, South Dakota, the Virgin Islands, Washington, West Virginia, and Wyoming. *See* ALA. CODE tit. 14, § 106 (1959); ALAS. STAT. § 11.40.120 (1971); C. Z. CODE tit. 6 § 2451 (1963); D.C. CODE § 22-3502 (1967) (as noted at the end of Chapter 3, the D.C. chief of police has agreed to a stipulation that this statute is inapplicable to private acts between consenting adults); IOWA CODE § 705.2 (1950); ME. REV. STAT. 17 §1001 (1964); ANN. CODE MD. art. 27, §§553, 554 (1971); MISS. CODE tit. 11, ch. 1, § 2413 (1956); N.M. STAT. 40A-9-6, 40A-29-3 (1964); GEN. STAT. N.C. §§ 14-177, 14-2 (1969); N.D. CENTURY CODE 12-22-07 (1960); OKLA. STAT. tit. 21 § 886 (1958); PA. STAT. 18 § 4501 (1963); LAWS P.R. tit. 33 § 1118 (1969); S.D. COMP. LAWS 1967, 22-22-21; V.I. CODE tit. 14 § 2061 (1964); REV. CODE WASH. 9.79.100 (1961); W. VA. CODE § 61-8-13 (1966); WYO. STAT. § 6-98 (1957). The maximum prison term allowed by Indiana is 14 years. *See* IND. STAT. 10-4221 (1956). The statutes of Florida, Tennessee, and Texas allow a maximum of 15 years. *See* FLA. STAT. §§ 800.01, 800.02 (1965, Supp. 1972) (the former, covering "the crime against nature," has, however, been declared unconstitutional; the latter statute, covering "unnatural and lascivious acts," authorizes a maximum imprisonment of 6 months); TENN. CODE 39-707 (1955); TEX. PENAL CODE art. 524 (1952). Michigan also allows a maximum of 15 years for anal sodomy but 5 years for other acts ("gross indecency"); however, if the offender is determined to be a "sexually delinquent person," the maximum is life imprisonment in both cases, a "sexually delinquent person" being "any person whose sexual behavior is characterized by repetitive or compulsive acts which indicate a disregard of consequences or the recognized rights of others" or the use of force or aggressions against children under 16. *See* MICH. COMP. LAWS ANN. §§ 750.158, 750.338, 750.338a, 750.338b, 750.10a (1968). Twenty years is the maximum punishment in Georgia, Nebraska, Ohio (under the old law), and Rhode Island. GA. CODE ANN. § 26-2002 (1970); REV. STAT. NEB. 28-919 (1964); OHIO REV. CODE 2905.44 (1953); GEN. LAWS R.I. § 11-10-1 (1969). Three other states—Arizona, Massachusetts, and New Jersey—authorize a maximum prison sentence of 20 years for anal sodomy, but 5 years (Arizona and Massachusetts) and 3 years (New Jersey) for other kinds of acts. *See* ARIZ. REV. STAT. ANN. §§13-651, 652 (Supp. 1971); ANN. LAWS

Mass. ch. 272, §§34, 35 (1968); N.J. Stat. 2A: 143-1, 2A: 115-1, 2A: 85-7 (1969). In Arkansas the statutory maximum is 21 years. See Ark. Stat. 41-813 (1964). In Missouri and Montana, although the statute sets a minimum term of imprisonment, it sets no maximum, so presumably the maximum is life. See Mo. Stat. § 563.230 (1953); Rev. Code Mont. 94-4118 (1969). The same situation prevails in California with respect to anal sodomy. See Cal. Penal Code §§ 286, 671 (West 1970). But a maximum of 15 years is set by the statute proscribing oral copulation. See Cal. Penal Code § 288a (West 1970). In Vermont, since anal sodomy is a crime only by virtue of common law, there being no statute fixing a penalty, it has been held that either a fine or imprisonment or both may be imposed in the discretion of the court. See State v. LaForrest, note 25, Chapter 2 supra. So presumably a sentence of life imprisonment could be imposed in Vermont for this crime. For oral copulation, however, the Vermont statutes prescribe a maximum of 5 years' imprisonment. See Vt. Stat. tit. 13, §2603 (1958).

8. Robinson v. California, 370 U.S. 660, 667 (1962). The best general treatments of the eighth amendment and the cases interpreting it are Note, *The Effectiveness of the Eighth Amendment, An Appraisal of Cruel and Unusual Punishment*, 36 N.Y.U.L. Rev. 846 (1961), and Note, *The Cruel and Unusual Punishment Clause and the Substantive Criminal Law*, 79 Harv. L. Rev. 635 (1966). The most exhaustive analysis of the historical meaning of the clause is found in Granucci, *"Nor Cruel and Unusual Punishments Inflicted": The Original Meaning*, 57 Cal. L. Rev. 839 (1969).

9. See the dissenting opinion in Weems v. United States, 217 U.S. 349, 701–9 (1910). Actually, the dissenting justices argued that the clause inhibited (1) the infliction of truly barbaric bodily punishments, (2) the infliction in unusual degree of bodily punishments not inherently cruel, and (3) the infliction of nonbodily punishments in a degree exceeding that authorized by statute. They would therefore find no basis in the clause for quarreling with any term of imprisonment a legislature might see fit to authorize for a crime. But if (3) constitutes the clause's only limitation on terms of imprisonment, it is superfluous as a constitutional protection because courts are already precluded by the separation-of-powers provisions of the Constitution from disregarding legislative maximums on penalties.

10. 356 U.S. 86 (1958).

11. "To be sure, imprisonment for ninety days is not, in the abstract, a punishment which is either cruel or unusual. But the question cannot be decided in the abstract. Even one day in prison would be a cruel and unusual punishment for the 'crime' of having a common cold." 370 U.S. 660, at 667 (1962).

12. Until 1972 Delaware continued to prescribe whipping as a punishment for crime. A state court upheld this mode of punishment against an eighth-amendment challenge. See State v. Cannon, 190 A.2d 514 (Del. 1963). But a federal appellate court ruled that it does constitute cruel and unusual punishment. See Jackson v. Bishop, 404 F.2d 571 (8th Cir. 1968).

13. A few states still provide for sterilization of certain criminals, but this may evade the reach of the eighth amendment if conceived as a measure for eugenics rather than punishment. *Compare* Skinner v. Oklahoma, 316 U.S. 535 (1942), *with* Buck v. Bell, 274 U.S. 200 (1927). However, the notion that complex antisocial

behavior can be traced to genetic defect is far more questionable now, from the scientific standpoint, than it was when *Buck v. Bell* was decided.

Recent years have seen several efforts, both in law journals and in the courts, to persuade judges to hold that the death penalty is inherently cruel and thus outlawed by the eighth amendment. The most ambitious of these is Goldberg & Dershowitz, *Declaring the Death Penalty Unconstitutional*, 83 HARV. L. REV. 1773 (1970). The Supreme Court of California so ruled, but under a comparable provision of the California constitution. People v. Anderson, 6 Cal.3d 628, 100 Cal. Rptr. 152, 493 P.2d 880 (1972). This decision lost its prospective force when the voters of California on November 7, 1972, approved a referendum proposition amending the state constitution to authorize the death penalty. The United States Supreme Court held that the death penalty for the defendants in the cases before it constituted cruel and unusual punishment, but it did not outlaw the penalty per se. Furman v. Georgia, 408 U.S. 238 (1972).

14. 144 U.S. 323.
15. *Id.* at 339–40.
16. 217 U.S. 349 (1910).
17. 217 U.S. at 367, 384.
18. *See* note 9 *supra*.
19. *See*, for example, the following statements:
    A punishment out of all proportion to the offense may bring it within the ban against "cruel and unusual punishments."
Robinson v. California, 370 U.S. 660, 667 (1962) (Justice Douglas concurring).
    But when the Court was confronted with a punishment of 12 years in irons at hard and painful labor imposed for the crime of falsifying public records, it did not hesitate to declare that the penalty *was cruel in its excessiveness* and unusual in its character [citing *Weems*].
Trop v. Dulles, 356 U.S. 86, 100 (1958) (Chief Justice Warren's opinion for the Court) (emphasis added).
    Then, too, a cruelly disproportionate relation between what the law requires and the sanction for its disobedience may constitute a violation of the Eighth Amendment as a cruel and unusual punishment, and, in respect of the States, even offend the due process clause of the Fourteenth Amendment.
Lambert v. California, 355 U.S. 225, 231 (1957) (Justice Frankfurter dissenting). *See also* Rudolph v. Alabama, 375 U.S. 889 (1963), in which Justices Goldberg, Brennan, and Douglas dissented from a denial of certiorari. The short opinion by Mr. Justice Goldberg urges that the case should have been heard to determine if the death penalty for rape, where human life was neither taken nor endangered, violates the cruel and unusual punishment clause. His opinion suggests two approaches to this question: (1) The comparative approach—Does the death penalty in this circumstance violate "standards of decency more or less universally accepted," but with reference to worldwide practice, not merely that of the American states? (2) A "legislative ends" approach—Is the penalty not reasonably necessary to attain legitimate penal goals, of which he lists only three (deterrence, isolation, and rehabilitation)? It is plain from the opinion that these justices regard the eighth amendment as prohibiting excessively harsh quantums

of punishment. A number of state court and lower federal cases give this same meaning to the eighth amendment or to its equivalent in state constitutions. *See, e.g.,* State v. Evans, 245 P.2d 788 (Idaho 1952), and cases cited therein. A careful and thoughtful analysis and review of the law and authorities is found in *In re* Lynch, 8 Cal.3d 410, 503 P.2d 921, 105 Cal. Rptr. 217 (1972), in which the Supreme Court of California invalidated, under the cruel or unusual punishments clause of the California constitution, a statute authorizing life imprisonment for a second conviction of indecent exposure.

The opinions of various justices in the death penalty case—Furman v. Georgia, *supra* note 13—likewise demonstrate general acceptance of this application of the cruel and unusual punishment clause. *See, e.g.,* 408 U.S. at 279–81, 323–27, 331–32, and 456–61.

20. "The whole inhibition [of the eighth amendment] is against that which is excessive either in the bail required, or fine imposed, or punishments inflicted." O'Neil v. Vermont, 144 U.S. 323, 340 (1892) (dissenting opinion). Granucci, *supra* note 8, demonstrates rather convincingly that the cruel and unusual punishments clause of the English Bill of Rights, from which the virtually identical provisions of the Virginia Declaration of Rights and the eighth amendment were successively copied, was in fact directed against excessively harsh punishments, rather than against barbarous *modes* of punishment such as burning, disemboweling, and the like.

21. *See, e.g.,* State v. Peters, 78 N.M. 224, 430 P.2d 382 (1967).

22. Packer, *Making the Punishment Fit the Crime,* 77 Harv. L. Rev. 1071, 1076 (1964).

23. *Compare* United States v. Rosenberg, 195 F.2d 583 (2d Cir.), *cert. denied,* 344 U.S. 838 (1952), *with* Schmidt v. United States, 177 F.2d 450 (2d Cir. 1949), and United States *ex rel.* Bongiorno v. Ragen, 54 F.Supp. 973 (N.D. Ill. 1944), *aff'd,* 146 F.2d 349 (7th Cir.), *cert. denied,* 325 U.S. 865 (1945).

24. *See* note 10 *supra.*

25. 356 U.S. at 101.

26. *See* note 12, Chapter 1 *supra.*

27. *Ibid.*

28. *See* note 7 *supra.*

29. In some of the countries to be mentioned, private consensual adult behavior, though generally lawful, may be criminal if prostitution is involved. The same is true of some of the American states that have legalized such conduct.

30. *See* N. St. John-Stevas, Life, Death and the Law 329 (1961) [hereinafter cited as St. John-Stevas]; Wolfenden Report, Report of the Committee on Homosexual Offences and Prostitution app. III (authorized Amer. ed. 1963) [hereinafter cited as Wolfenden]; Hammelmann, *Homosexuality and the Law in Other Countries,* in They Stand Apart 143, at 156 (J. T. Rees & H. V. Usill eds. 1955) [hereinafter cited as Hammelmann].

31. *See* St. John-Stevas 331; Wolfenden app. III; Hammelmann 158.

32. *See* St. John-Stevas 330; Wolfenden app. III; Hammelmann 158.

33. *See* St. John-Stevas 328; Wolfenden app. III; Hammelmann 157.

34. *See* St. John-Stevas 330; Wolfenden app. III; Hammelmann 157.

35. *See* St. John-Stevas 328; Wolfenden app. III; Hammelmann 161.

36. *See* St. John-Stevas 332; 4 Excerpta Criminologica No. 1389 (1964); Hammelmann 158–59.

37. *See* St. John-Stevas 331; Wolfenden app. III; 4 Excerpta Criminologica No. 1388 (1964); Hammelmann 159–60; Encyclopedia of Sexual Behavior 919 (rev. ed. A. Ellis & A. Abarbanel 1967).

38. For Hungary, *see* Criminal Code of the Hungarian People's Republic §§278–80 (1962), and 8 Excerpta Criminologica No. 482 (1968); for Czechoslovakia, *see* D. J. West, Homosexuality 76 (rev. ed. 1968), and 4 Excerpta Criminologica No. 1385 (1964).

39. *See* note 19, Chapter 2 *supra*.

40. *See* W. Parker, Homosexuals and Employment 16 (1970) (pamphlet published by the Corinthian Foundation, San Francisco).

41. *See* N.Y. Times, May 10, 1969, at 1, col. 1. The change became effective September 1, 1969.

42. *See* N.Y. Times, May 16, 1969, at 1, col. 1. The change became effective July 1, 1969.

43. *See* The Advocate, June 9, 1971, at 1; Vector, Aug. 1971, at 43.

44. *See* N.Y. Times, July 11, 1971, at 9, col. 1.

45. *See Law Reform in Norway*, One Magazine, July/Aug. 1972, at 4–5.

46. *See* St. John-Stevas 330; Wolfenden app. III.

47. *See* Turkish Criminal Code §§414–47, 576 (1965).

48. *See* D. J. West, Homosexuality 76 (rev. ed. 1968).

49. In Eire, the British statutes making buggery and acts of gross indecency criminal offenses are still in force. These statutes are the Offenses Against the Person Act, 1861, §61, and the Criminal Law Amendment Act, 1885, §11. Letter from D. Quigley, Attorney General's Office, Dublin, Eire, to the author, Dec. 11, 1969. Presumably, the same legal situation prevails in Northern Ireland, since the reform act passed by the British parliament in 1967 limited its application to England and Wales.

50. In Scotland, sodomy is an offense at common law, and acts of gross indecency are a statutory offense under the Criminal Law Amendment Act, 1885, § 11, which was made applicable to Scotland by §15. *See* Wolfenden para. 77.

51. *See* Wolfenden paras. 51, 72, 77, 136–43.

52. *See* 4 Excerpta Criminologica No. 1390 (1964).

53. *Ibid*.

54. *Ibid*.

55. Criminal Code of the RSFSR, art. 121, in H. J. Berman, Soviet Criminal Law and Procedure—the RSFSR Codes 196 (1966).

56. Since information on foreign criminal laws is so difficult to come by, this inquiry has been limited to the European nations and Canada, these countries being ones likely to share America's cultural traditions. No comprehensive survey of laws on this subject around the world has ever been made.

The information I have on countries beyond Europe and Canada is incomplete and, in some cases, unverified. Much of it, together with the information on Portugal and Iceland presented in the text, is drawn from an unpublished research paper prepared at the University of London by Mr. P. J. Richardson and also from my personal correspondence with him. The paper is entitled "The

Homosexual and the Law—A Comparative Study." I include it here to give as full a picture as possible. Homosexual acts in private between consenting adults—and deviate heterosexual acts, a fortiori—are not a crime in Japan, Korea, Mexico, Argentina, Uruguay, Egypt, or the Sudan. Some such acts are, however, criminal in Australia, New Zealand, the Republic of South Africa, Ethiopia, Morocco, Algeria, Lebanon, Pakistan, India, Thailand, and Colombia. Although a provision of the Israeli Penal Code does cover private consensual acts between adults, such acts by instruction of the Attorney General have not been prosecuted since 1949. The statutes of Australia, New Zealand, South Africa, and India seem merely to have copied the former English law on buggery, but in those countries, as in the United States, the statute has often been enlarged by judicial decision to include acts such as fellatio. In Morocco, Algeria, Pakistan, and perhaps Lebanon as well, the laws against sodomy appear to be a throwback to the ancient Muslim religious codes. In three of those countries the major Western influence was French law, which does not criminalize private adult consensual behavior.

57. *See* WOLFENDEN paras. 13, 52, 61 and 62.

58. Model Penal Code § 207.5, Comment at 278–79 (Tent. Draft No. 4, 1955).

59. National Association for Mental Health, Position Statement on Homosexuality and Mental Illness, approved by the Professional Advisory Council, Sept. 17, 1970, and by the Executive Committee, Oct. 17, 1970.

60. National Institute of Mental Health, Final Report of the Task Force on Homosexuality (1969), published in SIECUS NEWSLETTER, Vol. VI, No. 3, at 3 (Dec. 1970).

61. *See* the proposed new Federal Criminal Code §§1643-44, in FINAL REPORT OF THE NATIONAL COMMISSION ON REFORM OF FEDERAL CRIMINAL LAWS (1971).

62. These recommendations in the states listed are to be found in their respective drafts of proposed new criminal codes. The drafts are on file in the offices of the American Law Institute, Columbia University Law School, New York, New York.

63. *See* Ploscowe, *Report to the Hague: Suggested Revisions of Penal Law Relating to Sex Crimes and Crimes Against the Family*, 50 CORNELL L. Q. 425 (1965).

64. The recommendations of the commissions of these states—New Hampshire, Texas, Montana, and California—may be found by consulting their respective drafts of new criminal codes on file in the offices of the American Law Institute, Columbia University Law School, New York, New York. The California committee chairman's proposal is found in section 9303 of Cal. Senate Bill No. 1506, introduced July 25, 1972.

65. *See* 45 J. ST. B. CAL. 560 (1970).

66. This conclusion is borne out by the only large-scale study done to date. See Note, *The Consenting Adult Homosexual and the Law: An Empirical Study of Enforcement and Administration in Los Angeles County*, 13 U.C.L.A. L. REV. 644, 688 n. 17, 708 n. 142 (1966). This study found that almost invariably the only prosecuting witnesses in these cases were police officers. So did the study by Barry Copilow and Thomas Coleman mentioned in note 5, Chapter 8 *supra*.

67. *See* cases cited in Note, 36 N.Y.U. L. REV. 846, at 852 n. 38 (1961). The cases in opposition to this view are cited *id*. 852 n. 39. See also the federal cases

cited *id.* 852 n. 40. A recent case in Kentucky held that life imprisonment without the possibility of parole is generally permissible as a penalty for forcible rape but is unconstitutionally excessive *as applied* to a 14-year-old juvenile offender. Workman v. Commonwealth, 429 S.W.2d 374 (Ct. App. Ky. 1968).

68. An interesting recent case aptly illustrating the differences between these bases for appellate supervision of sentences is Faulkner v. State, 445 P.2d 815 (Alas. 1968). Three judges of the Supreme Court of Alaska participated in the decision. One held that the supreme court had previously determined it lacked inherent power to correct a lower court's abuse of discretion in sentencing, but that the penalty imposed in this case was so excessive as to violate the cruel and unusual punishment clause of the Constitution. A second held that the sentence was not unconstitutionally excessive, but that the supreme court had inherent power to supervise sentencing by lower courts and should overturn the sentence here imposed as an abuse of discretion. The third took the position that the supreme court had no inherent power to correct abuses in sentencing by lower courts, and that if the legislatively authorized range of punishment was not constitutionally objectionable (as in this case), no sentence imposed within that range could contravene the cruel and unusual punishment clause. Thus, although the sentence was overturned, the case hardly stands for any definite proposition. Another case in which it is unclear whether the decision rests upon unconstitutional excessiveness or upon the appellate court's inherent power to correct lower-court abuse of discretion is United States v. McKinney, 427 F.2d 449, 455 (6th Cir. 1970).

69. Obviously, constitutional review under the eighth amendment of every criminal sentence, to determine if it is proportional to the gravity of the offense in light of individual circumstances, might impose a tremendous burden on appellate courts and particularly on the federal courts. This seems to be the thrust of Mr. Justice Black's reference to the eighth in Mishkin v. New York, 383 U.S. 502, at 517 (1966).

70. 438 F.2d 786 (4th Cir. 1970), *cert. denied,* 408 U.S. 942 (1972). *Cf.* Rudolph v. Alabama, note 19 *supra.*

71. 5 Cal. App.3d 865, 85 Cal. Rptr. 718 (1970).

72. 5 Cal. App.3d at 876-77, 85 Cal. Rptr. at 725.

73. 102 Ariz. 377, 430 P.2d 139 (1967).

74. 430 P.2d at 143.

75. 266 N.C. 295, 145 S.E.2d 899 (1966).

76. 145 S.E.2d at 902.

77. 368 S.W.2d 774 (Tex. Crim. App. 1963).

78. 368 S.W.2d at 775.

79. 234 F.Supp. 333 (W.D.N.C. 1964).

80. 483 P.2d 309 (Ct. App. N.M. 1971).

81. 234 F.Supp. at 337.

82. Actually, the federal court ordered Perkins's release unless within 60 days the state should choose to retry him. But the basis for its overturning of his conviction was that he had been deprived of the effective aid and assistance of counsel, who had been allowed only about two working hours to prepare his

defense. Whether he was retried and, if so, his ultimate fate at the hands of the state court I have been unable to discover.

83. *See* Bickel, *Homosexuality as Crime in North Carolina*, THE NEW REPUBLIC, Vol. 151, Dec. 12, 1964, at 5–6.

84. State v. Frederick, 74 N.M. 42, 390 P.2d 281 (1964); Starkey v. Cox, 73 N.M. 434, 389 P.2d 203 (1964).

85. McCutcheon v. Cox, 71 N.M. 274, 377 P.2d 683 (1967).

86. 483 P.2d at 311.

87. State v. Peters, 78 N.M. 224, 430 P.2d 382 (1967).

88. 78 N.M. at 227, 430 P.2d at 385.

89. *In re* Lynch, note 19 *supra*, demonstrates that this proposition is indefensible.

11

Conclusion

The cardinal principle of the American framework of government is majority rule, and rightly so. We are committed to the notion that the best government is a government of the people, by the people, and for the people. Yet everyone with any political sophistication realizes that the majority is no monolith, but rather an ever shifting coalition of diverse groups with divergent interests. Each group, in order to achieve some or all of its goals, must ally itself with others, offering support for some of their goals in order to obtain their support for its own in return. The end result is generally an accommodation or compromise not entirely satisfactory to anybody—a sort of common denominator that expresses the general will to the extent such a thing can be said to exist at all.

Besides the impossibility of achieving consistent agreement on policy, and the cumbersomeness of the process by which any agreement is reached, a government by majority rule has one great drawback. It is not only possible, but probable, that this coalition called the majority will exclude certain "discrete and insular minorities"[1] over the long run and subject them to gross unfairness on a regular and systematic basis. In American society such a pervasive and systematic discrimination has existed against blacks, which is only now being progressively eliminated. An equally pervasive and systematic discrimination has existed and still exists against the minority group called homosexuals.

Minorities so excluded usually possess some characteristic shared by none of the groups constituting the majority, which arouses great antipathy in those groups. Such minorities become the "other"—scarcely recognized as fellow human beings and co-participants in the same society. In the case of blacks, that character-

310

istic is a different skin color. In the case of homosexuals, it is a different sexual orientation. The antipathy of the majority to this peculiar factor characteristic of such a minority will generally bar the latter completely from the give-and-take of the political process and thus from protecting itself through legislation. When such a total exclusion occurs, the only protection against whatever damage the majority may see fit to wreak on the minority lies in the guarantee of fundamental civil rights and liberties enshrined in the Constitution and enforceable by resort to the courts. The Bill of Rights and the fourteenth amendment supply this guarantee.

Although the elimination of racial discrimination is still far from complete, it is well on its way. It owes much to federal and state civil rights legislation, but few would deny that this legislation was triggered by the work of the United States Supreme Court in applying with increasing vigor the constitutional guarantee of equal protection of the laws. Surely, the legislative success could not have been achieved without the substantial support of non-blacks who began to feel greater and greater empathy with the blacks' plight. But this empathy must be attributed in large part to the soul-searching the Supreme Court's decisions forced many whites to undergo on the question of racial discrimination. Undoubtedly, the legislative achievements also owe a great deal to the massive increases that have taken place in the blacks' own voting power and political organization. It is questionable, however, whether such increases would have occurred but for the sense of growing security the blacks derived from the protective decisions of the Court. In other words, the courts, through their power to invalidate the majority's handiwork under the Bill of Rights and the fourteenth amendment, may possess not only the sole means by which such a minority can protect itself against unfair discrimination by the majority but also the only voice of conscience to which the majority can be forced to listen. By compelling the majority to reevaluate its deepest prejudices in light of the great principles of liberty and equality for all enunciated in the Constitution, the courts thus effectively promote the ideal resolution of the problem—for the majority willingly to concede the minority its rights.

These principles—no deprivation of liberty without due process of law, and equal protection of the laws— are vague generalities that give no specific guidance to a court concerning the circumstances under which the majority may have violated them. In the final analysis, the only guidance is the court's own informed and enlightened conscience. And no one would quarrel with the proposition that this power of constitutional invalidation should be used sparingly. The achievement of any social objective, even the objectives of liberty and justice for all, should be left to the political process to the maximum degree possible.

If we assume that an enlightened and informed conscience dictates that homosexuals should be free, like the rest of society, to live their lives in security and without fear, as long as they do not hurt others, is this goal likely to be achieved through political action? The answer is no. In order for a minority to achieve its aims by means of the political process, it must assert itself through political activity, and this requires its members, first of all, to identify themselves. As far as the blacks are concerned, this initial step did not have to be taken. The color of one's skin cannot be easily hid. The members of such a minority are already identified, whether they like it or not. Not so the homosexuals. They bear no physical mark of the characteristic on which the discrimination against them is based. The vast majority of them can, and do, pass for heterosexuals in their usual contact with the rest of society. By identifying themselves as members of the minority, they risk everything short of life itself—friends and acquaintances, jobs, even liberty.

The difficulty of taking such a step is well illustrated in the New York Times Magazine article in which author Merle Miller declared his own homosexuality.[2] In this article Miller recounts how assiduously he avoided all connection with homosexual civil rights, while serving on the Board of the American Civil Liberties Union and aiding other similar causes right and left.[3] His declaration was, without doubt, an act of considerable courage, but he himself notes that he dared take it only at a point in life at which he was so independently established that its potential repercussions could hardly affect him seriously. Few homosexuals are that securely established. Even those who are can scarcely face with equanimity the prospect of the drastic change in attitude that disclosure of their orientation may produce in their family, friends, associates, and acquaintances. Increasing numbers of homosexuals, particularly in the younger age groups, are willing to identify themselves and work publicly for the securing of their rights, but their numbers are still insignificant.[4]

The ultimate question is how much longer American society will continue to deny these people their basic human dignity. If the legislatures are left to their own initiatives, it may be decades. The objective of this book has been to demonstrate that persuasive arguments can be made now for constitutional invalidation of that bulwark of antihomosexual legislation—the sodomy laws—on which rests much of the edifice of other discrimination against these people. It remains only to find judges with enough human sympathy to apply these arguments and *compel* reform. If reform is attained in this way, it may very well happen that liberation of the "perverts" of America will prove to be the liberation of the rest of American society as well. The state would finally be expelled from a sanctuary to which it should never have been admitted in the first place—the intimate private lives of its citizens. In any event, we could at least begin writing *finis* to another chapter in the long history of man's inhumanity to man.

NOTES

1. These are the words of Harlan Fiske Stone, quoted from the third paragraph of his famous footnote in the *Carolene Products* case. *See* note 7, Chapter 5 *supra*.

2. N.Y. Times, Jan. 17, 1971 (Magazine), at 9. This article has been republished in book form by Random House, together with an "afterword," as M. MILLER, ON BEING DIFFERENT (1971).

Understanding what it is like to be a homosexual can be difficult for heterosexuals, because the experience is so completely outside their ken. In this regard, Miller's book is quite useful. Novels may also help to bridge the gap. Two fine ones have recently been published, one British, the other American: *Maurice*, by E. M. Forster; and *What Happened*, also by Merle Miller. Forster's book, though written in 1913–14, was not published until after the author's death in 1970. Its publication is a significant event, not only because it is one of the few works with a homosexual theme by a major novelist but also because it ends happily—an unthinkable idea in the publishing world of previous years. Miller's book, with a more recent setting, is remarkable both for its style (it is beautifully written) and for its extraordinary psychological insight. Several other novels provide valuable glimpses of the existential predicament of the homosexual. These include *Giovanni's Room*, by James Baldwin; *The Occasional Man* and *Quatrefoil*, by James Barr; *Totempole*, by Sanford Friedman; *A Meeting by the River* and *A Single Man*, by Christopher Isherwood; *City of Night*, by John Rechy; and *The City and the Pillar Revised*, by Gore Vidal. Two brilliant and sympathetic efforts at depicting homosexual love in the ancient world are *Fire from Heaven* and *The Persian Boy*, by Mary Renault, novels in which, in sequence, she reconstructs the life and character of Alexander the Great. Also notable is *Memoirs of Hadrian*, by Marguerite Yourcenar, who has created an "autobiography" of the great Roman emperor by that name. Several of Renault's other novels also deal with the same theme, among them *The Charioteer* and *The Last of the Wine* (the latter also set in ancient Greece).

3. Two quotations from Miller's article make the point dramatically:

The American Civil Liberties Union recently has been commendably active in homosexual cases, but in the early fifties, when homosexuals and people accused of homosexuality were being fired from all kinds of Government posts, as they still are, the A.C.L.U. was notably silent. And the most silent of all was a closet queen who was a member of the board of directors, myself.

N.Y. Times, Jan. 17, 1971 (Magazine), at 10, col. 3.

I once belonged to 22 organizations devoted to improving the lot of the world's outcasts. The only group of outcasts I never spoke up for publicly, never donated money to, or signed an ad or petition for were the homosexuals. I always used my radio announcer's voice when I said "No."

Id. at 57, col. 1.

4. A number of books have recently appeared that describe the "gay liberation" movement, its organizations and activities. Many of these are personal statements by participants in the movement, and therefore much more reliable and illuminating than some of the "outsider" reporting by sensational journalists published in prior years. Among these recent books that portray current attitudes and goals are D. TEAL, THE GAY MILITANTS (1971); A. BELL, DANCING THE GAY LIB BLUES—A YEAR IN THE HOMOSEXUAL LIBERATION MOVEMENT (1971); J. MURPHY, HOMOSEXUAL LIBERATION: A PERSONAL VIEW (1971); D. ALTMAN, HOMOSEXUAL OPPRESSION AND LIBERATION (1971); J. ONGE, THE GAY LIBERATION MOVEMENT (1971); A. ALDRICH, TAKE A LESBIAN TO LUNCH (1972)); L. CLARKE & J. NICHOLS, I HAVE MORE FUN WITH YOU THAN ANYBODY (1972); S. ABBOT & B. LOVE, SAPPHO WAS A RIGHT-ON WOMAN (1972); K. TOBIN & R. WICKER, THE GAY CRUSADERS (1972); P. FISHER, THE GAY MYSTIQUE (1972); P. LYON & D. MARTIN, LESBIAN/WOMAN (1972); T. PERRY, THE LORD IS MY SHEPHERD AND HE KNOWS I'M GAY (1972); and THE GAY LIBERATION BOOK (L. Richmond & G. Noguera eds. 1972). Some of these books are valuable simply because they present the homosexuals' own views of themselves, which serve to counterbalance the portraits drawn by heterosexual psychotherapists. A brief summary of the movement up to about 1968 appears in Cantor, *The Homosexual Revolution*, in THE NEW SEXUAL REVOLUTION 85 (L. A. Kirkendall & R. N. Whitehurst eds. 1971). An excellent up-to-date review of the movement's history, problems, and prospects is provided by L. HUMPHREYS, OUT OF THE CLOSETS (1973). Four earlier books describing homosexuals and their "world" from the insider's viewpoint, but which generally exhibit a rather more apologetic and self-deprecatory attitude, are D. W. CORY, THE HOMOSEXUAL IN AMERICA: A SUBJECTIVE APPROACH (2d ed. 1960); D. W. CORY, HOMOSEXUALITY: A CROSS-CULTURAL APPROACH (1956) (an

anthology of earlier writings about homosexuality, several by English and other European authors); D. W. CORY, THE LESBIAN IN AMERICA (1964); and D. W. CORY & J. P. LEROY, THE HOMOSEXUAL AND HIS SOCIETY: A VIEW FROM WITHIN (1963).

The majority of homosexuals will not involve themselves in the gay liberation groups' efforts to improve their situation. W. CHURCHILL, HOMOSEXUAL BEHAVIOR AMONG MALES 193–94 (1967). Arno Karlen estimates that the total membership of homophile organizations in the United States is about ten thousand. A. KARLEN, SEXUALITY AND HOMOSEXUALITY—A NEW VIEW 516 (1971). And doubtless only part of this figure represents a hard core of real activists. Their numbers, however, are growing, and the importance of the movement should not be underestimated. "Although homophile organizations, whether male or female, constitute and represent a very small minority of the total homosexual population, they achieve social significance by the role they assume in openly protesting the status assigned to homosexuals by the larger society." Hooker, *Sexual Behavior: Homosexuality,* in 14 INT'L ENCY. SOCIAL SCIENCES 231 (1968).

Statutory Appendix

ALASKA

ALAS. STAT. § 11.40.120 (1971): "Sodomy: A person who commits sodomy is, upon conviction, punishable by imprisonment for not less than one year nor more than ten years."

CALIFORNIA

CAL. PENAL CODE § 286 (West 1970): Sodomy: Punishment. "Every person who is guilty of the infamous crime against nature, committed with mankind or with any animal, is punishable by imprisonment in the state prison not less than one year."

CAL. PENAL CODE § 286.1 (West 1970): Voluntary participation in act of sodomy. Aiding and abetting the same. Penalty. "The provisions of Section 286 notwithstanding, in any case in which defendant, voluntarily acting in concert with another person, by force or violence and against the will of the victim committed sodomy upon a human being, either personally or by aiding and abetting such other person, such fact shall be charged in the indictment or information and if found to be true by the jury, upon a jury trial, or if found to be true by the court, upon a court trial, or if admitted by the defendant, defendant shall suffer confinement in the state prison from five years to life."

CAL. PENAL CODE § 287 (West 1970): Penetration sufficient to complete the crime. "Any sexual penetration, however slight, is sufficient to complete the crime against nature."

CAL. PENAL CODE § 288 (West 1970): Crimes against children. A felony. "Any person who shall willfully and lewdly commit any lewd or lascivious act including any of the acts constituting other

316

crimes provided for in the part one of this code upon or with the body, or any part or member thereof, of a child under the age of fourteen years, with the intent of arousing, appealing to, or gratifying the lust or passions or sexual desires of such person or of such child, shall be guilty of a felony and shall be imprisoned in the State prison for a term of from one year to life."

CAL. PENAL CODE § 288.1 (West 1970): Same. Restriction as to suspended sentence. "Any person convicted of committing any lewd or lascivious act including any of the acts constituting other crimes provided for in Part 1 of this code upon or with the body, or any part or member thereof, of a child under the age of 14 years shall not have his sentence suspended until the court obtains a report from a reputable psychiatrist as to the mental condition of such person."

CAL. PENAL CODE § 288a (West 1970): Sex perversions. "Any person participating in the act of copulating the mouth of one person with the sexual organ of another is punishable by imprisonment in the state prison for not exceeding fifteen years, or, by imprisonment in the county jail not to exceed one year; provided, however, whenever any person is found guilty of the offense specified herein, and it is charged and admitted or found to be true that he is more than 10 years older than his coparticipant in such an act, which coparticipant is under the age of 14, or that he has compelled the other's participation in such an act by force, violence, duress, menace, or threat of great bodily harm, he shall be punished by imprisonment in the state prison for not less than three years. The order of commitment shall expressly state whether a person convicted hereunder is more than 10 years older than his coparticipant and whether such coparticipant is under the age of 14. The order shall also state whether a person convicted hereunder has compelled coparticipation in his act by force, violence, duress, menace, or threat of great bodily harm."

CAL. PENAL CODE § 288b, (West 1970): Voluntary participation in act of oral copulation. Aiding and abetting the same. Penalty. "The provisions of Section 288a notwithstanding, in any case in which defendant, voluntarily acting in concert with another person, by force or violence and against the will of the victim participated in an act of oral copulation, either personally or by aiding and abetting such other person, such fact shall be charged in the indictment or information and if found to be true by the jury, upon a jury trial, or if found to be true by the court, upon a court trial, or if admitted by the defendant, defendant shall suffer confinement in the state prison from five years to life."

CONNECTICUT

[From GEN. STAT. CONN. (Supp. 1969)]

Sec. 53a-65. Definitions.   As used in this part, the following terms have the following meanings:

(1) "Sexual intercourse" has its ordinary meaning and occurs upon any penetration, however slight. Its meaning is limited to persons not married to each other.

(2) "Deviate sexual intercourse" means (a) sexual contact between persons not married to each other consisting of contact between the penis and the anus, the mouth and the penis, or the mouth and the vulva, or (b) any form of sexual conduct with an animal or dead body.

(3) "Sexual contact" means any touching of the sexual or other intimate parts of a person not married to the actor for the purpose of gratifying sexual desire of either party.

(4) "Female" means any female person who is not married to the actor.

(5) "Mentally defective" means that a person suffers from a mental disease or defect which renders him incapable of appraising the nature of his conduct.

(6) "Mentally incapacitated" means that a person is rendered temporarily incapable of appraising or controlling his conduct owing to the influence of a narcotic or intoxicating substance administered to him without his consent, or owing to any other act committed upon him without his consent.

(7) "Physically helpless" means that a person is unconscious or for any other reason is physically unable to communicate unwillingness to an act.

(8) "Forcible compulsion" means physical force that overcomes

earnest resistance; or a threat, express or implied, that places a person in fear of immediate death or serious physical injury to himself or another person, or in fear that he or another person will immediately be kidnapped.

Sec. 53a-66. Lack of consent. (a) Lack of consent results from (1) forcible compulsion or incapacity to consent; or (2) where the offense charged is sexual contact, any circumstances, in addition to forcible compulsion or incapacity to consent, in which the victim does not expressly or impliedly acquiesce in the actor's conduct.

(b) A person is deemed incapable of consent when he is (1) less than sixteen years old; or (2)) mentally defective; or (3) mentally incapacitated; or (4) physically helpless.

Sec. 53a-67. Affirmative defenses. (a) In any prosecution for an offense under this part in which the victim's lack of consent is based solely upon his incapacity to consent because he was mentally defective, mentally incapacitated or physically helpless, it shall be an affirmative defense that the defendant, at the time he engaged in the conduct constituting the offense, did not know of the facts or conditions responsible for such incapacity to consent.

(b) When the alleged victim's age is an element of an offense under this part, it shall be an affirmative defense that the actor reasonably believed the alleged victim to be above the specified age, except when the alleged victim is less than fourteen years of age.

(c) In any prosecution for an offense under this part, it shall be an affirmative defense that the defendant and the alleged victim were, at the time of the alleged offense, living together by mutual consent in a relationship of cohabitation as man and wife, regardless of the legal status of their relationship.

Sec. 53a-68. Corroboration; exceptions. A person shall not be convicted of any offense under this part, or of an attempt to commit such offense, solely on the uncorroborated testimony of the alleged victim, except as hereinafter provided. Corroboration may be circumstantial. This section shall not apply to the offense of sexual contact in the third degree, nor to the offenses of prostitution, patronizing a prostitute, promoting prostitution or permitting prostitution.

Sec. 53a-69. Time limitation for complaint. No prosecution may be instituted or maintained under this part unless the alleged offense was brought to the notice of public authority within three months of its occurrence or, where the alleged victim was less than sixteen years old or incompetent to make complaint, within three months after a parent, guardian or other competent person specially interested in the alleged victim learns of the offense.

Sec. 53a-70. Sexual misconduct in the first degree: Class D felony. (a) A person is guilty of sexual misconduct in the first degree when he has sexual intercourse with another person, or engages in deviate sexual intercourse with another person or causes another person to engage in deviate sexual intercourse, and (a) the other person is less than twenty-one years old and the actor is his guardian or otherwise responsible for general supervision of his welfare; or (b) the other person is in custody of law or detained in a hospital or other institution and the actor has supervisory or disciplinary authority over him.

(b) Sexual misconduct in the first degree is a class D felony.

Sec. 53a-71. Sexual misconduct in the second degree: Class A misdemeanor. (a) A person is guilty of sexual misconduct in the second degree when: (1) Being a male, he engages in sexual intercourse with a female without her consent; or (2) he engages in deviate sexual intercourse with another person without the latter's consent; or (3) he engages in sexual conduct with an animal or dead body.

(b) Sexual misconduct in the second degree is a class A misdemeanor.

Sec. 53a-75. Deviate sexual intercourse in the first degree: Class B felony. (a) A person is guilty of deviate sexual intercourse in the first degree when he engages in deviate sexual intercourse with another person or causes another person to engage in deviate sexual intercourse: (1) By forcible compulsion, but it shall be an affirmative defense to prosecution under this section that the other person had previously with consent engaged in deviate sexual intercourse with the actor; or (2) who is incapable of consent by reason of being physically helpless; or (3) who is less than fourteen years old.

(b) Deviate sexual intercourse in the first degree is a class B felony.

Sec. 53a-76. Deviate sexual intercourse in the second degree: Class C felony. (a) A person is guilty of deviate sexual intercourse in the second degree when he engages in deviate sexual intercourse with another person or causes another person to engage in deviate sexual intercourse by forcible compulsion.

(b) Deviate sexual intercourse in the second degree is a class C felony.

Sec. 53a-77. Deviate sexual intercourse in the third degree: Class D felony.   (a) A person is guilty of deviate sexual intercourse in the third degree when he engages in deviate sexual intercourse with another person or causes another person to engage in deviate sexual intercourse, and (1) the other person is incapable of consent by reason of some factor other than being less than sixteen years old or (2) he is nineteen years old or more and the other person is less than sixteen years old.

(b) Deviate sexual intercourse in the third degree is a class D felony.

Sec. 53a-82. Prostitution: Class A misdemeanor.   (a) A person is guilty of prostitution when such person engages or agrees or offers to engage in sexual conduct with another person in return for a fee.

(b) Prostitution is a class A misdemeanor.

Sec. 53a-83. Patronizing a prostitute: Class A misdemeanor.   (a) A person is guilty of patronizing a prostitute when: (1) Pursuant to a prior understanding, he pays a fee to another person as compensation for such person or a third person having engaged in sexual conduct with him; or (2) he pays or agrees to pay a fee to another person pursuant to an understanding that in return therefor such person or a third person will engage in sexual conduct with him; or (3) he solicits or requests another person to engage in sexual conduct with him in return for a fee.

(b) Patronizing a prostitute is a class A misdemeanor.

Sec.53a-84. Sex of parties immaterial.   In any prosecution for prostitution or patronizing a prostitute, the sex of the two parties or prospective parties to the sexual conduct engaged in, contemplated or solicited is immaterial, and it shall be no defense that: (1) Such persons were of the same sex; or (2) the person who received, agreed to receive or solicited a fee was a male and the person who paid or agreed or offered to pay such fee was a female.

INDIANA

IND. STAT. 10-4221 (1956): "Sodomy.—Whoever commits the abominable and detestable crime against nature with mankind or beast; or whoever entices, allures, instigates or aids any person under the age of twenty-one [21] years to commit masturbation or self-pollution, shall be deemed guilty of sodomy, and, on conviction, shall be fined not less than one hundred dollars [$100] nor more than one thousand dollars [$1000], to which may be added imprisonment in the state prison not less than two [2] years nor more than fourteen [14] years."

KANSAS

KAN. CRIM. CODE 21-3505 (1971 Supp.): "Sodomy. Sodomy is oral or anal copulation between persons who are not husband and wife or consenting adult members of the opposite sex, or between a person and an animal, or coitus with an animal. Any penetration, however slight, is sufficient to complete the crime of sodomy. Sodomy is a class B misdemeanor."

KAN. CRIM. CODE 21-3506 (1971 Supp.): "Aggravated Sodomy. Aggravated sodomy is sodomy committed: (a) with force or threat of force, or where bodily harm is inflicted on the victim during the commission of the crime; or (b) With a child under the age of sixteen (16) years. Aggravated sodomy is a class B felony."

MASSACHUSETTS

ANN. LAWS MASS. c. 272, § 34 (1968): "Sodomy and Buggery. Whoever commits the abominable and detestable crime against nature, either with mankind or with a beast, shall be punished by imprisonment in the state prison for not more than twenty years."

ANN. LAWS MASS. c. 272, § 35 (1968): "Unnatural and Lascivious Acts. Whoever commits any unnatural and lascivious act with another person shall be punished by a fine of not less than one hundred nor more than one thousand dollars or by imprisonment in the state prison for not more than five years or in jail or the house of correction for not more than two and one half years."

NORTH DAKOTA

N. D. CENTURY CODE 12-22-07 (1960): " 'Sodomy' defined—Punishment.—Every person who carnally knows in any manner any animal or bird, or carnally knows any male or female person by the anus or by or with the mouth, or voluntarily submits to such carnal knowledge, or attempts sexual intercourse with a dead body, is guilty of sodomy and shall be punished by imprisonment in the penitentiary for not less than one year nor more than ten years, or in the county jail for not more than one year. Any sexual penetration, however slight is sufficient to complete this crime."

TEXAS

TEX. PENAL CODE art. 524 (1952): Sodomy. "Whoever has carnal copulation with a beast, or in an opening of the body, except sexual parts, with another human being, or whoever shall use his mouth on the sexual parts of another human being for the purpose of having carnal copulation, or who shall voluntarily permit the use of his own sexual parts in a lewd or lascivious manner by any minor, shall be guilty of sodomy, and upon conviction thereof shall be deemed guilty of a felony, and shall be confined in the penitentiary not less than two (2) nor more than fifteen (15) years."

UTAH

[From UTAH CODE (1969 Supp.)]

76-53-22. Sodomy.—1. Every person who is guilty of sodomy, committed with mankind with either the sexual organs or the mouth, shall be deemed guilty of a misdemeanor, and upon conviction may be punished by imprisonment in the county jail for not more than six months, or a fine of not exceeding $299, or both, except when the act of sodomy is:
(a) Between an adult and minor.
(b) With a victim incapable, through lunacy or any other

unsoundness of mind, whether temporary or permanent, of giving legal consent.

(c) With a victim who resists, but whose resistance is overcome by force or violence.

(d) With a victim who is prevented from resisting by threats of immediate and great bodily harm, accompanied by apparent power of execution, or by any intoxication, narcotic or anaesthetic substance administered by or with the privity of the accused.

(e) With a victim at the time unconscious of the nature of the act, which fact is known to the accused.

(f) With a victim who submits in the belief that the person committing the act is a legal spouse, and this belief is induced by any artifice, pretense or concealment practiced by the accused with intent to induce such belief.

(g) Between a human being and any animal.

2. Any person found guilty of committing an offense in subsection 1 (a) through (g), may be imprisoned in the state prison for not less than three nor more than twenty years.

3. For the purposes of this act, adult shall be any person having attained the age of eighteen years; a minor is a person under the age of eighteen years.

Table of Cases

Index